Napier and Wheat's
Recovering Damages for Psychiatric Injury

Second Edition

Kay Wheat, BA, Solicitor

D1342338

OXFORD
UNIVERSITY PRESS

OXFORD

UNIVERSITY PRESS

Great Clarendon Street, Oxford OX2 6DP

Oxford University Press is a department of the University of Oxford.
It furthers the University's objective of excellence in research, scholarship,
and education by publishing worldwide in

Oxford New York

Auckland Bangkok Buenos Aires Cape Town Chennai
Dar es Salaam Delhi Hong Kong Istanbul Karachi Kolkata
Kuala Lumpur Madrid Melbourne Mexico City Mumbai Nairobi
São Paulo Shanghai Taipei Tokyo Toronto

Oxford is a registered trade mark of Oxford University Press
in the UK and certain other countries

Published in the United States
by Oxford University Press Inc., New York

First edition published by Blackstone Press 1995

Second edition first published 2002

British Library Cataloguing in Publication Data
Data available

Library of Congress Cataloging in Publication Data
Data available

ISBN 1-1841 741 337

1 3 5 7 9 10 8 6 4 2

Typeset by Montage Studios Limited, Tonbridge, Kent
Printed in Great Britain
on acid-free paper by
Antony Rowe Limited, Chippenham, Wiltshire

Foreword to the First Edition
by The Honourable Mr Justice Wright

The law on the recoverability of damages for psychiatric injury – 'nervous shock' in lawyers' language – is currently in a state of considerable flux. It has rightly been described by the Master of the Rolls as being 'one of the most vexed and tantalising topics in the modern law of tort'. Two conflicting policy considerations can clearly be seen at work in the judgments in the various actions which have emerged from the Piper Alpha and Hillsborough disasters. On the one hand, there is the natural desire to compensate those who, as a result of the fault of another, have been exposed to horrific experiences or images, and have suffered psychiatric injury, often of a life-shattering nature, as a result. On the other hand there is the equally understandable perception of a need to contain such claims, so easily made and so difficult to verify, within clearly identifiable and if necessary even arbitrary bounds. Only in such a way, it is said, can the courts and the public, in the form of tax – and premium – payers be protected from a rising flood of increasingly remote and suspect claims by opportunist plaintiffs. The degree of public interest in the topic is underlined by the recent publication of Law Commission Consultation Paper No 137 on Liability for Psychiatric Illness, as recently as March of this year.

In such circumstances it is clear that this book comes pat upon its moment. As is to be expected from its authors, they argue the case for a liberal approach to the whole question in a cogent and forthright manner, and this book will unquestionably be regarded as a major asset by those who seek to push back the boundaries within which claims for damages in cases of this nature can be entertained.

But quite apart from this particularly topical aspect of their work, the authors have in this book provided practitioners in the field, whether legal or medical, with a work of reference which will provide them with valuable guidance over the whole extent of a topic which is, understandably, regarded by many as daunting in the extreme. They are to be congratulated for reducing the technicalities, both legal and medical, into manageable scope in language which is not merely approachable but indeed very readable. As such, I am sure that this book will find its way onto the shelves, certainly of all those who are concerned in any way with the advancement of claims for compensation for psychiatric injury before our courts, and of many others besides. I am very happy to commend it to its readers.

Michael Wright
April 1995

Summary of Contents

Contents

Acknowledgments

The author and publishers would like to thank the following for permission to reproduce copyright material:

Legal Studies & Services: the *Herald of Free Enterprise* arbitrations which first appeared in the *Personal and Medical Injuries Law Letter* in June 1989.

Bruno Press (New Orleans LA): C. B. Scrignar, *Post-Traumatic Stress Disorder: Diagnosis* (1988).

American Psychiatric Association (Washington DC): *American Psychiatric Association's Diagnostic and Statistical Manual* (DSM IV–TR) (2000).

Preface

Since the publication of the first edition of this book in 1995, there have been some significant developments in the area. Most importantly, the House of Lords has examined psychiatric injury on two further occasions in the cases of *Page v Smith* [1995] 2 WLR 644 and *White v Chief Constable of South Yorkshire Police* [1999] 2 AC 455. Whilst *Page v Smith* appeared to follow a liberal approach by rejecting the need for limiting factors in primary victim cases, it has nevertheless introduced a rigidity into the law by drawing a stark contrast between primary and secondary victims. Somewhat depressingly, *White* has similarly endorsed a rigid fixing of the boundaries in psychiatric injury claims. The other developing area is that of psychiatric injury claims in the employment field, often referred to as stress claims. There have also been some important cases in the law of negligence and the responsibility of public authorities, from *X v Bedfordshire County Council* [1995] 3 WLR 152 onwards. Substantial rewriting has therefore been necessary to incorporate these developments into the text.

As far as the diagnosis and statistical manuals are concerned, the fourth edition of the American Psychiatric Association's manual has been text revised but there are no major revisions which affect this text.

Thanks are due particularly to Terry Hanstock, information specialist at Nottingham Trent University, for all his help in locating cases and tracking down other information, often at extremely short notice, and to the editorial staff at Oxford University Press for their support and encouragement.

The law is as stated at 1 June 2002.

K. Wheat

Table of Cases

Table of Statutes

Table of Statutory Instruments

Introduction

Canst thou not minister to a mind diseas'd,
Pluck from the memory a rooted sorrow,
Raze out the written troubles of the brain,
And with some sweet oblivious antidote
Cleanse the stuff'd bosom of that perilous stuff
Which weighs upon the heart?

(*Macbeth*, act V, scene iii)

When Macbeth asked this question after embarking on the traumatic experience of multiple murder, he was probably exhibiting the despair of someone suffering the classic symptoms of post-traumatic stress disorder ('PTSD'). Whilst we will be cautious about having sympathy for Macbeth, we may be more sympathetic to, say, Samuel Pepys, who was greatly disturbed by his experience during the Great Fire of London, writing diary entries such as 'much terrified in the nights nowadays with dreams of fire and falling down of houses' (15 September 1666). The term 'the piercing of the mental skin' is a vivid metaphor to describe the effect of trauma on the human psyche. It is so well known that frightening experiences can have damaging and sometimes long-term effects upon the mind that it is surprising there should ever have been any doubt whether the courts should order compensation for those effects in the same way as physical injury to the person has been compensated. However, such injury has been treated with a great deal of circumspection by the courts, particularly in the case of *negligently* inflicted psychiatric injury.

There has been considerable development in this area of the law over recent years, due mainly to two factors. The first is the increasing recognition by lawyers and judges of psychiatric injury as a genuine and non-trivial form of damage, and the second is, tragically, the spate of disasters which occurred from the 1980s onwards such as the Bradford football stadium fire in 1985; the capsize of the *Herald of Free Enterprise* ferry in 1987, which was the same year as the King's Cross Underground fire; the sinking, near Athens, of the ship *Jupiter*, carrying holidaying schoolchildren, and the Piper Alpha oil rig blaze, both of which took place in 1988; the 1989 disasters at Hillsborough football ground and on the River Thames when the dredger *Bowbelle* sank the *Marchioness* riverboat; and the train crashes from the late 1990s onwards at Southall, Ladbroke Grove, Selby and Hatfield.

The horrific nature of these events resulted not only in physical injuries, but also, in numerous cases, the suffering of psychiatric illnesses by victims, their loved ones and witnesses to the events. As litigation ensued, much was learnt by lawyers and judges alike of the awful psychiatric consequences which can result from experiences such as these. The law developed on two important fronts. Firstly, the seminal House of Lords decisions in *Alcock v Chief Constable of the South Yorkshire Police*[1], *Page v Smith*,[2] *White v Chief Constable of South Yorkshire Police*[3] and secondly, at grassroots level there was much learnt about the handling and evaluation of the claims of individual victims.

It is important to stress that psychiatric injury can result from situations far less catastrophic than events such as the above. Every day, small-scale horrific happenings occur which affect perhaps only one or two people and do not even merit a mention in a local newspaper, but can have devastating consequences on those affected. Sometimes one of those consequences will be a psychiatric illness.

This book is about compensation for psychiatric injury, including 'nervous shock' claims. 'Nervous shock' is the expression used to describe a claim for psychiatric injury in the tort of negligence. Although the terminology is archaic and has no medical meaning, it is a useful form of shorthand to differentiate such claims from psychiatric injury claims in, say, intentional torts such as assault or in claims in contract, or claims against employers for psychiatric illnesses brought on by stressful working conditions.

Throughout the book the term 'psychiatric injury' is used. In other contexts the term 'psychological' as opposed to 'psychiatric' might be encountered. The terms are not mutually exclusive, nor are they precise; but psychiatric refers to medical conditions and, usually, to be compensatable, the condition must be more than 'mere distress'.

The purpose of this book is to outline the present state of the law in this area, and to provide some practical assistance to lawyers who may be dealing with such claims. It is also hoped that it may be of interest to doctors and other health care professionals working in the field.[4]

It is worth summarising here the essential requirements of a nervous shock claim. First, the claim must be for damages for a *recognizable* psychiatric injury.

---

[1] [1992] 1 AC 310.   [2] [1995] 2 WLR 644.   [3] [1999] 2 AC 455.
[4]For an excellent and very detailed analysis of claims for psychiatric injury in tort see N Mullany and P Handford, *Tort Liability for Psychiatric Damage* (London: Sweet & Maxwell, 1993).

A nervous shock claim may also arise in one of the following circumstances: (a) the claimant has also suffered physical injury, or has been foreseeably at risk of physical injury or has had a reasonable fear of being physically injured; (b) the claimant has suffered because of injury to another or has had a reasonable fear of injury to another person when that person stands in a special relationship to the claimant, and when the claimant has witnessed, through his or her unaided senses, the causative event or its immediate aftermath. In the case of (b) the event itself must be sufficiently upsetting to cause distress to the person of ordinary fortitude but the principle that one must take one's victim as one finds him applies equally in nervous shock claims.

Apart from evidential and causation problems, there is less room for contention about a claim when the plaintiff has also suffered physical injury, but difficulties arise in the other cases, particularly when the plaintiff has suffered through concern for a third party. The main cases are considered in relation to these areas.

Although nervous shock claims are probably those which cause most problems, it must not be forgotten that other torts can result in psychiatric injury, for example, the intentional infliction of mental distress as in *Wilkinson v Downton*,[5] and assault, and, of course, damages can be awarded in contract if the resulting injury was within the contemplation of the parties to the contract. Chapter 1 sets the claim in its legal context, looking at the general principles of negligence, other areas of tort, and contract.

Chapter 2 is concerned with the sorts of psychiatric injury which may occur, and also provides a brief history of the development of the recognition of general 'reactive' psychiatric disorders, such as PTSD. It must be stressed that PTSD is by no means the only disorder which can result from trauma, and, given the courts' demand for a properly diagnosed psychiatric illness to be established, it is dangerous to assume that because PTSD has not been diagnosed then the plaintiff is not able to establish a claim. However, PTSD is described in some detail because, by its very nature, it is *only* caused by trauma.

Chapter 3 looks at the practical problems which can arise in identifying the sufferer. It is worth stressing that, however distressing the experience, some people will not suffer any psychiatric injury. It is not the purpose of this book to encourage lawyers to find psychiatric problems where there are none. However, it must also be said that those who do suffer may not realize it, or may feel embarrassed about admitting it as many people see this as a sign of weakness, and need to be dealt with in a sensitive and sympathetic way. This chapter also considers some of the more common forms of questionnaire used by psychologists to make initial assessments of potential sufferers.

[5] [1897] 2 QB 57.

Chapter 4 examines the 'shock' cases, ie where the injury is caused by the witnessing of a single, sudden and shocking event or its immediate aftermath. By way of contrast, examples of events are given that have been held not to fall into this category. Chapter 5 deals with those cases where psychiatric injury has been caused by non-shocking states of affairs, such as the failure of local authorities to, for example, take children into care to avoid them being subjected to sex abuse.

Chapter 6 is about employers' liability in respect of psychiatric injuries, excluding 'shock' claims which are, since the decision of the House of Lords in *White v Chief Constable of South Yorkshire Police*, subject to exactly the same control mechanisms as any other form of action in negligence. Principally, the employment cases are about stressful working conditions, bullying and similar forms of treatment by employers, and discrimination claims.

Chapter 7 examines the principles of assessing damages and looks at quantum in detail in a number of cases, whilst chapter 8 is concerned with civil procedural matters which may be particularly pertinent to psychiatric injury.

Finally, Chapter 9 examines shortcomings in the present law and considers ways in which it may be reformed, and possible future developments.

1

The Legal Context

This chapter outlines the legal framework in which a claim in respect of psychiatric injury may arise. The various elements of a claim will be examined in more detail in subsequent chapters.

Claims for damages for psychiatric injury can arise in both contract and tort. They can arise with or without physical injury. The majority of claims

will arise from situations of sudden trauma, such as industrial or transportation accidents, where the claim will usually be in tort. However, claims for
psychiatric injury need to be understood within the legal framework which
allows or disallows a claim for such damage, regardless of the context.

In the law of negligence, claims for damages for psychiatric injury have for
many years been described as claims for 'nervous shock', but this has no
medical meaning, and has been largely superseded by the term 'psychiatric
injury'. However, it is still convenient shorthand to describe psychiatric
injury caused by negligence and is a useful reminder of the rule that *generally*
damages will be awarded only if the illness was caused by shock, ie, the
causal event must be of a type generally thought of as 'shocking'.

In nervous shock cases there are special limitations on the categories of
people who can claim. The limitations do not apply in other torts because there
are no reasons of policy to restrict claims, ie the torts arise, in varying degrees,
from deliberate acts, even though there might be no intention to cause harm,
as for example in nuisance. In negligence there is not the same degree of
control over actions; most people would very much wish not to be negligent,
but, inevitably, from time to time, are liable to be careless. The perceived need
to limit the circumstances in which a claim may be made, however, arises in the
area of employers' liability. In *White v Chief Constable of South Yorkshire*[1] the
House of Lords confirmed that the nervous shock limitations apply just as
much to employees as to other claimants in negligence. However, in
non-shock cases, the pre-existing relationship of employer and employee gives
rise to an obligation to care for the health of the employee and that includes his
mental health. The fact that the duty is both tortious and contractual makes no
difference to the standard of care but there are some differences between
claims brought in tort and contract. Further issues arise in the employment
context in relation to the statutory protections provided by the law relating to
discrimination and dismissal; recovering damages for psychiatric injury caused
by employment conditions will be explored in Chapter 6. There are some
circumstances in which damages can be recovered for injury suffered as a result
of 'non-shocking' circumstances outside of the employment context, which is
the subject of Chapter 5.

This introductory chapter will deal with general negligence principles; a
brief history of the 'nervous shock' claim and a general summary of the law.
The 'shock' cases will be dealt with in more detail in Chapter 4.

Generally, whatever the circumstances, in tort it must be established that
the claimant has suffered some recognizable psychiatric injury as opposed
to, what can be called, ordinary mental distress. Certainly this is the case in
negligence, but not, for example, in intentional torts or in nuisance.[2] In

---

[1] [1999] 2 AC 455.
[2] See *Bone v Seale* [1975] 1 WLR 797, CA, and *Campbelltown City Council v Mackay* (1989)
15 NSWLR 501.

breach of contract cases, damages can be awarded for both a recognized psychiatric illness and for ordinary mental distress depending on the terms of the contract and the circumstances of its breach.

NEGLIGENCE

Before looking at the special problems which arise when claiming for psychiatric injury, it is essential to see the claim in the general context of the concepts of foreseeability, remoteness and proximity.[3]

Duty of care and remoteness

It is worth stating the legal truism that in order to establish an action in negligence, the claimant must show that the defendant owes the claimant a duty of care, that the defendant is in breach of that duty, and that the plaintiff has suffered damage as a result. Again, returning to basic legal principles, the duty of care has been said to be owed to the defendant's neighbours, who are 'persons who are so closely and directly affected by my act that I ought reasonably to have them in contemplation as being so affected'.[4] Is saying that a duty of care is owed to a person because that person may suffer harm if the defendant is negligent the same as saying that the possibility of the person suffering harm is foreseeable? If it is not foreseeable then they are not neighbours: the defendant does not owe the person a duty of care. But *if* harm is foreseeable it will not necessarily follow that the person will recover damages for injury or loss caused (in the factual sense of 'caused') by the defendant's action. There will be cases when the damage is said to be too remote (that is, there is no legal causation): although the action factually caused the injury or loss, there is no legal causation. See, for example, the seminal case on this point — *Overseas Tankship (UK) Ltd v Morts Dock & Engineering Co, The Wagon Mound (No 1)*,[5] in which a careless oil spillage which was ignited by a spark in open water and destroyed a wharf by fire, undoubtedly satisfied the test of factual causation but failed the legal causation test of remoteness of damage. 'A defender is not liable for a consequence of a kind which is not foreseeable. But it does not follow that he is liable for every consequence which a reasonable man could foresee.'[6] In other words, foreseeability is a necessary condition for liability in the tort of

---

[3] For a full analysis of these concepts see H L A Hart and T Honoré, *Causation in the Law*, 2nd ed (Oxford: Clarendon Press, 1985). See in particular *Hughes v Lord Advocate* [1963] AC 837, HL; *Overseas Tankship (UK) Ltd v Morts Dock & Engineering Co Ltd* [1961] AC 388, PC; *Overseas Tankship (UK) Ltd v Miller Steamship Co Pty No 2* [1967] 1 AC 617, PC.

[4] *Donoghue v Stevenson* [1932] AC 562, per Lord Atkin at 580.   [5] [1961] AC 388.

[6] *McKew v Holland & Hannen & Cubitts (Scotland) Ltd* [1969] 3 All ER 1621, per Lord Reid at 1623.

negligence, but it is not a sufficient condition if the damage caused is too remote.

The language can be perplexing and there is no doubt that the concepts of foreseeability and remoteness can be used to mean exactly the same thing. Certainly the cases show the interchangeable use of these concepts; sometimes confusingly; sometimes in a more straightforward fashion, as per Lord Denning MR:

The more I think about these cases, the more difficult I find it to put each into its proper pigeon-hole. Sometimes I say: 'There was no duty'. In others I say: 'The damage was too remote'.[7]

So, in order to establish the existence of a duty of care foreseeability is a requirement. In other words, in order to establish a claim at all one has to show that a duty of care was owed to *this* claimant whose presence should have been foreseen by the defendant. In a road traffic accident, another user of the highway would be said to be owed a duty of care, as the likelihood of his or her presence on the highway is reasonably foreseeable, and personal injury or physical damage to his or her vehicle are foreseeable types of damage.[8] However, psychiatric injury is not regarded by the courts as 'physical' damage and hence the separate criteria (to be considered in detail in due course) which have to be satisfied in order to establish a claim for such injury.

Was the alleged damage too remote? To establish that the damage, of whatever kind, was not too remote, either (a) it has to be a direct, and foreseeable, physical consequence of the accident; or (b) it is a foreseeable consequence, even though it arises indirectly. An example of the latter is the case of the rescuer. A person who comes along to the scene of an accident and helps to rescue the injured and thereby also suffers injury could not say that his injuries are a direct physical consequence of the negligent behaviour of the person who caused the accident, but the likelihood of a rescuer being involved was foreseeable.[9]

To return to the specific issue of psychiatric injury, the practical application of these concepts can be seen in the case of *King v Phillips*[10]. The facts were that a taxi driver had backed his vehicle into a small boy on a tricycle. The injury to the boy and damage to his tricycle were slight but his mother heard him scream and, looking out of an upstairs window some 70 to 80 yards away, saw the tricycle under the taxicab but could not see the boy. She ran downstairs and into the road, and she met the

---

[7] *Spartan Steel & Alloys Ltd v Martin & Co (Contractors) Ltd* [1972] QB 27; and see also below on the issue of public policy.

[8] *Donoghue v Stevenson* [1932] AC 562.

[9] See Chapter 4 for further discussion of the position of rescuers.

[10] [1953] 1 QB 429, CA.

boy running towards her. She suffered psychiatric injury attributable to the shock of that incident. It was held that no legal wrong had been done to the mother (as opposed to the child). This was because no 'hypothetical reasonable observer'[11] could reasonably have anticipated that injury, either physical or psychiatric, could have been caused to her by the backing of the taxi without due attention. Accordingly, the driver owed no duty to the mother and was not liable to her for negligence. Denning LJ said:

What is the reasoning which admits a cause of action for negligence if the injured person is actually struck, but declines it if he only suffers from shock? I cannot see why the duty of a driver should differ according to the nature of the injury. . . . If he drives negligently with the result that a bystander is injured, then his breach of duty is the same, no matter whether the injury is a wound or is emotional shock. . . . If you view the duty of care in this way, and yet refuse to allow a bystander to recover for shock, it is not because there was no duty owed to him, nor because it was not caused by the negligence of the driver, but simply because it was too remote to be admitted as a head of damage.

A different result is reached by viewing the driver's duty differently. Instead of saying simply that his duty is to drive with reasonable care, you say that his duty is to avoid injury which he can reasonably foresee. . . . Then you draw a distinction between physical and emotional injury, and impose a different duty on him in regard to each kind of injury, with the inevitable result that you are driven to say there are two different torts — one tort when he can foresee physical injury, and another tort when he can foresee emotional injury. I do not think that that is right. There is one wrong only, the wrong of negligence.[12]

One may be forgiven for thinking at this stage that the unfortunate Mrs King was going to recover damages, but Denning LJ (who was supported by both other members of the Court of Appeal) went on to say:

. . . I think that the shock in this case is too remote to be a head of damage. It seems to me that the slow backing of the taxicab was very different from the terrifying descent of the runaway lorry.[13] The taxicab driver cannot reasonably be expected to have foreseen that his backing would terrify a mother 70 yards away, whereas the lorry driver ought to have foreseen that a runaway lorry might seriously shock the mother of children in the danger area.[14]

It is likely that this case would be decided differently today; suffice to say that there is an uncomfortable element of subjectivity in the notion that the slow inexorable backing of a motor vehicle towards a child is less shocking than the swift progress of a larger motor vehicle towards an area where

---

[11] Applying the test laid down in *Bourhill v Young* [1943] AC 92, HL; see page 34.

[12] [1953] 1 QB 429, at 439–40.

[13] Here reference was being made to the case of *Hambrook v Stokes Brothers* [1925] 1 KB 141, where a woman recovered damages following the shock she received when she saw a lorry run away downhill towards an area where she had just left her children. See below, page 33.

[14] ibid, at 442.

children are likely to be. It must also be remembered that the case was decided in the days when the psychiatric injuries complained of were always described as 'nervous shock', and it may have influenced the sort of events that the courts would regard as capable of causing shock that was not too remote a consequence. However, it does illustrate the conceptual acrobatics which judges are apt to indulge in when considering the wider effects of an initial negligent event by employing the filtering devices of foreseeability or remoteness to avoid liability 'in an indeterminate amount for an indeterminate time to an indeterminate class',[15] or avoid cases presenting enormous evidential difficulties. This may be linked to the question of public policy which features significantly in claims for psychiatric injury. Put simply the courts have seen it as their duty to envisage floodgates[16] and to keep them firmly locked.

It is arguable that there is no public policy justification for imposition of otherwise unjustifiable restrictions on claims for psychiatric injury. However, there are several possible reasons for the public policy arguments. For example, it could be said to be unfair (ie, as a matter of general morality) to extend the potential liability for, say, a momentary lapse of concentration to a vast and possibly ruinous extent; or it could be said that its effect upon the liability of insurers with the inevitable and dire consequences for everyone in terms of availability and cost of insurance would be disastrous. It is instructive, however, to consider the speech of Lord Edmund-Davies in *McLoughlin v O'Brian*:

My lords, the experiences of a long life in the law have made me very familiar with this 'floodgates' argument. I do not, of course, suggest that it can invariably be dismissed as lacking cogency; on the contrary, it has to be weighed carefully, but I have often seen it disproved by later events. It was urged when abolition of the doctrine of common employment was being canvassed, and it raised its head again when the abolition of contributory negligence as a total bar to a claim in negligence was being urged.

... I remain unconvinced that the number and area of claims in 'shock' cases would be substantially increased or enlarged were the respondents here held liable.[17]

The proximity test

All important is the related concept of 'proximity'.[18] It was used by Lord Atkin to explain the 'neighbour principle', ie, my neighbour is someone to whom I stand in a particular relationship of 'proximity'.[19] There is nothing

---

[15] Per Cardozo CJ in *Ultramares Corporation v Touche* (1931) 174 NE 441, at 444.

[16] See *McLoughlin v O'Brian* [1983] 1 AC 410, HL, especially at 430 and 438.

[17] ibid, at 425.

[18] The term appears to have been first used in *Thomas v Quartermaine* (1887) 18 QBD 685, at 688.

[19] See *Donoghue v Stevenson* [1932] AC 562, HL, and also *Home Office v Dorset Yacht Co Ltd* [1970] AC 1004.

in that case to suggest that proximity adds anything to the concept of foreseeability (my neighbour is someone who will be foreseeably damaged by my negligence). However, the concept has been responsible for the current limitations on recovering damages for psychiatric injury occasioned by shock.

A comparable area where the proximity issue defeats claims in negligence is in the area of economic loss and it is worth a short digression to consider such cases as being illustrations of the way in which the proximity test has been considered by the courts.

It is an established general principle that a claim in negligence for pure financial loss is not allowable,[20] and that it would only follow on the heels of physical damage, eg, if the electricity suppliers damage a cable on a manufacturer's property then the manufacturer will be able to claim pecuniary loss following upon this physical damage; the manufacturer will have no such claim if the electricity supply is interrupted by a power cut unaccompanied by physical damage. However, the tort of negligence has been widened to include some cases of pure economic loss, where some special relationship exists between the parties.[21] In the well-known negligent misstatement case of *Hedley Byrne & Co Ltd v Heller & Partners Ltd*[22] the House of Lords held that in principle there was no difference between physical loss and financial loss, and that a duty to take care in the making of statements existed whenever there was a special relationship, ie, where the inquirer was trusting the other to exercise a reasonable degree of care, and when the other knew or ought to have known that the statement would be relied on by the inquirer.

This issue is illustrated by *Caparo Industries plc v Dickman*[23] in which shareholders who purchased more shares and implemented a company takeover in reliance on an inaccurate and misleading auditor's report brought an action against the auditors alleging that they had been negligent in auditing the accounts, that the respondents had relied upon the accounts, and that the auditors owed them a duty of care either as potential bidders for the company or as existing shareholders. It was held that there were three criteria for the imposition of a duty of care — foreseeability of damage, proximity of relationship and the reasonableness or otherwise of imposing a duty.[24] The court went on to state that when a statement was put into general circulation, there was no general relationship of proximity with those who may read it, and so no duty of care was owed by the auditors to the

---

[20] See *Spartan Steel & Alloys Ltd v Martin & Co (Contractors) Ltd* [1972] QB 27.

[21] See *Weller & Co v Foot & Mouth Disease Research Institute* [1966] 1 QB 569 and *Spartan Steel and Alloys Ltd v Martin & Co (Contractors) Ltd* [1972] QB 27.

[22] [1964] AC 465.   [23] [1990] 2 AC 605.

[24] The use of the concept of 'the reasonableness or otherwise of imposing a duty' is another way of allowing a number of considerations (usually of policy) to influence whether there is a duty of care.

public at large, or to shareholders who read accounts for the purpose of buying shares with a view to a profit.

The proximity requirement is well illustrated by the House of Lords case of *Murphy v Brentwood District Council*.[25] The case concerned the liability of a local authority for the approval of plans for a defective foundation to the plaintiff's house. Lord Bridge of Harwich said:

> If a builder erects a structure containing a latent defect which renders it dangerous to persons or property, he will be liable in tort for injury to persons or damage to property resulting from that dangerous defect. But if the defect becomes apparent before any injury or damage has been caused, the loss sustained by the building owner is purely economic.... These economic losses are recoverable if they flow from breach of a relevant contractual duty, but, here again, they are not recoverable in tort in the absence of a special relationship of proximity ....[26]

A relative newcomer to the list of liability-restricting concepts employed by the appellate courts is the concept of 'assumption of responsibility' whereby, in pure economic loss cases, liability will arise only if the defendant has assumed responsibility towards the claimant.[27] This is unsatisfactory if interpreted literally (liability would depend upon the choice of the defendant) and if not so interpreted it seems to add nothing to the already problematic notion of proximity. Fortunately it has not infiltrated the area of personal injury, and in the Scottish case of *Gibson v Orm*[28] it was specifically said that 'assumption of liability' was not useful in cases of personal injury and death.

The proximity test in relation to psychiatric injury

What effect does the proximity issue have on a claim for psychiatric injury? Such a claim can either be ancillary to another claim, eg, physical damage to either property or person, or it can stand on its own. If there is physical damage then the claim for associated psychiatric injury is an allowable claim provided the psychiatric injury was actually caused by the tortious event, and, of course, that the defendant is liable in tort for the event. Proximity should not, therefore, be an issue in cases where physical injury has also been caused to the plaintiff.

In what kind of case can psychiatric injury arise in the absence of physical injury? To take first of all the case of a bereavement, there are no damages available in negligence for 'ordinary' grief.[29] (In certain cases, of course, bereavement damages can be claimed under the Fatal Accidents Act 1976, but these relate to financial loss and not personal injury.) This is because grief is a normal human emotion and therefore there is no damage. However great the distress, a widow, for example, will not recover damages for her grief upon the loss of her husband. If, however, she suffers from a

---

[25] [1991] 1 AC 398.   [26] ibid, at 475.
[27] See *Williams v Natural Life Health Foods Ltd* [1998] 2 All ER 577.
[28] (1999) SC 420.   [29] See *Hinz v Berry* [1970] 2 QB 40, CA.

recognizable psychiatric illness,[30] she still cannot recover, unless a number of conditions pertained at the time of the event that killed him, ie, she can show the required degree of proximity to the event.

What are the conditions at the time of the event? She must have either been involved in the event itself, eg, in the same motor vehicle as her husband (if she suffers physical injury then she can claim regardless of the proximity issue), or she must have witnessed the event or its *immediate aftermath*. In Chapter 4 precisely what the immediate aftermath may mean will be examined, but it is a way of saying that she must have been sufficiently proximate to the event.

To take another example, a motorist is travelling down the motorway when he comes upon speed restrictions, and police warning signs. Eventually in a queue of traffic he travels past the scene of a dreadful accident which has obviously only just happened because the fire and ambulance crews are still there attending the injured. He continues on his journey, but the incident he has just seen, which was also seen by many other motorists who have driven past it, has an extremely distressing effect upon him, so much so that he is later diagnosed as suffering from a recognizable psychiatric illness directly attributable to the scene he witnessed. Can he claim damages in respect of this illness and how will the proximity issue affect his claim? He will be able to say that he witnessed the immediate aftermath of the event, but he will have to satisfy the second limb of the proximity test (satisfied by the widow in the first example): he will have to show that his relationship to one or more of the injured or killed is sufficiently close, ie, sufficiently proximate. If he had recognized his wife's car as one of the damaged vehicles then that would suffice. If he had recognized his fiancée's car in the same way, then that *may* suffice. If he had recognized his next-door neighbour's car then that probably would not suffice. If there was no 'relationship proximity', i.e. he will be a 'mere bystander' and he will almost certainly not be successful.

Suppose the accident happens rather differently. Our motorist was waiting in a queue of traffic on a bridge, say, over the motorway, upon which there is heavy traffic in both directions. He sees a petrol tanker travelling along the motorway, away from the bridge. The tanker careers across on to the opposite carriageway and bursts into flames. Vehicles become out of control, themselves bursting into flames, overturning, colliding with others. There is general mayhem. The motorist is some distance away from the bridge so he is in no danger himself nor does he perceive himself to be. He is horrified by what he sees and, as a result, suffers psychiatric injury. He has no reason to believe that anyone close to him is anywhere near the accident, nor indeed are they. The question here is whether there are circumstances which are sufficiently horrific to cause

---

[30] Of course, the cause of her illness must relate to the trauma of the event and not just to the loss of her husband: *Hinz v Berry* [1970] 2 QB 40, CA.

psychiatric injury to one who witnesses them even if they have no relationship to any one of the participants. Atkin LJ in *Hambrook v Stokes Brothers*[31] suggested that there was no reason why a bystander should not be able to claim, and in *Alcock v Chief Constable of South Yorkshire Police*[32] there was speculation about the type of event which would be sufficiently horrifying to justify the mere bystander recovering damages. However, this possibility received a setback in the Court of Appeal in the case of *McFarlane v E E Caledonia Ltd*[33] when it overturned the first-instance decision to award damages to a worker who witnessed the explosions and fire on the Piper Alpha oil rig from a support vessel approximately 550 yards away. Stuart-Smith LJ said:

In my judgment both as a matter of principle and policy the court should not extend the duty to those who are mere bystanders or witnesses of horrific events unless there is a sufficient degree of proximity, which requires both nearness in time and place and a close relationship of love and affection between plaintiff and victim.[34]

Whether or not on the facts of this particular case, the Court of Appeal was entitled to reject the claim, this statement of general policy was not articulated in the House of Lords' decision in *Alcock v Chief Constable of the South Yorkshire Police*[35].

It is surely no coincidence that the early cases of claims for psychiatric injury concern pregnant women who, as a result of shock, have miscarried or given birth to disabled children.[36] In such cases physical damage is present. No doubt the distress would have been just as great if the plaintiffs concerned had not been pregnant, or if they had been fortunate enough to have had healthy babies, but their distress would not have been perceived to be physically measurable. There is interesting research being undertaken which may show that psychiatric injury can actually be identifiable in the chemical composition of the nervous system (see page 72). If this is scientifically established and then accepted by the courts then, by showing physical injury, the need for proximity to time and place, and to a relationship, will, or, at least should, disappear.

Causation

Once it has been established that there is a breach of the duty of care in negligence, it still has to be shown that there has been damage caused by this

[31] [1925] 1 KB 141, CA.   [32] [1992] 1 AC 310.   [33] [1994] 2 All ER 1.   [34] ibid, at 14.
[35] See, in particular, the judgments of Lord Oliver at [1992] 1 AC 310, 416, Lord Keith at 397, and Lord Ackner at 403.
[36] *Dulieu v White & Sons* [1901] 2 KB 669; *Bourhill v Young* [1943] AC 92; *Hambrook v Stokes Brothers* [1925] 1 KB 141.

breach. Generally it is said that causation is a question of fact and remoteness of damage is a question of law, but the issues are often very closely related. The simple test of causation is the 'but for' test,[37] ie, would the damage have occurred but for the defendant's negligence. However, this is complicated by factors such as intervening causes, competing causes, third-party acts and unreasonable acts of the claimant. These issues are explored further in Chapter 7. Causation was one of the issues considered by the Court of Appeal in *Page v Smith*.[38] This concerned a plaintiff who had previously suffered from the condition known as myalgic encephalomyelitis ('ME') and was subsequently involved in a fairly minor road accident. He suffered no physical injury but the judge at first instance accepted that the accident had caused the plaintiff's ME to recur. In the Court of Appeal, Ralph Gibson LJ said:

The point at which, for my part, the reasoning and conclusion of the judge on the issue of causation appear to be unsatisfactory is in his application of his finding about the degree of severity of the collision to the reasoning and opinions of the doctors. . . . It seems to me that the submissions for the defendant must be accepted, namely that there was no clear evidence from any witness to the effect that other cases had been observed or reported in which an accident causing no physical injury, and no more 'nervous shock' than some immediate fright, had caused either the onset or serious or permanent worsening of symptoms of ME. I am unable to accept that the evidence before the court is sufficient to justify a holding that the accident in probablity caused or materially contributed to the plaintiff's condition.[39]

It is interesting to speculate whether the judgment would have been the same if the disorder suffered by the plaintiff had been a reactive depression or post-traumatic stress disorder ('PTSD'), or whether the scepticism which surrounds the condition of ME was a factor which influenced the court. The House of Lords (see further page 38) sent the case back to the Court of Appeal to consider whether the judge at first instance, who had found in favour of the plaintiff, had used the wrong causation test and/or had reached the wrong conclusion on the facts.[40] The Court of Appeal found that the judge had been wrong to refer to the increase in the *risk* that the plaintiff's symptoms would be aggravated but he had correctly concluded, on the basis of *McGhee v National Coal Board*,[41] that the negligence was a material cause of the aggravation itself. It was found that on the basis of the medical evidence before him, the judge was entitled to conclude that the ME could, and had been, aggravated by the trauma.

Causation was the problem which faced the Court of Appeal in *Calascione v Dixon*.[42] The plaintiff had come upon the motorcycle accident which had

---

[37] See *Barnett v Chelsea & Kensington Hospital Management Committee* [1969] 1 QB 428.
[38] [1994] 4 All ER 522.   [39] ibid at 537.   [40] [1995] 2 WLR 644.   [41] [1973] 1 WLR 1.
[42] (1993) 19 BMLR 97.

killed her 20-year-old son. She did not immediately realize his involvement, but shortly afterwards drove to his house and discovered what had happened. She was taken to the hospital where, after a while, she was told her son was dead, and, upon identifying his body, she found that her son was barely recognizable (the trial judge suggested that there had not been time to clean him up 'very successfully'). However, subsequent events also played a part in her resulting psychiatric conditions. The defendant was charged only with driving without due care and attention (although he had been speeding and on the wrong side of the road), and the plaintiff's attempt, via a private prosecution, to convict him of causing death by dangerous driving failed. The defendant was eventually convicted of the lesser offence and fined £250 and awarded five penalty points. The plaintiff sued under the Law Reform (Miscellaneous Provisions) Act 1934 and the Fatal Accidents Act 1976, and on her own behalf in respect of nervous shock. She was suffering from two illnesses: PTSD and pathological grief disorder. The trial judge held that the former had been caused by witnessing the accident, but the latter, which was the more serious condition, was attributable to the later events relating to the prosecutions. The Court of Appeal refused to interfere with this decision, holding that the judge had applied the correct test, ie that the 'shock' of the event must be the cause, and that, on the evidence, it was not the cause of the pathological grief disorder. The evidence given at trial had suggested that her sense of injustice at what had happened was a crucial part of her condition and that had been as a result of the lenient treatment of the defendant.

In *Vernon v Bosley (No 1)*[43] the plaintiff suffered psychiatric injury after he witnessed the death of his two children when the car in which they were being driven by their nanny plunged into a river. The issues before the Court of Appeal were quantum of damages and whether the psychiatric injury had been caused by the shock of witnessing the event or by the fact of the death of the children. Like Mrs Calascione, the plaintiff had suffered a pathological grief reaction and the defendant's argument was that even if he had not witnessed the tragedy he would still have suffered in the same way. Evans LJ, supported by Thorpe LJ (Stuart-Smith LJ dissenting on the assessment of factual causation) acknowledged that damages are not awarded for so-called normal grief (according to Evans LJ, because such damage is too remote, but surely the better justification is that if it is a normal reaction, there is no damage, an essential element of the tort of negligence; see further Chapter 2). However, it was also stated that in such a case, there would inevitably be an element of normal grief and disentangling this from a compensatable pathological reaction would be difficult. In the light of this difficulty the court stated that, on the basis of *Bonington Castings v Wardlow*,[44] it was enough that the resulting psychiatric illness was

---

[43] [1997] 1 All ER 577.   [44] [1956] AC 613.

substantially caused by witnessing the event, even if there may have been another causal factor involved.

The earlier Court of Appeal decision of *Hinz v Berry*[45] had taken a different approach in saying that an estimate should be made of what the plaintiff would have suffered in any event to compare with the condition of the plaintiff after the shock. The approach in *Vernon v Bosley* is surely to be preferred as it avoids the evidential problems referred to, and it also avoids a potentially offensive situation where someone in a very close and devoted relationship would recover less compensation than someone in a less close relationship because, in the former case, their 'normal' grief would have been that much more.

The eggshell-skull rule

Page v Smith was also about the application of what is variously known as the 'eggshell-skull' or '*talem qualem*' rule, that one takes one's victim as one finds him: 'If a man is negligently run over or otherwise negligently injured in his body, it is no answer to the sufferer's claim for damages that he would have suffered less injury, or no injury at all, if he had not had an unusually thin skull or an unusually weak heart.'[46] This applies as much to psychiatric injury claims as it does to claims for physical injury, ie, once some psychiatric injury is foreseeable then, even if the claimant is suffering from some pre-existing susceptibility which results in much more severe illness than in the 'normal' person, there can be recovery for *all* psychiatric injury because it is damage of the same *kind*. What is *not* the case, however, is that if the claimant is of a psychologically vulnerable disposition then, no matter how trivial the event, if it produces the necessary psychiatric illness, the claimant can recover. The law distinguishes between 'primary' and 'secondary' victims. A primary victim is usually defined as someone within the range of foreseeable *physical* injury and a claimant can recover damages for psychiatric injury in such circumstances. If, however, he is a secondary victim then the 'normal fortitude' rule will apply, although there is an argument that the rule should only apply to 'mere bystanders' (see further page 101). In order for the claim to succeed at all, the event itself must be such that a person of normally phlegmatic disposition would be likely to be affected. This was established in *Bourhill v Young*.[47] Lord Wright said:

No doubt it has long ago been stated and often restated that if the wrong is established the wrongdoer must take the victim as he finds him. That, however, is only true ... on the condition that the wrong has been established or admitted. The

---

[45] [1970] 2 QB 40.   [46] *Dulieu v White & Sons* [1901] 2 KB 669, per Kennedy J at 679.
[47] [1943] AC 92.

question of liablity is anterior to the question of the measure of the consequences which go with the liability.[48]

There is no contradiction with the *talem qualem* rule. It is simply that injury of that type must be foreseeable. An example given in that case of unforeseeable *physical* injury illustrates the position. Lord Wright said:

One who suffers from the terrible tendency to bleed on slight contact, which is denoted by the term 'a bleeder', cannot complain if he mixes with the crowd and suffers severely, perhaps fatally, from being merely brushed against. There is no wrong done there.[49]

It must be stressed, however, that *Bourhill v Young* was about a 'mere bystander'. Primary victim cases are now treated differently since *Page v Smith*, and earlier cases have acknowledged the possibility of devastating consequences following relatively trivial incidents such as *Brice v Brown*[50] (see page 193) which concerned a woman who suffered minor injuries in a road accident, and whose daughter suffered a very bad laceration to her forehead. Clearly it was a much more distressing accident than the one in which Mr Page was involved, but nevertheless it was a relatively minor accident, though Mrs Brice developed a most severe psychiatric condition as a result of it.

However, the law at present is that the secondary victim vulnerable to injury of this type will recover nothing if the event itself would not be distressing or shocking to the person of average mental resilience because it would not have been foreseeable that distress or shock would have been experienced. Once it has been established that the event is distressing or shocking then, by application of the egg-shell skull rule, the vulnerable plaintiff will recover for the injury caused, however severe. This is assuming, of course, that factual causation can be proved. A pre-existing condition can have an effect upon the level of damages awarded in certain circumstances. This will be further considered in Chapter 6.

OTHER AREAS OF TORT

Although a psychiatric injury claim will usually arise in negligence, it may arise in a number of other tortious areas. It is essential to remember that the restrictions which we have been considering above apply only to *negligence* and if it is possible to plead another cause of action this may have enormous advantages for the plaintiff. The tort of deceit for example, could result in

---

[48] ibid, at 109–10.   [49] ibid, at 109.   [50] [1984] 1 All ER 997.

psychiatric injury. One of the earliest cases where damages were awarded was *Wilkinson v Downton*,[51] where, as a practical joke, the defendant had falsely represented to a married woman that her husband had met with a serious accident whereby both his legs were broken, as a result of which the woman suffered serious shock.

Other torts where psychiatric injury may result include false imprisonment, malicious prosecution, defamation, intimidation and breach of stutory duty. It is important to remember, of course, that the various limiting factors which apply in nervous shock cases, ie psychiatric injury caused by negligence, do not apply in the intentional torts.

INJURIES CAUSED BY INTENTIONAL ACTS

Deceit

The case of *Wilkinson v Downton*[52] established liability for psychiatric injury caused by a deliberate, as opposed to negligent, act of the defendant. Liability was established on the basis that this was a *wilful* act calculated to cause harm to the plaintiff. A claim in negligence for such damage would not have been allowable given the state of the law at that time. There is some force in the argument that *Wilkinson v Downton* liability is now of limited interest only, given the development of liability in negligence for psychiatric injury. However, it must be noted that the advantage of it is that, unlike a claim in negligence, it is not necessary to show that the injury was caused by some sudden impact or trauma upon the senses (see further the decision of the House of Lords in *Hunter v Canary Wharf*[53] discussed below). In *Wilkinson v Downton*, of course, liability was established on the basis of a statement only.

It can also be said that the limitations placed upon liability in negligence by the concept of remoteness of damage are not appropriate in the case of intentional acts. If a certain result is intended, can it ever be said to be too remote? However, practical difficulties may arise inasmuch as although the *act* may be intentional, its *consequences* may not have been. Would recklessness as to the consequences suffice? It is also a moot point whether, in relation to an intended act, there is a requirement that the plaintiff has suffered a recognizable psychiatric illness. If it can be established that the result was intended then it could be argued that non-medical mental distress would suffice.

In the case of *Powell v Boladz*[54] the issue was an alleged intentional falsification of medical records. The plaintiff was the parent of a child who

[51] [1897] 2 QB 57.   [52] [1897] 2 QB 57.
[53] [1997] 2 WLR 684.   [54] [1998] Lloyd's Rep Med 116.

died of a rare disease, which GPs and hospital staff had failed to diagnose. Liability was admitted and damages paid for the death of the child. However, the father then went on to issue further proceedings in respect of a psychiatric condition which he developed as a result of the GP's alleged removal and falsification of the child's medical records which related to the child's death. The action was brought: (a) in negligence on the basis that the parent was owed a duty of care; (b) in trespass to the person on the basis that it was a variant on the tort established in *Wilkinson v Downton*; and (c) on the basis of the tort of conspiracy to injure by unlawful means in relation to the economic loss suffered by the parent as a result of his unsuccessful appeal to the Secretary of State. At first instance the judge struck out the claim as disclosing no cause of action. An appeal was dismissed by the Court of Appeal. As far as the first proposed cause of action was concerned, the court found that there was no duty of care owed to the parent of a patient as there was not a sufficiently proximate relationship between the doctor and the parent. Although the parent was also a patient of the GP, a duty of care only existed in respect of treatment given to him, the parent. As to the second proposed cause of action, the court held that there was no *Wilkinson v Downton* claim because there was no statement, known to be false, which was made with the intention of causing the injury. Intention to injure could not be imputed to the doctor as he did not have the necessary degree of foresight to appreciate the consequences of his actions. Finally, as to the third cause of action, it had not been established that the conspiracy was aimed or directed at the plaintiffs, and, in any event, it had to be actionable by the plaintiff; the fact that it might be a crime or a breach of contract with a third party was not enough.

In *Wong v Parkside Health Trust*[55] the plaintiff had suffered harassment by various colleagues as a result of which she suffered both physical and psychiatric injuries, and she successfully brought a private prosecution for assault against one of them. She went on to bring a claim against him for 'intentional harassment' and a claim against their employer on the basis of vicarious liability. At first instance her claim against her colleague was struck out on the basis that, before the Protection from Harassment Act 1997 there was no cause of action at common law and, because there had already been a prosecution, any allegation of intentional infliction of harm was excluded from consideration under section 45 of the Offences Against the Person Act 1861. The Court of Appeal dismissed her appeal, as, following the exclusion of her claim under the 1861 Act, all that remained were her allegations that the colleague had been rude and unfriendly, and an intention to cause harm could not be imputed.

---

[55] [2001] EWCA Civ 1721.

Harassment

Following *Khorasandjian v Bush*[56] it seemed that harassment might be regarded as a new tort, or a specific aspect of the tort of nuisance (see *Burris v Azadani*[57]). The plaintiff was subjected to persistent telephone calls from a former lover. By a majority, the Court of Appeal held that her action to obtain an injunction under the tort of nuisance should succeed, despite the fact that she had no interest in the property in which she lived (she lived with her parents in their home), basing their decision on the fact that it would be absurd for her success or otherwise to depend upon the precise nature of her interest in the property in which she lived. Although *McCall v Abelesz*,[58] had denied a remedy in tort in respect of landlord harassment, this was on the basis that an action would lie for breach of covenant for quiet enjoyment. However, the possibility of harassment claims via the tort of nuisance was relatively short-lived because in the decision of the House of Lords in *Hunter v Canary Wharf*,[59] *Khorasandjian v Bush* was disposed of in the following fashion:

In truth, what the Court of Appeal appears to have been doing was to exploit the law of private nuisance in order to create by the back door a tort of harassment which was only partially effective in that it was artificially limited to harassment which takes place in her home ... In any event, a tort of harassment has now received statutory recognition: see the Protection from Harassment Act 1997.[60]

In consequence, it was held that only a person with an interest in land could sue in nuisance.

As referred to in Lord Goff's judgment, since *Khorasandjian v Bush* the Protection from Harassment Act 1997 has created a statutory tort of harassment (as well as a criminal offence), when the perpetrator engages in 'a course of conduct which amounts to harassment'.

Intimidation

Coercion is an essential element of intimidation, and it is therefore, by its very nature, intentional. An example of the sort of situation where psychiatric injury or general distress could well result is illustrated by *Godwin v Uzioqwe*[61] which concerned a 16-year-old girl who had been brought from Nigeria to work as a domestic servant and who had been treated as a drudge for two and a half years, with no proper food, clothing or social life. Damages of £20,000 were awarded for deprivation of these life essentials.

---

[56] [1993] QB 727.   [57] [1995] 4 All ER 802.   [58] [1976] QB 585, CA.
[59] [1997] 2 WLR 684.   [60] ibid, per Lord Goff at 695.   [61] The Times, 18 June 1992.

Breach of statutory duty

This is briefly considered in relation to non-shock cases in Chapter 5. A claim can be brought if, upon the construction of the relevant legislation, it is appropriate to infer a private action for damages. The precise nature of the relationship between negligence and the tort of breach of statutory duty is by no means clear because liability can be strict, or it can effectively add nothing to the approach in an ordinary negligence claim. However it was raised in connection with the Piper Apha oil rig disaster following the failure of the claims for damages for psychiatric injury brought by Mr McFarlane. The plaintiff subsequently brought an action against his solicitor and counsel for failing to plead (in addition to the claim in negligence), breach of statutory duty (regulation 32 of the Offshore Installations (Operational Safety, Health and Welfare) Regulations 1976).[62] In *McFarlane v Wilkinson*[63] the Court of Appeal held that although the regulations were intended to ensure the safety of those near the rig as well as on it, it was not enough to show that the breach caused the injury. He had to show that it was likely, not merely possible, that the breach would cause him injury, in order to obtain protection under the regulations. It was correct, therefore, to state that a claim for breach would not have enhanced the claim in negligence.

Other intentional torts

Clearly, any of the intentional torts such as false imprisonment, trespass, malicious prosecution and defamation which result in psychiatric injury should attract compensation, subject to foreseeability and causation issues being satisfied. In *Harrison and Hope v Chief Constable of Greater Manchester*[64] (a county court case) the plaintiffs were a mother and son whose house was searched by the police, pursuant to lawfully issued search warrants. The judge found that the police were entitled to enter the property under section 17 of the Police and Criminal Evidence Act 1984, but not to search. He awarded both plaintiffs damages (£1,000 each) for trespass, but the PTSD of the son was not compensated because of a failure of causation. It was found that he would have so suffered in the event of a lawful entry without the search of his bedroom.

Assaults

The criminal law has acknowledged that an assault can exist in a psychological form: in *R v Chan-Fook*[65] it was held that it is not necessary for direct

---

[62] SI 1976/1019. [63] [1997] 2 Lloyd's Rep 259. [64] [1995] CLY 1846.
[65] [1994] 1 WLR 689.

physical force to be applied to a person for an assault occasioning actual bodily harm to exist, and this was affirmed by the House of Lords in *R v Ireland, R v Burstow*[66] and extended to the offence of grievous bodily harm contrary to section 20 of the Offences Against the Person Act 1861. In *Burstow* the argument surrounded the word 'inflict' and whether it required the application of physical force. This was perhaps the most well known of the recent 'stalker' cases. There was no doubt about the requirement of grievous bodily harm being satisfied: the victim was suffering from a serious depressive illness such that she feared for her life at the hands of the defendant. The court took a strong, purposive approach to the legislation: in 1861 psychiatric injury may well not have been anticipated by the draftsman of the Act, but subsequent developments had shown that distinctions between physical and psychiatric harm were not clear cut, and it made no sense to extend psychiatric injury to actual bodily harm and not to grievous bodily harm. *Ireland* confirmed that threats made over the telephone can constitute an assault if they are sufficiently 'immediate'.

COMPENSATION FOR CRIMINAL INJURIES

It is appropriate to consider criminal injuries separately because in most cases the victim will not seek compensation through an ordinary civil action but will pursue a claim through the statutory criminal injuries scheme.

As originally introduced in 1964, the scheme was wholly administrative and there was no legal right to compensation, although decisions were judicially reviewable. The scheme is now (for injuries received on or after 1 April 1996) governed by the Criminal Injuries Compensation Act 1995. The Criminal Injuries Compensation Authority considers applications for compensation from victims of 'criminal injuries' or from dependants if the victim dies. There is a review procedure if the applicant rejects the first decision made, thereafter there is an appeal to the Authority. There is no definitive list of 'criminal injuries' but the scheme effectively adopts the categories which resulted from the operation of the old administrative scheme: a crime of violence (including arson, fire-raising and poisoning), trespass on the railway, the apprehension or attempted apprehension of an offender or the prevention or attempted prevention of an offence. In addition, section 109(1)(a)(ii) of the Criminal Justice Act 1988 states that a personal injury is a criminal injury when it is directly attributable to conduct constituting an offence which requires proof of intent to cause death or

---

[66] [1998] AC 147.

personal injury or recklessness as to whether death or personal injury is caused. It has been held that committing suicide is not a crime of violence (*Craig v CICB*[67] and *R v CICB, ex p Webb*[68]).

Paragraph 9 of the scheme states:

For the purposes of this Scheme, personal injury includes physical injury (including fatal injury), mental injury (that is, a medically recognised psychiatric or psychological illness) and disease (that is, a medically recognised illness or condition). Mental injury or disease may either result directly from the physical injury or occur without any physical injury, but compensation will not be payable for mental injury alone unless the applicant:

(a)   was put in reasonable fear of immediate physical harm to his own person; or

(b)   had a close relationship of love and affection with another person at the time when that person sustained physical (including fatal) injury directly attributable to conduct . . . And

(i)   that relationship still subsists (unless the victim has since died), and

(ii)   the applicant either witnessed and was present on the occasion when the other person sustained the injury, or was closely involved in its immediate aftermath;

(c)   was the non-consenting victim of a sexual offence (which does not include a victim who consented in fact but was deemed in law not to have consented); or

(d)   being a person employed in the business of a railway, either witnessed and was present on the occasion when another person sustained physical (including fatal) injury directly attributable to an offence of trespass on a railway, or was closely involved in its immediate aftermath.[69]

It is interesting to consider this provision in relation to the Australian case of *Fagan v Crimes Compensation Tribunal*[70] on the interpretation of the Criminal Injuries Compensation Act 1972 of Victoria, which resulted in damages being awarded to a boy who was aged five when his mother was murdered, and who suffered 'nervous shock' as a result. He was at school at the time of the murder, and the case hinged on the interpretation of the statute concerned; in particular, whether the injury was 'by or as a result of the criminal act'. The High Court held that the tribunal considering the application had erred in applying the common law principle of remoteness rather than simply looking at the words of the Act. If the latter approach was taken then it had to be said that the child had suffered his psychological injury as a result of a criminal act. Could a similar interpretation be made of being 'closely involved in its immediate aftermath'? Personal injury is 'directly attributable' if the incident from which the injury arose would be

---

[67] The Scotsman, 23 December 1992.   [68] [1987] 1 QB 74.

[69] It should be noted that, generally, unless taking an exceptional risk, those engaged in law enforcement activities are exempt from the scheme, save for the provisions of this sub-paragraph.

[70] (1982) 150 CLR 666.

considered by a reasonable person who knew all the facts to be a substantial cause of the injury, but not necessarily the only cause.[71]

Someone who witnesses the violent killing or injuring of another and who suffered psychiatric injury as a result of that will satisfy the 'directly attributable' condition. In *R v CICB, ex p Johnson*[72] the Queen's Bench Divisional Court held that the direct attributability test did not function according to the same criteria as the reasonable foreseeability test for nervous shock. The case concerned a woman who was psychiatrically injured after discovering the body of a friend who had died as a result of a violent crime. The court held that psychiatric injury (as opposed to mere shock) had to be proved as did causation, but *not* foreseeability.

It is not necessary that the offender should have been convicted, but the Board may withhold or reduce compensation if an applicant has not taken, without delay, all reasonable steps to inform the police or other appropriate authority of the circumstances of the injury with a view to bringing the offender to justice. However, it is appreciated that in the case of young children, they may have been too young or too frightened to know what to do, and there is a discretion in such cases. In addition, the requirement that the parties have stopped living together for good (see below) may not be strictly applied, although compensation will not be paid if there is any likelihood that the perpetrator of the crime will benefit from it.

The resulting injury can be physical or psychiatric and must be directly attributable to the criminal offence. Accidental injuries, even if caused by a road traffic accident where a road traffic offence has been committed, are excluded. As far as violence within the family is concerned, under paragraph 16 of the scheme if the applicant and the person who injured the applicant were living together in the same household at the time of the incident, compensation cannot be paid unless the person who caused the injury has been prosecuted (unless there are good reasons why this could not happen) *and* the parties have stopped living together for good. The award is subject to reduction on the basis of the applicant's conduct or character.

It should be noted here that the *conduct* constitutes an offence, whatever actual damage is caused, and the key elements are intention or recklessness. In the case of *Brown*,[73] a woman who suffered head injuries and 'psychological problems' when a raw potato thrown at a fellow employee missed him and hit her instead was found to be a victim of a crime of violence as this was regarded as a case of transferred malice and it did not matter that the woman had not reported the matter to the police. For that reason, compensation is not payable in respect of road traffic accidents except where the injury is due

---

[71] See *R v Criminl Injuries Compensation Board, ex p Ince* [1973] 1 WLR 1334, CA.
[72] The Times, 11 August 1994.
[73] 12 February 1993, CICB Appeal Board, Leicester.

to a deliberate attempt to run the victim down. The scheme specifically includes arson and poisoning, and it includes sexual abuse such as rape, incest and buggery, and also indecent assault. A person engaged in law enforcement activity is covered by the scheme. It is interesting to note the specific inclusion of the offence of trespass on a railway so as to cover the cases of shock produced in railway workers who came upon cases of suicide or attempted suicide, and drivers of trains that have hit people attempting suicide. If the victim is subjected to fear either of physical injury[74] or incarceration, or fear for a loved one or whatever fear may be induced by the criminal act and this causes psychiatric injury, then the victim is entitled to compensation under the scheme if the injury is 'directly attributable'.

As far as time limits are concerned, claims should be made as soon as possible and in any event within two years of the incident (it used to be three years), except that in exceptional cases this requirement can be waived. Cases involving children are often treated as exceptional.

The significant difference between the old and new schemes is that formerly compensation was calculated on the basis of tort calculations of damages, whereas now there is a tariff scheme for particular types of injury, graded according to the severity of the injury. There is not, however, a calculation to take into account the subjective factors which might make the injury particularly more debilitating for this particular applicant. Compensation is also given for loss of earnings and expenses. As far as psychiatric injury is concerned, the tariffs are as follows:

Disabling, but temporary mental anxiety, medically verified	£1,000
Disabling mental disorder, confirmed by psychiatric diagnosis	
lasting up to 28 weeks	£2,500
lasting over 28 weeks to one year	£4,000
lasting over one year but not permanent	£7,500
Permanently disabling mental disorder confirmed by	
psychiatric prognosis	£20,000

In *R v Criminal Injuries Compensation Appeals Panel, ex p Bennett*,[75] the court upheld the decision of the Criminal Injuries Compensation Appeals Panel that a mental disorder was not 'disabling' for more than 28

---

[74] See the Criminal Injuries Compensation Board's *Report* (1983), p 20, for a case where compensation was awarded to a young girl who had been forced into prostitution by threats of violence.

[75] 10 July 2000, QBD (Jackson J).

weeks. The victim had been subjected to an attack with an iron bar and had developed PTSD. The Panel had awarded her £2,500 on the basis that her condition had not been disabling for a longer period of time. The court held that, whilst the Panel, described as having 'considerable expertise' had to take into account the medical evidence produced, were not bound to agree with everything. The Panel had been correct in attaching some significance to the fact that the victim had returned to work within three months. A mental disorder was 'disabling' if it significantly impaired a person's functioning in some important aspect of his or her life and the standard to be adopted was that of 'the ordinary person adopting a sensible view of life'.

CONTRACT

Put simply, the purpose of damages for breach of contract is to put the injured party in the position which would have obtained if the contract had been properly performed. Damages are awarded to compensate for loss caused by the breach which the parties, at the time of entering into the contract, would expect to arise from a breach. The rule is well-known and was first formulated in *Hadley v Baxendale*,[76] in which Alderson B said:

Where two parties have made a contract which one of them has broken, the damages which the other party ought to receive in respect of such breach of contract should be such as may fairly and reasonably be considered either arising naturally, ie, according to the usual course of things, from such breach of contract itself, or such as may reasonably be supposed to have been in the contemplation of both parties, at the time they made the contract, as the probable result of the breach of it.[77]

Injury of a psychiatric nature, therefore, would have to be a natural consequence of the breach, ie, what reasonable persons entering into the contract would believe to be a likely consequence of the breach, or it would have to be a consequence of the breach given what the parties knew or should have known at the time the contract was made. However, in a personal injury case (including psychiatric injury) this rule does not apply. For an injured railway passenger, for example, any claim for physical or psychiatric injury would be founded in tort and so the rule in *Hadley v Baxendale* would not apply.[78] Similarly for cases of medical negligence when the plaintiff is a private paying patient the claim would be in contract, whereas in NHS cases, it would be founded in tort.[79] Specific issues relating to contract claims will be considered in Chapters 5 and 6.

---

[76] (1854) 9 Ex 341.   [77] ibid, at 354.
[78] See *Phillips v London & South Western Railway Co* (1879) 4 QBD 406.
[79] It was held in *Pfizer Corporation v Ministry of Health* [1965] AC 512 that where services are provided pursuant to a statutory obligation there is no contractual relationship.

However unforeseeable the damage may have been in tort, as long as the special circumstances can be shown to exist in *this* contract, the claim is allowable. Furthermore, as in tort, once this has been established, it does not matter if the extent of the psychiatric injury is far greater than either party could have anticipated. The distinction is that once the *type* of damage is accepted as being within the contemplation of the parties then it does not matter that the *extent* of the damage was not so contemplated.[80] However, arguments do arise over the difference between type and extent of damage, and sometimes the distinction is not made out. It is always important to remember that regardless of whether one is pursuing a claim in contract or in tort, one will be facing limitations which, in both cases, have been devised by the courts to avoid extending the area of liability to an unacceptable extent.

ORDINARY MENTAL DISTRESS

Often when psychiatric injury is considered, reference will also be made to 'shock' in its colloquial and non-medical sense. Most people involved in, say, a road traffic accident, would say they felt shocked by it. Anyone who receives news of the injury of a loved one will be distressed; a close bereavement will cause grief. All these are examples of non-medical distress. Is it possible to claim damages for such conditions?

Ordinary mental distress in tort

Ordinary mental distress is not generally compensatable in tort. However, there are a number of torts where, by their very nature, mental distress is an esential component, such as defamation (injury to feelings), malicious prosecution, false imprisonment, deceit, injurious falsehood and assault. In *Bone v Seale*,[81] the Court of Appeal considered the appropriateness of awarding damages for distress in nuisance. The nuisance concerned was a noxious odour which had been present for some twelve years or so, but in respect of which there had been no provable diminution in the value of the plaintiff's property. The trial judge had awarded £6,000 in damages, but this was reduced by the Court of Appeal to £1,000. Drawing a parallel between such a case and personal injury cases, Stephenson LJ said:

Is it possible to equate loss of sense of smell as a result of the negligence of a defendant motor driver with having to put up with positive smells as a result of a

---

[80] *H Parsons (Livestock) Ltd v Uttley Ingham & Co Ltd* [1978] QB 791, CA; *Victoria Laundry (Windsor) Ltd v Newman Industries Ltd* [1949] 2 KB 528; *Koufos v C Czarnikow Ltd* [1969] 1 AC 350.

[81] [1975] 1 WLR 797.

nuisance created by a negligent neighbour? There is, as it seems to me, some parallel between the loss of amenity which is caused by personal injury and the loss of amenity which is caused by a nuisance of this kind.[82]

It may be that other torts such as trespass to property, trespass to goods, etc are capable of giving rise to damages for mental distress if the appropriate set of circumstances prevailed. Statutory torts such as breaches of the Sex Discrimination Act 1975 or the Race Relations Act 1976 might give rise to, as an allowable head of damages, compensation in respect of injury to feelings.[83] In *Racz v Home Office*[84] damages for mental distress were awarded for misfeasance in public office.

What of damages for ordinary mental distress in negligence? In one sense damages are always awarded for mental distress if there is some physical injury because in such a case there are damages for pain and suffering, both of which are forms of mental distress. If, however, we look for a separate head of damage to cover mental distress or shock or grief or anger, or any other similar aspect of non-medical distress, then we look in vain. It has been held by the Court of Appeal in the case of *Nicholls v Rushton*[85] that a plaintiff involved in a motor accident who had suffered no physical injury, but had suffered a nervous reaction falling short of an identifiable psychiatric illness, could not recover damages: unless there was physical injury no question of damages for mental suffering, fear, anxiety and the like arose.

The House of Lords considered damages for fear in *Hicks v Chief Constable of the South Yorkshire Police*.[86] The case concerned two victims of the Hillsborough football stadium disaster, who had died of traumatic asphyxia. Their personal representatives brought actions for damages for pre-death injuries. The post-mortems showed no evidence of any physical injuries attributable to anything other than the fatal crushing that had caused the asphyxia, which, it was said, would have caused loss of consciousness within seconds and death within five minutes. It was held therefore that it could not be proved on the balance of probabilities that they had sustained any pre-death physical injuries. There was also argument as to whether damages for physical injuries should be increased on the account of the terrifying circumstances in which they were inflicted. Lord Bridge of Harwich said that it was perfectly clear law that fear by itself, of whatever degree, was a normal emotion for which no damages could be awarded. This is the same principle which denies the sufferer from 'ordinary' grief any damages for this normal emotion, which principle has a long and continuing

---

[82] ibid, at 803–4.
[83] See the Sex Discrimination Act 1975, s 66(4), and the Race Relations Act 1976, s 57(4); and see further Chapter 6.
[84] [1994] 2 AC 45.   [85] The Times, 19 June 1992.   [86] [1992] 2 All ER 65.

history.[87] Similarly, it was held in *Reilly and another v Merseyside Regional Health Authority*,[88] that claustrophobia and fear, even when they produced physical reactions such as sweating and vomiting, were within the normal human emotional experience and would only be compensatable if they amounted to a recognizable psychiatric condition. However, it should be noted that there is a recognizable psychiatric condition known as 'acute distress reaction', which is of short duration, and there appears no reason why damages should not be awarded for this, albeit in a modest sum. In other words, if so-called 'ordinary shock' is definable medically, then on the present law damages must surely be allowable. If the appropriate diagnosis had been made in *Nicholls v Rushton* then the plaintiff should have recovered damages.

Ordinary mental distress in contract

Where breach of contract has caused mental distress the crucial questions are whether the mental distress was a natural consequence of the breach of contract or whether it was within the contemplation of the parties that the breach would result in such distress. The history of damages claims shows a robust approach by the courts. In *Addis v Gramophone Co Ltd*,[89] it was held that damages for the wrongful dismissal of a servant could not include compensation for his injured feelings, however harsh and humiliating his dismissal had been. In a professional negligence case, Lord Denning MR said:

It can be foreseen that there will be injured feelings; mental distress; anger; and annoyance; but for none of these damages can be recovered.[90]

This view remained paramount until 1971 when a Scottish case[91] awarded damages for distress and disappointment to a bride who had no photographs of her wedding day following the breach of contract of the photographer commissioned to attend. In the important decision of *Jarvis v Swans Tours*,[92] the well-known case of the solicitor disappointed with his holiday, it was held that damages could be recovered for disappointment, distress, annoyance and frustration. As McGregor points out, 'the predominant object of the contract was the provision of some mental satisfaction ... by the giving of pleasure',[93] and in the subsequent case of *Heywood v Wellers*,[94] 'some mental satisfaction ... by the removal of distress'. The

---

[87] See, *Alcock v Chief Constable of the South Yorkshire Police* [1992] 1 AC 310, per Lord Ackner at 401.

[88] The Independent, 29 April 1994.   [89] [1909] AC 488, HL.

[90] *Cook v Swinfen* [1967] 1 WLR 457, CA, at 461.

[91] *Diesen v Samson* 1971 (Sh Ct) 49.   [92] [1973] QB 233.

[93] *McGregor on Damages*, 15th edn (London: Sweet & Maxwell, 1988).

[94] [1976] QB 446, CA.

Heywood case concerned an action against a solicitor by his former client, who had asked him to bring proceedings for a non-molestation order, and it was held that both solicitor and client would have contemplated that a failure by the solicitor to perform the contract would result in vexation, frustration or distress.

However, in *Channon v Lindley Johnstone*[95] the Court of Appeal declined to award damages for inconvenience, distress and disappointment following the negligence of solicitors in the conduct of matrimonial proceedings the outcome of which was described as being 'highly unsatisfactory, if not ruinous to the claimant'. The trial judge had awarded damages for loss of a chance and £10,000 for inconvenience, distress and disappointment but the Court of Appeal held that the solicitor's retainer did not amount to a contract to protect the claimant from mental distress or to procure for him a particular beneficial result.

The House of Lords has recently considered the matter of contractual damages for mental distress in the case of *Farley v Skinner*.[96] The plaintiff instructed a surveyor to prepare a report in respect of a property he wished to buy and, because of its proximity to Gatwick airport, he had specifically asked him to report on aircraft noise. The report was positive in this respect and the claimant purchased the property. It turned out that the property was close to a navigation beacon and aircraft were stacked up there waiting to land. He decided to remain living at the property but sued for damages for diminution of value of the property and for impairment of his use and enjoyment of it. In the event, it was found that the property had not reduced in value, but damages of £10,000 were awarded for the second part of the claim. The House of Lords upheld the award. It was stated that damages for non-pecuniary matters could be awarded in circumstances in which it has been made clear to the other party to the contract that the matter was important to the claimant, and that it was a specific term of the contract.

In 1975 Lawton J awarded damages to a former employee who claimed damages in respect of mental distress following breach of the contract of employment since it would have been in the contemplation of the parties that the breach, without reasonable notice, would expose the plaintiff to vexation, frustration and distress.[97] However, in the later case of *Bliss v South East Thames Regional Health Authority*,[98] the Court of Appeal overruled that decision stating that no such damages could be awarded in contract. It may be argued, with some ingenuity on the part of lawyers, that all successfully and properly completed contracts will contain some element of mental

---

[95] 2002 WL 347091.   [96] [2001] UKHL 49.
[97] *Cox v Philips Industries Ltd* [1976] 1 WLR 638.   [98] [1987] ICR 700.

satisfaction, and no doubt this is something the courts would not wish to encourage, and would explain the reason for the decision in *Bliss*.

The issue was revisited by the House of Lords in the case of *Johnson v Unisys*[99] where the claimant had brought an action for breach of contract against his former employer. He alleged that he had suffered a mental breakdown as a result of the way in which he was dismissed. His claim was rejected on the basis of the principle in *Addis v Gramophone Co Ltd*, and the decision in *Cox v Phillips Industries Ltd* was disapproved. (See further Chapter 6.)

In *McConville and Others v Barclays Bank and Others*,[100] it was held that damages were not recoverable for worry and distress caused to bank customers arising from allegedly unauthorized debits from their accounts through automatic telling machines.

NERVOUS SHOCK IN ENGLISH LAW: A BRIEF HISTORY

Having looked at the legal framework in which the claim for psychiatric injury sits, it is proposed to give such claims their historical setting, with a brief look at the major English cases which have established psychiatric injury as a valid head of damage, and the way in which the legal concepts discussed above have been employed in these cases. It is important to note that the expression 'nervous shock' is used to emphasize the fact that the restrictions imposed as the law has developed in the cases below, apply to claims in negligence (non-employer cases) only.

Two early non-English cases merit a mention not least because of their contrasting decisions on the same point. The first is a Privy Council case, *Victorian Railways Commissioners v Coultas*,[101] in which it was held that there are no damages for nervous shock that is unaccompanied by physical injury. The second is the Irish case of *Bell v Great Northern Railway Co of Ireland*,[102] in which damages were awarded for nervous shock despite the absence of physical injury.

Dulieu v White & Sons[103]

This Court of Appeal case is one of the earliest English cases to consider the claim in some detail. The facts concerned a publican's wife, Mrs Dulieu, who was standing behind the bar of the public house, when a horse van was driven into the public house by the defendant's servant. Mrs Dulieu was pregnant at the time, and following this incident she was prematurely

[99] [2001] 2 WLR 1076.   [100] The Times, 30 June 1993.   [101] (1888) 13 App Cs 222.
[102] (1890) 26 LR Ir 428.   [103] [1901] 2 KB 669.

delivered of a brain-damaged child. She recovered damages, not for the birth of the brain-damaged child, but for her own 'illness' brought about by the shock sustained from the incident. The negligent driving of the defendant's servant was not doubted; the issue was whether damages could be recovered for shock, and, if so, under what circumstances. First, it is interesting to note the reason given for preferring the term 'nervous' as opposed to 'mental' shock. Kennedy J said:

... I venture to think 'nervous' is probably the more correct epithet where terror operates through parts of the physical organism to produce bodily illness. ... The use of the epithet 'mental' requires caution, in view of the undoubted rule that merely mental pain unaccompanied by any injury to the person cannot sustain an action of this kind.[104]

It can be seen that this is a long way off from the concept of purely psychiatric injury. His lordship went on to say that if the fear, as opposed to impact:

is proved to have naturally and directly produced physical effects ... why should not an action for those damages lie just as well as it lies where there has been an actual impact? It is not, however, to be taken that ... every nervous shock ... gives a cause of action. ... The shock, where it operates through the mind, must be a shock which arises from a reasonable fear of immediate personal injury to oneself.[105]

So there is a great deal of emphasis on the shock having produced physical injury and the restriction imposed that fear for *oneself* is essential (this is no longer good law). The case contains a good statement from Kennedy J on the policy question:

... I should be sorry to adopt a rule which would bar all such claims on grounds of policy alone, and in order to prevent the possible success of unrighteous or groundless actions.[106]

Hambrook v Stokes Brothers[107]

The defendants' lorry was left at the top of a steep and narrow street unattended, with the engine running. The lorry, being inadequately secured, ran down the hill at great speed. Mrs Hambrook was walking up the hill when she saw the lorry running away towards the spot where she had just left her children. She was immediately afterwards informed by a bystander that a child answering the description of one of her children had been injured, and that the child was in a state of some distress. She later discovered that one of her children had indeed suffered serious injury. She was pregnant at the time, and the shock was said to have caused a severe haemorrhage and she died some two and a half months after the incident. Damages were recovered on the basis that the shock received was caused by *what she saw with her own eyes* and not by what she was told by the bystander.

---

[104] ibid, at 672–3.   [105] ibid, at 675.   [106] ibid, at 681.   [107] [1925] 1 KB 141, CA.

Dulieu v White & Sons was disapproved on the basis that the fear did not have to be for oneself. The legal argument as to why Mrs Hambrook's estate should recover damages went as follows. A duty of care is owed to all those using the highway; the breach of duty does not necessarily take place when a user is struck or injured, it can take place before then, ie, when the lorry was left in such a condition that it could run away. The fact that the particular injury which Mrs Hambrook suffered was not contemplated is irrelevant: if the act might cause damage, then it is immaterial that it was not damage of the exact kind caused. As a matter of policy, it was decided that it would not be right that a mother frightened only for herself would recover, hereas a selfless mother concerned only for her child would not. Hence the disapproval of *Dulieu v White & Sons*. Atkin LJ went on to say:

Personally I see no reason for excluding the bystander in the highway who receives injury in the same way from apprehension of or the actual sight of injury to a third party.[108]

The law has still to catch up with this generous *dictum*.

Bourhill v Young[109]

The 'pregnant fishwife' case. Mrs Bourhill was a passenger on a tram and had alighted at a stop. She was about to collect her fish basket from the driver's platform, when she heard the noise of the impact between a motor cycle which had been travelling in the same direction as the tram and a motor vehicle which was turning into the road occupied by the tram. She was some 50 feet away from the collision. She subsequently saw the blood of the cyclist on the road. Her child was stillborn a month later owing to the shock sustained. The House of Lords held that she was not entitled to recover damages. The example of the 'hypothetical reasonable driver' was cited and it was held that such a driver would not have foreseen that in this case the plaintiff would suffer shock. The duty of the road user to avoid inflicting injury by shock was maintained, this being to such persons as he may reasonably foresee, but as she was not within the area of potential danger, there was no duty owed to her. In other words, she was not in fear for herself being physically injured, and, of course, she was not in fear for a loved one. When Lord Porter spoke of the 'customary phlegm' he said:

It is not every emotional disturbance or every shock which should have been foreseen. The driver of a car or vehicle, even though careless, is entitled to assume that the ordinary frequenter of the streets has sufficient fortitude to endure such incidents as may from time to time be expected to occur in them, including the noise of a collision and the sight of injury to others, and is not to be considered negligent towards one who does not possess the customary phlegm.[110]

---

[108] ibid, at 157.   [109] [1943] AC 92, HL.   [110] ibid, at 117.

McLoughlin v O'Brian[111]

This House of Lords decision examined the tort of nervous shock in some depth and will be looked at further in Chapter 4. The plaintiff was a woman who claimed damages for psychiatric injury following an accident involving her husband and children. She did not witness the accident itself, but, on arriving at the hospital, was confronted with a distressing scene of physical suffering. The two main areas considered by their lordships were, first the issue of proximity in space and time to the accident itself, and secondly whether policy issues were such as to defeat such a claim. The plaintiff had failed in her claim at first instance, and the Court of Appeal had dismissed her appeal on the basis that although it was foreseeable that a wife and mother in her position would suffer injury by shock, policy considerations were such that the duty of care was limited to those at the scene of the accident. The House of Lords allowed the plaintiff's appeal. On the issue of proximity in space and time, it was held that it was sufficient if the plaintiff witnessed the event itself *or its immediate aftermath*. Whichever is experienced, however, the experience must be through the unaided senses of the plaintiff, although some speculation was made as to whether experience through simultaneous television broadcast would suffice.

On the policy question, their lordships did not see that this would defeat a claim, largely because the risk of the floodgates opening was not regarded as a serious one: 'However liberally the criterion of reasonable foreseeability is interpreted, both the number of successful claims in this field and the quantum of damages they will attract are likely to be moderate'.[112]

Alcock v Chief Constable of the South Yorkshire Police[113]

On 15 April 1989 a football match was due to be played at the Sheffield Wednesday football stadium at Hillsborough, Sheffield. It was the semi-final of the FA Cup between Liverpool and Nottingham Forest. The Leppings Lane end of the ground had been reserved for Liverpool supporters. South Yorkshire police were organizing the crowds of supporters and negligently allowed too many into the Leppings Lane end. The result is well known. After only about six minutes, the match was abandoned due to the mayhem caused by the overcrowding on the terraces. Over 400 people were injured in the resulting crush, and 95 people were killed. The match was due to be broadcast live. Instead, the live broadcast showed the scenes of panic and chaos as supporters desperately tried to disengage themselves from a terrifying, volatile mass of people tragically confined in the 'pens' on the terraces. The broadcast appeared to have complied with the standards imposed by the requirements of broadcasting guidelines not to show pictures of suffering by recognizable individuals. The broadcast was

---

[111] [1983] 1 AC 410.   [112] ibid, per Lord Bridge at 441.   [113] [1992] 1 AC 310.

recorded for later transmission on news programmes. Many of the television viewers that afternoon and evening had friends and relatives at the match.

Action was brought by a number of plaintiffs against the Chief Constable of South Yorkshire who admitted negligence in respect of the deaths and physical injuries. The psychiatrically injured plaintiffs included people, both with and without physical injuries, who had been present at the match, and people who had witnessed the televised scenes both live and on news bulletins subsequently transmitted. The controversial cases were (a) where the plaintiffs were present at the match, received no physical injury and did not claim that they received psychiatric injury as a result of being involved in distressing scenes, but that their psychiatric injuries were a result of losing a relative in the disaster, and (b) those who were not present at the match but claimed psychiatric injury as a result of seeing the television broadcast in the full knowledge that their relative was present at the match. In other words, the cases which caused the Court of Appeal and House of Lords such concern were those which raised the tortuous problems of both proximity to the event and proximity in terms of relationship to a killed or injured person.

It will be recalled that it was established by the House of Lords in *McLoughlin v O'Brian* that a person who had witnessed 'the immediate aftermath' of a distressing event could recover damages and, in that case, Lord Wilberforce suggested that 'whether some equivalent of sight or hearing, eg, through simultaneous television, would suffice may have to be considered'.[114]

Due consideration came in *Alcock*, but it was decided that, given the television broadcasting guidelines, those who saw a disaster on television could not be considered to have suffered nervous shock induced by seeing or hearing the event since they were not in sufficient proximity to the event and would not have suffered shock in the sense of a sudden assault upon the nervous system. Lords Ackner and Oliver did, however, admit the possibility of television placing the spectator in the required degree of proximity, using the example given by Nolan LJ, when the case had been before the Court of Appeal, of live television pictures of a hot-air balloon containing a number of children, floating across the sky and suddenly bursting into flames. It was suggested by Lord Ackner that the impact of this image upon the television spectators could be as great, if not greater, than if they had been present at the scene of the accident.[115] This image and the reason for choosing it have caused some bemusement although it is accepted that a very similar situation occurred in real life when the *Challenger* space shuttle burst into flames shortly after its launch on 28 January 1986, and this event was broadcast simultaneously. The assertion that seeing this image on television would be more horrific than being present at the event itself is, of course,

---

[114] [1983] 1 AC 410, at 423.   [115] [1992] 1 AC 310, at 405.

based upon the purely subjective assessment of the judges concerned, and it is odd that such speculation should have been made. A less subjective reason for the alleged potency of such an image may well be that it would leave no doubt in the minds of the spectators that the occupants of the balloon would perish. Yet it is somewhat ironic when one considers that this would be a situation where this conclusion would be reached by *reasoning* as opposed to an instinctive reaction, and it is clear the impact of an event is not necessarily governed by the witness's rational response. It may be that their lordships did not want to reject absolutely and unequivocally all possibility of liability for an experience through an audiovisual medium, and this speculation was their way of saying the door was still slightly ajar. Even so Lord Oliver was cautionary:

... any further widening of the area of potential liability to cater for the expanded and expanding range of the media of communication ought, in my view, to be undertaken rather by Parliament, with full opportunity for public debate and representation, than by the process of judicial extrapolation.[116]

However, see the speech of Brennan J in *Sutherland Shire Council v Heyman*[117].

So what did *Alcock* say about the proximity of relationship to the dead, injured or, indeed, almost-injured person? In England and Wales no remoter relative than a parent or a spouse has successfully claimed for psychiatric injury, save for rescuers and others who fall into categories of special, but non-intimate relationship (see pages 102–106). It was accepted that cases involving more distant relatives may be admitted, albeit after being subjected to careful scrutiny. Lord Jauncey of Tullichettle stated:

I do not consider that it would be profitable to try and define who such others might be or to draw any dividing line between one degree of relationship and another.... the proper approach is to examine each case on its own facts in order to see whether the claimant has established so close a relationship of love and affection to the victim as might reasonably be expected in the case of spouses or parents and children.[118]

The Court of Appeal considered both the position of the rescuer and the mere bystander in *McFarlane v E E Caledonia Ltd*.[119] The plaintiff was employed as a painter on an oil rig in the North Sea and on the night of the massive Piper Alpha oil rig explosions he was on a support vessel 550 metres away. As a result of what he saw he suffered psychiatric injury. His position as a rescuer was considered and rejected on the basis that he was not involved in the rescue operation beyond helping to move blankets and assisting two walking injured. He also claimed, that, regardless of his involvement in the rescue, he should recover as a mere bystander because

---

[116] ibid, at 417.   [117] (1985) 157 CLR 424.   [118] [1992] 1 AC 310, at 422.
[119] [1994] 2 All ER 1.

the event was exceptionally horrific. The Court of Appeal rejected this argument stating that a 'close' relationship was necessary for a witness to recover.

The case of *Alcock* has set out the parameters of nervous shock cases, although by no means with complete clarity (see, for example, the primary/secondary confusion evidenced in *Page v Smith* examined in full below). However, despite the fact that it might be regarded as the definitive statement of the law as far as secondary victims are concerned, the outcome for some of the plaintiffs might have been very different. Brian Harrison and Robert Alcock who both witnessed the horrific events unfold, lost relatives (Alcock, a brother-in-law, Harrison, two brothers) but did not succeed because there was no evidence presented to show that they were in relationships of close love and affection. It is important to note that their presence at the ground meant that they satisfied the first requirement of the secondary victim test, ie proximity in space and time to the traumatic event, and that they were not automatically excluded from satisfying the second requirement, ie a close tie of love and affection; it was simply that the evidence did not substantiate this.

Page v Smith[120]

At the time of his road accident in July 1987 the plaintiff had been a sufferer from myalgic encephalomyelitis ('ME') and was recovering from an episode of the illness which had commenced in March 1987. He was hoping to return to work in September of that year. The accident happened when the defendant drove his car across the road in front of the plaintiff. Neither of the parties nor the defendant's passenger suffered any physical injury. The plaintiff did not report feeling particularly shocked by the incident and drove home afterwards. (There was some suggestion that the trial judge formed the view that the accident was fairly serious because Mr Page's car was a 'write off'. It was subsequently acknowledged that this might simply have related to the age of the motor vehicle and not the severity of the damage.)

About three hours after the accident Mr Page experienced symptoms of a nature that indicated that his condition was resurfacing and, at the time of the trial, he was regarded as a permanent invalid. The main issue for consideration by the House of Lords was whether it was foreseeable that someone in his position would suffer psychiatric injury. Related to this was the question as to whether the plaintiff was a person of normal fortitude and whether that is relevant to the foreseeability point. In other words, although physical injury was foreseeable even though, in the event, it did not occur, it had to be decided whether foreseeability of *psychiatric* injury was a separate requirement. The majority of the House of Lords (Lords Lloyd, Ackner and

---

[120] [1995] 2 WLR 644.

Browne-Wilkinson) held that, as Mr Page was a primary victim, the two types of injury did not have to be considered separately. It was enough that he was at risk of *personal* injury. Lords Keith and Jauncey dissented on the basis that, under the circumstances, it was unforeseeable that the plaintiff would suffer injury by shock.

The main majority judgment was that of Lord Lloyd. He said that although foreseeability of physical injury is not necessary in nervous shock cases (ie, in certain circumstances secondary victims can recover), it is sufficient. There was no need for psychiatric injury to be foreseeable as a separate form of injury: 'It could not be right that a negligent defendant should escape liability for psychiatric injury just because, though serious physical injury was foreseeable, it did not in fact transpire.'[120] He went on to say: 'There is nothing in *Bourhill v Young* to displace the ordinary rule that where the plaintiff is within the range of foreseeable physical injury the defendant must take his victim as he finds him.'[122]

However, this 'ordinary rule' had, until then, applied only to cases of physical injury, because rightly or wrongly, psychiatric injury had always been treated differently requiring distinct foreseeability. In his dissenting judgment Lord Keith had referred to the *ex post facto* approach to nervous shock cases, ie deciding what was foreseeable with the benefit of hindsight. Although Lord Lloyd accepted that the *ex post facto* rule applied in secondary victim cases on the basis that one needs to know the outcome of the event before one can say whether shock should have been foreseen, this had no place in primary victim cases: 'To introduce hindsight into the trial of an ordinary running-down action would do the law no service.'[123] Physical proximity is, therefore, everything. The primary victim can recover damages for a totally debilitating psychiatric condition because there was a risk (however small) of physical injury (however trivial). Lord Jauncey's dissenting judgment gave the, perhaps sexist, example of someone reversing their car into a tight parking space and bumping into another parked car containing 'a woman prone to hysteria'. There is no physical injury. 'Is B to be compensated because A should have foreseen that a hysterical woman might be in the car and therefore sustain a shock from a minor bump? Common sense would loudly say *No*'.[124]

Lord Lloyd deals with this in his judgment by saying that in those circumstances there would be no foreseeability of physical injury. This may be the case, but what of a scenario where the woman is in a stationary car and the other car hits her travelling at 10 mph? The only way in which these cases can be distinguished is by deciding them ex post facto, which is precisely what Lord Lloyd says is not to be done in primary victim cases.

---

[121] ibid, at 667.   [122] ibid, at 672.   [123] ibid, at 667.   [124] ibid, at 657.

White v Chief Constable of South Yorkshire Police (on appeal from Frost v Chief Constable of South Yorkshire Police)[125]

The case concerned police officers who were on duty at the Hillsborough football ground on 15 April 1989 when, due to the negligence of the police, ninety-five spectators were crushed to death and over four hundred people were injured. The officers had all suffered psychiatric injury as a result of their varying degrees of involvement in the event. The Court of Appeal by a majority found in favour of all but one of the officers, on the basis that they were akin to employees[126] (one plaintiff also fell into the rescuer category) and therefore, unlike the relatives of the victims who were also present at the ground, they were owed a pre-existing duty of care. The concept of primary and secondary victims set out in *Page v Smith* was irrelevant because it did not concern rescue situations and, importantly, as the purpose of distinguishing between primary and secondary victims was to apply limiting criteria to the latter, they did not apply when there was a pre-existing duty of care, as here.

The decision was an unattractive one inasmuch as the different treatment of these police officers compared with the unsuccessful plaintiffs in *Alcock* who searched for their relatives at the football ground that day, displayed a blatant lack of fairness. The result was that those who purchased tickets for a football match, and attended at the ground on the assumption that they would be safe, were in a disadvantaged position compared with those police officers who were paid to be there.[127]

On appeal, Lords Steyn, Hoffmann and Browne-Wilkinson found that an employer's duty to protect his employees' health and safety was subject to the 'usual' rules in nervous shock cases, and allowed the appeals. Furthermore, for a rescuer to succeed, he must be within the range of foreseeable physical injury or reasonably believe himself to be. Lord Griffiths agreed in respect of the claims *qua* employee, but upheld the decision of the Court of Appeal in respect of those officers who were deemed to be rescuers. He did not accept that a rescuer had to be in physical danger, although went on to state that if the rescuer is in no physical danger it will only be in exceptional cases that personal injury in the form of psychiatric injury will be foreseeable.

Lord Goff disagreed with the interpretation of Lord Lloyd's judgment in *Page v Smith*. Lord Lloyd was not saying that the presence of someone within the range of foreseeable physical injury was necessary, it was merely sufficient. In other words, there can be primary victims, for example, employees and rescuers, who are not within the range of physical injury.

---

[125] [1999] 2 AC 455.

[126] Although not technically employees, police officers were in the same position and this aspect of the case was never in contention in either the Court of Appeal or the House of Lords. See further the Police Act 1964, s 48.

[127] See, eg, K Wheat, '*Frost*: More Confusion and Unfairness in Psychiatric Injury Claims' [1998] MJLS 32.

Lord Steyn said that the 'narrow formulation' of Lord Lloyd in *Page v Smith* had been designed with a view to fix the boundaries of the law:

In any event, the decision . . . was plainly intended, in the context of pure psychiatric harm, to narrow the range of potential secondary victims. The reasoning of Lord Lloyd and the Law Lords who agreed with him was based on concerns about an ever widening circle of plaintiffs.[128]

Yet this is not consistent with Lord Lloyd's concern that, although as he saw it, there was no scope in that case to take the law forward, there should be no step backwards. Furthermore, if the decision was intended to have the restrictive result anticipated by Lord Steyn, it would have been open to the House of Lords to find that presence within the range of foreseeable physical injury was *necessary*, but not *sufficient*, thus still imposing a requirement that the psychiatric injury itself still had to be foreseeable. However, since *White*, rescuers are now in the same position as mere bystanders. In other words unless they can show they are within the range of foreseeable physical injury they cannot recover damages. All victims must either be primary victims, however minor the injury, or slight the risk of physical injury, or must achieve some sort of 'physical' relationship with the accident, as well as having a degree of 'relational proximity'.

The elements of a claim for psychiatric injury in negligence can be summarized as follows. First, if there is also physical injury then, subject to any difficulties which might arise from the point of view of causation, the claim for the psychiatric injury will not be contentious. Secondly, where there is no physical injury, then a distinction has been made between 'primary' and 'secondary' victims.

If the victim is a primary victim then, since *Page v Smith*,[129] there are no limiting factors; the claimant will be treated in the same way as a claimant who has physical injuries.

If the victim is a secondary victim then he must be present at the event which has been responsible for causing the injury, or at its immediate aftermath, and the event has to be such as to have a shocking effect upon the senses, and to be of a sufficient magnitude to be likely to cause psychiatric injury to a person of 'normal fortitude'. He must also have a close relationship of love and affection with one or more primary victims.

In cases of both primary and secondary victims, the claimant must have suffered a recognizable psychiatric illness.

Why would it be so wrong to use the same approach to nervous shock cases in the case of both primary and secondary victims? In *Page v Smith* Lord Lloyd distinguished primary and secondary victim cases on the basis that certain control mechanisms are necessary in secondary victim cases to

---

[128] [1999] 2 AC 455, at 497.   [129] [1995] 2 WLR 644.

avoid 'liability towards all the world'. This risk, he stated, is not present in cases of physical injury. However, in the case of a widespread contamination case the extent of the liability for physical injury could be huge. The emphasis on physical proximity neither corresponds to the way in which physical injury can occur in the real world, nor to some point of principle, although Lord Lloyd's judgment does suggest that this case represents a principled approach:

In *McLoughlin v O'Brian* your Lordships had the opportunity to take the law forward by holding that the claimant could recover damages for nervous shock, even though she was two miles away at the time of the accident. No such opportunity offers in the present case. But it is at least as important that the law should not take a step backwards. This would, I fear, be the result if the decision of the Court of Appeal were allowed to stand.[130]

Yet, in *Page v Smith* we find the drawing of a bright line which places primary victims in the winning category and reinforces the handicapped nature of the secondary victim.

The distinction between primary and secondary victims is, in itself, problematic. In its 1998 report, the Law Commission recommended that the courts should abandon attaching practical significance to the classification.[131] However, judges still refer to it, and it is referred to in the subsequent chapters of this book. Nevertheless it should be noted that in many cases it is by no means clear who falls into the respective categories, and it is arguable that it is simply not applicable in non-shock cases. What can be said is that if a claimant can fit him/herself into the category of primary victim then the chances of a successful claim are significantly increased.

---

[130] [1995] 2 WLR 644.
[131] *Liability for Psychiatric Illness* (Law Com No 249) (London: The Stationery Office, 1998), para 554.

2

The Injury

In Chapter 1, reference has been made to psychiatric injury resulting from a variety of distressing experiences. Damages are awarded in negligence only if a recognizable psychiatric disorder has resulted, and it is proposed to look at such disorders which can occur as a result of such experiences. This has been stated in many cases, for example *McLoughlin v O'Brian*,[1] but this did not stop a trial judge from awarding a wife damages for 'ordinary shock' after witnessing her husband's injuries a year later (*Whitmore v Euroways Express Coaches Ltd*).[2] However, the requirement that there be a recognizable psychiatric injury is now so well known that such awards are unlikely to be given again (although see below, with regard to 'acute stress reaction'). Caution should also be exercised in dealing with the expression 'nervous breakdown'. Although this was referred to without disapproval in the case of *Walker v Northumberland County Council*,[3] it is a general lay expression, at most referring to behavioural manifestations of a condition rather than the condition itself.[4]

A few words should be said about the terminology. Sometimes 'recognized psychiatric injury' is used, sometimes 'recognizable psychiatric injury'. The latter is preferable as, arguably, it covers a wider range of injury. For example, there have been a number of cases[5] where damages have been recovered for pathological grief, yet it can be described generally as an adjustment disorder. The Law Commission, for example, use the expression 'recognizable',[6] as did the New Zealand Court of Appeal in *Van Soest v Residual Health Management Unit*[7] where it was acknowledged that medical opinion was not fixed and a definition should not be based on diagnostic classifications which might become out of date.

In Chapter 5 the case of *Phelps v Hillingdon London Borough Council*[8] will be examined in some detail, but for the purposes of this chapter its interest is in the 'injury' for which damages were claimed. The plaintiff's dyslexia had not been diagnosed by an educational psychologist and it was alleged that, as a result of this, she had not received the educational provision that she required. It was accepted that the failure to ameliorate a condition was 'injury' for the purposes of the claim. Lord Slynn quoted[9] with approval Sir Thomas Bingham in *E (A minor) v Dorset County Council*:[10]

---

[1] [1983] AC 410.   [2] The Times, 4 May 1984.   [3] [1995] 1 All ER 737.
[4] The importance of precision when pleading psychiatric injury is highlighted by *Rorrison v West Lothian College* (2000) SCLR 245, where the Scottish Outer House said that pleadings should give fair notice that a claimant intended to prove a recognizable psychiatric illness and to specify what it was; a general reference to a 'nervous breakdown' would not do.
[5] See, eg, *Vernon v Bosley (No 1)* [1997] 1 All ER 577.
[6] Liability for Psychiatric Illness (Law Com No 249) (London: The Stationery Office, 1998).
[7] [2000] 1 NZLR 179.   [8] [2001] 2 AC 619.   [9] ibid, at 664.
[10] [1995] 2 AC 633.

If . . . a plaintiff can show (1) that the adverse consequences of his congenital defect could have been mitigated by early diagnosis of the defect and appropriate treatment or educational provision; (2) that the adverse consequences of his congenital defect were not mitigated because early diagnosis was not made, or appropriate treatment not given or provision not made, with resulting detriment to his level of educational attainment and employability; and (3) that this damage is not too remote I do not regard the claim for damage to be necessarily bad.[11]

Dyslexia is a recognizable disorder (classified, for example, in the tenth revision of the World Health Organization's *International Statistical Classification of Diseases and Related Medical Problems*[12] ('ICD–10') at F81), and therefore failure to diagnose is like any other failure to diagnose a psychiatric or, indeed, a physical condition. The difference, of course, is that in the case of most conditions left undiagnosed, there will be some form of 'suffering', rather than simply being at a disadvantage. However, once it is recognized that there is some form of personal injury, then damages for economic loss flow from it, and those were the important damages as far as the claim in *Phelps* was concerned.

In *King v Bristow Helicopters Ltd, Morris v KLM Royal Dutch Airlines,*[13] the House of Lords had to consider the meaning of 'bodily injury' in Article 17 of the Warsaw Convention on International Carriage by Air 1929, which deals with compensation claims against carriers. It was held that a psychiatric condition developed by a passenger as a result of an accident on board an aircraft did not fall within the definition of 'bodily injury'. However, if the condition caused a physical condition, such as a peptic ulcer, or could be shown to have brought about physical changes to the brain's structure then compensation could be awarded. It was said that 'bodily injury' was a change in part or parts of the body which were sufficiently serious to be capable of being called an 'injury' (Lords Nicholls, Mackay and Hobhouse). Lords Steyn and Hope dissented, concluding that bodily injury involved strict liability for manifested physical injury and that it excluded mental injury or illness.

The word 'damage', however, was given a wider interpretation in *Black v Baer Corp*[14] by the Scottish Outer House, in relations to a claim under the Merchant Shipping (Oil Pollution) Act 1971 (s 1(1), s 20) and the Merchant Shipping Act 1974 (s 4(1)), where it was held that 'psychological' damage could not be regarded as being excluded from the scope of the provisions, but this was in relation to the psychological effect of physical injuries caused by oil pollution.

In *Chief Adjudication Officer v Faulds,*[15] the House of Lords held that the investigation of a series of fatal incidents did not constitute an 'accident' in

---

[11] ibid, at 703.   [12] See further www.who.int/whois/icd10.   [13] [2002] 2 WLR 578.
[14] 1999 SLT 1404.   [15] [2000] 1 WLR 1035, HL.

order for an award of industrial injuries disablement benefit under s 94(1) of the Social Security Contributions and Benefits Act 1992 to be made. A fire officer had been discharged on medical grounds after suffering post-traumatic stress disorder ('PTSD') following an investigation into a number of fatalities. Psychological injuries did not fall within a prescribed industrial disease under the Social Security (Industrial Injuries) (Prescribed Diseases) Regulations 1985, awards of benefit could only be made when there had been an industrial accident. It was stated that, if this were not the case, benefit would be available for any stress-related disorder arising in the course of employment, which was not the intention of Parliament.

Before considering specific disorders, it may be helpful to look at the way in which mental disorders are classified, and the way in which the terminology is used. It must be stressed that this is a brief and unsophisticated excursion through a very difficult area, with the intention only of setting the claim in its proper context. Difficult questions of psychiatric categorization, techniques of diagnosis, suitability of treatment and so on are all the province of the medical experts whom the lawyer will instruct. It is hoped, however, that the following introduction will be of some help to the lawyer who is unfamiliar with psychiatric concepts.

CLASSIFICATION OF MENTAL DISORDERS

The work of physicians[16] in the eighteenth and nineteenth centuries led to the distinction between mental disorders which were caused by physical damage and those which were not so attributable. Those which have physical causes are 'organic', and those which have not are 'functional'. The functional group can be further divided into 'psychoses' and 'neuroses'. Generally it is true to say that psychoses are serious mental illnesses when the sufferer loses touch with reality whereas neuroses are less serious and less disruptive of 'normal' life. Schizophrenia is a psychotic illness, as is manic depression. However, depression is a widely used term which can be part of a number of illnesses, such as neurotic depression, or part of a personality disorder or an adjustment disorder. Because so-called psychotic conditions have little in common, save for their severity and loss of touch with reality many psychiatrists feel it is not useful to refer to them collectively.[17] Indeed, ICD–10, unlike previous editions, does not use the traditional division of neuroses and psychoses at all. However, it is outside the scope of this book to look at the merits or otherwise of the distinction.

[16] eg, William Battie, *A Treatise on Madness* (London, 1758).
[17] See M Gelder, D Gath and R Mayou, *Concise Oxford Textbook of Psychiatry* (Oxford University Press, 1993) p 46.

Generally speaking most psychiatrists would agree that, in addition to psychoses and neuroses there are adjustment disorders, which can have similar symptoms to some neuroses but are dealt with separately because they have a different aetiology, ie, cause. Finally, there are personality disorders, various forms of sexual dysfunction and substance abuse, and illnesses which are specific to children which are categorized separately.

Mental disorders have, of course, been classified over a very long period of time, and in a number of ways in the medical literature, but in the diagnostic context there are two main glossaries or guides to mental disorders: the *Diagnostic and Statistical Manual of Mental Disorders* published by the American Psychiatric Association, the revised fourth edition of which was published in 2000, ('DSM–IV–TR'); and *The ICD 10 Classification of Mental and Behavioural Disorders: Clinical Descriptions and Diagnostic Guidelines* which is part of the tenth revision of the *International Statistical Classification of Diseases and Related Health Problems* mentioned above, which was ('ICD–10') World Health Organization's published in 1992. There is some controversy in the field of psychiatry as to the usefulness in practice of such categorizations which inevitably fall short of proving a satisfactory classification system for all sufferers. However, both DSM–IV and ICD–10 have a number of residual categories for psychiatric disorders which do not fit precisely into the more specific categories. Unless otherwise indicated, all references to DSM–IV refer to the revised edition.

Basic classification

Psychiatric textbooks adopt different systems of classification but tend to follow the system below. This is based upon that contained in the second edition of the *Concise Oxford Textbook of Psychiatry*, by Gelder, Gath and Mayou (1988).

    Personality disorder
    Mental impairment
    Organic psychoses (underlying physical cause detected)
    Functional psychoses (schizophrenia; affective psychoses; no underlying physical cause detected, although may be present)
    Neuroses
    Adjustment disorder
    Other disorders (includes alcohol and drug dependence, sexual deviance/dysfunction etc, and disorders specific to childhood)

This is a very basic list and the formal classification systems are much more complicated, particularly DSM–IV–TR, which on the face of it, bears little resemblance to the above. That is not surprising as the formal classification systems are designed to assist the psychiatrist in diagnosis and treatment, and not as a broad description of mental illness.

Referring back to our broad classification system, there follows a brief description of the disorders concerned.

Personality disorder

This term is used to describe those who exhibit abnormal behaviour which is not attributable to either a mental illness or an intellectual impairment, and is said to have arisen through an 'uneven' development of their personality from childhood. Various 'types' of personality have been defined including the hysterical, obsessional, paranoid and depressive. Broadly speaking, a personality disorder does not necessarily have any causal connection with trauma or stress, although some may say that it can be environmentally induced by, say, the experiences of childhood. For example, studies have shown that clinical descriptions of borderline personality disorder have great similarities with descriptions of chronic post-traumatic stress disorder, and particularly so when the victim has been subjected to repeated trauma over a long period of time, in cases of, say, repeated sexual abuse.[18] It is also acknowledged that in a small proportion of sufferers from PTSD, an 'enduring personality change' can occur (see Chapter 7). Furthermore, it is important to note that someone with a pre-existing personality disorder who is subjected to trauma or stress can seriously react to that incident and be, what may be thought to be, disproportionately affected by it. In other words they can be said to have an 'eggshell personality'. See *Brice v Brown*[19] (see page 193).

Mental impairment

This is essentially characterized as learning disability and refers to cases where intellectual impairment has been present since childhood (as opposed to dementia, where the onset is in adult life). It has no specific relevance to traumatically induced psychiatric disorder.

Organic psychoses

Organic psychoses are those psychoses (not neuroses) caused by physical disease or damage to the brain or nervous system, and therefore they can be caused by *physical* trauma and form part of a personal injury claim in the usual way. In *W v Hardman*[20] it was accepted that a minor head injury had been causative of the claimant's subsequent development of schizophrenia.

Functional psychoses

Schizophrenia and some severe depressive illnesses are psychotic illnesses, but, as indicated above, psychotic illnesses are very difficult to define. They

---

[18] See J L Herman and B A van der Kolk, 'Traumatic Antecedents of Borderline Personality Disorder' in A van der Kolk (ed), *Psychological Trauma* (American Psychiatric Press, 1987).
  [19] [1984] 1 All ER 997.   [20] [2001] 7 CL 447, Leeds county court.

have severe symptoms, and are said to be characterized by lack of insight by the patient, but this is an imprecise attribute, given that there can be some insight in, for example, schizophrenic patients, and some lack of insight in some so-called neurotic patients. Sometimes trauma can be associated with a psychotic illness, but, as Scrignar says,[21] at best the link is tenuous. A person suffering from a psychotic illness can, of course, be adversely affected by trauma, and if that is the case, then the medical expert involved will have to address the effect, the treatment and the prognosis, whilst taking into account the psychotic illness. This may be an extremely difficult task. As Scrignar says: 'During legal proceedings, mental health professionals may feel that they are trying to untie the Gordian knot as they attempt to explain to the court the relationship of trauma, schizophrenia and PTSD'.[22] In *Mount Isa Mines Ltd v Pusey*[23] it was found that discovering the badly burned body of a workmate had caused the plaintiff to develop schizophrenia.

Neuroses
This is a very wide category of mental disorder, and divides into many different subcategories, such as anxiety disorder, phobic disorder, obsessional neurosis. One or more of these conditions can be caused by distressing experiences. ICD–10 states that:

the term 'neurotic' is still retained for occasional use and occurs, for instance, in the heading of a major group (or block) of disorders F40–48, 'Neurotic, stress-related and somatoform disorders'.[24]

It goes on to state at the introduction to F40, that: 'mixtures of symptoms are common (coexistent depression and anxiety being by far the most frequent), particularly in the less severe varieties of these disorders often seen in primary care'.

Neuroses can vary from minor emotional disruptions, ie, everyday emotional reactions in a slightly exaggerated form, to quite serious disorders.

In DSM–IV, PTSD is classified as an anxiety disorder.

Adjustment disorder
This is separately categorized here because of its *specific* aetiology. ICD–10 states that these are:

states of subjective distress and emotional disturbance, usually interfering with social functioning and performance, and arising in the period of adaption to a significant life change or to the consequences of a stressful life event.

[21] C B Scrignar, *Post-traumatic Stress Disorder*, 2nd edn (New Orleans, LA: Bruno Press, 1988), p 120.

[22] ibid, p 121.   [23] (1970) 125 CLR 383.

[24] Somatoform disorders are those which exhibit physical symptoms with no detectable physical cause.

It can include a grief reaction. DSM–IV states that: 'The essential feature of this disorder is a maladaptive reaction to an identifiable psychosocial stressor, or stressors'.

In ICD–10, PTSD is classified under the category of reaction to severe stress and adjustment disorders.

Other disorders

Included here is alcohol and drug dependence which can be the eventual outcome of alcohol and drug use following a distressing experience.

AETIOLOGY

Aetiology is concerned with all causes of mental disorder. Psychiatric disorders can be genetically determined or they can occur as a result of a naturally occurring disease, or they can be brought about by an external stimulus. The latter type of disorder can be said to be environmentally induced, and the main concern of this book is with certain external causes of mental disorder. In reality many mental disorders are caused by a complex interaction of external causes, genetic or similar predisposition, and physical illness. Psychiatrists classify causes as follows, although again a warning is appropriate that this is a general description only, and, inevitably, oversimplified.

Predisposing factors

First there are the factors in the individual's physical make-up, determined by genetic, biological and similar considerations. Secondly, there are the factors of the individual's personality. It has been seen that one type of mental disorder is a personality disorder, but an individual does not have to be suffering from a personality disorder to have a predisposing personality factor. Most people can be classified in a very rough and ready way as having a particular type of personality. This can affect the way in which they will react to external factors such as stress. See further below. McFarlane has stated that, even in the case of devastatingly bad disasters, the incidence of PTSD is rarely more than 50 per cent and, he suggests, this must be due to some pre-existing factors in the personalities of those affected.[25] There are a number of theories as to why this should be, but not a great deal of practical research.[26] For the purposes of recovering damages, however, the presence of such general pre-existing factors, even on the assumption that they can be

---

[25] A C McFarlane, 'Vulnerability to Post-traumatic Stress Disorders' in M E Wolfe and A D Mosnaim (eds), *Post-traumatic Stress Disorder: Etiology, Phenomenology and Treatment* (Washington, DC: American Psychiatric Press, 1990).

[26] See, eg, Ruth Williams, 'Personality and Post-traumatic Stress Disorder' in W Yule (ed) *Post-Traumatic Stress Disorders: Concepts and Therapy* (Chichester: John Wiley & Sons, 1998).

identified, will not limit the damages recoverable, and furthermore, neither will a specific vulnerability *unless* the resulting psychiatric condition has been caused to a secondary victim in circumstances where a person of normal fortitude would have suffered nothing at all. That there might be a general predisposition in a significant proportion of the population, however, might raise doubt as to what could be normal fortitude, but it will be seen that normal fortitude is a legal, not a psychiatric, concept.

Precipitating factors

These include the external factors with which we are concerned in this book, such as trauma, and they also include physical factors such as cerebral tumours or the effect of drugs. A physical factor can have physical effects but also psychological effects due to the stress placed upon the individual concerned. This should be noted in particular in relation to head injury cases.

Perpetuating factors

These are factors which prolong the duration of the disorder concerned, and essentially will be secondary factors, such as the loss of a job which will prolong the original disorder. Stress can be a precipitating factor or a perpetuating factor.

Factual causation is essential for any action in damages to succeed. Jaspers[27] has formulated three criteria for deciding whether a psychological state is a reaction to events. First, the precipitating factors (often called stressors) should be sufficiently severe and closely related to the onset of the psychological state; secondly, there must be some clear connection between the stressor and the stress reaction; and thirdly, the reaction should disappear when the stressor is removed, unless of course there are perpetuating factors maintaining it. Although this sounds fairly obvious, it is important to bear it in mind, because there will often be socio-economic consequences of psychiatric injury (loss of job, inability to keep up friendships etc), which will interact with the resultant disorder and affect diagnosis, prognosis and recovery.

Other perpetuating factors can be aspects of the claimant's personality, but the research in this area is not extensive.[28] In any event, one would normally expect any excessively detrimental symptoms attributable to personality to be compensatable under the principle that one takes one's victim as one finds him, but see the case of *Jeffries v Home Office*[29].

[27] K Jaspers, *General Psychopathology*, trans J Hoenig and M W Hamilton (Manchester: Manchester University Press, 1963), p 392.
[28] See Williams in Yule (n 26 above).   [29] [1999] CLY 1414.

HISTORY OF THE ILLNESS

Before going on to consider in more detail the relevant disorders which have been mentioned above, there follows a brief account of the history of traumatically induced psychiatric illness, which has been described by a variety of names depending upon the circumstances in which it has been inflicted.

The early history gives two notable instances in which psychological problems follow trauma; the first being the somewhat predictable circumstance of war, and the second in the less obvious situation of railway accidents.

To deal with the latter first, one of the most influential of the early doctors writing on the topic was John Eric Erichsen, Professor of Surgery at University College Hospital, London, who, in 1875, wrote *On Concussion of the Spine: Nervous Shock and Other Obscure Injuries of the Nervous System in Their Clinical and Medico-legal Aspects*. Although this deals with a variety of injuries to the spine resulting from falls and accidents of many different types, he comments that the most frequent cause, and certainly the cause of the most severe injuries is a railway collision. It is important to stress that he was referring to 'injuries' which normally have no obvious physical cause. His central thesis was that in trauma 'concussion of the spine' occurred causing molecular changes in its structure and inflammation of tissue. Although there was little in the way of pathological evidence available for most of the injuries, he did refer to the case of a man who died three and a half years after being involved in a railway accident in which, apparently, he suffered no external sign of injury. The post-mortem revealed signs of chronic inflammation of the brain, and the spinal cord.

The condition of spinal concussion or 'railway spine' as it came to be known was not always accepted by doctors and was attacked by Herbert Page who was surgeon to the London and North-West Railway. He attempted to discredit Erichsen and denied the existence of the condition of 'spinal concussion'. Instead, he introduced the concepts of 'nervous shock' and 'functional disorders', particularly by citing cases where manifestations of shock are greater in cases which caused the victim greater fright.[30]

Page seemed to identify fear as the prime cause of the disorder, and concluded that fear would probably be statistically greater, the more alarming the accident. In those days railways were, of course, the fastest way of travelling. Speeds which, at the beginning of the twenty-first century, would seem almost quaintly slow, could, no doubt, produce great alarm. If

---

[30] See M R Trimble, *Post-Traumatic Neurosis* (Chichester: Wiley, 1981) for a good account of the history of diagnosis of traumatically induced disorders.

this is considered in conjunction with the size and powerful appearance of railway locomotives, then it is understandable that they could induce considerable fear into those who may have been involved in even the most minor incident. Charles Dickens, for instance, was involved in a railway accident which left him with a great fear of rail travel.[31]

The other early experiences concerned war, the American Civil War being perhaps the first example of the recording of manifestations of psychiatric injury. Neurasthenia (physical and mental exhaustion) and other symptoms such as pains in the chest, breathlessness and weakness were recorded (da Costa's syndrome, known more usually today as neurocirculatory asthenia). The First World War produced, of course, countless cases of 'shell-shock' (although the rather crude assumption that it was literally due to the effect of exploding shells as opposed to the exposure to the multifarious horrors of war has long since been discredited), and by the end of the war there were over twenty army hospitals in the UK dealing specifically with shell-shock.[32] Again, the Second World War produced psychiatric casualties, but not of the same magnitude as in the First. Sophisticated diagnosis has developed since then. Despite this, it was still the case that a great number of Vietnam war veterans remained undiagnosed for many years.[33]

In more recent history, both the Falklands and Gulf wars have produced victims of psychiatric illness directly attributable to their war experiences.

There are also a number of major civilian disasters, which have produced large-scale victims of stress, such as the Australian bushfires, the American Buffalo Creek flood, and events such as the capsize of the *Herald of Free Enterprise* ferry near Zeebrugge in 1987. These have resulted in various studies of the effects of major stress, disaster management and other areas.[34]

POST-TRAUMATIC STRESS DISORDER

The most commonly known psychiatric illness following trauma or stress is post-traumatic stress disorder ('PTSD'), although it must be emphasized that it is by no means the only disorder which can manifest itself, and practitioners acting for claimants should be alert to any suggestion by the defence that because PTSD is not present then any psychiatric disorder which is present is not related to the event concerned.[35]

---

[31] L T C Rolt, *Red for Danger* (London: Bodley Head, 1955).

[32] M Stone, 'Shellshock and the Psychologists' in W F Bynum, R Porter and M Shepherd (eds), *The Anatomy of Madness*, vol 2 (London: Tavistock, 1985).

[33] M J Friedman, 'Post-Vietnam Syndrome: Recognition and Management' *Psychosomatics*, vol 22 (1981).

[34] See B Raphael, *When Disaster Strikes* (London: Unwin Hyman, 1990).

[35] See the judgments of Thorpe and Evans LJJ in *Vernon v Bosley (No 1)* [1997] 1 All ER 577 where it was specifically stated that PTSD should not be adopted as the yardstick in psychiatric injury claims.

DSM–IV and DSM–IV–TR

It was not until 1980, when the third edition of the American Psychiatric Association's *Diagnostic and Statistical Manual* ('DSM–III') was published that PTSD was finally accorded a diagnostic heading. As already indicated the current Manual is DSM–IV, and PTSD is disorder number 309.81. PTSD is classified as an anxiety disorder. DSM–III R, 309.81, states:

The essential feature of Post-Traumatic Stress Disorder is the development of characteristic symptoms following exposure to an extreme traumatic stressor involving direct personal experience of an event that involves actual or threatened death or serious injury, or other threat to one's physical integrity; or witnessing an event that involves death, injury, or a threat to the physical integrity of another person; or learning about unexpected or violent death, serious harm, or threat of death or injury experienced by a family member or other close associate (Criterion A1). The person's response to the event must involve intense fear, helplessness, or horror (or in children, the response must involve disorganized or agitated behaviour) (Criterion A2). The characteristic symptoms resulting from the exposure to the extreme trauma include persistent re-experiencing of the traumatic event (Criterion B), persistent avoidance of stimuli associated with the trauma and numbing of general responsiveness (Criterion C), and persistent symptoms of increased arousal (Criterion D). The full symptom picture must be present for more than one month (Criterion E), and the disturbance must cause clinically significant distress or impairment in social, occupational, or other important areas of functioning (Criterion F).

Traumatic events that are experienced directly include, but are not limited to, military combat, violent personal assault (sexual assault, physical attack, robbery, mugging), being kidnapped, being taken hostage, terrorist attack, torture, incarceration as a prisoner of war or in a concentration camp, natural or manmade disasters, severe automobile accidents, or being diagnosed with a life-threatening illness. For children, sexually traumatic events may include developmentally inappropriate sexual experiences without threatened or actual violence or injury. Witnessed events include, but are not limited to, observing the serious injury or unnatural death of another person due to violent assault, accident, war, or disaster or unexpectedly witnessing a dead body or body parts. Events experienced by others that are learned about include, but are not limited to, violent personal assault, serious accident, or serious injury experienced by a family member or a close friend; learning about the sudden, unexpected death of a family member or a close friend; or learning that one's child has a life-threatening disease. The disorder may be especially severe or long lasting when the stressor is of human design (eg, torture, rape). The likelihood of developing this disorder may increase as the intensity of and physical proximity to the stressor increase.

The traumatic event can be re-experienced in various ways. Commonly the person has recurrent and intrusive recollections of the event (Criterion B1) or recurrent distressing dreams during which the event is replayed (Crierion B2). In rare instances, the person experiences dissociative states that last from a few seconds to several hours or even days, during which components of the event are relived and the person behaves as though experiencing the event at that moment (Criterion B3). Intense psychological distress (Criterion B4) or physiological reactivity (Criterion B5) often occurs when the person is exposed to triggering events that resemble or symbolize an aspect of the traumatic event (eg, anniversaries of the traumatic event; cold, snowy weather or uniformed guards for survivors of death camps in cold climates; hot, humid weather for combat veterans of the South Pacific; entering any elevator for a woman who was raped in an elevator).

Stimuli associated with the trauma are persistently avoided. The person commonly makes deliberate efforts to avoid thoughts, feelings, or conversations about the traumatic event (Criterion C1) and to avoid activities, situations, or people who arouse recollections of it (Criterion C2). This avoidance of reminders may include amnesia for an important aspect of the traumatic event (Criterion C3). Diminished responsiveness to the external world, referred to as 'psychic numbing' or 'emotional anesthesia', usually begins soon after the traumatic event. The individual may complain of having markedly diminished interest or participation in previously enjoyed activities (Criterion C4), of feeling detached or estranged from other people (Criterion C5), or of having markedly reduced ability to feel emotions (especially those associated with intimacy, tenderness, and sexuality) (Criterion C6). The individual may have a sense of a foreshortened future (eg, not expecting to have a career, marriage, children, or a normal life span) (Criterion C7).

The individual has persistent symptoms of anxiety or increased arousal that were not present before the trauma. These symptoms may include difficulty falling or staying asleep that may be due to recurrent nightmares during which the traumatic event is relived (Criterion D1), hypervigilance (Criterion D4), and exaggerated startle response (Criterion D5). Some individuals report irritability or outbursts of anger (Criterion D2) or difficulty concentrating or completing tasks (Criterion D3).

The diagnostic criteria are reproduced in Appendix 1.

ICD–10

The World Health Organization classification in ICD–10 at category F43 lists disorders which are reactions to severe distress, and adjustment disorders. Post-traumatic stress disorder is defined as follows:

... a delayed and/or protracted response to a stressful event or situation (either short or long-lasting) of an exceptionally threatening or catastrophic nature, which is likely to cause pervasive distress in almost anyone (eg natural or man-made disaster, combat, serious accident, witnessing the violent death of others, or being the victim of torture, terrorism, rape, or other crime). Predisposing factors such as personality traits (eg compulsive, asthenic[36]) or previous history of neurotic illness may lower the threshold for the development of the syndrome or aggravate its course, but they are neither necessary nor sufficient to explain its occurrence.

Typical symptoms include episodes of repeated reliving of the trauma in intrusive memories ('flashbacks') or dreams, occurring against the persisting background of a

---

[36] A personality disorder characterized by low energy.

sense of 'numbness' and emotional blunting, detachment from other people, unresponsiveness to surroundings, anhedonia, and avoidance of activities and situations reminiscent of the trauma. Commonly there is fear and avoidance of cues that remind the sufferer of the original trauma. Rarely, there may be dramatic, acute bursts of fear, panic or aggression, triggered by stimuli arousing a sudden recollection and/or re-enactment of the trauma or of the original reaction to it.

There is usually a state of autonomic hyperarousal with hypervigilance, an enhanced startle reaction, and insomnia. Anxiety and depression are commonly associated with the above symptoms and signs, and suicidal ideation is not infrequent. Excessive use of alcohol or drugs may be a complicating factor.

The onset follows the trauma with a latency period which may range from a few weeks to months (but rarely exceeds six months). The course is fluctuating but recovery can be expected in the majority of cases. In a small proportion of patients the condition may show a chronic course over many years and a transition to an enduring personality change.

It is interesting to note that in the earlier edition of DSM (DSM–III R) the definition of PTSD was such that the sufferer had to have experienced an event that is outside the range of usual experience (ie, outside the range of such common experiences as simple bereavement, chronic illness, business losses, and marital conflict), but that this requirement is no longer necessary under the DSM–IV classification. This recognizes the diversity of ways in which human beings can experience and be affected by stress, and is therefore to be welcomed. It also supports the view that, the earlier definition reflected the need to construct a diagnosis of symptoms which assisted the litigation process in 'shock' cases.[37]

Acute stress reaction

Both ICD–10 and DSM–IV also describe acute reactions to stress which are what the lay person would regard as 'shock'. Such phenomena are short-term reactions only, but it is worth bearing in mind that they are specific psychiatric disorders, and *in consequence should be compensatable*. In DSM–IV, 'acute stress disorder' is classified at 308.3. In ICD–10 (at F43) the diagnostic guidelines for 'acute stress reaction' include daze, disorientation, agitation, sweating and breathlessness, usually lasting only two or three days. In cases such as *Nicholls v Rushton*,[38] where the plaintiff had suffered a nervous reaction which was described as 'falling short' of a recognized psychiatric injury, it may be that the plaintiff could be properly diagnosed as suffering from one of these short-term disorders and could recover damages. The diagnostic criteria are reproduced in Appendix 1.

---

[37] See Williams in Yule (n 26 above).   [38] The Times, 19 June 1992.

'The three Es'

Scrignar, in his book *Post-Traumatic Stress Disorder*,[39] uses the definition of PTSD in DSM–III R and describes the specific sort of 'trauma' which is necessary as a stressor to precipitate PTSD by reference to 'the traumatic principle'. This, he says, is:

any environmental stimulus which poses a realistic threat to life or limb, impacting on one, or more likely a combination of the five sensory pathways to the brain, if perceived as a serious threat to one's life or physical integrity, whether it produces physical injury or not, can be regarded as a trauma and precipitate a PTSD in a vulnerable individual. The central factor in the development of PTSD is not necessarily the type or duration of the environmental trauma, but whether the trauma poses a realistic threat to life or limb, and a person is consciously aware and has a full appreciation of the potential for serious injury or death to self or others. Also vital and a natural consequence is an intense activation of one's autonomic nervous system following exposure to the traumatic event.[40]

The activation of the autonomic nervous system produces extremely intense, and frequent or persisting, anxiety; 'pathologic' anxiety. Scrignar says that anxiety is pathologic when the autonomic nervous system discharges: (a) so intensively that it renders an individual incapable of speech, movement or thought; (b) unpredictably and frequently in an attack-like manner; and (c) so regularly that chronic anxiety is the result. He describes five levels of anxiety, level 1 being normal, level 2 being mild symptoms of edginess, tension, feelings of nerves, up to symptoms at panic level (level 5) of acute and intense feelings of impending doom, going crazy, going out of control, dying, or other thoughts of a cataclysmic nature.

Scrignar then goes on to identify the three sources of pathologic anxiety, what he calls the three Es. The first is the environment, ie, the stressor which precipitates the PTSD. The definition at DSM–IV, 309.81, states that the stressor must also pose a threat to one's physical integrity, or a threat of serious harm to one's children, spouse, close relatives, or friends; or witnessing the destruction of one's home or community; or seeing another person who has recently been seriously injured or killed. The use of the word 'serious' in the definition is also difficult; who decides what is serious? Presumably it must be the plaintiff, ie, the test must be subjective. The ICD–10 classification is no more helpful on this point, stating that PTSD is a response to a stressful event or situation 'of an exceptionally threatening or catastrophic nature, which is likely to cause pervasive distress in almost anyone', and also refers to the example of an accident as a 'serious' accident. At this point it is worth stating again that just because the criteria of PTSD are not satisfied, it does not mean that the plaintiff's claim will fail. One or

[39] n 21 above.   [40] ibid, pp 13–14.

more other psychiatric disorders can be present. (See further the reference to Adjustment Disorder in the PTSD diagnosis criteria in DSM–IV in Appendix 1.) It is also worth stating that *if* what is a relatively minor, say road accident, or perhaps a 'near-miss', *appears* to the victim to be extremely threatening, then this 'extremely threatening event' (or howsoever it is described) can be markedly distressing to almost anyone, so if the other symptoms of PTSD are there, then it appears that the definition can be satisfied in such a case.

Scrignar's second 'E' refers to encephalic events, also called cognitions, and concern thoughts, visual images, flashbacks, assumptions, beliefs, perception of external events and dreams. These encephalic events are always necessary for a diagnosis of PTSD to be made, and are what distinguish it from other anxiety disorders. The definition refers to them as recurrent and intrusive recollections of the event, recurrent and distressing dreams of the event and sudden feelings that the event was recurring. Scrignar calls them the videotapes of the mind, and they can be played back every day for months or years, keeping the trauma fresh in the mind. Such 'playbacks' can be triggered by physical sensations: Dr Morgan O'Connell, psychiatrist of the Royal Naval Hospital, Haslar has described the case of one young man on the *Herald of Free Enterprise* whom he treated. Every time he stood at the bar in a pub he experienced these distressing flashbacks. It was discovered that he had been in the bar on the ferry at the time of the capsize; bottles of spirits were spilt, leaving an intense smell of alcohol, by which he was surrounded for some time after the capsize. The smell of spirits would bring back the images of the capsize with a vivid intensity.

Finally, Scrignar's third 'E' stands for endogenous events, which are physical sensations. These can be particularly difficult to differentiate from physical sensations produced by organic causes, particularly if the plaintiff was already ill before the event, or suffered actual physical injury at the event. If it is eventually established that the cause of the sensations is non-organic, then until the plaintiff accepts this, the PTSD will not be treatable.

These physical sensations remind the plaintiff of the event, which set off the encephalic events, ie, the intrusive thoughts, dreams etc, which produce symptoms of anxiety (activation of the autonomic nervous system), which results in tension and unpleasant physical sensation, which reminds the plaintiff of the event, and so on. In other words, it has what Scrignar calls a 'spiral effect'.

These, then, are the characteristics of PTSD. Survivor guilt, which was included as a characteristic in DSM–III has since disappeared from the revised edition, but it is still thought to be an important factor.[41]

---

[41] See W Yule, 'The psychological sequelae of disasters and resulting compensation', *Practical Reviews in Psychiatry*, series 2, no 9 (1990), p 6.

It is, perhaps, pertinent at this stage to enquire how frequently the specific criteria of PTSD will occur. Professor William Yule, and others at the Institute of Psychiatry, London University carried out assessments of forty-five adult survivors from the *Herald of Free Enterprise* disaster, and all but three reached the DSM–III (the edition of the manual at that particular time) criteria for PTSD. Many of them also satisfied diagnostic criteria for depression, anxiety and a pathological grief reaction. In his paper on the subject,[42] Professor Yule acknowledges that it cannot be concluded that 90 per cent of survivors suffered from PTSD, as the extent of the referral basis was not known, but he does conclude that comment is needed upon what was probably a high incidence, and goes on to cite Rachman,[43] who argued that extreme difficulties in emotional processing are associated with traumatic events in which the stimulus is intense, sudden (the *Herald* capsized in 45 seconds), dangerous (half the passengers were killed), prepared (ie, prepared fears of drowning), uncontrolled and unpredictable. An event such as the capsize of the *Herald* should, therefore, produce a high level of psychiatric disorder. Professor John Gunn and Professor P J Taylor, also of the Institute of Psychiatry, state that the crucial factor about the likelihood of development of a psychiatric disorder seems to be prolongation of uncertainty about the final extent of damage to be inflicted.[44] Again, in relation to the *Herald* case, many of the victims were in the water for a very long time, with no way of knowing whether they would ever be rescued. This research appears to conflict with the views of McFarlane (n 24 above), but the conflict may be more to do with the sampling used in this research.

An extremely important factor for the practitioner is the way in which the sufferer's avoidance response can mask PTSD altogether. A study of 246 people exposed to an industrial disaster showed that those who were resistant to a first interview had suffered a higher degree of exposure to stress, and were more likely to have suffered from PTSD at the seven-month period than those who had agreed to a first interview. It was found that the resistance to interview was part of an avoidance response, and showed that without follow-up exercises the level of PTSD would have been under-estimated.[45] A plaintiff who steadfastly denies psychiatric injury, therefore, may not only still be a victim, but may be even more seriously affected than more vocal contemporaries.

ICD–10 states that symptoms should not generally be diagnosed as PTSD unless there is evidence that they arose within six months of the traumatic

---

[42] ibid.

[43] S Rachman, 'Emotional processing' (1980) 18 *Behav Res Ther* 51.

[44] J Gunn and P J Taylor (eds), *Forensic Psychiatry, Clinical, Legal and Ethical Issues* (London: Butterworth-Heinemann, 1993), p 897.

[45] L Weisath, 'Importance of high response rates in traumatic stress research' (1989) 80 *Acta Psychiatr Scand* 131.

event, but that a 'probable' diagnosis may be made if more than six months elapsed provided the clinical manifestations are typical and no alternative identification of the disorder is plausible. Similarly DSM–IV refers to delayed onset of PTSD, which delay can be a matter of years. Scrignar prefers the explanation that PTSD was there the whole time, but had not been diagnosed. There is some research to support this view, for example, a retrospective case review of 150 Israeli soldiers indicated that delay in seeking treatment explained most cases of apparently delayed-onset PTSD.[46] Suffice to say that the six-month period should be viewed with some caution. It is important to stress that we are here dealing with the diagnostic criteria for PTSD; other disorders have different patterns of development. For example, in ICD–10, at F62, enduring personality changes are dealt with, and it is stated that 'such enduring personality change is most often seen following devastating traumatic experience'.

The same degree of caution is necessary when it is considered that ICD–10 states that PTSD rarely lasts more than six months, although DSM–IV is unspecific as to duration. There have been a number of follow-up studies carried out. For example, 14 years after the Buffalo Creek disaster of 1972, a follow-up study was done of 39 per cent of the living survivors.[47] Three-quarters of the population had improved; less than 10 per cent had worsened. Of course, whether those who were still suffering were still suffering from PTSD rather than from, say, an enduring personality change, is debatable. It should be remembered that PTSD was not a recognized disorder in 1972, and diagnoses are made retrospectively on the basis of recorded clinical pictures. Follow-up studies, which are fairly infrequent in any event, can at present, therefore, give only an approximation of the duration of PTSD.[48]

OTHER DISORDERS

Neuroses

This is an enormous category of mental disorder. Neuroses can range from a very mild form of illness to an illness which severely disrupts the life of the sufferer. These include anxiety states, phobic states, some types of depression, obsessive compulsive disorder, somatoform disorders, and dissociative disorders. This discussion of other disorders is not intended to be in any way

---

[46] Soloman et al 'Delayed Onset PTSD among Israeli Veterans of the 1982 Lebanon War' (1989) 52 *Psychiatry* 428.

[47] Green et al 'Buffalo Creek Survivors in the Second Decade: Stability of Stress Symptoms' (1990) 60 *Am J. Orthopsychiatry* 43.

[48] For a review of PTSD see O'Brien, 'The Validity of the Diagnosis of Post Traumatic Stress Disorder', December 1994 JPIL, p 257.

exhaustive, but contains general descriptions for the lay person of some of the disorders which can be environmentally induced and which may be induced particularly by trauma.

It has been acknowledged that environmental factors can play an important part in the development of neurotic disorders. A non-traumatic example is shown by studies that have indicated that workers on assembly lines report more neurotic symptoms than do comparable workers who have more control over their rate of work.[50] The ability of trauma to cause such symptoms is much less controversial.

The most common forms of neurotic illness after stress are anxiety states, phobic states and neurotic depression.

Persistent duress stress disorder

Although not presently included in the main diagnostic manuals, the possibility of a further diagnostic category of 'persistent duress stress disorder' ('PDSD') has been mooted in the correspondence pages of the *Australian Prescriber* by Maarten de Vries, who states that it carries the same features as PTSD in DSM–IV, save for the fact that there is no single traumatic event. However, Creamer and McFarlane have cautioned against introducing a new category of mental illness in the absence of evidence that it is a distinct entity and not adequately covered by existing categorizations.[49]

Anxiety states

ICD–10 gives no overall definition so it is useful to look at ICD–9 which said that they are:

Various combinations of physical and mental manifestations of anxiety, not attributable to real danger and occurring either in attacks or as a persisting state. The anxiety is usually diffuse and may extend to panic. Other neurotic features such as obsessional or hysterical symptoms may be present but do not dominate the clinical picture.

Attacks of anxiety are often accompanied by a variety of bodily (somatic) symptoms, such as palpitations, excessive sweating, breathlessness, faintness, a sinking feeling in the stomach, nausea and shakiness. If anxiety attacks are very severe, then the sufferer can go into a panic. The sufferer

---

[49] See M de Vries, letter to the editor and comments by M Creamer and A McFarlane (1999) 22 Aust Prescr 1999 32–4 (available at www.australianprescriber.com/magazines/vol22no5/letters.htm).

[50] D E Broadbent, 'Chronic Effects from the Physical Nature of Work' in B Gardell and G Johansson (eds), *Working Life* (London: Wiley, 1981).

may also have a persistent fear of some unfocused, unspecified disaster occurring.

If the anxiety has a particular focus then it is classified as a phobic anxiety. The phobia can be specifically linked to a stressful event, such as fear of travelling in motor vehicles or a fear of water.

Depression

The use of this term can create considerable confusion. ICD–10 has a whole block of disorders (F30–F39) which are called 'mood (affective) disorders' and which include depressive disorders. These can be of a varying degree of severity, but ICD–10 says:

the individual usually suffers from depressed mood, loss of interest and enjoyment, and reduced energy leading to increased fatiguability and diminished activity. Marked tiredness after only slight effort is common. Other common symptoms are:

  (a)   reduced concentration and attention;
  (b)   reduced self-esteem and self-confidence;
  (c)   ideas of guilt and unworthiness; . . .
  (d)   bleak and pessimistic views of the future;
  (e)   ideas of acts of self-harm or suicide;
  (f)   disturbed sleep;
  (g)   diminished appetite.

Depression can be caused by distressing experiences, and in ICD–10 various types of depressive reaction are included as reactions to stress and adjustment reactions. They can, of course, accompany other psychiatric disorders also caused by stress or trauma.

Somatoform disorders

These are characterized by the presence of physical symptoms for which there is no demonstrable organic cause. Both DSM–IV and ICD–10 indicate that they can be associated with distressing experiences, but they are particularly difficult to treat because the patient will be unwilling to acknowledge that the physical symptoms are, in fact, psychological in origin.

A related matter is that psychiatric injury can have specific physical consequences, for example, it is thought that stress can have an adverse affect on the immune system.[51]

---

[51] Calabrese et al (1987) cited in Gunn and Taylor (n 44 above), p 933.

Dissociative disorders

These result in a partial or complete loss of the normal integration between memories of the past, awareness of identity and immediate sensations, and control of bodily movements, often associated closely in time with traumatic events.

Pathological grief

This phenomenon considerably occupied those involved in the *Herald of Free Enterprise* arbitration (see page 212). DSM–IV refers to 'normal bereavement', and says that 'a full depressive syndrome' is a normal reaction to the death of a loved one. That would include such things as poor appetite, weight loss, insomnia and feelings of depression. Guilt, if present, is chiefly about things done or not done by the survivor at the time of death; thoughts of death are usually limited to the person's thinking that he would be better off dead or that he should have died with the deceased person. The person generally regards the feeling of depressed mood as 'normal' although help with loss of appetite or insomnia may be sought. The duration of 'normal bereavement' is variable, particularly between different cultural groups. Pathological grief is grief beyond this 'normal' reaction. DSM–IV says that morbid preoccupation with worthlessness, prolonged and marked functional impairment and marked psychomotor retardation suggest that the bereavement is complicated by the development of a major depression. In ICD–10 grief reaction is described as an adjustment disorder, and can include depressive and anxiety reactions, which can be prolonged.

It was acknowledged by the arbitrators that an assessment of the difference between normal and pathological grief could only be done in a 'rough and ready fashion'. Because damages are not awarded for 'normal' grief, courts have the somewhat absurd task of trying to reduce damages by whatever part of the plaintiff's psychological state can be attributed to 'normal' grief only.[52]

The Court of Appeal endorsed this approach in *Vernon v Bosley (No 1)*[53] when it held that it was unnecessary to try to attribute part of the plaintiff's condition to 'normal grief' and part to his witnessing the aftermath of the accident. The same decision held that 'pathological grief' was a recognizable psychiatric illness.

Enduring personality changes

It is acknowledged that enduring personality changes can take place after extremely distressing experiences. ICD–10 at F62 defines such a change by

---

[52] See *Hinz v Berry* [1970] 2 QB 40 discussed at page 192.
[53] [1997] 1 All ER 577.

reference to the extremity of the stress, ie, it must be so extreme that it is unnecessary to consider personal vulnerability to explain its profound effect on the personality. Examples given of the sorts of extreme experiences are torture, disasters and hostage situations. Symptoms include a hostile or mistrustful attitude towards the world, social withdrawal, feelings of emptiness or hopelessness, a chronic feeling of being threatened and estrangement. It also states that long-term change in personality following short-term exposure to a life-threatening experience such as a car accident should *not* be included since recent research shows that such a development depends upon a pre-existing psychological vulnerability. An example of this can be seen in *Brice* v *Brown*[54] (discussed at p 193). In DSM–IV there is a category of disorder described as 'Personality change due to a General Medical Condition' (310.1), but it is not clear how this is different from, for example, a long-term anxiety disorder or reactive depression.

Overlap of disorders

Many victims will develop more than one psychiatric disorder. This should present no particular problem for the practitioner, but it will probably have created diagnostic and treatment problems, and make prognosis more difficult. This was one of the features of the *Herald of Free Enterprise* arbitrators (see further page 212).

Accident neurosis

In the next chapter allegations of malingering will be considered. There is another concept, well-known to litigators, often described as 'accident', 'compensation' or 'litigation' neurosis. It means that some or all of the claimant's symptoms relate to anxiety about the personal injury claim and will resolve after settlement. An interesting follow-up study[55] was carried out on some thirty-five plaintiffs who had exhibited perplexing physical symptoms which could not be shown to have organic causes. The follow-up was to see whether they recovered markedly once their damages claims had been settled. The practitioner will recognize this allegation: it was said that they were suffering from accident or compensation neurosis. The result of the study showed that few of the claimants had recovered and such recovery as did take place was unrelated to the time of compensation. Interestingly, what did emerge from the study was that it appeared that an important factor inhibiting the recovery process was over-protectiveness on the part of relatives. It appears that no useful conclusions can be drawn about this phenomenon.

---

[54] [1984] 1 All ER 997.
[55] Tarsh and Royston, 'A Follow-up Study of Accident Neurosis' (1985) 146 *Br J Psychiatry* 18 and R Mayou, 'Accident Neurosis Revisited' (1996) 168 *Br J Psychiatry* 399.

PREDISPOSITION

It is not surprising that there are types of personality which are more vulnerable to psychiatric injury. Scrignar says that predisposition to PTSD is correlated with pre-existing autonomic hyperactivity or anxiousness. The anxiety can be part of a specific anxiety disorder, or it can be brought about by biological factors such as extreme fatigue or chronic sickness, or through substance abuse. He goes on to say:

It must be concluded that no carefully controlled study has ever been conducted which definitively demonstrates that certain personality characteristics predispose a person to PTSD. Individuals with a higher than normal pre-morbid anxiety level apparently are more likely to perceive danger and develop PTSD. Whether a patient appears for psychiatric treatment depends more upon their personal coping skills and social support system.[56]

It is important to note Scrignar's conclusion that two patients with identical pre-morbid personalities, subjected to the same distressing experience, may deal differently with the stress, and that the way in which they do so can affect whether they develop PTSD. He does not define 'personal coping skills', but social support can be readily identified. A victim without a supportive family or friends will be more vulnerable, as will a victim who ostensibly has a great deal of support, but is a naturally reticent character and does not utilize that support to the full. Sadly, one of the characteristic reactions to stress is a wish to move away from the disaster site,[57] which can mean that a victim moves away from familiar surroundings, family and friends and unwittingly exacerbates the situation. Sometimes support can be overused, in the sense that the victim acquires 'learned helplessness' and loses the capacity to appreciate his or her potential for influencing events and the subsequent course of his life, and so clings to the support group.[58]

Research is inconclusive as to the predisposing effect of age, gender and cultural background. A curious factor is the effect of previous traumatic experiences. It may be thought that they would in some way 'prepare' the victim and leave him less vulnerable. Research, however, points towards the reverse being true. Research on the firefighters in the Australian bushfires showed that those who had suffered previous traumatic experiences suffered more than those without such histories.[59] The 'pint pot' syndrome may be relevant: the human psyche can only take so much battering; once the pot is

[56] See Scrignar (n 21 above), p 86.
[57] See Masserman cited in Gunn and Taylor (n 44 above), p 890.
[58] See M E P Seligman, *Helplessness: On Depression, Development and Death* (New York: Freeman, 1992).
[59] See McFarlane quoted in Gunn and Taylor (n 44 above), p 893.

full then further assault will result in overflow and breakdown. On the other hand those who have had little or no experience of distressing but 'normal' life events, eg, bereavement, job changes, moving home etc may also be vulnerable.[60] Research is also inconclusive as to whether previous trauma can prevent the victim avoiding subsequent incidences of trauma/stress — 'learned helplessness'.[61]

DIAGNOSIS

Understandably, many psychiatrists and psychologists are impatient with a requirement of a strict diagnosis. The human psyche is enormously complex; it will not always be possible to say that a number of complicated symptoms set upon what is always a unique personality will result in a clear diagnosis happily conforming to the pictures painted by the systems of classification. In fairness to those systems, the difficulties of diagnosis and overlap of disorders are acknowledged, and there are many 'unspecified' categories where the more specific diagnostic criteria are not satisfied. The crucial point from the practitioner's point of view is that a 'positive' psychiatric illness is diagnosed, even if there are understandable difficulties in precise classification. Professors Gunn and Taylor state:

The term 'positive psychiatric illness' can embrace the whole range of morbid emotional responses as well as the ordinary form of neurotic and psychotic disorders. The doctor thus must attempt to determine the existence of any psychiatric disorder and its relation to the incident. The court is more concerned with the existence of disorder in itself, its attribution, and its consequences than with the niceties of diagnosis and classification. Diagnostic terms should be used simply and conventionally, but it is unnecessary to follow slavishly definitions from textbooks and glossaries such as the DSM–III or ICD.[62]

An important point to note is that the reaction of the victim will not remain constant. Many studies have shown that the victim proceeds through a cycle of reactions. Gunn and Taylor review the literature, citing, first, the 'dazed' state, where victims seem unaware of their surroundings, then the euphoric state which is characterized by restlessness, altruism and perhaps relief at survival. The next stage is when reality impinges as the horror of what happened is recalled in detail. At this stage survival guilt and a sense of helplessness emerge.

Generally, it is thought that diagnosis can be difficult due to the fact that awareness of stress-related disorders is still fairly limited and patients may

[60] See Gunn and Taylor (n 44 above), p 894.
[61] Seligman coined the term, quoted by Gunn and Taylor (n 44 above), p 894.
[62] Gunn and Taylor (n 44 above), pp 102–3.

present a long time after the event. Their recollections of the event may be coloured by subsequent experiences; they may be obsessed with physical symptoms which are not organic or, upon the physical evidence, should not be causing the degree of pain or disablement complained of. There are constantly developing techniques to help in diagnosis. A number of self-assessment questionnaires are used by psychiatrists and psychologists, but which ones are used, and the degree of importance placed on each one will vary. Sometimes these are completed by the patient before seeing the expert, but sometimes the expert will want to interview the patient first, form an assessment and then ask for completion of the questionnaire(s) to confirm, or otherwise, the initial diagnosis. It is wise to note the preferences of the particular expert before exposing the potential patient to any of this type of documentation, and many of these questionnaires are subject to copyright restrictions.

An important difference between the ICD–10 and DSM–IV diagnostic criteria was highlighted by *Blackledge v London General Transport Services Ltd.*[63] This was an action brought under the Disability Discrimination Act 1995. An employment tribunal had to determine whether the applicant suffered from PTSD which constituted a mental impairment for the purposes of the Act. The Employment Appeal Tribunal upheld an appeal against the tribunal decision and preferred the ICD–10 criteria which state that generally PTSD should arise within six months of the traumatic event, whereas DSM–IV has no time limit and expects the diagnostician to specify if the onset of symptoms is at least six months after the stressor. The DSM–IV requirement that there should be significant distress or impairment of functioning was preferred. The Employment Appeal Tribunal held that this was not just a case of preferring one expert's evidence to that of another, but of conflating the diagnostic criteria of both DSM–IV and ICD–10. The Employment Appeal Tribunal also said that the tribunal had ignored the fact that ICD–10 is the classification recognized by the NHS.

In considering the sort of information that may be elicited from the patient in order to diagnose his condition and also to assess the type of treatment necessary, as well as the condition's prognosis, it is worth noting the list of headings in Chapter 10 of Scrignar's book on forensic evaluation: chronologic history; symptom inventory checklist; medical history; psychiatric history; medication; social history; antisocial behaviour; history of previous litigation; family history; personal history; and mental status examination (an assessment by the expert on the basis of the patient's mannerisms, speech patterns, thought processes and mood). It must be stressed that experts take different approaches, but the foregoing gives some indication of the sort of information which will be sought.

---

[63] [2001] WL 825 497.

TREATMENT

There are many ways in which victims of trauma can be helped. These include early screening for symptoms (gained through proper and immediate procedures implemented in the case of disasters), voluntary support groups and self-help, as well as the more conventional professional intervention. Whilst those who are victims along with others do not necessarily recover quicker than solitary victims, there is some advantage in knowing that others have suffered similar experiences so that relating to a peer group is probably helpful.[64] Sometimes relatively simple strategies have been used with significant success in helping the victims of disaster. After the Australian bushfires of 1983, a leaflet entitled *Coping with a Major Personal Crisis* was devised which listed the sorts of experiences and symptoms which a victim might expect to undergo, describing them as normal, and giving simple advice. This leaflet was used after the Welton air crash, when an aircraft collided with private houses in Lincolnshire, without loss of life, and the reaction to this was investigated.[65] The leaflet was circulated throughout the areas, 91 per cent of those who had received it had made some effort to read it, and 27 per cent had kept it. People appreciated the fact that someone was concerned, and also the attempt to normalize their experiences.

Some local-authority social services departments publish literature advising people of the likely feelings they may experience following traumatic experiences (see Appendix 3). The publication of a victims' newsletter also had beneficial effects following the Bradford fire and the *Herald of Free Enterprise* capsize. The newsletters would include requests for information, for contacts, poems and letters about loved ones who had died. Less than 2 per cent of victims rejected the newsletter whereas personal visits were refused by a large number. Victim support schemes can also be vitally important, although research shows that only about 1 per cent of those who report crime to the police are ever referred for help. In March 1986 there were, however, some 185,000 referrals.[66] Often this sort of help is enough; the mixture of practical advice, someone to talk to, and the reassurance that someone cares can resolve anxieties. Whoever supplies this service to victims, it is often described as counselling and can include informal counselling by social workers or more formal counselling by specially trained counsellors, such as bereavement counsellors, and can include one-to-one counselling and/or group therapy.

---

[64] Gunn and Taylor (n 44 above), p 939.

[65] Lalonde et al, 'Community Responses to a Near Disaster', presented at 1st European Conference on Post-traumatic Stress Studies, Lincoln 1988, cited in P E Hodgkinson, 'Technological Disaster: Survival and Bereavement' (1989) 29 *Soc Sci Med* 351.

[66] Gunn and Taylor (n 44 above), p 936, citing the work of Hough and Mayhew.

Being able to talk about the event can be just as important for professionals as 'civilian' victims. Specific debriefing sessions can be held for rescue workers who are subjected to stress over an extended period of time following a large-scale disaster. The debriefing sessions organized following the San Francisco earthquake in 1989 were twofold: initial 'defusing' a few hours after the rescue work began, and a day or so later a formal three- to five-hour session with a mental health professional.[67] Counsellors and others involved in the process may also require help.

Despite the apparent benefits of debriefing, participation should of course be entirely voluntary and confidential, and it should also be noted that that there is some controversy about its value as a formal psychological intervention. 'Formal debriefing' was developed by Mitchell in 1983 for debriefing emergency personnel.[68] Not a great deal of evaluation has been carried out, but some research has been critical of it, for example, Griffiths and Watts found that those who attended debriefing scored higher on the impact of events scale than those who did not.[69] However, this could be explained by the fact that those who attended had been exposed to greater distress. Debriefing is examined further below in Chapter 6.

The fact that the event affects possibly just one person does not, of course, diminish that person's need to discuss the event, if necessary with an appropriate mental health adviser. Again, fairly simple techniques can be effective, such as training in progressive muscle relaxation.

An interesting study was carried out following the *Herald of Free Enterprise* disaster to ascertain whether the viewing of human remains by the bereaved was helpful or harmful.[70] The conclusion was that those who view may be more distressed in the short term, but less distressed in the long term. It was also concluded that no one should be encouraged to view, as there will always be individuals who will be badly affected by it, but that those who wish to do so should not be prevented. It is strongly advocated that suitably qualified 'helpers' should be available at the time the decision is taken. It should, however, be noted that the actual sight of the body can be one of the triggering events of psychiatric injury.[71] Needless to say, there should be no suggestion that the decision to view the body is a *novus actus* breaking the chain of causation, the decision to view a body being part of the normal consequences of a death.

---

[67] See Armstrong et al, 'Debriefing Red Cross Disaster Personnel: The Multiple Stressor Debriefing Model', *Journal of Traumatic Stress* (October 1991) (4).

[68] J Mitchell, 'When Disaster Strikes: The Critical Incident Stress Debriefing Process' (1983) 8 *Journal of the Emergecy Medical Services* 36–9.

[69] J Griffiths and R Watts, *The Kempsey and Grafton Bus Crashes: The Aftermath* (East Lismore, Australia: Instructional Design Solutions, 1992).

[70] Hodgkinson et al, 'Viewing Human Remains Following Disaster: Helpful or Harmful?' (1993) 33 Med Sci Law 197.

[71] See *Hevican v Ruane* [1991] 3 All ER 65, QBD (decision reversed on appeal) (see further p 251).

Drug treatment

This will depend very much upon whether the victim is suffering from PTSD, or depression or some other psychiatric disorder. As far as PTSD is concerned, it seems to be acknowledged that drug treatment alone cannot resolve the problem.[72] Scrignar is neutral about the use of drugs in treating PTSD, stating that further research is necessary before conclusions can be drawn. However, he does consider the use of tranquillizers, antidepressants and sedatives. If depression is diagnosed as well as PTSD it is likely that antidepressants will also be given. The risk of diagnosing depression alone and masking as yet undiagnosed PTSD has been cautioned against in research.[73] There is also the danger of the prescription of drugs to those who may already be overusing alcohol and other substances to control their symptoms.

Psychological treatment

There are a large number of different theories and types of treatment which concentrate on altering behaviour and/or cognitive behaviour. Gunn and Taylor cite an example of behavioural treatment for morbid grief where patients who were taken through a period of guided mourning were compared with a control group who were encouraged to avoid thought of the deceased and given distraction techniques. Those who had been encouraged to write about their deceased loved ones and look at photographs of them improved significantly more than the control group.[74] The technique can be modified depending upon the trauma and resulting psychological state. For example, Dr Morgan O'Connell at the Royal Naval Hospital in Haslar encourages patients to produce collages based upon various memorabilia.

There are a number of different strategies used to treat patients psychologically. These include stress inoculation training, thought-stopping techniques, and other forms of what Scrignar calls encephalic reconditioning or cognitive restructuring, ie, ways of changing those distressing 'videotapes of the mind', and desensitization, which is a way of gradually re-exposing the victim to the scene of the trauma, or the phobic or anxiety-producing stimulus, such as water, car travel etc. Attribution theory is another way in which victims are encouraged to cope with a traumatic experience. According to this, the nature of the way in which an individual explains an event affects the way in which he will respond to it. Affirming that the explanation for the event is not the fault of the victim will help that victim to

[72] M J Friedman, 'Towards Radical Pharmacotherapy for PTSD' (1988) 145 *Am J Psy* 281.
[73] See Hodgkinson, 'Technological Disaster: Survival and Bereavement' (1989) 29(3) *Soc Sci Med* 351–6.
[74] Gunn and Taylor (n 44 above), p 938, citing the research of Mawson et al (1981).

come to terms with it, to allay feelings of guilt and shame. Joseph et al[75] concluded that there may be considerable scope for identifying vulnerable individuals and for improving distress by altering people's perceptions of the causes of significant events that took place during the disaster. Scrignar also refers to the usefulness of family conferences, sleep training, and assertiveness training.

One of the most recent treatments to be developed is 'Eye Movement Desensitization and Reprocessing' ('EMDR'). EMDR involves the targeting of distressing memories and thoughts by means of isolating negative images and associated thoughts. The patient then tracks a therapist's fingers which are moved across his path of vision. It is not clear precisely how this works but it has been suggested that it operates on a neurophysiological level.[76]

PROGNOSIS

There have been several follow-up studies undertaken in respect of victims of large-scale disasters,[77] but not enough, and not over a long enough period of time for any conclusions to be drawn from which useful generalizations can be made. Experts will make their prognoses on the basis of the severity of the symptoms, the degree of support the patient has, the way in which the patient has progressed, or not as the case may be, during the period from initial consultation to final report or trial, and so on. Often it will not be possible to say that the patient is cured; many of the techniques referred to above will be available to the patient throughout life to deal with anxieties, intrusive thoughts or images etc which *may* return from time to time. Knowing that these techniques have worked in the past can be of considerable comfort to the sufferer. Some experts will use the questionnaire system to see how the patient is progressing.

CHILDREN

Are there any special problems relating to children who are exposed to trauma? It was once thought that children did not suffer from PTSD. Conclusions have been drawn, however, that children as young as eight can

[75] 'Attributions and Symptoms after a Maritime Disaster' (1991) 159 *Br J Psychiatr* 542.

[76] See P Smith and W Yule, 'Eye Movement Desensitization and Reprocessing' in W Yule (ed), *Post-traumatic Stress Disorders: Concepts and Therapy* (Chichester: Wiley, 1999).

[77] See, eg, Gleser, Greg and Winget, *Prolonged Psychosocial Effects of Disaster: A Study of Buffalo Creek* (New York: Academic Press, 1981).

suffer the symptoms of PTSD.[78] The effects can go on for a number of years. Inevitably, the interaction with their parents can produce some confusing results, particularly if the parents have also been involved in the traumatic episode. Research has shown very different levels of distress reported by children when they were seen separately from their parents, after the *Herald* disaster, when children knew that their parents were trying to cope with their own distress.[79] Some differences, however, have been noted between adult and children's symptoms of PTSD; for example, it is more difficult to detect 'psychic numbing' in children. As Yule and Williams say: 'If anything, their pressing need to avoid situations that remind them of the accident drives them out of the house where it will be discussed and into a frenzy of social activities.' Clearly, this can mask psychological distress: it may well be thought that a child is unaffected if he appears to be full of energy and 'enjoying himself'. Yule and Williams also note with surprise the failure of teachers to note the problems the children were experiencing, but go on to say that this experience is similar to that in Australia following the bushfires, when McFarlane was thwarted in his attempts to study the children who saw the fires because schools would not co-operate saying it was best to let past things remain in the past. Another interesting point made by Yule and Williams is the value of group work with parents and children, considering that each may be trying to protect the other from their own distress.

Professor Yule worked with children who suffered in the *Jupiter* disaster (the ship carrying school children which sank near Athens in 1988) and gave valuable evidence in the case of *Gardner v Epirotiki SS Company & Others*.[80] The reference to PTSD and children in the DSM–IV diagnostic criteria should also be noted (see Appendix 1).

THE FUTURE

Research produced as long ago as 1929[81] concluded that stress produces physical changes to the nervous system. Subsequent research has continued to confirm that a number of complex neurochemical changes take place within the nervous system following conditions of acute stress,[82] and in

---

[78] W Yule, 'The Effects of Disasters on Children' (November 1989 11(6) *Association for Child Psychology and Psychiatry Newsletter*.

[79] Yule and Williams, 'Post-traumatic Stress Reactions in Children' (1990) 3(2) *Journal of Traumatic Stress*.

[80] [1995] 10(10) PMILL.

[81] W B Cannon, *Bodily Changes in Pain, Hunger, Fear and Rage: An Account of Recent Researches into the Function of Emotional Excitement* 2nd edn (New York: Appleton-Century-Crofts, 1929).

[82] H Anisman, 'Neurochemical Changes Elicited by Stress: Behavioral Correlates' in H Anisman and G Bigname (eds), *Psychopharmacology of Aversively Motivated Behavior* (New York: Plenum, 1978); D Krieger, 'Brain Peptides: What Where and Why' (1983) 22 *Science* 975.

1984, Bessel van der Kolk et al, produced a biological hypothesis that animals that have been exposed to 'inescapable shock' undergo changes in the chemical composition of their nervous systems, the extrapolation of which to humans suggests that opioid peptides play a vital role in the state of stress and its subsequent treatment and management.[83] This has fascinating and important implications for lawyers. One of the central problems in relation to establishing a successful claim for any form of psychiatric injury has always been that it is not 'physical' damage. If the future holds the possibility of producing evidence of actual physical damage to a claimant's neurochemical composition, then the question of proximity will disappear. There will remain, of course, the question of causation, but it would remove one of the most difficult obstacles to a claim, and put psychiatric injury on a par with ordinary physical damage. Similarly, research at the Institute of Psychology, King's College, London has resulted in the development of 'Vivid' (virtual in-vivo interactive dissection) which displays patterns of nerve connections inside the brains of living people.[84] Conventional MRI (magnetic resonance images) scanners, although they can produce images of the brain, cannot detect the nerve connections. At present the research is concentrating on the brains of schizophrenics, but clearly there is potential for examination, diagnosis and treatment of many other psychiatric conditions. This is all well into the future, but it could result in one of the most exciting developments in medical evidence.

More immediately, since the recognition over the past ten years of so of the extent of traumatically induced disorders, a considerable amount of work has been carried out, and it is hoped that more follow-up studies will be carried out. Increased information about the effect of trauma of all kinds upon psychological development should bring a greater understanding and awareness.

---

[83] B A van der Kolk et al, 'Post-traumatic Stress Disorder as a Biologically Based Disorder: Implications of the Animal Model of Inescapable Shock' in B A van der Kolk (ed), *Post-Traumatic Stress Disorder: Psychological and Biological Sequelae* (Washington, DC: American Psychiatric Press, 1984).

[84] See The Guardian, 18 January 2002, p 11.

3

Identifying the Claimant as a Sufferer

In this chapter some of the practical difficulties that may arise in identifying psychiatric injury are examined. This is of practical importance for lawyers because people who wish to pursue claims for physical injuries often do not realize the possibility that psychiatric injury may also be involved. In other circumstances, the client may claim to have suffered psychiatrically, and the lawyer may need to know how to proceed further. This chapter, therefore, aims to give some practical advice for circumstances such as these.

Although much of what follows is applicable to the non-shock cases, such as a workplace-induced disorder, it is suggested that there will be fewer identification problems in cases of ongoing 'stressful' circumstances.

THE IMPORTANCE OF IDENTIFICATION

Lawyers acting for both claimants and defendants should be aware of the difficulty of identifying psychiatric injury. Early identification will assist with the progress and settlement of the case. It may well be that the claimant is suffering from physical symptoms which are difficult to resolve; the specialists concerned may be unable to make a firm prognosis. In these circumstances, the defendant may be alleging an element of functional overlay (a much over-used term which has no clear meaning but is often deployed to suggest that there is a 'psychological' element to the plaintiff's physical symptoms), or even malingering, which will, no doubt, be strongly denied. These sorts of problems, and there are many variations on the theme, can delay settlement and increase costs. If there is some psychiatric injury then the sooner it is identified the better, so that it may be treated, and, it is hoped, resolved, and so that its relationship to the physical disorders can be clarified, and, again, it is hoped, resolved. Research shows that claimants are more interested in recovering their health than in receiving compensation.[1] The sooner the illness is identified the sooner the treatment can be done.

It is worth pausing here to consider the importance of tact on the part of the legal advisers involved. Most victims will not be aware that they are suffering from an identifiable illness. In the majority of cases they will have also suffered physical trauma, and may ascribe any difficulties they have to that. They may feel hostile towards the doctors treating the physical illness, believing them to be either incompetent or unsympathetic. Many will not wish to accept that they have a psychiatric disorder. This would be particularly so if the physical injury incurred was relatively minor; they may fear accusations of being weak and faint-hearted. There is no doubt that there is a fair amount of public opinion which would brand them so.[2] They may also fear the stigma and misery of being diagnosed as mentally ill and dread the treatment. The legal adviser should therefore approach the plaintiff with a fair degree of sensitivity and reassurance. It is important to stress that the phenomenon of psychiatric injury is well known, and that many others have suffered similarly without accusations of weakness, and, importantly, without being told that they are 'mad'. It is worth relating the following story which may be of help even with the most stiff-upper-lipped person.

On 12 December 1931 Winston Churchill was in New York on a lecture tour, when he was struck by a taxi whilst trying to cross Fifth Avenue. He suffered two cracked ribs, scalp wounds, slight injury to the pleural cavity and some general bruising. In other words, his injuries were minor ones. Rest was prescribed, and he and his wife went to the Bahamas, arriving for New Year. Some eight days or so later he experienced a nervous reaction, experiencing lack of concentration, a feeling of inadequacy, insomnia, apathy. He later wrote in the *Daily Mail*: 'I certainly suffered

[1] See the Law Commission report, *Personal Injury Compensation: How Much is Enough?* (Law Com No 225) (London: HMSO, 1994).
[2] See *Daily Telegraph* leader, 20 December 1990.

every pang, both physical and mental, that a street accident or, I suppose, a shell wound can produce'.

It has been subsequently stated by a professor of clinical psychiatry[3] that 'it can be surmised from documented evidence that Churchill not only suffered from physical injuries as a result of the car accident, but developed PTSD as well'. He went on to say 'Unlike most commoners, Churchill was able to quit work (depart from his lecture tour) to rest and recuperate in the Bahamas with his wife, personal secretary, a nurse and the rest of his entourage'. In other words Churchill was in the very best position to recover and yet even then he did not make an immediate recovery. It is extremely unlikely that most victims of PTSD and other reactive disorders will have any of these material and social advantages.

IDENTIFYING SYMPTOMS OF PSYCHIATRIC INJURY

In the case of a head injury, the claimant's lawyer should always be alert to psychiatric injury, but in all forms of injury, its possibility should be recognized. If the legal adviser is concerned that there may have been psychiatric injury amounting to an identifiable illness, what sort of signs might he look for?

It is vital to remember that a number of psychiatric injuries and conditions can be caused by trauma. Because of the detail of diagnostic criteria of PTSD, and because of the wide publicity received for PTSD in the wake of the *Herald of Free Enterprise* arbitrations and other recent disasters, it is tempting for the practitioner to think in terms of PTSD and little else. Certainly this condition has received, in recent years, the main focus of attention in psychiatric injury litigation. This is partly due to the prominence of PTSD in the traumatic effects caused to the victims in the spate of disasters in the late 1980s. It is also partly because PTSD is probably the most commonly diagnosed psychiatric injury in an accident situation. But, as we have said earlier, PTSD is not the only psychiatric injury and an open mind as to the possibility of a variety of psychiatric illnesses is, therefore, vital.

The claimant may have been involved in a 'disaster', by which we mean a major incident as defined, for example, by the Cranfield Disaster Preparedness Centre as:

Any situation resulting from natural or man-made catastrophe demanding total integration of the rescue, emergency services and life support systems available to those responsible for the affected areas together with the communication and transportation resources required to support relief operations.

---

[3] C B Scrignar, *Post-traumatic Stress Disorder* (New Orleans, LA: Bruno Press, 1988), p 83.

In such a case, it is possible that, before the victims seek legal advice they will have had discussions with social workers and doctors experienced in dealing with the effects of trauma. When they see a legal adviser for the first time they may have already told their story several times, and been made aware of the possibility of some psychiatric disorder developing. It is certainly to be hoped that they would have had such an opportunity, as the appropriate degree of care at this stage is essential if the victims are to cope socially and psychologically with the after-effects.[4] If this is the case, then they will already have been alerted to the possibility of psychiatric illness and it should be relatively easy to ask what, if any, steps have been taken to deal with this. Earlier messages about symptoms manifesting themselves, and the availability of help can be reinforced. The adviser will go on to point out that psychiatric disorder is a legitimate head of damage, and should be carefully assessed in a similar way to the physical injury (if any) suffered.

Regrettably, even in the case, of a major disaster, the medical and social service resources may not have been as readily available as desired. A victim may therefore seek legal advice 'cold', and it will be left to the legal adviser to consider for the first time the possibility of traumatically induced psychiatric injury. A number of local authorities have produced leaflets and similar literature for distribution in the aftermath of disasters (see Appendix 3).

Victims of incidents which fall short of being disasters will almost always seek legal advice totally unaware of possible psychiatric injury. It will be difficult to identify whether they are in fact suffering. It is relatively easy and acceptable for the adviser to tell someone who has been involved in a disaster that psychiatric injury is possible and to ask the appropriate questions to determine whether medical assessment is necessary. A victim of a relatively minor traffic accident will not immediately spring to mind as being a sufferer or potential sufferer. It would not be desirable to encourage practitioners or their clients to find illness where there is none, or to encourage pursuit of the psychiatrist's couch once the ambulance has gone out of sight. This is where the interviews with the client are so important for the plaintiff practitioner.

A large part of contact time will be taken up with straightforward factual questions of what took place — 'How fast do you think you were travelling?' etc — but it can be illuminating at the first interview simply to ask for a general description of what happened. It may be that the most distressing parts of the incident will either be described with emotion in some vividly remembered detail, or, just as significantly, there will be an avoidance of aspects of which the client simply cannot speak. These may be no more than warning signs for the adviser concerned (store them away and remember

---

[4] There are a number of texts which deal generally with disasters and their consequences for survivors. A good account is provided by B Raphael in *When Disaster Strikes* (London: Unwin Hyman, 1990).

them at future interviews, and see if the reaction is still the same), or they may be so obviously distressful that, at that stage, the possibility of psychological after-effects is broached with the client. Even then, the practitioner should not be assuming psychiatric injury. Most accidents produce ordinary shock and distress; in most cases, nothing more serious will develop, and the client should not be made to dread becoming psychiatrically ill as a natural consequence of his misfortune. By contrast, it should be remembered that even if the initial interview indicates the most phlegmatic of clients, one of the characteristics of PTSD is 'psychic numbing', which can mean that there is a *failure* of emotional response, easily mistaken for unconcern. Achieving the correct balance is not easy. The fact that others were affected more seriously than the client may produce great feelings of guilt, which will cause a suppression of memories and anxieties on the basis that he is lucky and should gratefully get on with his life. There is also the phenomenon of 'delayed onset' of PTSD recognized in DSM–IV and ICD–10 (see page 257), and defined as such if the onset of symptoms was at least six months after the trauma.

Claimant practitioners will be aware that frequently a client is accompanied by a spouse or other close relative or friend. If psychiatric illness is a possibility then it can be a great help for the legal adviser to elicit the views of someone close to the claimant who may be aware of personality changes since the incident, such as distressing dreams, increased irritability, or increased consumption of alcohol. Even if the claimant denies symptoms, by conscious or unconscious suppression, it is likely that the spouse or similar will not collude in this denial. For the same reason, it is usual for the expert psychiatrist or psychologist to want to see a close friend or relative of the victim.

Generally, the claimant's lawyers should simply be alert to the possibility of traumatically induced psychiatric disorder without being obsessive about it, and through the continuous lawyer–client relationship be sensitive to new indications of its existence, deterioration or (it is hoped) improvement.

POST-TRAUMATIC STRESS DISORDER

What of specific indicators? Having said that PTSD is only one of the psychiatric disorders which can result from trauma, it is an important one, on which a great deal of work has been carried out in recent years. As already noted, the main springboard for understanding the diagnostic criteria of PTSD is DSM–IV and ICD–10. From this Scrignar[5] has compiled a table of the cardinal characteristics of PTSD:

---

[5] Scrignar (n 3 above), pp 89–90.

(a) **Nervousness.** The person is apprehensive, on edge, tense, jumpy, easily startled, and fearful.

(b) **Preoccupation with the trauma.** The person talks a great deal about the accident, speculating that more serious injury or even death could have occurred.

(c) **Pain or physical discomfort.** The person complains of pain or physical discomfort that appears disproportionate to the actual injury incurred.

(d) **Sleeplessness.** The person complains of insomnia with resultant tiredness and fatigue.

(e) **Flashbacks and nightmares.** The person relives the trauma during flashbacks or nightmares with similar emotional reactions as if the accident were happening again. Intrusive thoughts related to the trauma are common.

(f) **Deterioration of performance.** The person experiences inability or difficulty in carrying out usual life activities such as work, family responsibilities, social and recreational activities, or any activity engaged in before the trauma.

(g) **Phobia.** The person experiences fearfulness and avoidance of the place where the accident occurred or extreme apprehension associated with some activity related to the trauma.

(h) **Personality change.** The person becomes withdrawn, moody, irritable, distracted, forgetful, and unlike his usual self.

(i) **Dudgeon.** The person gives expression to frequent unprovoked outbursts of anger with complaints about the carelessness of others and a retributive attitude. Quarrelsome behaviour may be evident.

(j) **Depression.** At some point following the trauma the person feels 'blue' or 'down in the dumps'. A loss of self-confidence, a pessimistic attitude, brooding about past events, or feeling sorry for self may be noted. Social withdrawal, lack of pleasure, and a look of sadness on the face of a person formerly cheerful and outgoing may be extant.

This account of the symptoms of PTSD may be more useful in understanding a client who has PTSD. It is also important to remember that in the *Herald of Free Enterprise* arbitration it was stressed that these are guidelines only. This should also be kept in mind when instructing experts.

These symptoms do, of course, have further effects, so that the plaintiff may have sought sleep and solace in alcohol which itself has caused physical illness.

All of these characteristics will affect the ability of the claimant to work. Loss of a job after the incident, if there is no other compelling reason, may therefore be an indicator. Again, all of these characteristics are likely to put a strain on relationships. Discord in marital or other close relationships can therefore be an indicator if it comes after the incident with no previous signs that the relationship was breaking down. Quarrelsome behaviour which is untypical of the claimant's previous behaviour may result in incidents of violence with or without the involvement of the police or prosecution. This may also be an indicator. An inability to concentrate and sleeplessness and, indeed, many of the other characteristics, may mean that the plaintiff has abandoned previously enjoyed hobbies and social activities.

What is clear from this interaction of symptoms is that, without diagnosis, the condition will worsen because the claimant's social circumstances will be progressively deteriorating. Recovery will be delayed if there is no adequate social and emotional support, which is unlikely to be the case if the claimant's marriage has broken down and he has quarrelled with family and friends. Financial matters will become an additional burden if a job is lost. The lack of a job and enjoyable social activities will mean that the claimant's time will be used almost exclusively to consider his unhappiness; there will be no distraction and no respite. The claimant's lawyer must be alert to identify these signs which will have a potentially major effect on the medico-legal analysis of the client's claim. Further if there is no possibility of a successful claim for legal reasons, the lawyer should advise the client about the possibility of medical assistance in the form of counselling and other treatment.

It is not suggested that the practitioner has to possess some unrealistic level of intuition, merely that he should be aware of the phenomenon of psychiatric injury and notice if an indicator presents itself.[6]

THE EFFECT OF PSYCHIATRIC INJURY ON PHYSICAL INJURIES

Psychiatric disorders can affect physical injuries in a number of ways. A claimant whose psychiatric disorder has not yet been recognized but who has some physical result of the incident can concentrate upon that as being the sole aspect of his unhappiness. Furthermore, the physical injury is itself a constant reminder of the trauma and, indeed, disproportionate pain or physical discomfort is a recognized characteristic of PTSD. A claimant will, for example, be far more troubled by a scar if seeing it always recalls the event which caused it, and the recollection of that event causes distress. The general 'knock-on' effect of psychiatric symptoms on social and financial circumstances can also mean that the claimant is not recovering quickly from the physical injuries. Of course, coping with the stress of financial

---

[6] For general observations and advice on dealing with traumatized clients, see G Peart, 'Case Management and Client Care for Solicitors and their Clients Litigating PTSD Claims Arising from Fatalities or Disaster Situations' [1999] 2 JPIL 113.

deterioration (which can lead to social problems) is a common consequence of physical injury alone, and care needs to be taken not to confuse signs of such stress with psychiatric disorder; in that case what is needed is an interim payment, not the help of a psychiatrist.

USE OF QUESTIONNAIRES FOR ASSESSMENT

Those who treat psychiatric injury, whether psychiatrists or psychologists, use a number of questionnaires to assess their patients. The General Health Questionnaire (GHQ) was designed to be a self-administered screening test. It focuses on breaks in normal function, ie, normal for that person, and therefore concentrates on two major areas: first the inability of the patient to continue his normal functions, and secondly, the appearance of new phenomena of a distressing nature. Examples of the questions are:[5]

HAVE YOU RECENTLY:

been able to concentrate on whatever you're doing?	Better than usual	Same as usual	Less than usual	Much less than usual
felt capable of making decisions about things?	More so than usual	Same as usual	Less so than usual	Much less capable
been getting scared or panicky for no good reason?	Not at all	No more than usual	Rather more than usual	Much more than usual

The GHQ consists of thirty questions and it stresses the importance of all thirty questions being answered. It must be said, however, that the GHQ is a closed clinical document and may be purchased only by those with medical or psychology qualifications though it is possible that a psychologist who purchases it may give it to a lawyer for controlled use with the client. This may be particularly useful as a screening mechanism where the client may be reluctant to visit a psychiatrist or psychologist because of the 'stigma' associated with doing so. Indeed, particularly in the case of children, or very nervous clients, this may be appropriate as a sensitive method of checking whether the client needs full medical assessment. Even so, it does not necessarily follow that the initial assessment by the claimant in conjunction with the practitioner will be welcomed by the expert. Some psychologists, for example, prefer to interview the plaintiff *before* the GHQ or any other clinical questionnaire is completed as they believe more telling results can be obtained this way. It is, therefore, important to liaise with the experts and deal with each case on an individual basis.

Other surveys which are, again, subject to copyright and various restrictions are:

---

[7] Extract from General Health Questionnaire 30 © David Goldberg 1978, reproduced by permission of the publisher, NFER-Nelson.

(a) **The Beck Depression Inventory**. This was designed to measure the behavioural manifestations of depression and in particular to provide a quantitative assessment of intensity. It is said to discriminate effectively between varying degrees of depression; it is also able to reflect changes in the intensity of depression after an interval of time.

(b) **The Revised Impact of Event Scale**. This questionnaire was specifically developed as a result of research into the characteristic experiences of individuals with PTSD related to a specific trauma. The fifteen items provide self-report data on the extent to which the person has experienced intrusive thoughts and exhibited avoidance behaviour in relation to a specific trauma during the previous seven days — ie, it focuses on a person's current response level.

(c) **The Beck Anxiety Inventory**. This measures the severity of anxiety in adults. It was constructed to measure symptoms of anxiety which are minimally shared with those of depression, such as those symptoms measured by the Beck Depression Inventory.

(d) **The Beck Hopelessness Inventory**. This measures the extent of negative expectancies about the immediate and long-range future. It is designed to measure the extent of negative attitudes held during the previous seven days.

(e) **The Structured Clinical Interview for PTSD (SCID)**. This is an interview checklist used to evaluate the presence or absence of PTSD, and has been held to be diagnostically reliable but poor in assessing severity of the disorder.

(f) **The Clinician Administered PTSD Scale (CAPS)**. This scale is designed to assess intrusive and distressing recollections of traumatic events and can also record sleep difficulties, irritability, outbursts of anger, poor concentration, hypervigilance and exaggerated startle response.[8]

GENUINENESS OF SYMPTOMS

'Malingerer' means someone who deliberately pretends to be suffering from an illness or disability usually, but not necessarily, for gain. Indeed, if a 'rational' motive is not present (another may be fear, eg, military deserters) then the person concerned is almost certainly suffering from what is classified in DSM–IV as a factitious disorder, which is deliberate feigning of symptoms, but is part of a personality disorder. Malingering is to be contrasted with functional disorders such as these. It is suggested that the problem of malingering can be dealt with satisfactorily by competent doctors and lawyers, and is no more prevalent in psychiatric disorder cases than it is in those of a physical nature.

[8] See Shepherd et al, 'Assessing General Damages: A Medical Model' (1994) 144 NLJ 162.

There is no doubt that, at times, genuineness of symptoms has unduly preoccupied participants in litigation, because where disorders which have no organic manifestation are concerned, there is a common conception that they are easy to feign, and difficult to detect. However, because no medical expert wishes to be successfully duped, and certainly not in the public forum of a court room, any expert should take great care to apply stringent checks in any case where malingering is an issue. It is worth the plaintiff's lawyer reminding the defence of this in appropriate cases, and also of the remark of Richard Asher:

The pride of a doctor who has caught a malingerer is alike to that of a fisherman who has landed an enormous fish and his stories (like those of the fisherman) many become somewhat exaggerated in the telling.[9]

Great care should be taken to ensure that the consequences of the injury to the claimant, such as a slow ability to return to normal life, are not written off as malingering. The Law Commission's report, *Personal Injury Compensation: How Much is Enough?*, stresses the fact that even so-called minor injuries can have profound effects on the lives of victims and their families, and that health and normal life were far more important than financial compensation.[10]

Indications of malingering include inconsistencies in the relating of the history of the 'illness', and possibly in the accounts of the traumatic event itself (although given the possibility of post-traumatic amnesia and non-chronological recollection of the event, the latter should be treated with care). In addition the longer the case is studied, the more likely the conclusions drawn will be accurate. Scrignar says:

the clinician must make a diagnosis based on history of a trauma, self-report of symptoms by patient, psychological tests, interviews with relatives or friends, review of records and mental status examination.[11]

DSM–IV states at V65.2 that:

Malingering should be strongly suspected if any combination of the following is noted:
(1)   medicolegal context of presentation, eg the person's being referred by his or her attorney to the physician for examination;
(2)   marked discrepancy between the person's claimed stress or disability and the objective findings;
(3)   lack of cooperation during the diagnostic evaluation and in complying with the prescribed treatment regimen;
(4)   the presence of antisocial personality disorder.

---

[9] R Asher, *Talking Sense: A Selection of his Papers*, ed Sir Francis Avery Jones (London: Pitman Medical Publishing, 1972).
[10] Law Commission (n 1 above), pp 204–14.   [11] Scrignar (n 3 above) p 145.

Item (1) should be disregarded for the purposes of this chapter, as we are specifically concerned with cases of referral by lawyers. Scrignar himself is cautious about (3) and (4).[12] Firstly, the genuinely ill can be contrary, although he does go on to say that in due course they can usually be persuaded to co-operate, whereas the malingerer, through fear of discovery, may continually try to thwart attempts to diagnose or treat. Secondly, he cautions: 'When evaluating patients, the clinician must be aware of the difference between antisocial personality disorder and intermittent antisocial behaviour; one must be suspicious of malingering in the former, while in the latter, the interpretation is not necessarily that of an unreliable scoundrel'.[13]

An interesting development in psychiatric diagnosis is that of 'script-driven imagery'. In this form of testing the subject meets with the psychiatrist who elicits specific information concerning events in the subject's past. From this information, a thirty-second 'script' is written and recorded for each event. The scripts are then played back to the subject, who is told to imagine the event described in the script as vividly as possible. Whilst this is taking place, the subject's heart rate, sweat gland activity, muscle tension, etc are measured. A value is ascribed to each measurement, both before and during the time the subject imagines the event. These values are then subjected to statistical analysis. In an American case in September 1993[14] the plaintiff was a woman who had been involved in a head-on collision. She developed nightmares, a fear of driving and other PTSD symptoms. Testing, by using script-driven imagery yielded a 99 per cent probability of PTSD.

It is important to be aware of other areas where malingering is sometimes alleged, eg, back injuries. Most practitioners, whether they are acting for the plaintiff or the defendant, would accept that such cases do not present all that often, and do not raise insuperable difficulties. In cases where malingering is suspected, then the usual steps are to interview the appropriate people with whom the plaintiff has contact, and look at any relevant social, work and, indeed, litigation history. There is a developing trend for the defence to use secretly made video recordings of the plaintiff, this is often found in a back injury case. Obviously, physical symptoms, or a lack of them, are easier to detect in cases of physical injury.

However, it is important not to become overly suspicious as to possible malingering. Richard Mayou has carried out research into the relationship between medical, psychological and social outcomes and attitudes to compensation in road traffic accidents. His findings suggested, first, that the amount of compensation recovered was relatively modest not least because

[12] ibid, pp 144–5.   [13] ibid, p 145.
[14] See Pitman et al 'Psychophysiologic Testing for Post-traumatic Stress Disorder', *Trial*, April 1994.

claimants were willing to settle quickly for small sums, and, secondly, that '[t]erms such as exaggeration, simulation or malingering are rarely appropriate'. Whilst concluding that there is a real possibility that a small proportion of people will fabricate and exaggerate, this should not prevent lawyers and doctors from being aware of the genuine suffering of the majority of claimants.[15]

THE CHILD VICTIM

It may be thought that the child who suffers from one or more psychiatric disorders is in some ways easier to identify, as usually a parent will be the child's mouthpiece, and will have been watching carefully the physical (if any) effects of the event, which attention will have made the psychological effects easier to identify. Even when there has been no physical injury a parent may have been particularly attentive following the child's exposure to trauma. It may also appear more appropriate to the claimant's lawyer to enquire whether the event has affected the child in a non-physical sense, and, of course, the risk of a parent not wishing to co-operate is unlikely.

On the other hand, studies have shown that parents and other carers tend to try and stifle the need of a child to talk about the distressing experience, and to reassure themselves that it has not adversely affected the child. William Yule, Professor of Applied Child Psychology at the University of London's Institute of Psychiatry, has argued that studies have shown that traumatically induced emotional disturbances in children are flawed in their methodology, and also says:

Another reason for the failure to recognize and report the severity of the effects of disasters on children is the understandable but misplaced reaction of adults who do not want to consider the horrors the children have faced. After some disasters, people in authority have prevented researchers interviewing children; schools have ignored the event or paid it cursory attention, arguing that children are getting over it and no good is done by bringing it all up again. The result is that children quickly learn not to unburden themselves to teachers who then take a long time to link the drop off in standards of work and impaired concentration with the intrusive thoughts the children are experiencing.[16]

There is less material on the effect of trauma on children and it was believed at one time that children did not suffer from, for example, PTSD. DSM–IV has this to say about children:

---

[15] R Mayou, 'Medico-Legal Aspects of Road Traffic Accidents' (1995) 36(6) *Journal of Psychosomatic Research* 789–98.
[16] 'The Effects of Disasters on Children' 11(6) *Association for Child Psychology and Psychiatry Newsletter* (November 1989).

Diminished interest in significant activities and constriction of affect both may be difficult for children to report on themselves, and should be carefully evaluated by reports from parents, teachers and other observers. A symptom of post-traumatic stress disorder in children may be a marked change in orientation toward the future. This includes the sense of a foreshortened future, for example, a child may not expect to have a career or marriage. There may also be 'omen formation', that is, belief in an ability to prophesy future untoward events.

Children may exhibit various physical symptoms, such as stomach-aches and headaches, in addition to the specific symptoms of increased arousal noted above.

One of the awards in the *Herald of Free Enterprise* arbitration concerned a 14-year-old boy whose mother and elder brother were killed; he, his father and sister survived. He was diagnosed as suffering from PTSD and a prolonged depressive adjustment disorder (see page 221). It is also instructive to read the judgment in *Gardner v Epirotiki SS Company & Others*[17], a case arising out of the sinking of the boat *Jupiter* near Greece in 1988. The plaintiff was 14 at the time and suffered the most terrifying experience when the boat was rammed by another vessel. She spent some time in the sea as she watched the *Jupiter* disappear into the water. She developed PTSD, together with severe depression, a generalized anxiety state, and phobia, particularly for water. Giving judgment for the plaintiff, Mr Justice Wright described her symptoms thus:

... since the events of October 1988 and to the present time she has suffered and continues to suffer, now at about monthly intervals, and if she gets very tired, of vivid dreams of the actual event with additional horror, such as the windows of the lounge coming in followed by the water. These nightmares cause her to awake feeling distressed and unwell. She also has other vaguer dreams of being trapped and in danger. She can usually sleep through these but wakes in the morning unrefreshed and unwell. Both these kinds of dreams are significantly more disturbing to her than the childish nightmares she used to have prior to the incident.

After the event she had a continuous headache for almost six months. This condition has significantly improved, but she still thinks that she gets rather more headaches than she should. On a number of occasions since October 1988 she has, whilst waking, experienced 'flash-backs', a sudden reaction or feeling as if the traumatic event were recurring, a phenomenon which is a particular feature of PTSD. She last had such an experience in the early part of 1992.

Quite apart from that, she is persistently bedevilled by intrusive thoughts of the traumatic events. Throughout the three years that she was at school after the accident, she had great difficulty sleeping. If she composed herself to sleep she found the thoughts, and the sensation of the noises, mental pictures and smells associated with the event bearing in on her so as to make her feel ill. She found that the only way to get to sleep would be to watch television until she went off or simply to read herself to sleep. Nothing less would suffice to distract her mind from the intrusive thoughts of the accident. Even now, while she is at University, she has difficulty getting off to

[17] (1995) 10(10) PMILL (January 1995).

sleep, and usually has to read for about an hour into the small hours before she can succeed. . . .

In order to keep the intrusive thoughts and feelings at bay, she has developed a technique which she describes as 'an internal monologue'. Sometimes she repeats what people are saying to her, and when she is not in conversation she sings songs to herself or keeps up a conversation with herself in order to keep her mind occupied. This technique requires a conscious effort on her part, and I entirely accept her when she says that she finds it exhausting. These intrusive thoughts, and the necessity to resort to this defensive technique and the impact upon her concentration have all, I am satisfied, had a catastrophic effect upon her educational attainments, and I shall have to return to this topic later.

I am satisfied that, as she describes, she suffers from a high degree of anxiety, which, as it so often is, is associated with a marked degree of irritability which her mother confirmed. She is hyper-anxious about losing articles, which she associates with the fact that she lost all her property in the accident, and she behaves irrationally if she mislays even an unimportant article. When it is found, she feels sensations of guilt. She suffers from a degree of claustrophobia and finds crowded places, particularly on public transport, difficult. Wherever she goes she finds herself looking for escape routes.

Her appetite has been diminished, and she has developed a well marked phobia for water. Even so mundane an operation as filling a bath induces intrusive thoughts in her, and she normally takes showers instead. While she is able to swim she can only do so if she concentrates on swimming lengths; she cannot enjoy being at the pool with her friends, as the sound of splashing and shouting upsets her.

Her summary of herself is that from a relatively placid outgoing stable character with no real anxieties, she has turned into an introverted neurotic worrier. She takes deliberate steps to avoid any 'triggering' experiences, and finds herself unable to watch scenes on the television or at the cinema involving water or indeed any catastrophes.

The plaintiff was awarded (*inter alia*) the sum of £17,500 general damages and the sum of £12,500 for future loss of earnings given the detrimental effect of the incident on her education.

Although the medical expert may make all the appropriate enquiries of schools and any other agencies involved, the lawyers involved should also be aware of these other sources of information on the child's behaviour, and be prepared to make enquiries. It is important not to rush a child's case because it is especially difficult to make an accurate prognosis for a child.

4

The Shock Cases

THE 'SHOCKING' CRITERION

The basic criteria for establishing liability in negligence for nervous shock cases were set out in Chapter 1. This chapter will expand the coverage of this area by examining a number of cases where there was found to be a sudden and shocking event which caused the claimant's psychiatric illness.

Establishing that the event fulfilled the 'shocking' criterion is crucial if the claimant has suffered psychiatric injury as a result of being a 'secondary victim', ie that he was necessarily outside the sphere of being personally at risk of physical injury. How crucial the shocking criterion is to establish primary victim status is debatable, as, since *White v Chief Constable of South Yorkshire Police*,[1] this now seems to depend upon simply being at risk of physical injury, regardless of one's perceptions. Under the crude 'limiting factors' imposed, the shock must come directly through one of the five senses, and not through the mediation of a narrator passing on bad news. It might be arguable that the claimant 'hears' the bad news, but this will not do. Hearing an explosion will probably suffice, but to be informed by a third party that the explosion has killed or injured one's entire family will not.

It has been pointed out that the diagnostic criteria of post-traumatic stress disorder ('PTSD') are exceptional in that the cause of the condition has been included as a defining characteristic.[2] However, it is uncontroversial that the claimant does not have to be suffering from PTSD, as any recognizable psychiatric illness shown to have been caused by the event will attract damages. Nonetheless, it is unfortunate that the diagnostic criteria relating to a condition which, clearly, can be the result of exposure to sudden trauma, should coincide with the artificial imposition of the shock requirement.

It is worth repeating that the majority of cases involving psychiatric injury will also involve actual physical injury to the plaintiff. In such cases, subject as ever to factual causation and proof of injury, there should be no difficulty in sustaining the psychiatric part of the claim. (It is also worth emphasizing the importance of considering the possibility of psychiatric illness following a head injury.)

PRIMARY VICTIMS

Alcock v Chief Constable of South Yorkshire Police[3] established a distinction between 'primary' and 'secondary' victims. Lord Oliver stated that a primary victim is someone who is physically injured or is within the range of foreseeable physical injury or reasonably believes that he is at risk, or is 'involved mediately'.[4] In *Page v Smith*,[5] the House of Lords removed the barriers to claims by primary victims by treating them like victims of physical injury. The requirement of foreseeability of psychiatric injury was abandoned once the claimant brought himself within the definition of a primary victim. However, the majority of the House of Lords in *White v Chief Constable of South Yorkshire Police*[6] chose to treat *Page v Smith* as meaning that, in order to be a primary victim, it was *necessary* rather than *sufficient* for the claimant to be within the range of foreseeable physical injury (or to

---

[1] [1999] 2 AC 455.

[2] See R Mayou, 'Psychological, Quality of Life and Legal Consequences of Road Traffic Accident Injury' [1995] JPIL 277.

[3] [1992] 1 AC 310.   [4] ibid, at 410.   [5] [1995] 2 WLR 644.   [6] [1999] 2 AC 455.

reasonably believe himself so to be). It was uncontroversial that the road accident in which Mr Page was involved was an 'impact' event; the controversy was that it was of a minor nature, that no one was injured, and that probably only someone lacking in 'normal' fortitude would be affected by it in the sense of developing a medical condition, as opposed to, perhaps, suffering a brief period of 'normal' distress. The result in *Page v Smith* might have been curious in this respect, but *White* has now made it unfair in the sense that it has simultaneously opened up the scope for psychiatric injury claims (*anyone* at risk of *any* sort of physical injury in *any* type of situation can claim damages for psychiatric injury of *any* degree of severity), while also narrowing it (if you are just outside that area, then hard luck).[7]

However, in *Cullin v London Fire and Civil Defence Authority*,[8] the Court of Appeal refused to strike out a claim for damages for psychiatric injury sustained following the witnessing of an unsuccessful attempt to resuscitate a colleague. The court stated that it was possible that the claimant could satisfy the *White* and *Page v Smith* requirements. Importantly, the court also stated that, for the purposes of deciding whether a claimant was the primary victim of an accident or incident, that accident or incident had to be regarded broadly. Similarly in *Campbell v North Lanarkshire Council*,[9] the Scottish Outer House refused to strike out a claim for damages for psychiatric injury arising from an explosion at the workplace when the pursuer was just a few yards away. The defender alleged that he was not a rescuer, nor did he have a tie of love or affection, not had he feared for his own personal safety. The judge held that the action would only be dismissed where the court was satisfied that even if the pursuer proved all he averred, he was still bound to fail, and, again, importantly, actions for psychiatric injury were apt to raise difficult issues and could rarely be dismissed in a summary fashion. It is important, however, to note that both these cases were interlocutory applications, and might merely reflect judicial concern not to dismiss claims without hearing the evidence.

Fear for oneself

Although it is now uncontroversial law, it should be remembered that one of the earliest cases in England on 'nervous shock', *Dulieu v White & Sons*,[10] established the principle that damages could be recovered for the condition which had been produced by fear for *oneself* and indeed that case stated that *only* fear for *oneself* would do. In consequence, the case of 'the accident I almost had and *thought I was going to have*' can result in a successful claim for damages for psychiatric injury. It will, of course, have to

---

[7] See the judgment of Lord Goff in White, ibid, at 479–80.   [8] [1999] PIQR P314.
[9] 2000 SCLR 373.   [10] [1901] 2 KB 669.

satisfy the foreseeability requirements. The incident itself need not be distressing to a person of ordinary fortitude,[11] so long as the claimant is a primary victim (and that is satisfied if there is reasonable fear for oneself). A word of caution is appropriate here, however, as it has already been pointed out that damages are not recoverable for 'shock' in the general sense; there must be an recognizable psychiatric illness. The great majority of near-misses will not, it is hoped, result in any such illness. Those that do should have no difficulty as far as proximity is concerned, subject to the additional requirements of factual causation and proof of injury. Normally, the fact that one fears for oneself is enough to establish a sufficiently close physical proximity. However, it must be reasonable to fear for oneself. The reasonableness of the fear will be demonstrated either by the fact that the plaintiff was within the physical area of the risk or by the fact that the nature of the event (sudden, dramatic etc) was such as to make the claimant reasonably fear for his own safety. This was considered by the Court of Appeal in *McFarlane v E E Caledonia Ltd*[12] where it was found that the claimant could not reasonably have been in fear for his own safety when he was on a support vessel which was some 550 metres away from the Piper Alpha oil rig which exploded in the North Sea in 1988. Stuart-Smith LJ said:

The [support vessel] was never in actual danger ... If indeed the plaintiff had felt himself to be in any danger, he could have taken refuge in or behind the helicopter hangar, which was where non-essential personnel were required to muster. The judge [at first instance] thought it was entirely understandable that the plaintiff and other non-essential personnel should wish to see what was happening on the Piper Alpha. I agree with this. What I do not agree with, is that someone who was in truth in fear of his life from spread of the fire and falling debris should not take shelter. Only someone who is rooted to the spot through fear would be unable to do so. The plaintiff never suggested that; he accepted that he had moved about quite freely and could have taken shelter had he wished.[13]

In the case of *Schofield v Chief Constable of West Yorkshire Police*[14] the plaintiff was held by the Court of Appeal to be a primary victim when, in her presence, a fellow police officer negligently discharged a gun. They had gone to a house where four guns had been found. Without warning, the officer had fired the gun into some bedding material. Immediately before he did this, the plaintiff, realizing what he was about to do, had moved to protect the women who had reported the matter to the police. The plaintiff developed PTSD. It was held that her involvement meant that she was not just a mere bystander but someone who the officer knew or should have known would be exposed to a risk of physical injury, and so she should be regarded as a primary victim. Clearly it seems that, in view of her actions, she

---

[11] See *Bourhill v Young* [1943] AC 92, HL, at 117.   [12] [1994] 2 All ER 1.
[13] ibid, at 11.   [14] [1999] ICR 193.

could, regardless of the actual threat to her physical integrity, be regarded as reasonably in fear for herself. (The House of Lords in *Hicks v Chief Constable of the South Yorkshire Police*[15] identified fear 'of whatever degree' as a normal human emotion and not therefore compensatable unless, of course, it is causative of a recognizable psychiatric illness.)

As stated above, following the majority decision of the House of Lords in *White*, it is arguable that the test is now that the claimant must actually be within the range of foreseeable physical injury, rather than that he must fear for himself. Nevertheless, it could be said that 'fear for oneself' is still an essential element in a primary victim case, as it is difficult to envisage circumstances in which a claimant is within the range of foreseeable physical injury which results in psychiatric injury, but did not actually fear for himself. A possible example would be some form of 'delayed reaction' when, after the event, the claimant realized what might have happened and this *subsequent* realization caused the psychiatric condition. Indeed, it seems that something very much like this happened to Mr Page in the *Page v Smith* case. In these circumstances, however, there would still be something akin to fear for what might have happened to oneself. In *Hambrook v Stokes*,[16] it will be recalled, the court rejected 'fear for oneself' as the sole basis for claiming damages for nervous shock in the absence of physical injury. Quite rightly, the court recognized that it would be wrong not to acknowledge the importance of the moral worthiness of concern for others, and hence, fear for others became an acceptable causative agent of nervous shock. Curiously, and, perhaps sadly, the current situation with regard to the disparity between primary and secondary victims is against the spirit of those sentiments. This was, of course, acknowledged by Lord Goff in *White*, who described the scenario of the two civilian rescuers at a train crash, both bravely entering the train wreckage, one at each end of the train, one unknowingly being at physical risk, the other not. The result of the majority decision in *White*, would mean that the first one can recover damages if he develops a psychiatric condition as a result of his involvement, while the latter cannot.[17]

Imagined harm to oneself

The plaintiff must normally experience at least part of the event through his unaided senses. So, for example, a claim for damages was disallowed when the plaintiff, who worked at a school, suffered psychiatric injury as a result of realizing that she had narrowly escaped being attacked and possibly killed by a burglar who entered the school at a time when she would have been on duty had she not swapped her shift with another.[18]

---

[15] [1992] 2 All ER 65.   [16] [1925] 1 KB 141.
[17] [1999] 2 AC 455, per Lord Goff at 487–8.
[18] *Wilks v Haines* [1991] Aust Torts Rep 81-078.

Primary victims: medical cases

On any sensible interpretation of 'primary victim', patients who are subjected to medical treatment which goes wrong, should be regarded as primary victims, although it will be seen in the context of the 'fear for the future' case of *The Creutzfeldt-Jakob Disease Litigation Group B Plaintiffs v The Medical Research Council and the Secretary of State for Health*[19] the judge declined to define the recipients of the human growth hormone as primary victims.

It is not surprising that the main area of professional negligence where personal injury of a psychiatric nature has arisen is medical negligence. The reason for this is clear: if there is a breach of a duty of care or a breach of a contractual term then it will usually be discovered through physical injury, and, of course, once this has been shown, then any associated (ie, factually caused) psychiatric injury will form part of the claim too.

A medical negligence claim can arise in a contractual situation, where the patient is paying privately, or in tort, if the patient is in receipt of NHS treatment. It is, of course, well established that a duty of care exists. The *locus classicus* of 'standard of care' is in *Bolam v Friern Hospital Management Committee* where McNair J directed the jury as follows:

[a doctor] is not guilty of negligence if he has acted in accordance with a practice accepted as proper by a responsible body of medical men skilled in that particular art.[20]

In other words, the standard is the standard of a responsible medical practitioner and the fact that there are doctors who would have treated the patient differently does not matter. The standard concerned is objective, and takes no account of the particular doctor's level of skill or experience.[21]

Broadly speaking, the problem of causation is more difficult in medical negligence cases than in ordinary personal injury actions, the reason being that, usually, there will already be some injury or disease present. For example, in *Robinson v Post Office*,[22] the plaintiff sued the Post Office after suffering an injury received in the course of his employment, and also sued the doctor who administered an anti-tetanus injection without carrying out the appropriate test for an allergic reaction. Mr Robinson suffered from such a reaction, but it was found that even if the test had been administered properly, it would not have resulted in Mr Robinson's reaction being known in time.[23]

Frequently, the situation will be complex, and it will be impossible to say whether a particular cause was operating or not. In such cases the courts

---

[19] [2000] Lloyd's Rep Med 161; and see further Chapter 5.

[20] [1957] 1 WLR 582, at 587, and see *Bolitho v City & Hackney Health Authority* [1997] 4 All ER 771.

[21] See *Wilsher v Essex Area Health Authority* [1986] 3 All ER 801, CA.

[22] [1974] 1 WLR 1176.

[23] See also *Rance v Mid-Downs Health Authority* [1991] 1 QB 587.

should normally take the view that the plaintiff succeeds if, on the balance of probabilities, the negligent act materially contributed to the injury or disease.[24]

However, the situation can become further complicated when causation is considered before the damage suffered is identified, as in the case of *Hotson v East Berkshire Health Authority*.[25] Due to the defendant's negligent treatment, the child plaintiff had suffered an injury which the trial judge found to be 75 per cent likely to occur anyway. On this likelihood, the judge awarded the child 25 per cent of his damages. The House of Lords rejected this approach, and said that the 75 per cent likelihood finding meant that on the balance of probabilities the judge had found that the negligence had *not* caused the injury. This meant that the plaintiff recovered nothing. What the plaintiff had suffered, however, was what is known as 'the loss of a chance', ie, the chance in this case of receiving treatment which *may* have benefited him. Clearly the defendant's negligence caused *that* particular loss, and the decision in *Hotson* has been criticized on this basis.[26]

Causation is likely to be less of a problem with psychiatric injury, which is not usually a likely consequence of medical treatment. However, difficulty could arise in cases where the treatment was itself for a psychiatric condition, or in sensitive operations such as sterilizations, where there could be some psychiatric consequences. It is important to remember here that if there are possible consequences which are likely to be grave and adverse whether physically or otherwise, the doctors concerned are under a duty to inform the patient of these consequences, and failure to do so will give rise to a cause of action in negligence.[27] Of particular relevance here is the fact that the obtaining of the patient's consent alone may not be enough. This is illustrated by *Wells v Surrey Area Health Authority*.[28] Mrs Wells was due to give birth to her third child by Caesarean section, and it was the hospital's practice to offer a sterilization operation at the same time if the woman already had two or three children. Mrs Wells consented to the sterilization operation whilst she was in labour, but later regretted it. She sued alleging assault on the basis that she had not been in a position to give valid consent. This was rejected by the court, but she succeeded in negligence as it was held that counselling is an important preliminary to sterilization and the hospital had been negligent in failing to give her proper advice about it.

If psychiatric injury is suffered as a result of negligent treatment resulting in physical injury, then the requirement that the outcome must be

---

[24] See *McGhee v National Coal Board* [1973] 1 WLR 1 and *Wilsher v Essex Area Health Authority* [1988] AC 1074, HL.
[25] [1987] AC 750.
[26] See, eg, M A Jones, Textbook on Torts, 7th edn (London: Blackstone Press, 2000), p 216.
[27] See *Sidaway v Bethlem Royal Hospital Governors* [1985] 1 All ER 643.
[28] The Times, 29 July 1978.

sufficiently shocking or distressing to the person of average emotional constitution ('normal fortitude') need not be satisfied so long as the patient is regarded as a primary victim. In particular, it should also be considered that even if the mishap was minor, it could result in phobic anxiety about medical treatment, particularly if an operative procedure has gone wrong whilst the patient was unconscious. In *Ackers v Wigan Health Authority*,[29] however, there was no question of the mishap being minor. The plaintiff had a Caesarean section operation to deliver her first child. She was not adequately anaesthetized, and was aware during the whole of the operation, but unable to indicate this due to the effect of the muscle relaxant administered before the operation. The operation lasted one and a quarter hours and she was in great pain and fear. As a result of this, she suffered a severe reactive depression, suffering from mood changes, irritability, insomnia, and a phobia about hospitals and anaesthetics. She was terrified when she learnt that her second child would be born by a Caesarean section, and she became frightened of further pregnancy, which adversely affected her sexual relationship with her husband. She also felt unable to face necessary surgery for other ailments which resulted in additional pain and discomfort. Although the prognosis was fairly optimistic, it did involve a course of therapy which would mean reliving her experiences which would be very unpleasant. She was awarded £12,000 in respect of general damages, wholly for psychiatric injury and £1,700 for the cost of future psychiatric treatment.

In *Biles v Barking Health Authority*[30] the plaintiff was diagnosed as suffering from PTSD as a result of a sterilization operation carried out when she was nineteen. The operation turned out to have been unnecessary, and she underwent many operative procedures in an attempt to conceive. She had a tender scar across her lower abdomen. Her sexual function was impaired, although the prognosis in respect of this was good. At the time of trial she had been suffering from PTSD for seven years, her symptoms being depression and anxiety.[31] However, in *Kerby v Redbridge Health Authority*,[32] no damages were recoverable for 'dashed hopes' after the death of a baby (it was held that this was to avoid 'double recovery' as there was also a claim available under the Fatal Accidents Act 1976).

In *Kralj v McGrath*[33] the plaintiff was admitted to hospital for the birth of her twins. One of the babies was lying in a transverse position in the womb, and the obstetrician put his arm inside the plaintiff in an attempt to turn the child around by manipulation of its head. These efforts were not successful

---

[29] [1986] CLY 1048.   [30] [1988] CLY 1103.

[31] See also *Smith v Barking* [1994] 5 Med LR 285, where damages for depression were recovered after failure to warn of risk of tetraplegia; and *Grieve v Salford Health Authority* [1991] 2 Med LR 295, where damages were awarded for depression following a negligently caused stillbirth.

[32] [1993] 4 Med LR 175.   [33] [1986] 1 All ER 54.

and the baby was later delivered by Caesarean section. The child was born with severe disabilities as a result of the obstetrician's attempt to turn it and died some eight weeks later. The plaintiff and her husband already had one child and intended to have three. The claim for damages included a claim for aggravated damages due to the obstetrician's conduct and a claim for grief arising out of the loss of the child and a claim for the financial loss of having another child to replace the dead child.

The claim for aggravated damages did not succeed.[34] It was also held that she was not entitled to damages for grief, but she had seen the child in its disabled condition and was entitled to damages for nervous shock caused by this and by hearing what had happened to it (this may be contrasted with the refusal of the courts to award damages when shock had been caused by hearing from a third party of the death or injury to a loved one, whereas here Mrs Kralj recovered because of *what had been done to her*).

Furthermore, it was held that she was entitled to have those damages increased if, because of her grief at the loss of the child it would be more difficult for her to recover from her own injuries. She also recovered the financial loss which would result from a future pregnancy.

It should be noted here that not all medical malpractice actions are actions in negligence. A patient who has not been informed of the broad nature of the physical examination or surgical procedure which is carried out by a doctor cannot be said to have consented and the subsequent examination or surgery will constitute a battery, which has been defined as a non-consensual touching.[35] Damages for psychiatric injury are recoverable in battery, and punitive damages in such cases are discussed in Chapter 7.

SECONDARY VICTIMS

As outlined above, where damages are sought for psychiatric injury caused by witnessing injury to another it is common to regard the other person as the primary victim, and the claimant in the psychiatric injury case as the secondary victim. However, it must be stressed that the secondary victim in this context is someone to whom a duty of care is owed and *not*, for example, a person who suffers financially when his business partner is injured and unable to work, someone to whom no duty is owed and who cannot be compensated. The claimant in the psychiatric injury case has an action in his own right which is independent of the action of the so-called primary victim.[36]

[34] See Chapter 7 for further discussion of damages.
[35] *Chatterton v Gerson* [1981] QB 432.
[36] See *Videan v British Transport Commission* [1963] 2 QB 650: duty owed to rescuer even though no duty to the victim who was a trespasser.

A secondary victim in 'shock' cases must satisfy three conditions: (1) he must witness the event itself or its immediate aftermath ('event proximity'); (2) the event must be one which would be sufficiently distressing to an individual of normal fortitude; and (3) he must be in a close relationship of love and affection with one or more primary victims ('relationship proximity').

Event proximity

'Event proximity' means that the secondary victim must witness either the accident itself or its immediate aftermath, and that the experience of the accident or immediate aftermath must normally be by sight or hearing. In *Benson v Lee*,[37] a decision of the Supreme Court of Victoria, a mother went to the scene of an accident 100 yards away from her home, where her child was injured. She accompanied the child to hospital where he was pronounced dead. It was held to be foreseeable that she would go to the accident and suffer shock which resulted in mental illness.

The whole concept of 'event proximity' was explored in much detail in the case of *McLoughlin v O'Brian*.[38] Mrs McLoughlin's husband and three children were all involved in a road accident. At the time Mrs McLoughlin was at home and, some two hours after its occurrence, was informed about the accident by a neighbour who took her to the hospital two miles away. When she arrived there she was informed that one child had been killed, and she was allowed to see her husband and the other children. She claimed that the shock of seeing them resulted in severe psychiatric illness. The court at first instance and the Court of Appeal had both found against her, holding that, since she had not been at or near to the scene of the accident, she was not entitled to recover damages for the resultant shock. The House of Lords allowed her appeal. It was accepted that proximity to the accident should be close both in time and space because the claim is essentially for shock-induced illness. However, it was held that to insist upon the plaintiff seeing or hearing the event directly was impractical and unjust, and that someone who comes very soon upon the scene should not be excluded. The crucial part of Mrs McLoughlin's case was the state in which she found her husband and children. It appeared that they had yet to be given any attention at the hospital. Lord Wilberforce summarized what she experienced:

She was taken down a corridor and through a window she saw Kathleen, crying, with her face cut and begrimed with dirt and oil. She could hear George shouting and screaming. She was taken to her husband who was sitting with his head in his hands. His shirt was hanging off him and he was covered in mud and oil. He saw the appellant and started sobbing. The appellant was then taken to see George. The

---

[37] [1972] VR 879.   [38] [1983] 1 AC 410.

whole of his left face and left side was covered. He appeared to recognise the appellant and then lapsed into unconsciousness. Finally, the appellant was taken to Kathleen who by now had been cleaned up. The child was too upset to speak and simply clung to her mother. There can be no doubt that these circumstances, witnessed by the appellant, were distressing in the extreme and were capable of producing an effect going well beyond that of grief and sorrow.[39]

It was this sort of scene which impressed the court as being sufficiently 'shocking' to be part of the 'immediate aftermath' of the accident.

It is essential to note from *McLoughlin v O'Brian* that the 'immediate aftermath' is not calculated in a strictly temporal sense. Whilst for most practical purposes the further away from the accident one is in time, the less likely the 'immediate aftermath' criteria are likely to be satisfied, it is not necessarily going to be so in every situation. Mrs McLoughlin was some two hours or more away from the time the collision took place when she experienced its effects. However, the appearance of her family was largely unchanged from that time.

In *Chester v Waverley Corporation*[40] the High Court of Australia rejected the claim of a mother psychiatrically injured when, in her presence, the dead body of her child was recovered from a flooded trench which had not been fenced properly by the defendant authority. The injury was held not to be foreseeable. However, the date of this case should be noted and it should no longer be regarded as good law in the light of the much later Australian High Court case of *Jaensch v Coffey*, where Deane J considered the meaning of 'aftermath' in some detail:

The facts constituting a road accident and its aftermath are not, however, necessarily confined to the immediate point of impact. They may extend to wherever sound may carry and to wherever flying debris may land. The aftermath of an accident encompasses ... the extraction and treatment of the injured. In a modern society, the aftermath also extends to the ambulance taking an injured person to hospital for treatment and to the hospital itself during the period of immediate post-accident treatment ... In the present case ... the aftermath of the accident extended to the hospital to which the injured person was taken and persisted for so long as he remained in the state produced by the accident up to and including immediate post-accident treatment.[41]

Consequently, if the claimant sees the primary victims either at the scene of the accident, or elsewhere, in a state of physical dishevelment or distress and pain, would this satisfy the criteria concerned, even if this is many hours later? On the basis of *Jaensch v Coffey*, there is no reason why a claim should not succeed, but the decision in *Alcock v Chief Constable of South Yorkshire*

---

[39] ibid, at 417.   [40] (1939) 62 CLR 1.   [41] (1984) 155 CLR 549, at 607–8.

Police[42] is not encouraging in this respect inasmuch as the 'eight hours or so' which had elapsed between the incident and the time that Mr Alcock identified his brother-in-law at the mortuary was said to have removed the identification outside of the 'immediate aftermath'.[43] It is clearly arguable that the identification of bodies *can* be regarded as part of the immediate aftermath on the *Jaensch v Coffey* test, and the 'hearing bad news' cases in Australian and South African jurisdictions which go far beyond this.[44]

In *Palmer v Tees Health Authority*,[45] the mother of a murdered child claimed that within fifteen minutes of discovering that her daughter had not returned from a trip to the shops she believed that her daughter had been abducted (she had good reason to claim this as she was aware that a convicted child molester had been rehoused in her neighbourhood and she had raised concerns about this with the local social services). The Court of Appeal rejected the claim that this realization was a sudden shocking event: the event was the abduction and murder which she did not witness.[46]

It could be argued that perception of the event through senses *other* than sight and sound, for example, smell and touch, would be sufficient. One of the diagnostic criteria for PTSD in the fourth edition of the American Psychiatric Association's *Diagnostic and Statistical Manual of Mental Disorders*[47] ('DSM–IV') concerns the exposure to internal or external cues that symbolize or resemble an aspect of the traumatic event and this is not sense specific. Whilst such an experience would no doubt occur under very unusual circumstances, on the authorities cited above (*McLoughlin v O'Brian; Jaensch v Coffey*), it would satisfy the criteria concerned. Scrignar[48] describes the experiences of a coroner's assistant attending the scene of an air crash, where the stench of burning flesh was a strong factor in the experience of trauma.

The trauma-inducing event witnessed by a plaintiff may take place before any accident occurs, or, indeed, even if little or no injury is suffered as a result of it. *Dooley v Cammell Laird & Co Ltd*[49] illustrates this. Mr Dooley, a crane driver, operating the defendant's crane, was loading a full canvass sling of material from a quay into a ship's hold when he saw the rope begin to break. He attempted to move the crane so that if the material fell it would fall into the sea, but before he could achieve this the rope broke and the load fell into the hold. As a result he suffered sciatica and 'nervous shock'. The claim for damages for both these injuries was accepted by Donovan J, who

---

[42] [1992] 1 AC 310.   [43] ibid, per Lord Ackner at 405.

[44] See *Coates and Another v Government Insurance Office of New South Wales* (1995) 36 NSWLR 1; *Reeves v Brisbane City Council* (1995) 2 Qd R 661; *Barnard v Santam Bbk* (1999) (1) SA 202, discussed further in Chapter 5.

[45] [2000] PIQR P1.   [46] See further Chapter 5.   [47] Washington, DC, 1994.

[48] C B Scrignar, *Post-Traumatic Stress Disorder*, 2nd edn (New Orleans, LA: Bruno Press, 1988), p 60.

[49] [1951] 1 Lloyd's Rep 271.

stated that it was obvious that if one is loading material in this way, and if men are working on the deck or in the hold, then they may become injured or killed and that:

if the driver of the crane concerned fears that the load may have fallen upon some of his fellow workmen, and that fear is not baseless or extravagant, then it is ... a consequence reasonably to have been foreseen that he may himself suffer a nervous shock.[50]

This was picked up in *Alcock* as being a legitimate case of recovery of damages because the plaintiff thought that he might have caused injuries to others.[51]

Since *White* it is doubtful as to how the case of *Carlin v Helical Bar*[52] would be decided, although the decision is refreshingly simple. In that case, the plaintiff was employed as a crane driver. Owing to the negligence and breach of statutory duty of the defendant, a man was crushed to death by the crane operated by the plaintiff, through no fault of his. He recovered damages for his subsequent condition brought on by a fear of causing injury to others. His success appears to have been based purely upon event proximity without the need for some special relationship with the victim. In such a situation, it is possible to argue either that, by reason of the circumstances there is a 'relationship' which justifies a finding of liability, or by stretching the definition of 'primary victim' (which, since *White*, is doubtful). In the Irish case of *Curran v Cadburys*[53] a woman who feared that she had killed a colleague in a conveyor-belt accident, which was caused by the negligence of her employer, recovered damages. The judge regarded her as a primary victim, as she was 'in the eye of the storm' when the accident took place, although there was no suggestion that she was at risk of physical injury herself.

Normal fortitude

The test is whether the event itself is such that a person of normally phlegmatic disposition would be *likely* to be affected. This is not always easy to reconcile with the rule that one takes one's victim as one finds him. However, it is important to note that the rule is not about foreseeability and remoteness of damage, but is about foreseeability and duty of care. Was it foreseeable that a person in this situation would suffer psychiatric injury so as to be owed a duty of care? Once that is established, then the tortfeasor must indeed take his victim as he finds him. This was considered at length in the case of *Bourhill v Young*. Lord Wright said:

Does the criterion of reasonable foresight extend beyond people of ordinary health or susceptibility, or does it take into account the peculiar susceptibilities or

---

[50] ibid, at 277.   [51] [1992] 1 AC 310, per Lord Oliver at 408.   [52] (1970) 9 KIR 154.
[53] The Irish Times, 21 December 1999.

infirmities of those affected which the defendant neither knew of nor could reasonably be taken to have foreseen? . . . A blind or deaf man who crosses the traffic on a busy street cannot complain if he is run over by a careful driver who does not know of and could not be expected to observe and guard against the man's infirmity.

. . . whether there is duty owing to members of the public who come within the ambit of the act, must generally depend on a normal standard of susceptibility.[54]

Of course, once it has been established that the situation would have been shocking to one who possesses normal susceptibility, then the fact that *this* particular plaintiff reacted in a way which could not have been foreseen, for example because of an 'eggshell personality', does not affect liability or damages any more than susceptibility to physical injury affects liability for negligently causing physical injury.

It is important to stress that the requirement only applies to secondary victims: *Page v Smith*.[55] However, it can give rise to difficulties if, for policy reasons, the court does not wish to describe someone as a primary victim. For example, it will be seen in Chapter 5, that there were a number of successful claims for damages by plaintiffs who had been given the human growth hormone as children, and had developed psychiatric illnesses when it was revealed that they might have been exposed to Creutzfeldt-Jakob disease ('CJD') and that the condition, which has a long latency period, might develop in the future. In these cases, the judge preferred to categorize the plaintiffs as secondary victims, even though common sense would be much more likely to see them as primary victims, ie those persons who actually received the drugs, which might cause them illness. Although the condition of CJD is appalling and the normal fortitude rule would be highly unlikely to defeat such a claim, a similar scenario could arise with much lesser medical conditions. It is arguable that the primary/secondary victim distinction should not apply at all in these non-shock cases.[56] Nevertheless, in the CJD cases at least, the distinction between primary and secondary victims has been maintained, and, indeed, the requirement of 'normal fortitude' has been incorporated into the criteria.[57] Arguably, a better way of looking at the situation is to argue that the rule only applies to mere bystanders, inasmuch as the concept originates in *Bourhill v Young*, which was about the liability of a tortfeasor to a bystander and was about duty and not damage. In other words, in, for example, the CJD litigation it should have been clear that a duty was owed to the claimants in respect of CJD or any other physical injury, and therefore owed in respect of illness caused by reasonable fear of it.

---

[54] [1943] AC 92, at 109–10. [55] See, eg, Lord Lloyd at [1995] 2 WLR 644, 675.
[56] See Chapter 5.
[57] In *The Creutzfeldt-Jakob Disease Litigation Group B Plaintiffs v The Medical Research Council and the Secretary of State for Health* [2000] Lloyd's Rep Med 161, per Morland J at 168.

Relationship proximity

As stated above, beyond satisfying the requirement of proximity to an event which would be sufficiently distressing to an individual of normal fortitude, a successful claimant must normally also show 'relationship proximity'. The secondary victim (the claimant) must normally stand in a certain relationship to the primary victim.

Generally, the relationship is likely to be one of some intimacy. The only examples of successful claims so far in the United Kingdom are those of spouses or the parent–child relationship, although a parent–foster-child relationship has been involved, without specific comment.[58] Persons in similar 'quasi' relationships should not have difficulty establishing their claims if the emotional ties are more or less identical with those in the formally legalized relationship. Here, therefore, would be included cohabitees, children not formally adopted but treated as the natural children of the party concerned,[59] siblings who can establish especially close ties, and step-parents and stepchildren. The inclusion of cohabitees is the most obvious, but can present problems. A court may, for example, be reluctant to consider a claim when the parties' relationship is of short duration and their period of cohabitation is short. However, there is no doubt that a relationship of identical or shorter length would not be queried if the parties were formally man and wife. The test will be the strength of the relationship. Similarly, a homosexual couple living together should be treated the same as heterosexual cohabitees. In the case of *Dunphy v Gregor*[60] the New Jersey Supreme Court held that an unmarried cohabitant could recover damages after witnessing her partner being hit by a car and being dragged 240 feet down a road.

Do the parties have to be living together? Again, a couple engaged to be married, particularly if their relationship is of some duration, can hardly be held to be in a different category to those who have recently chosen to live together. And why should there be a requirement that they be formally engaged at all?

Must siblings be of a certain age to justify their claim? It would be a harsh judge indeed who denied the claim of a minor child who witnessed the distressing death of the sibling to whom he was devoted. And if that devotion survives into adulthood, why should the sibling be denied his claim simply because they are no longer children? There are many other close relationships: grandparents and grandchildren; aunts and uncles and their nieces and nephews; devoted platonic friendships, and so on.

---

[58] *Hinz v Berry* [1970] 2 QB 40, CA.

[59] See *Long v PKS Inc*, Lloyd's List, 16 April 1993, California, where a foster-mother recovered damages.

[60] 642 A 2d 372 (NJ 1994).

The judgment in *Alcock v Chief Constable of South Yorkshire Police*[61] sent a clear message that categories would not be devised and boundaries would not be drawn. If there is evidence of an intimate relationship, and the injury is proved and the legal requirements satisfied, then no relationship is excluded. In *Burdett v Dahill* (2002), a case heard at Sheffield county court, the defendant had applied for summary judgment on the basis that the claimant had no realistic prospect of succeeding in his claim for damages for PTSD. The claimant, who was physically uninjured, developed PTSD after witnessing the death of a friend. The claimant and his friend were walking along a dark country road in the early hours of the morning, both very drunk. Cars coming from both directions hit the claimant's friend and he died instantaneously. His Honour Judge Swanson upheld the district judge's decision to dismiss the defendant's application. It was said that the claimant had a realistic chance of showing that either he was a primary victim and/or that he was bound to the deceased by close ties of love and affection. The Law Commission has recommended[62] that there should be a fixed, statutory list of relationships which would give rise to an irrebuttable presumption that the relationship is close enough to result in the psychiatric injury.

Although the courts have not considered anything other than a relationship of close love and affection, a relationship of proximity might arise in a number of ways. Suppose you are cutting long grass at the front of your house with a scythe. There is no fence between you and the highway, but you are well away from the footpath. You are swinging the scythe to and fro in the normal way, when a small child of perhaps two or three who, due to the negligence of the local authority employee to whom the care of the child has been entrusted, suddenly rushes towards you at the precise moment that you are swinging the scythe in the direction of the oncoming child. You make every attempt to control the scythe, but cannot avoid causing the child dreadful injuries. You suffer psychiatric injury. This, arguably, would establish the necessary relationship proximity, should you be inclined to take action against the local authority concerned.[63] This illustration may be somewhat fanciful, but it shows that there are exceptions to the rule that the relationship must be an intimate one. In *Alcock v Chief Constable of the South Yorkshire Police*, Lord Oliver considered the problem of involuntary participants in a negligently caused event, concluding that the fact that the defendant's negligence has brought the plaintiff into the event is enough to establish a relationship of proximity and all that remains to be considered is foreseeability of the type of damage caused.[64]

---

[61] [1992] 1 AC 310.

[62] The Law Commission, *Liability for Psychiatric Illness* (Law Com No 249) (London: The Stationery Office, 1998); see further Chapter 9.

[63] See *Carmarthanshire County Council v Lewis* [1955] AC 549 where the House of Lords considered the liability of a local authority for escaped schoolchildren.

[64] [1992] 1 AC 310, at 408.

It is arguable that the plaintiff recovered damages in *Dooley v Cammell Laird & Co Ltd*[65] because he was in a special relationship to those likely to be injured: the essential element in that case was that the plaintiff was put in the position of believing that *his* actions would have been the cause of any injury to his fellow workers. A novel approach was taken by the High Court of Singapore in *Pang Koi Fa v Lim Djoe Phing*,[66] a secondary victim case, where it was found that because the surviving spouse in a medical negligence claim blamed herself for having persuaded her husband to accept the negligent advice, she could recover damages for psychiatric injury because she was a participant in the medical treatment. The Australian case of *Mount Isa Mines Ltd v Pusey*[67] allowed recovery of damages by a plaintiff who, after an explosion, discovered the badly burned body of his workmate and subsequently developed a schizophrenic condition.[68]

The fundamental problem with the concept of relationship proximity is that the courts have only considered relationships of love and affection, and therefore a secondary victim who is not in such a relationship is regarded as a mere bystander. It is arguable that there should be another category of relationship whereby, although there may not be a tie of love and affection in the family sense, there is a bond of some other significance. Such a category may include, for example, colleagues who work together closely and depend upon one another (particularly in dangerous or hazardous occupations, where a mistake can risk the lives of many colleagues).

Often the claimant in such circumstances can establish himself as a primary victim, as in the case of *Young v Charles Church (Southern) Ltd*,[69] where the plaintiff witnessed the death by electrocution of a colleague. Although there was a breach of statutory duty (the Construction (General Provisions) Regulations 1961), and, said the Court of Appeal, common law liability too, the defendant argued that the plaintiff was merely a bystander. The Court of Appeal held that liability extended to injury which could have been foreseen, and that the plaintiff was 'lucky' not to have been electrocuted himself. This case was decided before *White* but the fact that the court held that he was lucky to escape means that after *White* it would almost certainly be decided in favour of the plaintiff, ie he would be classified as a primary victim. To extend the meaning of relationship proximity would bring into the category of successful secondary victims people like the plaintiff in the case of *Hunter v British Coal Corporation*.[70] He was in a mine with a colleague, driving along a roadway when he hit a water hydrant,

---

[65] [1951] 1 Lloyd's Rep 271.   [66] [1993] 3 SLR 317.   [67] (1970) 125 CLR 383.
[68] See also *Wigg v British Railways Board*, The Times, 4 February 1986, where a straightforward foreseeability approach was taken in the case of a train driver — in front of whose train a person had thrown himself — who suffered a heart attack when he found the body on the railway line.
[69] (1998) 39 BMLR 146.   [70] [1999] QB 140.

causing it to leak. He and the colleague tried to turn it off, but were unable to do so. The plaintiff went to find a hose to divert the water and the hydrant then exploded killing his colleague. (The defendant was negligent in failing to maintain the roadway.) The plaintiff did not witness the actual explosion, nor his colleague's death, but he developed a depressive illness and suffered from 'survivor guilt' nonetheless. He failed in his action in damages.

The case of *Duncan v British Coal Corporation*, which was heard by the Court of Appeal at the same time as *Frost v Chief Constable of South Yorkshire Police*[71] (heard under the name *White v Chief Constable of South Yorkshire Police* in the House of Lords). It concerned a colliery deputy who went down to the coalface to deal with an accident at Rossington colliery in 1990. One of his team had been crushed by a machine, and despite attempts at resuscitation the miner was dead. The deputy developed a psychiatric illness, the fact of which was not disputed by the defence. The Court of Appeal rejected the plaintiff's claim on the basis that he was not geographically close to the incident. Rose LJ, who supported the claim of the police officers at Hillsborough on the basis that there was a pre-existing duty of care owed to the officers by the Chief Constable who had caused the disaster (a view that was rejected by the House of Lords), stated that the first aid that Mr Duncan gave was plainly within the terms of his contract of employment. However, as far as the police officers were concerned, presumably their duties that day were part of their contracts of employment. No doubt the colliery deputy was employed to give first aid, but is there any difference between him and the officers, save for the fact that when he arrived at the scene the accident had already happened? Whatever happened to the immediate aftermath?

In *Robertson v Forth Road Bridge Joint Board (No 2)*,[72] a case heard by the Scottish Court of Session, two employees developed psychiatric injuries after they had witnessed the death of a workmate when he was blown off the Forth road bridge as a result of their employer's negligence. The court found that they were mere bystanders, and, as such, the employer's duty of care extended no further than the general duty to non-employee bystanders. Rose LJ had doubted the correctness of this decision in *Frost*, although Henry LJ distinguished it on the basis that, because the whole event was over so quickly, there might not have been time for the witness-employees to participate in it.

In *Mount Isa Mines v Pusey*[73] the High Court of Australia took a much more liberal approach which would admit of a wider category of claimants who do not satisfy the 'love and affection' test. In that case, the plaintiff heard an explosion in the building in which he was working. He went to the scene and saw an electrician being severely burnt. He supported the

---

[71] [1997] 1 All ER 540.　　[72] 1996 SLT 263.　　[73] [1970] 125 CLR 383.

electrician, with whom, it is important to note, he was not acquainted, out to an ambulance. He succeeded in his claim for psychiatric injury damages purely on the basis that it was foreseeable that another employee in the building would go to the scene. Walsh J referred to the employee being 'within the area of potential danger' or 'within the area of risk'.[74] This was not a physical area of risk (the plaintiff would not satisfy the *White* test now of being within such an area) but within the area where, foreseeably, a fellow employee might go. *Mount Isa*, a 'rescue case', was approved by the Court of Appeal in *Frost* but, of course since the House of Lords' decision in *White* it cannot be regarded as good English law. In *Mount Isa* the judgments of Windeyer J and Walsh J make it clear that they were not deciding this case purely on the basis that both the victim and the plaintiff were employed by the same employer, but purely on the basis of foreseeability.[75] The case was not, however, giving carte blanche to mere bystanders, but restricting liability towards those who might reasonably be expected to go to the scene.

It is arguable that it would be desirable to categorize such people as participants, in the sense that they are engaged in common activities and might feel a sense of responsibility towards their colleagues, or feelings of affection which might not be strong enough to satisfy the 'close tie of love and affection' requirement. This would widen the category of 'involuntary participants' referred to by Lord Oliver in *Alcock*,[76] defined as those people who, through the negligence of another, believe that they have caused the death or injury of another. The plaintiff in *McFarlane v E E Caledonia*,[77] who was on a support vessel some 550 metres away from the blazing Piper Alpha oil rig and who, although not a 'rescuer', carried out some helpful activities, could not really be regarded as a 'mere bystander' but he was treated thus by the Court of Appeal.

Fear for injury to another: real and imagined

As in the case of the claimant's fear for injury to himself, fear of injury to another must be induced by the unaided senses of the plaintiff. In *Hambrook v Stokes Brothers*[78] the plaintiff suffered psychiatric injury as a result of apprehending injury to her children after she saw a runaway lorry go downhill towards the place where she had just left them. Shortly afterwards she was told by a bystander that one of her children had been hit. It was held by the court that recovery of damages was possible only on the basis that the injury was caused by the sight of the runaway lorry and not by the communication of bad news.

In *King v Phillips*[79] although the incident (a taxi backing towards a place in the road where the plaintiff believed her child to be playing) was perceived

---

[74] ibid, at 412.   [75] ibid, at 404, and 412.   [76] [1992] 1 AC 310, at 408.
[77] [1994] 2 All ER 1.   [78] [1925] 1 KB 141.   [79] [1953] 1 QB 429.

by the plaintiff's unaided senses, she was held to be an unforeseeable plaintiff, being positioned some 70–80 yards away and looking out of the window of her home. This is a case which has attracted some criticism.[80]

In *Dooley v Cammell Laird & Co Ltd*,[81] discussed above, the plaintiff was operating a crane when the cable broke, causing a load to fall into the hold of a ship, and his psychiatric injury was wholly the result of his fear for the harm that may have been caused to his fellow employees below (in fact, no one was injured). The defendant was held to be liable.

To differentiate between real and imagined harm is illogical as Mullany and Handford state:

> Shock victims who genuinely and honestly believe that they have killed or injured another are for all intents and purposes in the same position as if the imagined facts were true — and provided that mistaken belief proved to be genuine and honestly held and causative of psychiatric injury, these types of case should be treated the same as any other.[82]

One might go on to say that the belief should be reasonable in all the circumstances, as it would be illogical to insist that fear for oneself must have reasonable grounds but fears for another need not. Fears, however, might not be reasonable, but irrational. (This topic is considered further in Chapter 5.)

Secondary victims: medical cases

In *Taylor v Somerset Health Authority*,[83] the psychiatrically injured party was the widow of the victim of medical negligence. After months of failure to diagnose and treat his heart disease, the plaintiff's husband suffered an unexpected and immediately fatal heart attack at work. He was taken to hospital and found to be dead. Shortly afterwards the plaintiff arrived at the hospital where she was told that her husband was dead. She was shocked and distressed. A few minutes later she identified her husband's body in the hospital mortuary which caused her further distress. As a result of these experiences she suffered a psychiatric illness. As a 'secondary' victim of the negligence Mrs Taylor had to satisfy the 'event proximity'. She failed to do so, firstly, because the judge held that there was no external, traumatic event, and secondly, because even if the fatal heart attack were found to be such an event, the communication of the bad news by the doctor was expressly excluded as a legitimate means of causation in *Alcock v Chief*

---

[80] See, eg, A L Goodhart, 'Emotional Shock and the Unimaginative Taxi Driver' (1953) 69 LQR 347.

[81] [1951] 1 Lloyd's Rep 271.

[82] Nicholas J Mullany and Peter R Handford, *Tort Liability for Psychiatric Damage: The Law of 'Nervous Shock'* (London: Sweet & Maxwell, 1993), pp 222–3.

[83] [1993] PIQR P262.

Constable of South Yorkshire Police,[84] and the subsequent identification of the body did not form part of the immediate aftermath of the event. It went to the fact of the death as distinct from the circumstances in which the death came about. However, the facts of *Jaensch v Coffey*[85] (albeit that it is an Australian case), should be noted in this regard: the plaintiff in that case recovered compensation after her husband was involved in an accident and she thought he was going to die. It seems that it was this concern about his death that caused her illness. To regard concern as to whether someone would die as being compensatable when the actual death is not, is absurd, and it is no answer to the absurdity to state that the 'immediate aftermath' can include visiting a 'dying' spouse, who in the event survives, whereas it cannot include visiting a hospital to identify a spouse's corpse.

In the case of *Sion v Hampstead Health Authority*,[86] the plaintiff had suffered a psychiatric illness as a result of the experience of sitting at his son's bedside for fourteen days watching him deteriorate and fall into a coma. The son was the victim of a road accident but the plaintiff's claim was in respect of negligent medical treatment. The Court of Appeal rejected his claim because there was no evidence of 'shock', no sudden appreciation by sight or sound of a horrifying event, but a continuous process. In particular, the court said, the son's death was not surprising but expected. A similar decision was made in *Taylorson v Shieldness Produce Ltd.*[87]

In *Tredget v Bexley Health Authority*,[88] a county court case, damages were recovered by parents who were psychiatrically injured by the circumstances of the birth and subsequent death of their child caused by medical negligence. His Honour Judge White found that the illnesses were caused by the shock, the sudden and direct appreciation of sight or sound of a horrifying event. However, in *Bunny Soon Heng Tan v East London and the City Health Authority*,[89] a different approach was taken by Her Honour Judge Ludlow at Chelmsford county court to the case of a man whose wife was treated negligently during the course of her labour. It was proposed to carry out a Caesarean section, but the child died before this could take place. The plaintiff was telephoned at work and asked if he wanted to be present when the stillborn child was delivered. He agreed to this and went to the hospital. After the birth he held the child and both he and his wife kept an all-night vigil beside the child's body. He subsequently fell in and out of work, eventually realizing that his inability to cope was due to the effect of the stillbirth (the issue other than 'shock' was whether he was suffering from anything amounting to a psychiatric illness, and the judge found that he was not). The judge found that the delivery of the stillborn child was not shocking in audio-visual terms, and that it was not unexpected because he

---

[84] [1992] 1 AC 310.   [85] (1984) 155 CLR 549 (High Court of Australia).
[86] [1994] 5 Med LR 170.   [87] [1994] PIQR 329.   [88] [1994] 5 Med LR 178.
[89] [1999] Lloyd's Rep Med 389.

had been telephoned to warn him of this and to ask if he wished to be present. As he was not present at the death and the stillbirth was not part of the death, his claim could not succeed. It is arguable that the wife's distressed condition and the arrangement for the birth were part of the immediate aftermath, but it appears from the judgment that the judge thought that there could be no aftermath to a death. The judgment particularly points up the crudity and insensitivity in this area of the law.

However, in *Walters v North Glamorgan NHS Trust* (2002),[90] a mother who suffered from pathological grief reaction recovered damages, even though her son's death took place over a period of thirty-six hours. The child became unwell when ten months old. The hospital failed to diagnose that he was suffering from acute hepatitis. It was accepted that, had they done so, the child would have been treated and probably would have survived. In the event, the mother, who was staying with the child in his hospital room, awoke to find him choking and vomiting blood. He had suffered a major epileptic fit and irreparable brain damage. He was transferred to another hospital, the mother travelling with him, and upon the advice of the second hospital agreed to the withdrawal of life support. Thomas J found that she was a secondary victim, but that she satisfied the 'event proximity' test inasmuch as the thirty-six hours from her seeing her son choking to the termination of life support was a horrifying event which she suddenly experienced. She recovered damages, *inter alia*, for pain suffering and loss of amenity of £16,000.

This less restrictive view has been taken in other jurisdictions. In the Californian case of *Ochoa v Superior Court (Santa Clara County)*,[91] the Supreme Court of California held that there was no need for a 'sudden, brief' event to succeed. It upheld the claim of a mother whose son was in a juvenile hall infirmary. During a visit she saw that he was very pale and seemed to be having convulsions. She was told that he only had flu, but he pleaded with her not to leave him. She was forced to leave, and never saw him alive again. She recovered compensation for her psychiatric injury. In the Singapore case of *Pang Koi Fa v Lim Djoe Phing*,[92] it was said that, in medical negligence cases, it would be rare to witness the act of negligence itself, only the result, and it would be wrong, therefore, to impose the requirement that there be a sudden, shocking event. In that case, the medical procedure took place in June 1985, and the plaintiff watched her daughter die from then until the following September.

In *G v North Tees Health Authority*[93] the plaintiffs were mother and child. The child had suffered from a skin complaint and in the course of the treatment the mother reported that the child was suffering from a vaginal

---

[90] QBD [2002] EWHC 321.   [91] (1985) 703 P 2d 1.   [92] [1993] 3 SLR 317.
[93] [1989] FCR 53, QBD.

discharge. A swab was taken, but, due to the negligence of the hospital it was mixed up with another one and it was reported that the swab from the child contained semen. The child was subjected to a very painful internal examination and was interviewed by social workers and police. Some four days later the mistake was discovered. The mother was already suffering from a phobic anxiety condition and this was exacerbated. The prognosis was good. The child suffered from nightmares and enuresis. She became preoccupied with sexual assaults and her genital organs, and developed a fear of both doctors and the police. The prognosis was similarly good, although it was thought that future gynaecological procedures might make her anxious. The mother and child were awarded general damages of £5,000 each. What was the status of the mother in terms of her right to receive damages? It might be argued that she too was a primary victim because, as the child's mother, she had responsibility for the child and that she might be regarded as having some responsibility for the alleged sex abuse. However, in *Powell v Boladz*,[94] the Court of Appeal held that there was no duty of care owed to the parent of a child *qua* parent, even if he was also a patient of the same doctor. A duty only arose in connection with treatment given to them. These issues were not explored at all in the case of *G*, because liability appears to have been admitted and the court decision was about damages only. On the other hand, the judge did refer to the damage to the mother's reputation, so he may have had in mind some kind of quasi-defamatory basis for damages.

A more straightforward case, *Waller v Canterbury and Thanet Health Authority*[95] concerned the suicide of a 20-year-old man whose parents discovered his body hanging by a rope. The parents had warned the hospital of his suicidal tendencies and had been assured he would be kept within the hospital ward. In breach of this assurance, he found his way into a disused building where his parents found him. They both suffered depressive illnesses as a consequence and recovered damages.

RESCUERS

There is a traumatic event of some kind, maybe a minor road accident, or maybe a large-scale industrial explosion or transportation disaster. It is well established that those who go to the scene, either as volunteer helpers or in their professional capacity as members of the emergency services, are vulnerable to both physical or psychiatric injury or indeed both. It is also well established that any injury they suffer is foreseeable. In *Haynes v Harwood*,[96] a police constable successfully claimed damages after he was

---

[94] [1998] Lloyd's Rep Med 116.   [95] [1993] CLY 1453 (Canterbury county court).
[96] [1935] 1 KB 146.

injured when he stopped a runaway horse on a crowded street. It was confirmed in *Baker v T E Hopkins & Son Ltd*,[97] that a duty is owed to rescuers. Morris LJ quoted with approval the American case of *Wagner v International Railway Co* in which Cardozo J famously said:

Danger invites rescue. The cry of distress is the summons to relief. The law does not ignore these reactions of the mind in tracing conduct to its consequences. It recognizes them as normal. It places their effects within the range of the natural and probable. The wrong that imperils life is a wrong to the imperilled victim; it is a wrong also to his rescuer.[98]

As to any possibility of the defence of *volenti* being raised, it has been stated that:

the doctrine of assumption of risk does not apply where the plaintiff has, under an exigency caused by the defendant's wrongful misconduct, consciously and deliberately faced a risk, even of death, to rescue another from imminent danger of personal injury or death, whether the person endangered is one to whom he owes a duty of protection, as a member of his family, or is a mere stranger to whom he owes no such special duty.[99]

Once it has been shown, therefore, that the defendant has been negligent towards the victims of an accident and that the requirements of foreseeability have been met in respect of those persons, then others who go to their aid will recover damages for any resulting physical injury, and psychiatric injury consequent upon it. As far as psychiatric injury alone is concerned, this has had a chequered history.

In *Chadwick v British Railways Board*[100] Mr Chadwick was a civilian rescuer, when a serious railway accident occurred some 200 yards from his home in Lewisham on 4 December 1957. He went to the scene immediately and stayed there helping in the rescue activities for some twelve hours. As a result of his experiences that night he suffered what was described as an 'anxiety neurosis'. He was described as a man who before the accident had been of 'a happy disposition' who 'got on extremely well with people'. Indeed he was described as being cheerful and responsible for allaying the fears of those railway passengers whom he comforted and helped that night. Mr Chadwick recovered damages against the British Railways Board for the psychiatric injury he received as a result of helping in that rescue. It was held that injury by shock was foreseeable in those circumstances; that the fact that someone would attempt to rescue the victims of the accident was foreseeable and that a duty was therefore owed to such persons; and that the fact that the risk run by the rescuer was not of the same kind as that run by the persons

---

[97] [1958] 1 WLR 993, CA.   [98] 232 NY Rep 176, at 180.
[99] A L Goodhart, 'Rescue and Voluntary Assumption of Risk' (1935) CLJ 192, 196.
[100] [1967] 1 WLR 912.

being rescued did not deprive the rescuer of his remedy; on the contrary, the very situation of a rescue involves unexpected things happening. Although a decision at first instance, *Chadwick* has been approved subsequently by the House of Lords in a number of cases, and in particular in *McLoughlin v O'Brian*[101] and in *Alcock v Chief Constable of the South Yorkshire Police*.[102]

However, since *White*, rescuers are in a different position. Now, recovery of compensation will depend upon the rescuer being a primary victim, ie someone who was at risk of physical injury.

> I too would accept that the *Chadwick* case was correctly decided. But it is not authority for the proposition that a person who never exposed himself to any personal danger and never thought that he was in personal danger can recover pure psychiatric injury as a rescuer. In order to recover compensation for pure psychiatric harm as a rescuer it is not necessary to establish that his psychiatric condition was *caused* by the perception of personal danger ... The plaintiff must at least satisfy the threshold requirement that he objectively exposed himself to danger or reasonably believed that he was doing so.[103]

This does, of course, avoid some of the problems as to how one defines a rescuer. Someone who runs to the scene of an accident, sees horrifying scenes and hears cries of pain coming from the victims, only then to run, say, to a telephone to raise the alarm, participating no further, will not be a 'rescuer' unless in so acting he is at risk of physical injury or reasonably believes himself to be. In *Wigg v British Railways Board*,[104] in which a train driver recovered for the psychiatric injury he suffered after searching for a passenger (a victim of the defendant's negligence) on the railway track and finding him dead. Tucker J said that although the plaintiff could be described as a rescuer, the presence of a train driver on the track was foreseeable anyway. Now, after *White*, would he have to show that he was at risk of physical injury? In *McFarlane v E E Caledonia Ltd*,[105] a worker on a support vessel in the Piper Alpha rescue operations who moved blankets and assisted two of the walking injured as they arrived on the support vessel failed in his claim and would fail now as he was not at risk of physical injury nor reasonably believed that he was exposed to such danger.

What of psychiatric injuries to the rescuer who is a member of the emergency services? In the case of *Ogwo v Taylor*[106] the House of Lords decided that there was no principle which precluded a professional fireman from recovering damages from a person who had negligently started a fire and in which the fireman was injured. It was decided that his injuries were foreseeable, and therefore he should recover compensation, but confirmed that the rescuer should not take unnecessary risks. In *Piggott v London*

---

[101] [1983] 1 AC 410.   [102] [1992] 1 AC 310.
[103] [1999] 2 AC 455, per Lord Steyn at 499.   [104] The Times, 4 February 1986.
[105] [1994] 2 All ER 1.   [106] [1988] AC 431.

Underground,[107] a total of £34,000 damages were awarded to four firemen who suffered psychiatric injury during the King's Cross fire in October 1987, the first time that damages had been awarded *primarily* for psychiatric rather than physical injuries. The latter award was not universally approved, as the *Daily Telegraph* leader of 20 December 1990 stated:

> The concept of seeking damages for stress incurred in the course of professional duties ... seems to us unworthy and distasteful. Indeed, we would argue that men and women who find the stresses of dangerous but respected and rewarding jobs too much to bear should simply seek different employment.

The writer of that piece perhaps did not see that there is no essential difference between this kind of claim and a claim by someone in a dangerous occupation for physical injury caused by the defendant's negligence. There is an implicit assumption in that piece that the firemen could in some way have avoided suffering this type of injury. Suffice to say that however dedicated the fireman or member of the other rescue crews may be, that is no bar to him pursuing his claim, if the facts are otherwise in his favour. Compensation for psychiatric injury suffered by rescuing a fireman was also made in *Hale v London Underground*,[108] where fourteen police officers settled their claims following the Hillsborough disaster and this produced another outraged editorial.[109]

It has been argued that the approach of the House of Lords in *White v Chief Constable of South Yorkshire*, although regrettable in not providing sufficient support for the principle of altruism, is defensible on the grounds of distributive justice (a point explicitly made by Lord Hoffmann), in that it removed an unjust disparity between the compensation of police officers and the refusal to compensate the relatives and was therefore mediating between the interests of broad aggregates of persons.[110] However, another view might be based upon one of Lord Steyn's reasons for continuing to make a distinction between physical and psychiatric injury, that being that the concern about the effect the possibility of such claims might have upon those who witness gruesome events: 'I do not have in mind fraudulent or bogus claims. In general it ought to be possible for the administration of justice to expose such claims. But I do have in mind the *unconscious* effect of the prospect of compensation' (emphasis in original).[111] The corollary of this is that, if rescuers are aware of the possibility of compensation then they should also be aware that they have to put themselves at risk in order to get it. Might this make them more effective rescuers? It is no use countering this

---

[107] *Financial Times*, 19 December 1990 (news item).
[108] The Times, 5 November 1992.   [109] See The Times, 4 February 1995.
[110] R Mullender and A Speirs, 'Negligence, Psychiatric Injury, and the Altruism Principle' (2000) 20(4) OJLS 645.
[111] [1999] 2 AC 455, at 494.

with the assertion that in the exigency of the moment, the rescuer is not, for one moment, cynically going to contemplate this, because to take such a stance is to support the view that rescuers, at least, should be compensated. Admittedly, Lord Steyn is concerned, not about malingering, but about the effect on recovery from psychiatric illness,[112] but nevertheless this can be said about all cases of psychiatric injury, and to bar rescuers who have, it has generally been thought, been eligible to claim since the 1967 case of *Chadwick*, smacks of unjustified parsimony.

However, although, arguably, cases like that of Mr Chadwick should be compensated, the essence behind the decision in *White* might be based on two other grounds. First, Mr Chadwick was a volunteer, and professional rescuers are different in two important respects, as stated by Lord Griffiths: 'The police are trained to deal with catastrophic incidents and reasonably well compensated under the terms of their service if they do suffer injury in the course of their duties.'[113] However, the House of Lords could not distinguish between professional and civilian rescuers without overruling its own decision in *Ogwo v Taylor*, which they would either have had to do on the basis that psychiatric injury is different to physical injury by adding further distinctions to the already tortuous boundaries of psychiatric injury claims in negligence, or by introducing the American 'fireman's rule' (ie no compensation for any form of injury) into English law which would have gone down particularly badly with the emergency services. The other ground which, it can be argued, is behind the *White* decision, is that by requiring a claimant to be within the range of foreseeable physical injury in order to qualify as a rescuer, the problem of deciding who, and who is not, a rescuer is circumvented. For example, the answer to the question 'can you rescue a dead body?' is 'yes, as long as you are at physical risk when you do it'. So far, so good, but the question then to be answered is whether someone was actually at physical risk, and, furthermore, the category will also include those who reasonably believe they are at physical risk. Is there a likelihood that courts will decide these points in favour of the claimant if they decide his is a deserving case?

Lord Goff's wider approach to those who are primary victims which is based on that of Lord Oliver in *Alcock* is arguably the better one. In particular, in relation to rescuers, Lord Goff said that Mr Chadwick was not attempting to rescue anyone, but was providing comfort to those trapped in the wreckage; his actions were laudable and his psychiatric injury was clearly foreseeable.[114] Consider for example the Canadian case of *Bechard v Haliburton Estate*.[115] There had been an accident involving a motorcyclist

---

[112] '[P]sychiatric harm . . . often endures until the process of claiming compensation comes to an end'; ibid.

[113] ibid, per Lord Griffiths at 464.   [114] [1999] 2 AC 455, at 484.

[115] (1992) 84 DLR (4th) 668.

who was lying in the middle of the road. The plaintiff, who was in a vehicle involved in the accident got out of the car. Another vehicle, driven by the defendant approached. The plaintiff was screaming and waving to him to stop, but he collided with the motor cyclist and killed him. The plaintiff recovered compensation for psychiatric injury because it was held that the defendant should have realized that an accident had occurred and foreseen that he might collide with victims of the accident. It was held that the plaintiff was performing a role similar to that of a rescuer. Now, an English court would have to find in such circumstances that there was a risk of physical injury or a perceived risk.

THE 'MERE BYSTANDER'

By the 'mere bystander' is meant someone who can establish 'event proximity' but has no special relationship with the primary victim.

Normally such a person has little hope of establishing a claim. In *Owens v Liverpool Corporation*,[116] damages were recovered by mourners at a funeral, who were relatives of the deceased, for shock caused by the negligence of a tram driver in damaging the hearse and upsetting the coffin. However, this is a curious case and very much at odds with the current legal framework. Indeed, referring to the case in *Alcock v Chief Constable of the South Yorkshire Police*, Lord Oliver said that 'it is doubtful how far the case, which was disapproved by three members of this House in *Bourhill v Young* [1942] 2 All ER 396 ... can be relied upon'.[117]

However, it is not entirely out of the question that a mere bystander should recover. As Lord Ackner also stated in *Alcock*:

why does it [the duty] not eventually extend to bystanders? As regards the latter category, while it may be very difficult to envisage a case of a stranger, who is not actively and foreseeably involved in a disaster or its aftermath, other than in the role of rescuer, suffering shock-induced psychiatric injury by the mere observation of apprehended or actual injury of a third person in circumstances that could be considered reasonably foreseeable, I see no reason in principle why he should not, if in the circumstances, a reasonably strong-nerved person would have been so shocked. In the course of argument your lordships were given, by way of an example, that of a petrol tanker careering out of control into a school in session and bursting into flames. I would not be prepared to rule out a potential claim by a passer-by so shocked by the scene as to suffer psychiatric illness.[118]

Lord Atkin, in *Hambrook v Stokes*, stated that he saw no reason why a bystander should not recover.[119] However, *McFarlane v E E Caledonia*

---

[116] [1939] 1 KB 394.   [117] [1992] 1 AC 310, at 412.   [118] ibid, at 403.
[119] [1925] 1 KB 141, at 157, CA.

Ltd[120] is not encouraging in this respect as the Court of Appeal held that witnessing the Piper Alpha oil rig explosions did not entitle the plaintiff to recover damages.

THE TORTFEASOR WHO CAUSES OR THREATENS SELF-INJURY

Assuming that the appropriate event proximity and relationship proximity are established, can a claimant recover damages for psychiatric injury caused by the negligence of the tortfeasor injuring himself or threatening his *own* safety? The *dictum* of Deane J in *Jaensch v Coffey*[121] that in order to succeed the injury must have been sustained 'as a result of the death, injury or peril of *someone other than the person whose carelessness* is alleged to have caused the injury'[122] (emphasis added) specifically precludes such a claim, but in *Alcock v Chief Constable of South Yorkshire Police* this wholly anomalous position was considered by Lord Oliver as being 'curious and wholly unfair'.[123] Until recently the question has not been in issue in the English courts (not being dealt with in *Bourhill v Young*[124] where there was insufficient proximity to the incident in which the defendant had injured himself negligently) but in Australia, on the authority of *Jaensch* it was said in *Harrison v State Government Insurance Office*[125] that damages could not be recovered. In that case a wife suffered minor physical injuries in a road accident in which her husband was killed and which was due to his negligence. Her claim for psychiatric injury was eventually allowed simply because it was impossible to separate the psychiatric injury caused by the accident itself and that caused by the shock of her husband's death.

The position has been clarified, albeit only to confirm the anomaly, by the case of *Greatorex v Greatorex*[126] where the claimant brought an action against his son who had negligently inflicted head injuries upon himself by driving carelessly and under the influence of alcohol. The claimant was a fire fighter who attended the scene of the accident and subsequently developed PTSD. Cazalet J had to determine the preliminary issue as to whether a duty of care was owed by someone whose self-inflicted injuries caused psychiatric injury to a witness. He found that no duty of care was owed because, for policy reasons, such cases would arise mainly when there was a close tie of love and affection and, therefore, there was potential for creating family strife by allowing such claims. Obviously claims arise for physical injuries between family members, for example where a car passenger is physically injured by the negligent driving of his spouse, and it has never been thought necessary

---

[120] [1994] 2 All ER 1.   [121] (1984) 155 CLR 549.   [122] (1984) 155 CLR 549, at 604.
[123] [1992] 1 AC 310, at 418.   [124] [1943] AC 92.
[125] [1985] Aust Torts Rep 80-723.   [126] [2000] 1 WLR 1970, QBD.

to restrict this in the interests of family harmony. Arguably, there is a difference inasmuch as here there would be a claim for an injury affecting the emotions rather than the body. It has not, however, been clearly articulated as to why that should be ruled out on grounds of policy. The other reason sometimes cited for disallowing such claims is that it interferes with the right of self-determination, which only makes sense where self harm is deliberate and not negligent.[127]

PSYCHIATRIC INJURY CAUSED BY DAMAGE TO PROPERTY

Whilst the majority of cases of traumatically induced psychiatric injury are caused by bodily injury to the claimant or someone sufficiently proximate to the plaintiff, or by fear of such injury, it is possible to recover damages in cases of property damage. In *Attia v British Gas plc*,[128] the defendants set fire to the plaintiff's house whilst installing central heating. There was no dispute that a duty of care was owed, the question was whether this type of damage, ie, psychiatric injury, was foreseeable, and it was held that it was. However, *Attia* is an odd case because the Court of Appeal held that, since the defendant owed a duty of care not to damage her house, the question as to whether psychiatric illness was foreseeable was a remoteness of damage question, ie duty did not arise. This goes against the general principle at the heart of 'nervous shock' claims, which is that *psychiatric* injury has to be foreseeable rather than just physical damage to self or physical damage to property. In the Australian case of *Campbelltown City Council v Mackay*,[129] the plaintiffs' house had collapsed over a period of time due to the negligence of the local council and the building contractors. In the New South Wales Court of Appeal, Kirby P said: 'The causes of action at common law should, in my opinion, be released from subservience to nineteenth-century science.[130] This is a piece of good advice from which the law would have benefited had the House of Lords taken it in *Alcock* and *White*. However, it was felt inappropriate for the New South Wales Court of Appeal to review the boundaries of nervous shock claims, and therefore, it was held that, in negligent property damage, damages could be awarded for vexation, worry and distress in the same sum as might have been awarded for psychiatric illness. In *Perry v Sidney Phillips & Son*,[131] the Court of Appeal awarded damages for vexation, distress and worry after a surveyor induced the plaintiffs to purchase a property with serious defects. In this approach would lie an answer to the *Attia* problem: damages could be awarded for this sort

---

[127] See the Law Commission recommendations discussed in Chapter 9.
[128] [1988] QB 304, CA.   [129] (1989) 15 NSWLR 501.   [130] ibid, at 503.
[131] [1982] 1 WLR 1297.

of distress in contract, rather than making an even bigger mess of negligence claims and psychiatric injury.

The precise nature of the relationship between the plaintiff and the property (for example, does the plaintiff have to have a proprietary interest?) has yet to be fully explored, but it may be that the courts would use some variant on the 'proximity theme' in order to decide whether to admit any claim. An interesting question is whether property can include animals. In *Davies v Bennison*[132] damages were awarded for the shock of seeing a pet killed, but the action was in trespass. However, in *Campbell v Animal Quarantine Station*[133] the Supreme Court of Hawaii awarded damages for 'mental distress to the owners of a boxer dog which died in the back of an overheated van on its way to a veterinary hospital'. There was no psychiatric injury.

---

[132] (1927) 22 Tas LR 52.   [133] 632 P 2d 1066 (Hawaii, 1981).

5

The Non-shock Cases

INTRODUCTION

Although in *Alcock v Chief Constable of the South Yorkshire Police*[1] the House of Lords stressed the necessity of the event-proximity requirement, it was recognized by Lord Oliver that 'It would be inaccurate and hurtful to suggest that grief is made any the less real or deprivation more tolerable by a gradual realisation'.[2] This chapter deals with those instances of psychiatric injury

---

[1] [1992] 1 AC 310.   [2] ibid, at 416.

which arise over a period of time so that there is no single 'shock'. This categorization is, like the 'shock' category, crude and there may be situations which are not easy to place into either pigeonhole. The distinction between 'shock' and 'non-shock' cases depends upon the historical development of nervous shock cases, rather than clear and principled differences in the way in which they should be approached in law, or indeed in any commonly understood approach to language. For example, someone who receives a telephone call giving bad news about the death or injury of a loved one, will receive a shock. They might remain in a 'state of shock' for some time afterwards, but this will be a non-shock case because there is no sensory perception of a situation which impacts upon the mind. Of course, the bad news is acquired through the sense of hearing, but, for the purposes of the law, it is a cognitive process, just as the reading of bad news in a newspaper or whatever, is cognitive and not sensory. Some instances of non-shock are genuinely so, ie there is no event either sensory or cognitive, which impacts upon the claimant, but rather a state of affairs which might persist for some time. Cases of occupational stress fall into this category, and are dealt with separately in Chapter 6. There are similar examples outside the employment situation. Psychiatric injury caused by the ongoing failure of an education authority to diagnose a learning disability, where the result is a deterioration in the claimant's condition and, perhaps associated depression, is such an example, as are the 'fear for the future' cases, where claimants, although currently well, have been exposed to some danger whereby there is a possibility that, in future, they will develop a serious medical condition.

The important feature of all these cases is that the distinction between 'primary' and 'secondary' victims is either not clear, or is unnecessary, but nevertheless courts continue to employ the terminology. As has been seen, the distinction is not clear either in a factual sense, nor in the sense that there is a consensus of legal opinion as to what constitutes 'primary' and 'secondary'. Further, the position of the law as so far established, is that foreseeability of psychiatric injury *per se* is not enough to ground a claim. However, that applies only in the case of shock claims. It will be noted, that this has not been applied rigorously outside that context.

STATUTORY BODIES IN RELATION TO THE PERFORMANCE OF THEIR DUTIES

X (Minors) v Bedfordshire County Council

Generally, those who provide services pursuant to duties imposed upon them by the state are not automatically found to be liable in a private law action if they fail to provide them, or provide them inadequately. The whole area is a difficult one and does not easily survive an analysis based upon principle.[3] The issue has arisen in the field of personal injury in the context of, for example, employers' liability (see Chapter 6) and in the provision of services, such as child protection, by local authorities. The major case in the context of local authority services is *X (Minors) v Bedfordshire County Council*.[4] This House of Lords case concerned a number of local authorities who, it was alleged, had failed in the provision of child protection and educational services. In the first category, was the case of X itself, where there had been a failure on the part of social services to take the necessary steps to obtain care orders in respect of abused children who subsequently claimed that they had suffered psychiatric illness as a result of that abuse. *M v Newham London Borough Council* was a case of misdiagnosis by a social worker and a psychiatrist of sexual abuse, where the child suffered psychiatric injury. In the second category were the cases typified by *E v Dorset County Council* where there were allegations that the local education authorities had negligently performed their statutory and common law duties in relation to special educational needs. It was found that there was no breach of statutory duty in any of the cases.

The next question to be considered was whether there was a breach of the common law duty of care. The House of Lords considered the threefold negligence test in *Caparo v Dickman*,[5] whereby the criteria are foreseeability, proximity and the test as to whether it would be just and reasonable to impose a duty of care. It was found that the first two were satisfied. However, on the third element, to impose a duty was said not to be just and reasonable because, first, the statutory system to protect children cut across different disciplines, such as the police, doctors and so on, and the actions of those involved would have to be isolated in order to allocate responsibility. Immense problems in trying to disentangle the involvement of each of the bodies concerned would arise. Secondly, the threat of litigation was held to be inappropriate given the fine line to be drawn between the competing interests in a child protection case (keeping the child with its family and protecting the child). Thirdly, it was held that to impose a duty of care would result in an over-cautious approach which would be detrimental in a general sense to the carrying out of the duties, and that, inevitably, there would be litigation which would be a drain on important resources. This might be regarded as a form of 'immunity' for local authorities, and, as such, would be unlawful following the decision of the European Court of Justice in *Osman v United Kingdom*.[6] However, the court went on to hold that if the workers (doctors, social workers, etc) were found to have personal duties

---

[3] See, eg, Michael A Jones, *Textbook on Torts* (London: Blackstone Press, 2000), ch 9.
[4] [1995] 3 WLR 152.   [5] [1990] 1 All ER 771.
[6] [1999] 1 FLR 93. There was held to be a breach of article 6(1) of the European Convention on Human Rights to give a 'blanket immunity' to the police from certain actions in negligence.

towards the claimants then the authorities who employed them could be vicariously liable. It is important to bear in mind that these cases were 'strike out' applications, and there were no decisions made by the House of Lords on the substantive merits of the respective cases.

Developments since *X (Minors) v Bedfordshire County Council*

There were, however, three significant cases after this that are pertinent to the psychiatric injury claim. The first is *Barrett v Enfield London Borough Council*,[7] which concerned a claim that a child had suffered psychiatric injury as a result of inadequate and inappropriate care in the hands of the local authority. Again, this was a strike out application heard by the House of Lords. The court held that, whilst normally a decision to take a child into care, being an exercise of a discretion pursuant to a statutory power, would not be justiciable, once the child was in care, it was arguable that the treatment of the child might give rise to liability on the part of a local authority. Further, the bar on a child suing his parents for negligent decisions in his upbringing did not apply to a local authority, which had to take decisions which a parent never had to take and which had trained staff to advise on such decisions, and that in all but the clearest cases it was important to see on the facts proved whether what was alleged was justiciable. Moreover, the question whether it was fair, just and reasonable to impose a duty of care was not to be decided in the abstract, on the basis of assumed hypothetical facts, but on the basis of what had been proved; and that, accordingly, the plaintiff was entitled to have his claim heard and the facts investigated.

In *W v Essex County Council*,[8] the authority placed a 15-year-old boy with a foster family. The boy was known to the placing authority as a sexual abuser but this information was not communicated to the family and some of the children were sexually abused by him. The foster parents suffered psychiatric injury. A majority of the Court of Appeal had held[9] that it was arguable that, once the local authority had given assurances that the boy was not a sex abuser, then it assumed a responsibility for the accuracy of such information. It could not be said that it would not be just and reasonable to impose a duty of care towards the children who had been abused. However, it was said that it would not be just and reasonable to impose a duty towards the parents because it would hamper the authority in carrying out its child protection duties. The House of Lords held that it was wrong to strike out the parents' claims, as, first, on the facts alleged, regardless of whether they

---

[7] [2001] 2 AC 550.   [8] [2000] 2 AC 592.
[9] *W v Essex County Council* [1999] Fam 90.

were ultimately found to be right or wrong, it was impossible to say that the claim would so clearly not succeed that it ought not to be pursued to trial. It was not sufficient for striking out purposes that W might struggle to prove their case, but rather to consider whether, if the facts were proved, the claim would nevertheless fail, Secondly, neither the case of *McLoughlin v O'Brian* nor the case of *Alcock* meant that the categorization of those claiming to be included as either primary or secondary victims was conclusive. It depended on the facts of each case and there was insufficient information at this stage to rule that these circumstances were outside the range of psychiatric injury currently recognized by the law.

In the European Court of Human Rights case of *Z v United Kingdom*,[10] where a local authority had failed to take timely steps to protect children when there was evidence of abuse, it was held that there had been a breach of article 3 (prohibition of torture and inhuman and degrading treatment) of the European Convention on Human Rights, and that could apply to treatment by private individuals, and there had also been a breach of article 13 (the right to an effective remedy) because there had been no procedure in force to enable them to obtain an enforceable award of compensation. The European Court had acknowledged that the multidisciplinary aspects of child protection could make the situation complex but that, in itself, was not enough to exclude liability.

In *Phelps v Hillingdon London Borough Council*[11] the House of Lords considered a number of claims all relating to the duties of local education authorities. The case of *Phelps* was the only one where there had been a decision on the substantive merits of the case. The others were all appeals from interlocutory decisions which were either strike out cases (*G (A Minor) v Bromley London Borough Council* and *Jarvis v Hampshire County Council*) or an application for pre-action discovery (*Anderton v Clwyd County Council*). In all four cases it was alleged that, as a result of the failure of the authorities to provide, or adequately provide, educational services for children with special needs, the children had suffered, either from 'psychological' problems, or they had remained without educational provision appropriate to their condition. The issues pertinent to all of them can be examined by a consideration of *Phelps*. The child in that case, who had a history of poor performance at a number of schools, had been referred, in 1985 at the age of twelve, to an educational psychologist employed by Hillingdon Borough Council. The psychologist assessed her reading and verbal skills and concluded that, although they were below average, the cause was emotional in origin, and that she did not require special schooling under the Education Act 1981. For the next three years she received remedial teaching but made no progress. Her parents then paid for private assessments, which found her

---

[10] [2002] 34 EHRR.   [11] [2001] AC 619.

to be severely dyslexic. Her claim was for breach of the common law duty of care, and the damages claimed were for her diminished prospects of congenial and remunerative employment, handicap in the job market and damages in respect of 'Anxious (Avoidant) Personality Disorder'.

Garland J, at first instance, had found that there was such a breach and had awarded her damages.[12] The Court of Appeal reversed this decision.[13] Stuart-Smith LJ stated that *X v Bedfordshire* had led to a proliferation of claims by its suggestion that there might be liability on the part of local authority officers, for which the local authority might be vicariously liable. Further, this would circumvent the 'immunity' justified by policy reasons in *X*. (It was unfortunate that this judgment was given just after the European Court of Human Rights in *Osman v United Kingdom*[14] had criticized such immunity.) Also, as *X* was about interlocutory applications, there was not enough information available to the House of Lords to consider properly the nature of the educational services provided. The Court of Appeal consider-ed them, however, and concluded that, unlike the services provided by health authorities, they were not set up for the use of members of the public, but for the use of the education authority in the discharge of its statutory duties. There had, therefore, been no 'assumption of responsibility' towards the child. It is difficult to see why this should be so, particularly in the light of cases such as *Kirkham v Chief Constable of Greater Manchester Police*,[15] where there was held to be an assumption of responsibility on the part of the police, and therefore an obligation to try to prevent the suicide of a prisoner. It could not be said that the police were providing some sort of service to those in custody, let alone members of the general public.

The House of Lords held that there could be individual liability, as there was no doubt that the psychologist had a duty of care. As far as 'assumption of responsibility' is concerned, Lord Slynn quite rightly pointed out that this 'phrase means simply that the law recognizes that there is a duty of care'.[16] It was clear that both teachers and parents would follow advice given, and the 'result of a failure by an educational psychologist to take care may be that the child suffers emotional or psychological harm, perhaps even physical harm'.[17] If there were to be no vicarious liability then this could only be the case if there were good policy reasons. In appropriate cases, authorities should be vicariously responsible because it is not likely to lead to unreasonably high standards (the *Bolam*[18] test ensures that standards are only of ordinary competence in the field), and it is not likely to hamper the authority in the provision of the services.

The trial judge had found that the appropriate standard of care had not been met because the usual test using the Wechsler Intelligence Scale for

---

[12] [1997] 3 FCR 621.   [13] [1999] 1 WLR 500.   [14] [1999] 1 FLR 193.
[15] [1990] 3 All ER 246.   [16] [2001] AC 619, at 654.   [17] ibid.
[18] *Bolam v Friern Hospital Management Committee* [1957] 1 WLR 582.

Children ('WISC') had revealed discrepancies and, once this had been revealed, the expert evidence indicated that it would then have been usual to seek an explanation, probably with the use of the Bangor Dyslexia Test, which had been in use since 1983. Secondly, the psychologist was negligent in failing to retest when the child failed to make progress. The House of Lords held that the judge had not erred in coming to the conclusion he did on the evidence available, nor in making the assumption that, had she been taught appropriately at school, ie as someone who was dyslexic, she would have been more literate than she was now. The other issue was the nature of the loss sustained. As has already been referred to in Chapter 2, these sorts of cases can give rise to difficulties in terms of what constitutes an 'injury', and the judge had taken the approach that failure to diagnose dyslexia is akin to a failure to diagnose a fracture or a psychiatric injury, and that 'injury' could constitute 'a failure to mitigate the adverse consequences of a congenital defect'. Damages were awarded by the trial judge (and not disturbed by the House of Lords), for the economic consequences of the failure to diagnose, but they were rejected by the trial judge in respect of Anxious (Avoidant) Personality Disorder, for reasons which appear to be largely to do with the evidence available.[19]

Lord Nicholls tackled the point that the decision might lead to 'gold-digging' actions brought on behalf of underachieving children. He was confident that courts could weed out hopeless claims, and warned that this case was not a green light for 'generalised educational malpractice', contrasting this with 'manifest incompetence or negligence comprising specific, identifiable mistakes'.[20] In any event, he noted, there are many things which cause children to underachieve and while the interaction of certain teachers and certain pupils might be poor, this would not in itself give rise to a claim.

Given the nature of the bullying of children, clearly psychiatric injury can be a foreseeable consequence of such behaviour. This was considered at first instance in *B–S v West Sussex County Council*.[21] Damages were claimed against the education authority for psychiatric injury caused by bullying at a maintained school for which the county council was responsible. It was held that, although schools were under a common law duty to safeguard the well being of children on school premises and to prevent bullying, that duty did not extend to bullying that occurred outside school, in this case on a bus whilst travelling to and from school. Using the three-stage test of *Caparo Industries plc v Dickman*,[22] outlined above, it was held that it would not be practical or fair to impose a greater duty on the school than to ensure that a pupil was not bullied at school. The duty was to prevent bullying on school

---

[19] 'In so far as it was an attempt to turn matters which do not sound in damages into psychiatric injury which does, I have no regard for it'; per Garland J at [1997] 3 FCR 621, 645.   [20] ibid, at 667–8.   [21] (2001) 3 LGLR 28.   [22] [1990] 2 AC 605.

premises. If the school chose to take an active stance against bullying outside of school, that was a matter of discretion.

In *Various Claimants v BACHL*,[23] the claimants recovered damages for personal injuries arising from physical and sexual abuse whilst staying in children's homes run by a private company, BAC Ltd. The staff had not been properly selected, trained or supervised; the company was vicariously responsible for these 'negligent' acts[24] and that discretion would be exercised to allow the actions to proceed under section 33 of the Limitation Act 1980. When assessing quantum in respect of psychiatric injury, the court accepted that the claimants had arrived at the homes having gone through a traumatic series of damaging experiences and in no case were the first defendants wholly responsible for the claimants' psychiatric problems suffered to date.

Somewhat different issues were considered in the case of *Leach v Chief Constable of Gloucestershire Constabulary*.[25] It concerned the police interviews of Frederick West, the man accused of a number of particularly gruesome murders. As the police believed him to be mentally disordered they required 'an appropriate adult' to be present at the interviews. They asked Leach, a voluntary worker for a project helping young homeless people, to act in this capacity. The only information she was given was his age. She brought an action against the police alleging that, as a result of her involvement she had suffered post-traumatic stress disorder ('PTSD').

Leach's allegations of negligence were that: (1) she should not have been invited or allowed to accept without being warned as to the nature of the case; (2) she should have been assessed as to her suitability; (3) she should have been offered counselling during, or shortly after her involvement; (4) she had been falsely advised that she would not have to testify at trial; and (5) there had been a general failure to care for her health and safety given the particularly harrowing nature of the offences. The trial judge struck out her claim on the basis that it was not in the public interest to impose a duty of care on the police when they were acting in accordance with the Code of Practice for the Detention, Treatment and Questioning of Persons by Police Officers under section 66 of the Police and Criminal Evidence Act 1984. The Court of Appeal, by a majority (Pill LJ dissenting), held that there was no duty towards an appropriate adult, who was not paid or employed by the police, and who was entirely voluntary and who could stop at any time. If there was a duty, then it would be detrimental to the police in carrying out their job of interviewing effectively. Further, it was said that:

---

[23] 26 June 2001, QBD.
[24] See *Lister v Helsey Hall Ltd* [2001] 2 All ER 769, HL, regarding vicarious liability, and see further Chapter 6.
[25] [1999] 1 WLR 1421.

When considering foreseeability, that person [the appropriate adult], if nothing more was known about him, had to be assumed to be a person of customary phlegm, but if the duty was broken, the victim would be treated as a primary victim, and if the victim in fact had an 'eggshell mind', then the police would be liable for all the harm suffered by a person with a mind in such a state.[26]

This could, however, have been avoided by the court simply stating either that the police should have given adequate warning and therefore would not have failed to meet the standard of care, or that the defence of *volenti non fit injuria* (voluntary assumption of risk) applied. Similarly, the other problem raised by Brooke LJ, that the courts would not be able to decide what should or should not be done to avoid the stressor which might trigger the illness, would also be avoided by warning the person in advance of the general nature of the alleged crimes. The court also said that because the subject matter here was 'harm to the mind' any new policy decisions should be taken by the House of Lords. This might come as news to many lawyers. Breaking new ground does not usually deter the Court of Appeal, as the example of the court's bold decision in the very difficult conjoined twins case.[27] Arguably, this caution reflects a general nervousness in the context of compensation for purely 'harm to the mind'.

Leach's claims were struck out with the exception, however, of the claim that she should have been given counselling, and there was liberty to restore the claim that there had been a general failure to care for her health and safety, if this was deemed appropriate at trial. (Her claim that she should not have been told that she would not have to testify was struck out on the basis that it stood or fell with the general duty of care, which, it was found, she was not owed.) Henry LJ made the rather odd remark (which he raised in support of the finding that there was no duty of care) that no one could predict the form the interviews would take, stating: 'There would not seem to be much risk, even to the most susceptible psyche, in a "No Comment" interview'. The fact that the refusal to comment might come at the end of a question which contained some harrowing material does not seem to have occurred to him.

Was this a policy decision? Clearly, it is undesirable for the police to have imposed upon them restrictions as to the sorts of material which can be included in questioning of suspects, but a decision that she should have been warned in advance would not have resulted in this. Perhaps the unspoken policy element concerned the availability of appropriate adults. If they are to be warned that the questions and answers might contain disturbing material, then perhaps the number of people willing to undertake such a role might dwindle to an unacceptable level.

---

[26]   ibid, per Brooke LJ at 1437.

[27]   *Re A (Children) (Conjoined Twins: Medical Treatment) (No 1)* [2001] Fam 147.

In *McNern v Commissioner of Police for the Metropolis*,[28] the claimant alleged that he had suffered PTSD as a result of police negligence in failing to execute a warrant of arrest until two years after it had been issued. He had been aware that a warrant had been sought but had been led to believe that no further action was to be taken against him. The Court of Appeal held that it was not reasonably foreseeable that an arrest on a warrant, even in the event of delayed execution, could give rise to a psychiatric illness. It was accepted that he had a vulnerable personality which had made matters worse for him, but that was held to be irrelevant to the issue of foreseeability because the police had been unaware of his vulnerability in that regard. It was said that if it was known that someone was vulnerable to psychiatric illness, the police may have to take special care as to how they effect the arrest.

Duties of authorities to warn

In *Palmer v Tees Health Authority*,[29] a claim for damages was brought by a mother, as administratrix of the estate of a 4-year-old victim of sexual abuse and murder, together with her own claim arising from her psychiatric illness. The claims were struck out and subsequent appeals dismissed. The woman had heard a rumour that a convicted child molester had been rehoused in her neighbourhood and she contacted social services to find out if this was true. She was assured that it was not. Shortly afterwards her child went to a local shop for ice cream and never returned. It was subsequently discovered that she had been sexually abused and murdered. The mother's claim was for PTSD and pathological grief reaction.

The Court of Appeal upheld the decision of Gate J to dismiss the claims. The claims failed because of lack of proximity. It was said that there was no relationship between the victim and the health authority who had failed to identify the dangerousness of the murderer. There had been a catalogue of blunders in dealing with him, blunders for which other agencies were also responsible. However, the essential proximity requirement was not satisfied. The claimant had tried to rely on the case of *Holgate v Lancashire Mental Hospital Board*,[30] where the facts were almost on all fours with the present case and where the plaintiff had been successful, but this argument failed because in *Holgate* the duty question had never been challenged, the argument had been about standard of care only. Furthermore, the case had been decided before the three-fold requirement of *Caparo Industries plc v Dickman*[31] had been set out. Stuart-Smith LJ held that there was another reason why the proximity requirement was necessary, and that was that it

---

[28] 18 April 2000, CA.   [29] [2000] PIQR P1.
[30] [1937] 4 All ER 19.   [31] [1990] 2 AC 605.

was only once a potential victim had been identified could they be warned. With respect, that does not justify imposing a proximity requirement because it means that, even though a health or police authority might realize its blunder, they are under no obligation to do anything about it until a potential victim is in sight.

In *Faya and Rossi v Almaraz*,[32] the Maryland Court of Appeals allowed an appeal against a decision of the trial court to dismiss complaints that a hospital should have warned them about the HIV-positive status of a surgeon who had operated on them. The defence had been that the risk of contracting the virus was minimal. The court held that, although it was a remote possibility that they had contracted the virus, the seriousness of the potential harm should also be considered. Here, of course, there were a finite number of identifiable patients, and it is likely that an English court would reach a similar conclusion.

Negligence in the provision of other services

This relates not only to 'professional' negligence, but to any situation when someone is engaged to carry out a particular task either specifically for remuneration for that task or in the context of the provision of some service concurrent or related to a commercial transaction. Actions for professional negligence in all fields can arise in both contract and tort. In most non-medical cases there is a contract between professional and client. There is implied into most contracts the expectation that the professional will carry out professional activities with reasonable skill and care unless there are express terms to the contrary.[33] This implied term is now embodied in section 13 of the Supply of Goods and Services Act 1982. The professional's tortious liablity arises by reason of the 'duty of care' principle, and any breach of a duty of care giving rise to foreseeable injury will impose tortious liability upon the professional who owed the duty. It is generally thought that a doctor treating an NHS patient has no contractual relationship with that patient,[34] and any action brought by the patient will be brought in tort on the basis of breach of duty of care.

The question whether a professional who has a contractual relationship is also concurrently liable in tort has been considered by the courts on many occasions and has given rise to conflicting decisions. On the one hand, it has been argued that, whatever the contractual provisions, it seems inconsistent to deny that there is also a duty of care, and on the other hand, that if the parties have entered into a detailed contract in the full knowledge of its

---

[32] (1993) 620 A 2d 327.

[33] The exception are contracts for finished articles, where it is more appropriate to say the implied term is that the article concerned will be fit for its purpose.

[34] See *Pfizer Corporation v Ministry of Health* [1965] AC 512.

implications, the law should not insist on adding something to this. It is no coincidence, therefore, that the cases which seek to deny concurrent liability are those concerned with purely commercial contracts.[35] In any event, it must be understood that any contractual term which purports to exclude liability for death or personal injury is void.[36]

The question of foreseeability of psychiatric damage is not a difficult one in, for example, the doctor–patient relationship. However, in other cases, if there is a breach of professional duty, whether it is a duty which has arisen through a contractual term or one imposed by the law of tort, then the connection between the breach and any subsequent psychiatric injury has to be established, factually of course, but also in the sense that legal causation must be proved. In other words the damage cannot be too remote. A claim in contract may succeed where one in tort would not, if the injury could be said to be within the contemplation of the parties to the contract, though the connection was too remote for liability in tort. The circumstances of the contract would have to be linked to the anticipated state of mind of the non-breaching party. In most professional contracts, of course, no such factors will be present. However, in the provision of legal services, there are a number of situations when the advice and action sought will be to alleviate or prevent a situation which is or is likely to cause psychiatric injury. It is essential, however, that the legal practitioner knows of the relevant factors or could reasonably be expected to know of them.

In *Heywood v Wellers*,[37] the plaintiff had instructed solicitors to bring proceedings against a man to prevent him from molesting her. As a result of negligence on the part of the solicitors, the proceedings were ineffective. Damages were awarded in respect of anxiety, vexation and distress. Similarly, in *Dickinson v Jones Alexander & Co*,[38] damages of £5,000 were awarded to the plaintiff for mental distress caused by the negligent failure of the defendant solicitors to remove her husband from the former matrimonial home and by negligent financial advice. At the time that the negligence took place, there was clear evidence that the plaintiff was suffering from the effects of the matrimonial situation which the defendants failed to alleviate, as they had a letter from her doctor saying she was 'suffering from an anxiety depression type of illness', and was being treated with tranquillizers, and that the doctor had no doubt that her condition had been brought on by her matrimonial situation. It appears that the £5,000 was awarded for 'non-medical' distress, but, had her condition been worse, then, upon the evidence available, she would probably have recovered for a specific psychiatric condition. The test, of course, is whether such damage would have been within the contemplation of the parties. In other words it will frequently be defeated as being damage which is too remote.

---

[35] See *Hai Hing Cotton Mill Ltd v Liu Chong Hing Bank Ltd* [1986] AC 80, PC.
[36] Unfair Contract Terms Act 1977, s 3.
[37] [1976] QB 446, CA.   [38] (1990) 6 PN 205.

Damages were recovered in *Malyon v Lawrance, Messer & Co.*[39] In that case the plaintiff sued his former lawyers for failing to issue proceedings in a road traffic case within the limitation period. He claimed damages, *inter alia*, for business losses brought about by his inability to cope due to prolongation of an anxiety neurosis. It was held that it must have been obvious to the defendants from the information they held about the plaintiff and his claim, that his condition was worsening due to delay, and damages were recovered.[40] However, generally, it must be said that damages will be recovered only where the specific risk is known or should have been known.

In *McLeish v Amoo-Gottfried & Co,*[41] damages were awarded to a plaintiff for mental distress caused by the negligence of a solicitor in the conduct of a criminal action, whereby he had been wrongly convicted of two charges of common assault on a police officer and a charge of possessing an offensive weapon. It was held that the very essence of the contract had been to ensure the plaintiff's peace of mind, and therefore it was foreseeable that he would suffer mental distress if the conduct of the case was negligent.

In *Martin McLoughlin v Grovers (a firm),*[42] it was held that a claim for damages for psychiatric illness allegedly caused by the negligent preparation of the claimant's criminal defence by his solicitors should not have been struck out as being too remote in contract, and unforeseeable in tort. The Court of Appeal said that, as far as foreseeability is concerned, the claimant should be regarded as a primary victim and the question of foreseeability should be considered in relation to the particular claimant and what the firm knew or should have known about him. The personality of the claimant was important in deciding foreseeability of psychiatric injury as was the potential for loss of the claimant's liberty in the case.

Al-Kandari v J R Brown & Co[43] concerned a firm of solicitors who negligently allowed their client to recover his confiscated passport, thereby enabling him to kidnap his children. When taking the children, he physically restrained his wife who suffered physical and psychiatric injury. The wife recovered damages from her husband's solicitors. French J held that a solicitor who had given an implied undertaking on behalf of a client, one object of which was to protect a third party, would owe a duty of care towards that third party who ought to be within the solicitor's contemplation as someone who was likely to be so closely and directly affected by his acts that it was reasonably foreseeable that the third party was likely to be injured by the solicitor's acts.

In *Gifford v Halifax Building Society,*[44] the Court of Appeal had to consider a claim for damages for psychiatric injury caused by the loss of a home, which, it was alleged, came about through negligent financial advice. The

---

[39] [1968] 2 Lloyd's Rep 539.   [40] See also *Wales v Wales* (1967) 111 SJ 946.
[41] The Times, 13 October 1993.   [42] 22 November 2001, CA.
[43] [1988] QB 665.   [44] 28 April 1995.

plaintiff and her husband had obtained an interest-only mortgage with no life insurance. Following the husband's death the property was repossessed because the plaintiff was unable to keep up the mortgage repayments. It was agreed that, as the plaintiff was a primary victim, subject to proof of causation, the only issue was whether the injury was foreseeable. However, the court found that there was nothing in the circumstances of the case to indicate that psychiatric injury was foreseeable.

Mullany has suggested that there could be liability in a *Spring v Guardian Insurance*[45] scenario for psychiatric illness caused by the negligent provision of a job reference:

if employers owe employees duties of care in relation to the proper preparation of references and are liable for economic loss consequent on the presentation of honest but unreasonably held opinions of employees' abilities, why would they not also be liable for consequential psychiatric injury?[46]

There is some force in this suggestion because economic loss is subject to control mechanisms in the same type of way as psychiatric injury.

In *Gonzalez v Metro Dade City Health Trust*,[47] the Supreme Court of Florida upheld a decision that there was no liability in damages to parents whose child had died and whose body was held in the hospital morgue, when they assumed it had been released to the funeral home for funeral arrangements to be made. There was no psychiatric injury , only 'mental anguish', and as such was uncompensatable in negligence. However, the court did confirm that damages for mental anguish could be recovered if the defendant's conduct was wilful (except for the fact that statute law in Florida provides immunity to its hospitals from an action in respect of a wilful, wanton or malicious conduct claim against one of its employees).

These circumstances are suggestive of the scandal at the Alder Hey Children's Hospital, where large numbers of organs were found to have been removed from the bodies of dead children and retained, often without the consent of their parents. There was no suggestion of negligence, and the law surrounding the use of body parts is murky. In the case of patients who have not expressed a wish that their organs be used after death (and that includes those who lack capacity such as most minor children), relatives must, by section 1(2) of the Human Tissue Act 1961, be consulted as far as it is reasonable to do so and they must agree to the organs being removed and used for transplantation or research. However, there is no penalty

---

[45] [1995] 2 AC 296.
[46] N Mullany, 'Fear for the Future: Liability for Infliction of Psychiatric Disorder' in N Mullany (ed), *Torts in the Nineties* (North Ryde: LBC Information Services, 1997).
[47] (1995) 651 So 2d 673.

prescribed by the Act for failure to comply, and it is hard to fit unauthorized removal or use of body parts into a recognized tort.[48]

There was considerable outrage at the revelation that children's body parts had, in some cases (but not all), been used without parental consent and proceedings have been issued,[49] although it is not clear upon what basis liability could be founded. As there was no negligence, and as there was no intention (presumably) to cause harm in the sense of *Wilkinson v Downton*,[50] the strongest argument will be in respect of breach of statutory duty, on the basis that since there is no criminal penalty contained within the Act it cannot have been the intention of Parliament that a civil action could not be brought. Presumably the parents are suing in respect of psychiatric injury. It has been argued that the secondary victim control mechanisms would apply in such a case, ie a sudden shocking event.[51] As the parents were not present when the organs were removed then such control mechanisms will not be satisfied. Unless the court were to take the same approach as Morland J in the Creutzfeldt-Jakob Disease ('CJD') cases[52] and award damages purely on the basis of foreseeability of injury then it is difficult to see how they could succeed. Furthermore, as will be seen below, the decision in the CJD cases depended very much on the particularly gruesome nature of the illness and there is no parallel in the Alder Hey case. Indeed, the children's organs might have been taken without consent, but the motive was to research on the diseases which killed the children, and the hoped-for outcome was to save lives not destroy them.[53]

In *Howarth v Green*,[54] Leveson J found that a stage hypnotist was liable for psychiatric injuries caused as a result of subjecting the claimant to a form of regression back to childhood, which had caused her to recall memories of child abuse at the age of eight. The injury was held to be foreseeable, not least because the model conditions for the terms of local authority's consent to a stage hypnosis performance under the Hypnotism Act 1952 specifically alluded to this.

BREACH OF CONFIDENCE

Professional advisers and others may receive information which is such that they are obliged to keep such information confidential. What if the adviser

[48] In *Dobson v North Tyneside Health Authority* [1996] 4 All ER 474 the Court of Appeal held that there was no duty of interment or disposal of a body and therefore no right of possession of the body by the deceased's next of kin.
[49] See *The Times*, 15 April 2000.   [50] [1897] 2 QB 57.
[51] A Grubb and I Kennedy, *Medical Law*, 3rd edn (London: Butterworths 2000), p 1849.
[52] *The Creutzfeldt-Jakob Disease Litigation Group B Plaintiffs v The Medical Research Council and the Secretary of State for Health* [2000] Lloyd's Rep Med 161, QBD.
[53] See R Colbey, 'Inappropriate Compensation' (2001) 151 NLJ 230, who argues cogently that compensation should not be paid but that, nevertheless, compensation will probably be paid without too much resistance because of the adverse publicity.
[54] 25 May 2001, QBD.

breaches that confidence, and such a breach causes psychiatric injury? As confirmed by *Attorney-General v Guardian Newspapers Ltd (No 2)*,[55] information is confidential if it is imparted in circumstances where the recipient has notice, or has agreed, that the information is confidential and where it would be just that he should be precluded from disclosure. In *Furniss v Fitchett*,[56] Mr and Mrs Furniss were both patients of Dr Fitchett. In May 1956 when relations between husband and wife were very strained, Fitchett gave the husband, to be passed to his solicitor, a document which summarized his observations about Mrs Furniss. The document concluded that she suffered from paranoia and subsequently, and unbeknown to Dr Fitchett, Mr Furniss used the letter in divorce proceedings. Mrs Furniss brought an action against the doctor, recovering, *inter alia*, damages for psychiatric injury. It was accepted that the letter was true, but it was held by the court that the duty of care owed to the patient was not limited to making sure the information was accurate. It also extended to the exercise of care in deciding whether to disclose the information at all. The duty to preserve confidences is not an absolute duty, and there will always be circumstances in which it will be possible to sustain the public interest defence.

In *Cornelius v de Taranto*,[57] a claim was brought in libel alleging that a psychiatric report prepared by a forensic psychiatrist for the purpose of assessing the viability of a potential personal injury claim and which contained a number of allegedly defamatory statements, had been disclosed to the plaintiff's GP and a consultant psychiatrist without her consent, and had consequently become part of her National Health Service records. The defence was one of justification in respect of all but one of the statements in the report. This was accepted on the basis that the statement which proved to be untrue had not caused significantly greater damage than the statements which were, in any event, true. However, Morland J also held that there was a fundamental obligation of confidentiality which had been breached and which entitled the claimant to damages in excess of a nominal sum for the significant mental distress caused by that breach of confidentiality, notwithstanding that the information had not been used in a manner detrimental to her.

TOXIC TRAUMA AND FEAR FOR THE FUTURE

Toxic trauma

Toxic trauma can be described as trauma which is caused environmentally but which is not perceived by one or more of the five sensory pathways to the

---

[55] [1990] 1 AC 109.   [56] [1958] NZLR 396.   [57] [2001] EMLR 12, QBD.

brain. Such trauma could be exposure to dangerous radiation levels or toxic substances of some kind. For any subsequent psychiatric illness to develop, it is essential for there to be cognitive awareness of the danger involved. Scrignar says:

As in other traumata which are perceived by one or a combination of the five senses, a variety of emotional responses can be expected. Some persons with good coping skills and a solid social support system would adapt quickly and experience no significant stress symptoms after four to six weeks. Others, who are 'worriers' and may have been suffering from a generalised anxiety disorder (GAD) prior to knowledge of exposure to invisible trauma, may have an exacerbation of the GAD or possibly develop a PTSD. Persons who develop a PTSD would have intrusive thoughts centring around exposure to the invisible trauma and its damaging effect upon their bodies, avoidance of all things believed to have been contaminated, and symptoms of increased arousal (anxiety). Encephalic events (cognitions) vivify the trauma, stripping away the cloak of invisibility. Official notification by governmental or medical officials of the hazards to health and the visible efforts and publicity attendant to populations in the danger area (warnings, evacuation, preventive measures, etc.) flesh out cognitions of dangerousness in the 'videotapes of the mind'. Accuracy of information and adequacy of preventive measures play an important role in a person's ultimate response to invisible trauma.[58]

There may be physical damage to the body's physiological structure caused by exposure to toxic substances which can have behavioural effects.

Tortious actions in respect of pollution in various forms are not uncommon. These can be in respect of negligence, nuisance, the rule in *Rylands v Fletcher*[59] or breach of statutory duty. Some of these actions can, of course, include a claim for damages for personal injury, although causation is always a difficult issue.[60] The interesting question is whether the law would allow a claim for psychiatric damage. If there is associated physical injury then there will be no need for the 'sudden impact' rule to be complied with. However, difficulties might arise in cases of those who develop psychiatric injury after exposure to toxic substances in respect of which there have been (as yet) no physical manifestations of poisoning. If there is immediate physical harm, but not to the plaintiff or those sufficiently proximate to him, the question of communication of bad news may be relevant.

Through exposure to the risk, even if there is no organic damage, awareness of the risk, and the possibility of illness developing, can produce psychiatric disorder. In respect of the latter, a number of particular claimants come to mind, such as those living within close proximity to places such as Sellafield, and other nuclear processing plants, and those who have

---

[58] C B Scrignar, *Post-traumatic Stress Disorders*, 2nd edn (New Orleans, LA: Bruno Press, 1988), pp 64–5.

[59] (1868) LR 3 HL 330.

[60] C Pugh and M Day, *Toxic Torts* (London: Cameron May, 1992).

been close to an industrial explosion such as the one which took place at Flixborough, near Scunthorpe, in 1974. At Flixborough twenty-nine people died and over one hundred were injured. Many homes in the vicinity were destroyed. After a fire and an explosion at the Walmsly Chemical Plant in Barking, East London, a major evacuation was organized as it was feared that a toxic cloud from the fire could contain significant levels of cyanates. At Bhopal, India, in 1984, a cloud containing methyl isocyanate escaped rapidly into the atmosphere at a time when the victims were sleeping and resulted in the deaths of around two thousand people, pulmonary oedema being the probable cause of death in most cases. Many physical disorders, such as blindness, occurred in those who survived. Then there was the incident at Three Mile Island, and, of course, Chernobyl. Many physical illnesses from such incidents take years to manifest themselves and it is little wonder that the cloud hanging over those who may eventually succumb to such illnesses can have serious psychological effects.

Is there any liability for psychiatric injury caused by a fear that physical illness will result from exposure to or proximity to such contamination? Mullany and Handford cite a number of cases[61] where psychiatric injury has resulted from situations akin to the *Donoghue v Stevenson*[62] scenario, but where the resulting injury was purely psychiatric. For example, in the Australian case of *Vance v Cripps Bakery Pty Ltd*,[63] the plaintiff recovered damages for a phobia caused by the realization that he had eaten bread containing a dead mouse; and in the Canadian case of *Curll v Robin Hood Multifoods Ltd*,[64] where the plaintiff was shocked by discovering a partly decomposed mouse in a bag of flour. In these cases there was no physical damage yet recovery was made for what, presumably, were justifiable fears.

There does not appear to be any difference between these sorts of cases and the case of a claimant who has suffered exposure to some form of environmental contamination but has not (as yet) been physically injured by it. There may never be any physical damage but if there is a significant risk of injury then why should the plaintiff not recover for suffering the fear of that injury? Claimants in this situation are sometimes described as 'the worried well' (see below, generally, for 'fear for the future' cases). The claimant will recover, of course, if the contamination is part of a traumatic event or its immediate aftermath which the plaintiff has experienced directly, but otherwise, despite the liberal Commonwealth decisions above, English law is unlikely to allow recovery, at least in negligence, unless there are particular limiting factors analogous to the CJD cases discussed below.

If the claimant has an interest in land and his use or enjoyment of that land has been interfered with by the contamination, does this make a claim in

---

[61] N Mullany and P Handford, *Tort Liability for Psychiatric Damage* (London: Sweet & Maxwell, 1993), p 213.
[62] [1932] AC 562.   [63] [1984] Aust Torts Rep 80–668.   [64] (1974) 56 DLR (3d) 129.

nuisance for psychiatric injury easier to sustain? It may do so, as the tort will turn on whether the defendant's use of the land was reasonable. In other words the defence that the defendant took all reasonable care is not available in the same way as it is in negligence. This distinction, however, may be more apparent than real. It was established in *Overseas Tankship (UK) Ltd v Miller Steamship Co Pty Ltd, The Wagon Mound (No 2)*[65] that in nuisance 'although negligence may not be necessary, fault of some kind is almost always necessary and fault generally involves foreseeability'. Furthermore, *Cambridge Water Co v Eastern Counties Leather plc*[66] confirms that only plaintiffs who can show that the damage of that type or kind was foreseeable can succeed in an action for nuisance or, indeed, for damage sustained under the rule in *Rylands v Fletcher*.[67]

In California it is possible to claim damages for fear of illness. In *Potter v Firestone Tyre & Rubber Co*,[68] the plaintiffs lived near the 125-acre Crazy Horse landfill site in Salinas, California. They discovered that toxic chemicals had contaminated their domestic water wells, and that the defendant company had been dumping toxic waste in violation of landfill regulations and the company's own policy. The California Supreme Court held that to recover damages for negligent infliction of emotional distress arising out of exposure to carcinogens in the absence of physical injury, claimants must establish, first, that they have been exposed to a toxic substance which threatens cancer and, secondly, that the fear stems from knowledge, corroborated by reliable medical or scientific opinion, that it is more likely than not that they will develop the cancer. However, the latter requirement was not necessary if the defendant's conduct amounted to oppression, fraud or malice.

Fear for the future

Potential claims for exposure to environmental contamination may well be described as 'fear for the future' cases. However, not all claimants are likely to be successful because of the continuing perceived need to keep control mechanisms in place to avoid a flood of claims. This is well illustrated by *Creutzfeldt-Jakob Disease Litigation Group B v The Medical Research Council and the Secretary of State for Health*.[69] The plaintiffs, handicapped by dwarfism, were, as children, injected in a clinical trial after 1 July 1977 with a human growth hormone ('HGH') that may have been contaminated with the virus which causes CJD. At an earlier hearing Morland J had held[70] that by 1 July 1977 the Department of Health should have suspended the HGH programme because of the risk of contamination. In the event the programme continued to run until 1985. Obviously those who had already developed CJD

---

[65] [1967] 1 AC 617.   [66] [1994] 2 WLR 53.   [67] (1868) LR 3 HL 330.
[68] Lloyd's List, 4 March 1994.   [69] [2000] Lloyd's Rep Med 161, QBD.
[70] *N and Others v UK Medical Research Council and Department of Health* [1996] 7 Med LR 309.

were able to recover damages for this condition, but these plaintiffs had not developed the condition, but feared that they might as the virus was capable of lying dormant for long periods of time. There were two ways of approaching the cases: they were either primary or secondary victims. The preliminary issue to be decided was whether the claims should proceed at all. On the facts it seems clear that the plaintiffs were primary victims. However, Morland J found that they were not primary victims on grounds of policy. To label such people as primary victims he considered would potentially open the floodgates to a large number of claims by very large numbers of people exposed to asbestos or radiation when there might be, say strict liability under statutory provisions, and where the realization of the exposure might come many years afterwards. The plaintiffs here were, therefore, secondary victims but their claims could succeed purely on the basis of foreseeability. The claims could go forward because there was close proximity between the doctors and the patients; there was a small number of victims; CJD was such an awful condition and was incurable, and the media interest in the cases meant that information forthcoming to the plaintiffs was sensational and unhelpful. Perhaps because of the risk of bad publicity, there was no appeal against this decision.[71]

In *Dickson v Bridge Hotel*,[72] a case heard in the Whitehaven county court, damages were awarded to a kitchen porter who suffered a needle-stick injury whilst working as a kitchen porter at a hotel when depositing a bin bag with discarded hypodermic syringes into a large bin. The physical injuries were minimal and comprised only a few needle pin pricks around the fingers of one hand. However, he feared that he might have contracted Hepatitis B or HIV. He underwent a number of tests and a course of immunization against Hepatitis. Four months after the accident, it was felt highly unlikely that he had contracted either disease but he required reassurance until a year after the accident, by which time the results of final tests were known. The case refers to the fact that he suffered 'psychological trauma'. His Honour Judge Philips found that the fear of infection with either disease was a very considerable one and should not be underestimated. In *Greenwood v Newalls Insulation Co Ltd*,[73] the plaintiff had been exposed to asbestos for two years from 1963. He developed asbestos-related pleural plaques which were diagnosed in early 1994. The agreed medical evidence was that the pleural plaques were asymptomatic, but he complained of chest pain and shortness of breath which he attributed to exposure to asbestos. There was a two per cent risk of him developing pleural disease sufficient to cause a disability; a one per cent risk of asbestosis; a three per cent risk of mesothelioma, and a

---

[71] See also the Australian case concerning fear of HGH and CJD, where, on an interlocutory application, the claim was allowed to proceed: *APQ v Commonwealth Serum Laboratories Ltd* (SC Vic No 8546 of 1993, 2 February 1995).

[72] (1999) 99(6) QR.

[73] [1999] CLY 1538, Sunderland county court (His Honour Judge Walton).

one to two per cent risk of lung cancer. He had also developed a psychiatric illness as a result of the diagnosis of pleural plaques and his perception that all his physical problems were due to asbestos. He recovered damages for the psychiatric illness. Without the development of the pleural plaques the plaintiff in this case would have been in the same position as one of the potential claimants that Morland J referred to, and for which reason did not want to classify such people as primary victims. Although only a county court case, it seems that the development of some physical condition albeit not one of those feared, was enough to distinguish such as case.

In all these cases there has been no suggestion that the fears were irrational. What of a case where it is? English law tends to stress reasonableness in such cases, for example, the requirement in a primary victim case that there is either real risk or physical injury, or that the victim reasonably believes him/herself to be at risk. Furthermore, it is arguable that if it is irrational it is unforeseeable. It should also be noted that in *Faya and Rossi v Almaraz*,[74] where the plaintiffs feared contracting HIV from an HIV-positive surgeon who operated on them, it was held that they could recover for their fear for their 'reasonable window of anxiety', ie the time between acquiring the information about the surgeon's HIV status and the negative results of the HIV tests. Presumably, therefore, any continuing fear that, for example, the test result was wrong, would have been considered unreasonable.

ACQUIRING INFORMATION OTHER THAN THROUGH THE UNAIDED SENSES OF THE CLAIMANT

Being told bad news

Generally there is no prospect of recovering damages if psychiatric injury results from being told bad news. This was established in *Hambrook v Stokes*.[75] However, there are a number of Commonwealth cases where damages have been recovered when the claimant has been involved in the same accident in which a loved one died and was informed of the death some time after the accident.[76] It may be that the difficulty in separating the shock of the accident from the shock produced by hearing of the death was at least partly responsible for these favourable decisions and partly the fact that the injury, or the immediate prospect of the injury, to the loved one, would have been witnessed by the claimant. However, there have been some later, very liberal decisions in other jurisdictions which have resulted in damages being

---

[74] (1993) 620 A 2d 327.   [75] [1925] 1 KB 141.
[76] See also the cases of *Andrew v Williams* [1967] VR 831 and *Kohn v State Government Insurance Commission* (1976) 15 SASR 255. See also the English case of *Schneider v Eisovitch* [1960] 2 QB 430.

awarded purely because the illness has resulted from being told the bad news. In *Coates and another v Government Insurance Office of New South Wales*,[77] damages were awarded by the New South Wales Court of Appeal to the children of a man killed by negligent driving. They had not been anywhere near the accident, but had suffered psychiatric illness after being informed of their father's death. The court simply rejected the view that it was essential to satisfy the 'event proximity' requirement. In *Reeve v Brisbane City Council*,[78] a similar decision was made by the Queensland Supreme Court, in respect of awarding damages to a widow, who was merely informed of the fatal accident. The South African Supreme Court of Appeal in *Barnard v Santam Bpk*,[79] upheld the claim for damages for psychiatric illness by a mother caused by being informed that her child had been killed in a bus accident. However, in English law there must be *some* perception with the unaided senses, in which case there is no bar to recovery just because the psychiatric injury may have been caused *partly* by hearing the news.

Television and radio broadcasts

The clear judicial disapproval in *Alcock v Chief Constable of the South Yorkshire Police*[80] of allowing recovery when a plaintiff suffered injury after a simultaneous television broadcast (far less for a recorded transmission) means that it would be an exceptional case which succeeded in this respect. The example given of such an exceptional case by Nolan LJ in the Court of Appeal in *Alcock* was that of children travelling in a balloon which suddenly burst into flames, the impact of which on live television would be as great or greater than the actual sight of the accident. Lord Ackner in the House of Lords in *Alcock* suggested that there could be 'many other such situations', so recovery has not been ruled out completely in the case of live broadcasts. However, it is clear that the wholly subjective speculations by judges as to what may be more or less shocking than real life, points up the inadequacies of the present state of the law. Furthermore, it is inexplicable why a live broadcast of, say, the balloon, is likely to be more shocking than a recorded broadcast which is seen by a plaintiff with no previous knowledge of the incident.

The insensitive communication of bad news

Presumably, a distinction can be drawn between false information and information which is true but which is communicated in a insensitive and thereby shocking manner?

---

[77] (1995) 36 NSWLR 1.   [78] [1995] 2 Qd R 661.
[79] (1999) (1) SA 202.   [80] [1992] 1 AC 310.

In *Alcock v Chief Constable of South Yorkshire Police*,[81] their Lordships referred to the broadcasting code of ethics, which the authorities could be expected to follow, and which code precluded them from showing the suffering of recognizable individuals. It was suggested that if this code was breached, this would be a *novus actus* breaking the chain of causation. Leaving aside the question of whether it would make any difference whether the breach of the code was *intentional* or not (it probably would under the tort in *Wilkinson v Downton*[82]), is there likely to be any obligation to communicate bad news in a particularly sensitive fashion? It was said in *Mount Isa Mines Ltd v Pusey*[83] that there is no duty to break bad news gently. In *A B v Tameside & Glossop Health Authority*,[84] the Court of Appeal held that there had been no negligence by the health authority when they had written to over 900 patients who had received obstetric treatment from a doctor who was later found to have been HIV positive. The allegation of negligence had been made by 114 patients who alleged that the news had been communicated in an insensitive manner, as a result of which they had suffered psychiatric illness. The letter had simply informed the patients of the HIV status of the doctor and advised them to undergo tests. A telephone counselling service was subsequently established, but not at the time the letters were sent out, and it was alleged that the news would have been better broken in person or that the telephone counselling service should have been available at the time the letters were received. The court held that there was no negligence simply because the health authority did not, with hindsight, select what might have been the better method of communicating the news. It has been argued that it was wrong for counsel for the defendant to concede that a duty might be owed in such a case, and, further, that it would be wrong to impose a duty in such a case, because, *inter alia*, it would be wrong to impose such constraints on people such as the police or social workers who have the difficult job of breaking bad news.[85]

However, in the Australian case of *Petrie v Dowling*,[86] damages were recovered by a mother who was told in a blunt manner by a nurse that her daughter was dead. This appears to be another example of a Commonwealth case which is considerably more generous than English case law.

Bad news which turns out to be untrue

Where false information is given due to negligence there is little in the way of English case law to support a claim. In *D v National Society for the*

---

[81] [1992] 1 AC 310.   [82] [1897] 2 QB 57.   [83] (1970) 125 CLR 383.
[84] [1997] 8 Med LR 91.
[85] S Dziobon and A Tettenborn, 'When the Truth Hurts: The Incompetent Transmission of Distressing News' (1997) 13(3) PN 70.
[86] [1992] 1 QdR 284.

Prevention of Cruelty to Children[87] Lord Denning MR distinguished between false information in the *Wilkinson v Downton*[88] sense, ie, when there is a deliberate deceit, and false information due to negligence. In the latter case it was said there would be no liability. The rule in *Hedley Byrne & Co Ltd v Heller & Partners Ltd*[89] has no application here either, as one of the essential elements of the tort of negligent misstatement is that the recipient of the information relied upon it, as opposed to simply received it. Could it be argued (somewhat tortuously perhaps) that the recipient relied upon it being true and therefore suffered loss on this basis? It seems unlikely. Having said that, there is a curious English case, *Allin v City & Hackney Health Authority*[90] (a county court case and thus only of limited authority), in which it appears the point was never specifically argued. The facts were that the plaintiff's baby was eventually born in a very poor condition after a difficult birth and was not expected to live. There was no negligence in the management of the pregnancy, birth or subsequent treatment of the child. The plaintiff alleged that she was told by two doctors that the baby had died, and there was an entry in the medical records which supported her account. About six hours afterwards she discovered that the baby was alive and, indeed, the child survived, albeit it with some disability. The plaintiff suffered psychiatric injury and recovered damages, not least because there was a concession from counsel that there was a duty of care. Clearly it was not a *Wilkinson v Downton*[91] situation as there was no intention to cause harm. It is arguable that damages for psychiatric injury could be awarded on the same principle as damages for economic loss are awarded for negligent misstatement on the basis of 'assumption of responsibility'.[92] However, it has been cogently argued by Jones that the juxtaposition of such a claim with the 'nervous shock' rules produces a 'bizarre consequence' which would be that someone:

who is correctly informed about the death of a loved one killed by the defendant's negligence has no claim against the person who killed that loved one for the psychiatric damage which results, whereas a person who is incorrectly, and negligently, informed that a loved one has died may have a claim for psychiatric harm against the careless informant, even though no one has died and there was no negligence in respect of the loved one.[93]

This is not a palatable result and, it is suggested, *Allin* must be regarded as a mistake.

---

[87] [1978] AC 171.　　[88] [1897] 2 QB 57.　　[89] [1964] AC 465.
[90] [1997] 8 Med LR 91.　　[91] [1897] 2 QB 57.　　[92] See Chapter 1.
[93] M Jones, 'Negligently Inflicted Psychiatric Harm: Is the Word Mightier than the Deed?' (1997) 13(4) PN 111.

6

Psychiatric Injury and Employment

INTRODUCTION

Since *White v Chief Constable of South Yorkshire*[1] it has been clear that in claims for psychiatric injury caused by 'shock' or 'impact' the same

---

[1] [1999] 2 AC 455.

limitations apply to shocking events caused by an employer's negligence as apply to situations where there is no pre-existing relationship between the claimant and the defendant. In other words, if the employee is not a primary victim, the secondary victim restrictions of proximity in time and space and proximity of relationship (in the sense of close ties of love and affection) apply. However, psychiatric injury can occur as a result of non-impact events, or a series of events, or a continuing state of affairs, and within the employment context, where there is a pre-existing relationship, there are obligations between employer and employees which are both tortious and contractual. There can, of course, also be some overlap in the sense that a persistent fear of, say, robberies, might be based upon having been involved in one at some point, but the important issue will be whether the employer is, in some way, in breach of the duty of care to provide a safe working environment, as opposed to being directly responsible for the 'shocking' robbery itself.

It is well established that an employer owes a duty of care towards its employees in respect of their health and safety.[2] This duty is personal and non-delegable.[3] Liability is not strict, as the employer is only required to take steps that are reasonable to protect health and safety. However, the duty does not depend upon personal fault on the part of the employer because vicarious liability may arise for the acts of employees, even where the employer has acted reasonably and could not have reasonably prevented the acts from taking place.

The employer's duty of care relates to the provision of a safe place of work, including safe plant and equipment; the provision of competent fellow-employees, and the provision of a safe system of work. An employer is vicariously liable for the negligent acts of its employees carried out 'in the course of their employment' (although, of course, the employees themselves are also liable, compulsory employer's liability insurance will mean that it usually makes financial sense to proceed against the employer).

Claims for damages for psychiatric injury resulting from an alleged breach of the duty to provide a safe place of work will typically concern accidents which, if causative of psychiatric injury, will either also involve physical injury or will be such that the employee concerned is a primary victim, ie, he is, or reasonably believes himself to be, at foreseeable risk of physical injury. (An example might be inadequately secured bank premises which thereby render the bank's employees more vulnerable to robberies.[4]) The same is

---

[2] Technically the police and members of the armed forces are not employees, but for the purposes of this chapter they are treated as such. See also *White v Chief Constable of South Yorkshire Police* [1999] 2 AC 455.

[3] See *Wilsons & Clyde Coal Co Ltd v English* [1938] AC 57.

[4] Note that there is some employee opposition to the new-style Job Centres because it is thought that the informal approach to jobseekers (open plan offices etc), does not offer sufficient protection to staff (see The Times, T2 supplement, 5 April 2002, p 4).

likely to be true in respect of an alleged breach of the duty to provide safe plant and equipment. Claims arising from an 'ongoing' state of affairs, or a 'one-off' non-shocking event will, however, generally arise in the context of the provision, or otherwise, of competent co-workers and a safe system of work. Such claims include the cases of so-called 'occupational stress' which can be complicated because employees may become distressed or ill simply because of the inherent nature of their job.

Although claims for psychiatric injury can give rise to difficulties it is uncontentious that an employer's obligation includes a duty to take reasonable care of the mental, as well as the physical, health of his employees (*Petch v Customs and Excise Commissioners*[5]). The existence of the duty is not in dispute, but there is only a duty to prevent *foreseeable* psychiatric injury and that can only be decided in relation to the particular circumstances of the employment.

OCCUPATIONAL STRESS AND THE DUTY AND STANDARD OF CARE

Occupational stress

The expression 'occupational stress' is used here largely because it is a concise way of referring to psychiatric conditions which develop as a result of the claimant's responses to working conditions. However, it is not an expression which has any particular meaning in a psychiatric sense[6] and, furthermore, 'stress' can simply mean 'pressure' and many workers respond favourably to it. In *Sutherland v Hatton*,[7] the Court of Appeal reviewed various reports which considered, and attempted to define, the problem.[8] For example, the court cited the report of a working party of the Health Education Authority entitled *Stress in the Public Sector: Nurses, Police, Social Workers and Teachers* (1988) which defined 'harmful' stress as 'an excess of demands upon an individual in excess of their ability to cope'.[9] The court also quoted the report of the Education Service Advisory Committee of the Health and Safety Commission, *Managing Occupational Stress: A Guide for Managers and Teachers in the Schools Sector* (1990) which stated that 'stress is a process that can occur when there is an unresolved mismatch between the perceived pressures of the work situation and an individual's ability to cope'. The booklet of guidance from the Health and Safety Executive, Stress at Work (1995) was described by the Court of Appeal as 'particularly helpful

---

[5] [1993] ICR 789.

[6] The *Concise Oxford Dictionary*, 8th edn (Oxford: Clarendon Press 1990), however, does refer to 'stress disease' which results from continual mental stress.

[7] [2002] 2 All ER 1.   [8] ibid, 7–8.   [9] Appendix 1.

in distinguishing clearly between pressure, stress, and the physical or psychiatric consequences':

There is no such thing as a pressure free job. Every job brings its own set of tasks, responsibilities and day-to-day problems, and the pressures and demands these place on us are an unavoidable part of working life. We are, after all, paid to work and to work hard, and to accept the reasonable pressures which go with that.

Some pressures can, in fact, be a good thing. It is often the tasks and challenges we face at work that provide the structure to our working days, keep us motivated and are the key to a sense of achievement and job satisfaction.

But people's ability to deal with pressure it not limitless. Excessive workplace pressure and the stress to which it can lead can be harmful. They can damage your business's performance and undermine the health of your workforce.[10]

The report defined 'stress' as:

the reaction people have to excessive pressures or other types of demand placed upon them. It arises when they worry that they cannot cope. It can involve both physical and behavioural effects, but these are usually short-lived and cause no lasting harm. When the pressures recede, there is a quick return to normal.

Stress is not therefore the same as ill-health. But in some cases, particularly where pressures are intense and continue for some time, the effect of stress can be more sustained and far more damaging, leading to longer-term psychological problems and physical ill-health.[11]

'Stress', as defined here, and accepted by the Court of Appeal, as being something very different from ill-health. The Court of Appeal went on to observe that stress can be most harmful where the employee feels powerless or trapped.

Post-traumatic stress disorder ('PTSD') was not generally recognized as a psychiatric disorder until 1980 when the American Psychiatric Association added PTSD to the third edition of its *Diagnostic and Statistical Manual of Mental Disorders* ('DSM-III')[12] classification scheme. There have been tentative moves to develop diagnostic criteria for a somewhat different disorder, persistent duress stress disorder ('PDSD'), a variation of PTSD which is caused by persistent or unrelenting stressors rather than a single, traumatic event and recognizes the fact that the cumulative effect of many lesser events can be just as damaging as the effect of one major trauma.[13]

---

[10] p 2.   [11] p 4.

[12] *Diagnostic and Statistical Manual of Mental Disorders*, 3rd edn (Washington, DC, 1980). The fourth edition ('DSM-IV') was published in 1994.

[13] See M de Vries, letter to the editor and comments by M Creamer and A McFarlane (1999) 22 Aust Prescr 1999 32–4 (available at www.australianprescriber.com/magazines/vol22no5/letters.htm).

The Australian case of *Gillespie v Commonwealth of Australia*[14] concerned a claim by a former diplomat in respect of a breakdown he suffered as a result of the living conditions in Caracas, Venezuela, where he had been posted by the Australian Foreign Affairs and Trade Department. His argument was not that he should not have been sent, but that he should have been prepared for the situation there beforehand. The claim failed because although the work involved a reasonably foreseeable risk of psychiatric harm, his particular vulnerability was not foreseeable, and, in any event, he would probably have gone to Venezuela in any event, so there was a failure of causation.

In *Petch v CEC*[15] the plaintiff was a former civil servant who suffered psychiatric illness, in consequence of which he was dismissed. He alleged that his illness had been caused by his employment. Dillon LJ stated:

unless senior management in the defendants' department were aware or ought to have been aware that the plaintiff was showing signs of impending breakdown, or were aware or ought to have been aware that his workload carried a real risk that he would have a breakdown, then the defendants were not negligent in failing to prevent the breakdown.[16]

The plaintiff was not successful, but the case had established the legitimacy of such a claim subject to the foreseeability requirement (*Petch* did not receive the same sort of publicity as *Walker*, discussed below, presumably because the claim ultimately failed).

In *Walker v Northumberland County Council*,[17] Colman J had to consider the circumstances of a social worker whose workload had increased as a result of a rise in the incidence of child abuse cases. He had complained about his workload and had said things such as 'I don't know how much longer I can go on like this', but despite being promised extra help none was forthcoming. He eventually took sick leave with what was described as 'a nervous breakdown'. Some months later he returned to work, again with assurances about a lessening of his workload, but received no additional help, and also had to deal with the paperwork that had built up in his absence. He became psychiatrically ill once more, and took retirement on the grounds of ill health. He sued in respect of both bouts of illness, but recovered compensation only for the second breakdown (albeit the more serious and valuable one in terms of level of damages). The judge held that the first breakdown was unforeseeable for two reasons. First, the employing authority had no previous experience of workers becoming ill through overwork. Secondly, there was nothing in the personality of Mr Walker to alert them to the possibility of this happening to him. Clearly, neither of these reasons applied to the second breakdown.[18]

---

[14] (1991) 104 ACTR 1.   [15] [1993] ICR 789, CA.
[16] ibid, at 796.   [17] [1995] 1 All ER 737, QBD.
[18] See also *Cowley v Mersey Regional Ambulance Service NHS Trust* (16 February 2001, QBD) where damages were recovered in very similar circumstances.

Fraser v State Hospitals Board for Scotland[19] involved a claim for damages for psychiatric harm suffered during the course of the claimant's employment, due to his employer's management style. He had suffered from moderately severe clinical depression which he claimed was a result of a punitive work regime, through being demoted and strictly supervised. The claim was unsuccessful on the basis that although it had been clearly established that an employer's duty did extend to the prevention of psychiatric harm, that duty did not extend to the prevention of commonplace negative emotions or normal human conditions, such as anxiety, stress, resentment or anger, since they were too remote from the concept of injury and were not sufficiently foreseeable. Notwithstanding that he was a primary victim, his claim failed because the employer could not have foreseen that its conduct might produce such a reaction. Opinion was reserved on the wider proposition that an employer owed a duty to take reasonable care not to make disciplinary decisions which might cause harm to an employee.

In *Collins v Woolwich plc*,[20] the plaintiff, who had been employed by Woolwich as a senior financial adviser, claimed damages against the defendant for psychiatric injury following a nervous breakdown. She had visited her GP in the spring of 1995 (visits that her employer was aware of), complaining of headaches and other symptoms. She went again in October 1995 and took a few days off work. When she returned in November, she had a nervous breakdown. Her argument was that her work was stressful in nature and her workload excessive with particular reference to the changes brought about by a reorganization in 1995, resulting in the introduction of a new line manager, mandatory examinations, the imposition of financial targets and monitoring of advisers' interviews. The plaintiff's argument was that her employer should have been aware of the risk of psychiatric harm and taken steps to avert or ameliorate it when she first told them that she was suffering from work-related stress. The defendant contended that there was nothing in the general job of a financial adviser which gave rise to a foreseeable risk of injury, nor anything specific about the job which created such a risk. Garland J rejected the claim, stating that the defendant did not know and could not be expected to know of any impending or actual emotional problems that the plaintiff had had prior to 26 October 1995. Furthermore, there were no steps that the defendant could have taken in October to avoid the resulting breakdown.

In *Levy v Allied Dunbar Assurance plc*,[21] the plaintiff had been employed by the defendant as a senior manager. He argued that an excessive workload and the behaviour of his line manager, which he alleged was intimidating, hostile and aggressive, amounted to a breach of his employer's duty of care

---

[19] 2001 SLT 1051.   [20] [1999] WL 1457312C, QBD.
[21] [2000] WL 33148711, QBD.

as a result of which he suffered stress-related injuries and was forced to give up work. The defendant disputed the factual allegations in relation to excessive workload, denied that the manager had behaved in the manner alleged and argued that it was unaware of his susceptibility to stress. The claim failed because, although the plaintiff had proved that he had suffered from a stress-related injury, he had not established that the line manager had behaved in the manner described. The burden of work placed on the plaintiff was also held not to be excessive because the defendant had been unaware of the plaintiff's susceptibility to stress and worry, and because the plaintiff had deliberately applied for, and was paid to perform, a high-pressure job.

In *Grant v Chief Constable of Grampian Police*,[22] a former policeman was injured after being struck by a baton during a training course. His right arm was only bruised but he developed a serious psychological condition which rendered him unfit for work and his employment was terminated. He argued that the occurrence of an injury indicated a failure on the part of the training course officers properly to look after his welfare and, even if the risk of injury had been inevitable, given the nature of the course, it was the duty of the officers to minimize that injury. The Chief Constable argued that there was no direct connection between the incident and the psychiatric illness, therefore it could not be shown that the illness was reasonably foreseeable. The claim was rejected by the court, on the basis that while there was no doubt that a duty of care was owed to a participant in the training exercise, he had failed to show that there was action that the officers could have undertaken that would have prevented the bruising and not reduced the necessary realism of the training course.

In *Armstrong v The Secretary of State for the Home Office*,[23] the claimant alleged that she had suffered PTSD following her duties as a prison officer in relation to the prisoner, Rosemary West, who was on remand, having been charged with ten counts of murder, along with her husband, Frederick West. He had committed suicide before the trial, and it was feared that she would do the same. Stringent procedures were put into place, therefore, to keep her under observation, and two officers were required to watch Rosemary West for twenty-four hours per day.

Mr Justice Owen posed three questions: did the work which the claimant was required to do create a reasonably foreseeable risk of psychiatric injury? If so, was the system of work in place a reasonable one? If there was a reasonably foreseeable risk of psychiatric injury and the system or work was not reasonable, did the failure to adopt a reasonable system cause the injury of which the claimant claimed? He answered the first question in the negative and therefore did not go on to deal with the second and third. He found that the claimant was treated no differently from the other prison officers (she claimed that she had been specifically encouraged to form a

---

[22] [2001] Rep LR 74, Scottish Outer House.   [23] [2001] WL 1347076, QBD.

friendship with West, and hence her devastation when she was convicted). Her principal officer and others became aware that she had become too closely involved with West, and, with hindsight, said the judge, it was probably not a good idea for her to attend court with West on the day she was sentenced. Nevertheless, he said that it was not foreseeable that her attendance there would give rise to psychiatric injury.

In *Waters v Commissioner of Police of the Metropolis*[24] the plaintiff, a police officer, appealed against the Court of Appeal's decision[25] dismissing her appeal against the Employment Appeal Tribunal's decision upholding the decision to strike out her statement of claim that the Commissioner of Police of the Metropolis had negligently failed to prevent her being victimized by fellow officers. She alleged that she had been sexually assaulted by a fellow officer whilst staying at police residential accommodation. Although the alleged assault took place whilst they were off duty, the plaintiff complained to the reporting sergeant and other officers, but no action was taken. In addition she also claimed that she had been totally ignored and reviled by fellow officers for making a complaint of sexual assault. The House of Lords allowed her appeal, stating that the statement of claim had raised an arguable case that should not have been struck out. The existence of a separate procedure under the Police (Discipline) Regulations 1985 did not rule out the possibility of a negligence claim being made. Where an employer knew that acts being done by some employees might cause physical or mental harm to another employee but did nothing to prevent such occurrences, it was arguable that such an employer was in breach of his personal duty to protect the victimized employee. Furthermore, it was in the public interest that such complaints were effectively dealt with so that women were not discouraged from joining the police force.*

In *Unwin v West Sussex County Council*,[26] a teacher recovered damages for the aggravation of her depression by her employer's failure to monitor her condition after it had been put on notice that she was suffering from stress. She had worked as a part-time teacher from 1986, and in 1996 a new principal was appointed who, she alleged, subjected her to bullying and harassment, in particular by treating her unsympathetically after a series of family bereavements. Eventually disciplinary proceedings were taken against her. Crane J found that the treatment had been unsympathetic but that it did not amount to bullying or harassment, and did not constitute a breach of duty in the sense that it was foreseeable that it would cause her to become ill. However, at the time of her treatment in 1996, the council was effectively on notice that she was suffering from depression, and she should

---

* Note the later case of *Chief Constable of Bedfordshire v Liversidge* [2002] EWCA Civ 894 where the Court of Appeal held that there is no vicarious liability on the part of Chief Constables for sex/race discrimination. The drafting error in the Race Relations Act 1976 has been corrected but, to date, not under the Sex Discrimination Act 1975.
[24] [2000] 1 WLR 1607, HL.   [25] [1997] ICR 1073.   [26] [2001] WL 825227, QBD.

have been monitored, which would have made a difference to the way in which she was approached. At the least, she should have been referred to the occupational health physician before instituting disciplinary proceedings.

A similar decision was made in *Witham v Hastings & Rother NHS Trust*[27] which concerned a senior nurse who had been off sick with post-natal depression. After eight months' sick leave she returned to work on the understanding that she would receive a lot of support. In the event, however, she was left, unaided, to supervise the closure of two hospital wards and the removal of some patients to a new hospital. After about nine months she took further sick leave for two months, but on return to work she felt that senior management thought she was exaggerating her workload, and this, and the pressure of the job itself resulted in a major breakdown in her health in mid-1997 and remained off sick until she was dismissed in May 1998. Tedd J held that the defendant had grossly dishonoured the arrangement for her return to work to be gradual and supported. It was reasonably foreseeable that, because of her previous depression, she would be vulnerable and that a lack of proper care could cause her ill health.

From the foregoing, it is clear that the courts are reluctant to find that there has been a breach of duty without some clear signal to the employer being ignored. The recent Court of Appeal decision in *Sutherland v Hatton*,[28] mentioned above, endorses this approach and, generally, provides some guidance on workplace 'stress' cases. The case concerned a number of conjoined appeals and the court took a pragmatic view of the employer's obligation, stressing that there are important differences between psychiatric and physical harm occasioned in the workplace. First, the employer is expected to know what is going on when this can be externally observed. However, it is less easy to know how individuals approach their work, prioritize and so on, and there is, therefore, far less scope for the employer to control the situation. Similarly, if the employee is vulnerable because of events in his personal life, the employer cannot be expected to be aware of this unless it is brought specifically to its attention. It was also acknowledged that, understandably, employees are not likely to want to present themselves as being vulnerable or unable to cope. If the standard of care is set too high, then this will have unwelcome effects on the employment market. Furthermore, if the employer makes too searching enquiries in an attempt to ascertain how the employee is coping, then more employees are going to be vulnerable to dismissal or demotion.[29] For these reasons, the Court of Appeal decided that, in the absence of plain indications of impending breakdown, the employer would not be liable. Only one of the four cases considered in *Sutherland v Hatton* was successful. Mrs Hatton and Mr Barber were both teachers. Mrs Hatton was under pressure due to her son's

---

[27] [2001] WL 1346938.   [28] [2002] 2 All ER 1.   [29] ibid, at 9.

illness but, said the Court of Appeal, the employer could not have known of this vulnerability, and, in any event, there was nothing that could have been done. Mr Barber was under pressure due to restructuring of work within the school, but he was under no more pressure than other teachers. Mr Bishop was under pressure because he could not adopt to new work methods, and, again, it was said that there was nothing that the employer could be expected to do about this. The only successful claimant was Mrs Jones, an administrative assistant at a local government training centre, who was expected to do the work of two or three people, and who tried to achieve this. She was also finding it difficult to make complaints about her situation due to the obstructive nature of her line manager. Psychiatric illness was held to be foreseeable.

What sorts of signs should an employer recognize? Given the central role of 'reasonableness' in negligence, the signs must surely be those which the average, reasonable employee would exhibit. However, there is also the question of the 'egg-shell' employee. It is implied by *Sutherland v Hatton* that, first, certain degrees of robustness are to be expected of employees in certain types of work, and that without clear warning signs an employer is entitled to expect an appropriate degree of robustness. Secondly, even with clear warning signs an employer will not be expected to keep an employee in employment if they are clearly incapable of doing a job which, inevitably, will subject the employee to certain sorts of stresses and strains, even such things as exposure to serious trauma, as, for example, in the case of those in the emergency services. *Sutherland v Hatton* suggests that the onus is on the employee to decide whether he is up to the job, but if it becomes clear that he is not, then dismissal on the ground of ill health will almost certainly be fair, subject to the employer going through the correct procedure.

This is not a licence for an employer to make unreasonable demands upon employees. If the demands were unreasonable, ie it was foreseeable that such demands would cause the average employee to break down, then the employer would be in breach of the duty of care. The Court of Appeal revisited these issues in *Young v The Post Office*[30] where it upheld the decision of the trial judge to award damages to an employee who had been extremely hard working and co-operative, but who was psychiatrically vulnerable due to an earlier breakdown brought on by stress at work, and where the employer had failed fully to implement a plan of flexible arrangements drawn up to assist him in his return to work. Where the breakdown or other psychiatric condition is due simply to the nature of the job, or the way in which the employee has approached the job, then without those plain indications there would be no liability. Cases in negligence, however, should

---

[30] [2002] EWCA Civ 661.

be contrasted with discrimination cases where the importance of employers taking positive steps to avoid it has been emphasized by the courts.[31]

A question that does arise is that, if an employee is found to be at risk, how does the employer handle such an employee? In *Sutherland v Hatton* the Court of Appeal declined to find that there should be specific systems in place to offer help. Hale LJ said that if 'knowledge advances to such an extent as to justify the imposition of obligations upon some or all employers to take particular steps to protect their employees from stress-related harm, this is better done by way of regulations imposing specific statutory duties.'[32] However, the court did state that, if there were schemes set up by an employer to offer advice and help on a completely confidential basis then it would be unlikely for that employer to be found liable.

Standard of care

Risk assessment is particularly pertinent to the statutory obligations of employers (see below), but essentially, breaching the duty of care in common law negligence is about failing to maintain a reasonable standard of care, and this will be judged by something akin to a risk assessment exercise which an employer should undertake to prevent injury in the workplace. When undertaking risk assessment, there are two principal considerations. First, what is the likelihood of something happening, and, secondly, if it does happen, how serious will it be? The Court of Appeal in *Sutherland v Hatton* specifically referred to the provision of confidential counselling, as being a good thing when employees were known to be suffering from 'stress', although did not go so far as to state that there was an obligation on employers to provide such schemes. That is not to say that, in a specific situation, where there is a plain indication to an employer of a need for some form of intervention, and, crucially, where there is some reasonable form of intervention which can be undertaken, that there might not be an obligation on an employer to provide that intervention.[33]

The Court of Appeal referred to 'confidential counselling'. However, 'counselling' can mean different things and may be carried out by people of varying degrees of competency and these factors in themselves might consist of a good reason for not making such schemes prescriptive.

---

[31] See *Porcelli v Strathclyde Regional Council* [1984] ICR 564, a Scottish Court of Session case where a 'hostile work environment' was recognized as being direct discrimination; and *Burton v De Vere Hotels* [1996] IRLR 596, in which the EAT held that although an employer was not responsible for the acts of third parties, steps should be taken to control them if it is within the power of the employer to do so.

[32] [2002] 2 All ER 1, at 10–11.

[33] In a non-negligence case, such as an assault, there might be an obligation. It was noted with something like disapproval in *Re Dassanayake* (CICA: Quantum: 2001) [2001] 5 QR 10 that a nurse was not offered counselling at the time that she was assaulted by one of the violent patients she was employed to care for.

'Employer intervention' has been examined in the Australian case of *Howell v State Rail Authority of New South Wales*.[34] The plaintiff, an assistant station master, was, as part of his contractual duties, required to supervise the transfer of any injured persons from any incident where an employee or member of the public is injured. A woman threw herself in front of a train and the plaintiff attended the scene. Shortly after he had arrived home he had brief telephone conversations with a psychologist instructed by the State Rail Authority Rehabilitation Service, but there was never any face-to-face contact. The claimant subsequently suffered from PTSD. He brought a claim against his employer, alleging, first, that he should have received pre-trauma counselling; secondly, that he should never have been exposed to the trauma; and, thirdly, that the conduct of the psychologist fell below the necessary standard of care.

The first two claims were dismissed by the judge, but he upheld the latter. However, of significance is the fact that the whole case proceeded upon the basis that debriefing would have been effective. There does not appear to have been any argument on the part of the rail authority that debriefing is controversial and there are those who say it is ineffective. The case went to appeal and was successful on the ground that there had been no evidence given that debriefing would have worked. In consequence, a retrial was ordered. At the retrial, Professor McFarlane, an eminent psychiatrist specializing in trauma, gave evidence that his cognitive behavioural programme should have been offered to the plaintiff and that this had a 70 per cent success rate. The defendant was found not to have met a reasonable standard of care. The waters were now pretty muddy, as, of course, McFarlane's proposed therapy is *not* the same as psychological debriefing. It is almost certain that no English court would decide that employers should provide something akin to McFarlane's therapy immediately after an employee has been exposed to trauma, particularly in the light of the decision in *Sutherland v Hatton*. If we recall the assessment of the standard of care in negligence by looking at the 'magnitude of the risk' and the cost of avoiding it, then therapy of this nature would, it is arguable, be far too expensive in the light of the risk of development of illness without it. Furthermore, the question must be asked as to whether, immediately after the traumatic incident, any form of psychological intervention can properly be described as 'treatment' given the absence of a diagnosis. It is arguable that Professor McFarlane's evidence was given with the benefit of hindsight, ie in the knowledge that this man went on to develop PTSD. The case also illustrates the way in which judges can get into difficulty over controversial non-physical treatments.

If an employer provides counselling, or, in appropriate cases, some more sophisticated form of debriefing, are employees under an obligation to

---

[34] This unreported case was before the Supreme Court of New South Wales on 7 June 1996, the Court of Appeal of NSW on 19 December 1996 and the Supreme Court of NSW on 7 May 1998.

participate in it? A refusal would, of course, be relevant to any later claim made by the employee either that the employer had not cared adequately for his or her health and safety and, of course, the employee would need to show that the debriefing that had been on offer was in some way defective and that some other form of intervention or therapy should have been on offer instead. It is likely, therefore, to be difficult for the employee to succeed on this basis. On the other hand, it is unlikely that there could be any obligation to participate. It was held in the *Herald of Free Enterprise* arbitrations that it was legitimate for those people traumatized by their experiences to refuse treatment for their PTSD on the basis that the treatment itself would be painful.[35] This is not to say, of course, that an employee who develops a condition that makes him incapable of doing his job, might not have to be suspended if he refuses to take sick leave, or is dismissed if the prognosis of his condition is poor.

In *Mulcahy v Ministry of Defence*[36] it was held that there was no liability on the part of the Ministry of Defence for injuries incurred by members of the armed forces in the course of actual military activities as opposed to training and day-to-day activities. The Court of Appeal ordered such a claim to be struck out as disclosing no reasonable cause of action. However, there might be a claim against the Ministry for failing to diagnose or treat a psychiatric illness suffered by war veterans.[37] Furthermore, it was held in *Matthews v Ministry of Defence*,[38] that section 10 of the Crown Proceedings Act 1947, which provides an immunity from an action in tort being brought by members of the armed forces following death or personal injury during the course of duty, as long as such a death or injury would attract a war pension, is incompatible with Article 6 of the European Convention on Human Rights which protects the right to a fair trial. Keith J held that such an immunity was a disproportionate way of dealing with the need to maintain efficacy and discipline within the forces.

LIABILITY OF THE EMPLOYER FOR DAMAGING INTERVENTIONS

Research on the efficacy of various forms of counselling and psychological debriefing has been patchy, and there is no consensus of opinion on its

---

[35] The *Herald of Free Enterprise* arbitrations first appeared in the *Personal and Medical Injuries Law Letter*, published by Legal Studies & Services, June 1989.

[36] [1996] 2 All ER 758.

[37] See J Beggs, 'Successfully Suing the MoD' (1994) 144 NLJ 369, and the actions being brought against the MoD by veterans of various war zones (eg Northern Ireland, Bosnia, the Falklands War) for failure adequately to prepare them for the experiences they suffered and failure to deal with the psychiatric consequences; see *The Times*, 5 March 2002, p 8.

[38] [2002] EWHC 13, QBD.

effectiveness, or even precisely what it should consist of.[39] In relation to pre-emptive interventions, it had been stated that: 'it must be concluded that the jury is still out on stress management training . . . Stressor reduction/ hazard control is, for several reasons the most promising area for intervention, although again there is not yet sufficient information to be confident about the nature and extent of their effectiveness.'[40] There has even been some research which has indicated that psychological debriefing can be harmful, although many would argue that such research is flawed.[41] A cautious employer might wonder whether there might be any liability for providing a 'negligent intervention'.

If counselling or debriefing is considered to be treatment then the standard will be governed by the *Bolam* test, that is, the standard will be that of the ordinarily competent counsellor or debriefer.[42] However, it is arguable that debriefing is not treatment, but rather some form of crisis intervention. Indeed, a strict interpretation of 'treatment' would not include debriefing because there is no diagnosed condition to treat.

Assuming, however, that debriefing is 'treatment', then it might be thought that the 'responsible body' referred to in *Bolam* will relate to the debriefer's own background. For example, if the debriefer is a counsellor who has undertaken a counselling course then it might be thought that the appropriate standard of care should be that of the ordinarily skilled counsellor. However, it is arguable that the debriefee should be aware of the counsellor's background and, perhaps relatively limited expertise, and, secondly, that the counsellor should be aware of his own limitations. As far as the second point is concerned, a fairly crude analogy can be drawn with, say, a physiotherapist who should be aware that the patient might have fractured bones and will need the appropriate attention beyond his expertise. Similarly, a counsellor should be aware that treatment might be required which he is incapable of providing. The importance of the debriefee knowing the exact nature and purpose of the debrief cannot be overestimated. A major problem is that different practitioners may mean different things by 'counselling' and 'debriefing'. The provision of such services therefore can reflect widely differing procedures, and an employer would be wise to choose assistance from a well-regarded source (for example, endorsed by the British Psychological Society), or, if in-house facilities are

---

[39] See, eg, R Canterbury and W Yule, 'Debriefing and Crisis Intervention', in W Yule (ed), *Post-Traumatic Stress Disorders, Concepts and Therapy* (Chichester: Wiley, 1998).

[40] Tom Cox, 'Stress Research and Stress Management: Putting Theory to Work' (HES Contract Research Report No 61/1993), p 73, para 5.4.

[41] S Wessely *et al*, 'A Systematic Review of Brief Psychological Interventions ("Debriefing") for the Treatment of Immediate Trauma Related Symptoms and the Prevention of Post Traumatic Stress Disorder' (1998) *The Cochrane Library*, issue 4, and J Kenardy, 'The Current State of Psychological Debriefing' (2000) 321 *British Medical Journal* 1032–3.

[42] *Bolam v Friern Hospital Management Committee* [1957] 1 WLR 582.

provided, then by someone suitably trained.[43] Nevertheless, an employee claiming that he has been exposed to negligent intervention will have to get over the hurdle of causation. To succeed a claimant would have to show that he is actually worse than if no intervention had been provided, which is a difficult requirement. He cannot argue that he has lost the chance of an opportunity to receive treatment without favourable statistics that he would have benefited from it.[44]

THE COURSE OF EMPLOYMENT

If damage is caused by a fellow employee in the ordinary course of carrying out his job, such as by doing his job incompetently, albeit without malice or any intention to cause harm, then establishing that the act or acts were carried out in the course of employment will often be problematic. The traditional test for deciding whether something is carried out in the course of an employee's employment is to ask whether the act was authorized, albeit that it was carried out in an unauthorized fashion. The classic example is the driver who drives negligently while making his authorized deliveries. This is simply an unauthorized way of carrying out authorized acts. It can be contrasted with a driver who makes an unauthorized detour, who is said to be on a 'frolic of his own'. However, when an employee is bullying or harassing a colleague, it might be thought that this is, for the most part, unauthorized. Of course, the implication of this analysis is that the grosser the behaviour, the less likely it is to be characterized as an act or acts done in the course of employment. While a bullying manager might just be found to be intimidating his subordinates in the course of his employment, could the same be said of a colleague who, in no position of authority, assaults a co-worker? This dilemma was addressed in *Jones v Tower Boot Co Ltd*.[45] The applicant had been subjected to racial taunts and acts of violence and brought an action against his employer.[46] The Employment Appeal Tribunal had held that there could be no vicarious liability for these acts because it could not possibly be in the course of someone's employment to carry out these sorts of acts. In what must be the right decision, the Court of Appeal held that the strict 'common law' interpretation of vicarious liability should not apply in this context, as the very purpose of the legislation was to prevent

---

[43] See, eg, N Tehrani, 'Introducing Trauma Care into an Organisation: From Theory into Practice', in Leather *et al* (eds), *Work-related Violence* (London: Routledge, 1999).
[44] *Hotson v East Berkshire Health Authority* [1987] 1 All ER 210.
[45] [1997] IRLR 168.
[46] There is statutory vicarious liability (subject to the proviso that the employer will not be liable if it did all that was reasonably practicable to prevent discrimination) under the Race Relations Act 1976, s 32, the Sex Discrimination Act 1975, s 41, and the Disability Discrimination Act 1995, s 58.

these sorts of things happening. There is a duty, therefore, on an employer to take positive steps to prevent harassment and other forms of discrimination.

As far as the common law is concerned, the House of Lords has now reviewed the concept of 'course of employment' in *Lister v Helsey Hall*[47] and reached a similarly liberal conclusion A number of schoolboys had been sexually abused by the school's warden, for which he received a seven-year prison sentence. An action was brought against the school alleging that it was vicariously liable for the acts of abuse. The facts were almost identical to an earlier Court of Appeal case, where it was held that a schoolteacher who abused a child on a school holiday, could not be said to be carrying out an authorized act in an unauthorized fashion.[48] However, in *Lister* the court re-examined this test (know as the *Salmond* test[49]), and concluded that it does not bar vicarious liability in such a case if there is a close connection between the acts which have been authorized and those which have not. In other words, the move is now towards the test for vicarious liability in discrimination cases, where essentially the test is whether the employee was at work at the time the acts took place. In the later case of *Balfron Trustees v Peterson and others*[50] (not a psychiatric injury case) Laddie J emphasized the argument in *Lister* that it was not so much the relationship between the employer and the negligent tortfeasor which had to be considered, but the relationship between the employer and the victim.

DEFENCES

Volenti non fit injuria

The defence of *volenti non fit injuria* is relevant here insofar as it relates to the extent to which an employee can consent to pressure at work. In *Smith v Baker*,[51] the House of Lords rejected the argument that an employee could assume the risk of the employer's negligence. It was acknowledged that employees do not often have a choice in the matter. In other words, it is no defence if the risk should be reasonably guarded against, so that if it cannot, the employer will not be negligent because the duty will not have been breached. *Johnstone v Bloomsbury*[52] concerned the excessive hours worked by a junior doctor. The case was only before the Court of Appeal on an interlocutory application and the issue was never fully litigated. Two things emerged from the case. The first was that section 2(1) of the Unfair Contract

[47] [2001] IRLR 472.   [48] *ST v North Yorkshire County Council* [1999] IRLR 98.
[49] The test having been set out originally in J W Salmond, *The Law of Torts: A Treatise on the English Law of Liability for Civil Injuries*, 1st edn (London: Stevens & Haynes, 1907).
[50] [2001] WL 1676904, Ch D.   [51] [1891] AC 325.   [52] [1991] 2 All ER 293.

Terms Act 1977 can apply in an employment contract, and, secondly, that, in principle, it was possible to argue that an employee was not always bound by the express terms in his employment contract. This is considered further below.

Contributory negligence

An employer is under an obligation to protect employees from their own negligence (*General Cleaning Contractors Ltd v Christmas*,[53]) but an employee can nevertheless be contributorily negligent if an employer has taken all reasonable steps to do this. Section 7 of the Health and Safety at Work Act 1974, which imposes duties on an employee to look after his or her own health and safety, should also be noted in this regard.

THE EMPLOYER'S STATUTORY DUTIES

In addition to his common law duties, an employer also owes concurrent duties to employees that are imposed by UK statute and European law. The main statute is the Health and Safety at Work Act 1974. The relevant European legislation is the European Framework Directive on the Introduction of Measures to Encourage Improvements in the Safety and Health of Workers at Work[54] and subsidiary directives. These have been incorporated into UK law by means of a set of regulations, commonly known as the 'Six Pack', which include the Management of Health and Safety at Work Regulations,[55] which is the most relevant to psychiatric illness claims. However, unlike the other five sets of regulations[56] these specifically state that it is not possible to sue for damages for breach of its provisions.[57]

In *Cross v Highlands and Islands Enterprise*[58] the pursuer committed suicide. His widow brought an action for damages from his former employer averring that the suicide was caused by the stress to which he was subjected at work, and that the employer had been negligent at common law. There was also an action for breach of duty under the Management of Health and Safety at Work Regulations 1992.[59] It was argued that, first, the common law duty of care of an employer needed to be interpreted in the light of the

---

[53] [1953] AC 180.   [54] Council Directive 89/391/EEC, OJ L183, 29.06.1989, p 1.
[55] SI 1999/3242.
[56] The Safe Use of Work Equipment, Provision and Use of Work Equipment Regulations 1998, SI 1998/2306; the Manual Handling Operations Regulations 1992, SI 1992/2793; the Workplace (Health, Safety and Welfare) Regulations 1992, SI 1992/3004; Personal Protective Equipment at Work Regulations 1992, SI 1992/2966; and the Health and Safety (Display Screen Equipment) Regulations 1992, SI 1992/2792.
[57] SI 1999/3242, reg 22 ('exclusion of civil liability').   [58] [2001] IRLR 336.
[59] SI 1992/2051 (revoked and replaced by SI 1999/3242).

European Framework Directive, and the standard of care of a competent person under the Directive, rather than that of a reasonably careful employer, should apply. Secondly, given the employer's knowledge of the possible effects of stress at work and in particular that the pursuer had been ill as a result of such stress, they were under a duty under regulation 3 to make an assessment of the risks at work. Thirdly, the employer was under a duty to take protective steps following the pursuer's return to work, and finally, although the regulations provided no civil right of action, they purported to implement the Framework Directive and such a right was required for proper implementation. The employer argued that psychiatric injury should be treated differently from physical injury and that only injury as a result of nervous shock was recoverable.

The employee had been employed as a senior training manager from 1990, based in a remote area. It was argued that he had begun to suffer from depression late in 1992, prior to the death of his mother in February 1993. In April 1993 he had approached his manager mentioning problems with his workload, and shortly after was certified unfit for work by his GP who identified 'stress' as the cause; he was certified as fit for work two months later. Shortly before returning to work, he attended a session with a stress adviser to whom he was referred by his personnel manager. He committed suicide two months after returning to work. The court held that it was right in principle to treat the risk of psychiatric injury in the same way as the risk of physical injury when considering the duty of care of an employer to protect his employees, and that nervous shock was not the only type of psychiatric injury that could give rise to an action in negligence, as this was a case concerning a primary victim. It was further held that it was common for statute and common law to impose different standards of care, and a pre-existing and co-existing common law duty setting a lower standard than the Directive did not need to be interpreted as if it were the vehicle for the implementation of the Directive. Given the limited extent to which the employer was aware of the severity of the illness and his continued vulnerability, there was no clear evidence that the job was objectively harmful to his health. In 1993 the code of practice relative to the regulations only dealt with physical health and safety, and in the absence of a general practice of carrying out risk assessment in relation to stress at work, the submissions on the impact of regulation 3 on the common law duty of care failed; the employer was under a duty to moderate the pursuer's workload on his return at least until it could be proved that he was coping, but the employer's evidence that this was done was accepted, and, in the light of the preamble and other Commission documents on health and safety it was clear that at the time of enactment the Commission did not intend to address the issue of the impact of stress at work on mental health in the Framework Directive.

THE IMPLIED CONTRACTUAL TERMS

As well as tortious claims, claims can also be brought in contract. In *White v Chief Constable of South Yorkshire Police*,[60] the House of Lords did not formally consider whether the contractual relationship added something to the position in tort when considering 'shock' psychiatric injuries, although Lord Steyn did state that 'the rules to be applied when an employee brings an action against his employer for harm suffered at his workplace are the rules of tort'.[61] Lord Hoffmann enigmatically stated that contractual liability 'obviously raises different questions' and left it at that.[62] In *Walker*, Colman J had rejected the usual 'policy' arguments against imposing a duty of care, on the basis that the tortious claim was set in a contractual framework.[63] The position, therefore, is far from clear. Nevertheless, a number of issues arise specifically in relation to contract. First, although there is an implied contractual duty on the part of the employer that it will care for the health and safety of its employees, there are also a number of other contractual duties that might give rise to a claim for psychiatric injury. Secondly, there is the question of whether the degree of foreseeability of psychiatric injury is different if a claim is brought in contract; in other words, if a breach and factual causation are proved, whether the employee fails on grounds of remoteness.

The House of Lords case of *Addis v Gramophone Co Ltd*[64] is authority for the proposition that an employee who is wrongfully dismissed, ie who is dismissed in breach of contract, cannot claim damages for the manner of the dismissal or for any injured feelings or for any loss to his reputation such as might make it difficult for him to obtain work. However, it is arguable that if it had been within the contemplation of the parties that the contract will provide a particular mental satisfaction i.e. over and above the satisfaction of the completion of the contract itself, then if there is a breach of contract so as to diminish that particular enjoyment, damages can be recovered, as in *Jarvis v Swan's Tours*.[65] In *Cox v Phillips Industries*[66] a former employee recovered damages for mental distress following a breach of contract by the employer. This was on the basis that such a result would have been in the contemplation of the parties at the time the contract was made.

The conventional *Addis* approach, however, was taken in *Bliss v South East Thames RHA*[67] where the plaintiff was a consultant orthopaedic surgeon. He became involved in a dispute with some of his colleagues, as a result of which he wrote a number of angry letters to them. As a result of this,

---

[60] [1999] 2 AC 455.   [61] ibid, at 497.   [62] ibid, at 505.
[63] *Walker v Northumberland County Council* [1995] 1 All ER 737, at 758.
[64] [1909] AC 488.   [65] [1973] 1 QB 233.   [66] [1976] 1 WLR 638.
[67] [1987] ICR 700.

the health authority referred his case to a panel of senior employees at the health authority who concluded that this was not pathological behaviour, but nevertheless required him to undergo a psychiatric examination. He refused and was suspended. After disciplinary proceedings brought by the defendant failed, the defendant lifted the requirement and the plaintiff was given time to decide on his future and was paid his salary. He subsequently consulted solicitors who wrote to the defendant alleging repudiation of the contract of employment and accepting it. Proceedings were brought claiming breach of contract. The Court of Appeal held that there was an implied term in the contract that the defendant would not, without reasonable cause, act in a manner likely to damage the relationship of confidence and trust, and the requirement for psychiatric examination was a repudiatory breach of that term. However, the claim for distress and injured feelings was rejected on the basis that in an action in contract, no damages could be awarded for injured feelings.

Addis was revisited by the House of Lords in *Mahmud v Bank of Credit and Commerce International SA*.[68] In that case former employees of the bank claimed damages for the 'stigma' which attached to them following the collapse of the bank and the discovery that it had been operating in a dishonest and corrupt manner. They claimed that, although they were unaware of this, they were nevertheless unable to obtain jobs because of their association with the bank. The House of Lords held that, subject to proof, the bank, by its activities, had been in breach of the implied term that the parties to the contract would not undermine the trust and confidence between the parties. It could have been argued that in the light of this, the court had moved one step closer to demolishing the *Addis* ruling and opening the door to claims for injury to feelings and psychiatric illness caused by the manner of the dismissal of an employee. In *Johnson v Unisys*,[69] the House of Lords considered this very issue. The plaintiff had worked for his employer for over twenty years and had become a director of the company. It was known that he suffered from work-related anxieties. Allegations were made about his conduct and in January 1994 he was summarily dismissed. He claimed statutory unfair dismissal and was successful, albeit that he was found to have contributed to his dismissal. He was awarded what was then the statutory maximum compensation of just over £11,500. It was agreed for the purposes of his case that the fact of his dismissal and the way in which he was dismissed had caused him to suffer a major psychiatric illness. He wanted to be compensated further in respect of this. The House of Lords gave different reasons for doing so, but they unanimously rejected his claim. Lord Steyn did so on the basis that he would fail on causation; Lords Hoffmann, Millett, Nicholls and Bingham on the

---

[68] [1998] AC 20.   [69] [2001] 2 WLR 1076.

basis that when Parliament had enacted the unfair dismissal legislation, it had intended to provide the sort of remedy that Mr Johnson was seeking and of which he had already availed himself, and that the loss which could be recompensed by unfair dismissal compensation was wide enough to cover compensation for distress, humiliation and so on.

In *Eastwood & Williams v Magnox Electric plc*,[70] the Court of Appeal had to consider the *Johnson* decision in relation to two employees who had been subjected to extremely unpleasant behaviour over a period of four, and twelve months respectively (the employer had persuaded co-workers to make false statements about them, and they were dismissed following disciplinary proceedings where allegations had not been substantiated). They had both successfully brought unfair dismissal cases, but were seeking damages in the ordinary civil court for breach of the implied trust and confidence term of the contract of employment. Their argument was that *Johnson* only applied to conduct by the employer in the actual dismissal. In their cases, the conduct alleged to be in breach of the implied term, had gone on before the contract came to an end. The Court of Appeal rejected this argument, stating that the manner and circumstances leading to a dismissal could extend back over a certain period, but that would be for the judge to decide. In this case the trial judge had considered this and had found against the claimants and the court was not prepared to interfere with this decision.

In *Transco plc v O'Brien*,[71] the implied term of trust and confidence was considered in relation to the content of redundancy packages. The ex-employee, unlike his colleagues, had not been offered a redundancy payment on enhanced terms. The defence was that there was no obligation to treat employees even-handedly and, in any event, the employee had not been offered the enhanced terms because the employer erroneously believed that he was not a permanent employee. The Court of Appeal held that an employer who treats an employee differently in this way, on 'capricious' grounds was in breach of its implied duty of trust and confidence. The expression 'capricious' was used in the earlier case of *United Bank Ltd v Akhtar*,[72] where it was said that purely capricious decisions could be in breach of the implied term, and that although there was no obligation on an employer to behave 'reasonably', neither party to the contract should behave in such a way as to prevent the other party from carrying out his part of the contract.[73]

The claimant in *Gogay v Hertfordshire County Council*,[74] was employed by the council as a care worker in a children's home, one of the residents of

---

[70] 22 March 2002, CA.   [71] [2002] EWCA Civ 379.   [72] [1989] IRLR 507.

[73] See also *White v Reflecting Roadstuds* [1991] IRLR 331 and *Western Excavating (EEC) v Sharp* [1978] QB 761, CA, where it was said that to imply a requirement of 'reasonableness' into a contract of employment would create uncertainty.

[74] [2000] IRLR 703, CA.

which was an 11-year-old girl who had been subjected to sexual abuse by her father. She also suffered from learning and communication difficulties. Her behaviour was highly sexualized and she was known to behave inappropriately towards adults in seeking their affection. She appeared to develop an obsession with the claimant and concerns were raised as to whether she was disclosing abuse by the claimant. The claimant became very concerned about this and asked not to be left alone with the child. She took sick leave for about ten days. The area manager offered her support and insisted that the child had made no allegations about her. Subsequently, during therapy sessions the child talked about the claimant in a way which led to a decision to investigate the matter under section 47 of the Children Act 1989 and the claimant was suspended. At the end of the investigation it was decided that the concerns had been unfounded and she was reinstated. However she was unable to resume work because of a depressive illness allegedly caused by her suspension. She brought a claim for loss of earnings and damages for personal injury, contending that the council had been in breach of the implied term of her contract of employment that it would not 'without reasonable cause conduct itself in a manner likely to destroy or seriously damage the relationship of confidence and trust'. At first instance, the judge found that the council had had no reasonable cause to conduct the section 47 investigation and therefore no reasonable cause to suspend her, and awarded damages of over £26,000. The Court of Appeal held that the section 47 investigation only required that the council have 'reasonable cause to suspect' that investigation was necessary, and therefore the court should be slow to intervene. The council had been justified in calling for an investigation, but the crucial issue in the appeal was whether it was justified in suspending the claimant. In the circumstances of the case, given the slim evidence against her, the council did not have reasonable cause for the action that it took and the severity of the allegations had had the effect of seriously damaging the employment relationship.

There is no reason why breaches of other implied terms which result in psychiatric injury should not be actionable in the same sort of way. For example, it has been acknowledged that there is an implied term that an employer must permit an employee to have the benefit of a grievance procedure (*W A Goold (Pearmak) Ltd v McConnell*[75]), and foreseeable psychiatric illness as a result of failure to do this should attract an award of damages. Similarly, breach of an express term of the contract, short of dismissal, such as a demotion should achieve the same result.

The case of *Garrett v London Borough of Camden*[76] concerned 'whistleblowing'. The plaintiff had been in dispute with his employer about a number of matters, but on appeal, he contended that he had been victimized

---

[75] [1995] IRLR 516.   [76] [2001] WL 542221.

which resulted in psychiatric illness, and that the victimization was a result of him blowing the whistle on financial impropriety within the local authority. The council commissioned a report into the allegations and whilst this concluded that there had been no financial impropriety, the report did conclude that there had been a failure to comply with various standing orders and codes of conduct. The Court of Appeal acknowledged that, in principle, there is nothing wrong with whistleblowing,[77] but that, on the facts, the judge had not erred in finding that that the whistleblowing did not result in him being victimized. The court stressed that this was not a claim for wrongful dismissal, ie a common law claim for breach of contract, or for statutory unfair dismissal.

Clearly, there is a difference between these sorts of cases where there is a breach of contract by the employer which falls short of actual dismissal and those cases where the employer does dismiss. It was acknowledged in *Gogay* that the difference between the decision in that case and the decision in *Johnson* is hard to reconcile. In other words, Mrs Gogay's employer was liable because she had been unjustifiably suspended, but, on the *Johnson* principle, they would not have been liable to pay damages at common law if she had been dismissed. However, the court stated that this should be remedied by Parliament.[78] It is worth noting that the judgment of Lord Steyn in *Johnson* does not result in this difficulty as he held that *Addis* does not rule out damages flowing from the manner of dismissal, and states that damages can be recovered for breach of the obligation of trust and confidence during, and at the end of the employment relationship.[79]

To some extent these cases reflect the tension between the traditional approach of English contract law and the recent emphasis on 'reasonableness' in the employment relationship, which has come about through the development of statutory unfair dismissal.[80] However, the traditional 'freedom of contract' approach is still applicable to commercial contracts where one can assume a rough equality of bargaining power, and the prevailing view is still that an employment contract fits into this category.[81]

The case of *Johnstone v Bloomsbury Health Authority* raised the question of the relationship between express and implied terms, which is at the heart of this dichotomy. Express terms can be said to be terms that the parties have

[77] The court referred with approval to the case of *Cornelius v London Borough of Hackney*, unreported, 18 January 1996, and it should also be noted that employees are protected from suffering detriment in cases of whistleblowing in appropriate circumstances (ie 'protected disclosures') by the Employment Rights Act 1996, s 47B.
[78] See the judgment of Lady Justice Hale at [2000] IRLR 703, 711.   [79] At 1089.
[80] Unfair dismissal law is currently contained within the Employment Rights Act 1996. Once an employer has shown the reason for the dismissal, he then has to go on and show that it was reasonable to dismiss the employee for that reason (s 98(4)).
[81] See *Western Excavating (EEC) v Sharp* [1978] QB 761, CA, and *United Band v Akhtar* [1989] IRLR 507, EAT.

freely entered into, and traditional approaches to contract law would say that the employee is bound by these. In *Johnstone* the employee was a junior doctor whose contract of employment required him to work for forty hours each week, with an obligation to work weekly overtime of up to an additional forty-eight hours. He claimed that this obligation caused him to become psychiatrically ill and he abandoned his career in medicine. He sued his former employer alleging that they were in breach of the implied term that the employer would care for the employee's health and safety. Given the express contractual term he had to show that the implied term could override the express term. The employer made an application to strike out the claim on the basis that it disclosed no cause of action. The Court of Appeal had to decide, therefore, whether, in principle, the claim could proceed to trial. Leggatt LJ held that, as a matter of law, an implied term could never override an express term of the contract. Stuart-Smith LJ held that it was arguable that it could. Browne-Wilkinson LJ held that on these particular facts, the plaintiff had an arguable case because the requirement to work overtime was couched in terms that only required the employee to work *up to* an additional forty-eight hours. As this implied an element of discretion on the part of the employer as to whether to require the employee to do this, then it was possible to argue that this discretion should be exercised in the light of the implied term relating to the employee's health and safety. By a majority of two to three, therefore, the claim was allowed to proceed. However, the implication of the judgment of Browne-Wilkinson LJ is that, if the contractual term had not been described in language which permitted this discretion, then he would have had to have taken the view of Leggatt LJ, ie that a clear, non-discretionary express term must prevail over an implied term. Dr Johnstone eventually settled out of court for a very modest sum, which suggests that he received some pessimistic advice about his prospects of success.

STATUTORY UNFAIR DISMISSAL

Since the Industrial Relations Act of 1971, there has been protection for employees with sufficient qualifying service from being unfairly dismissed.[82] There are a number of ways in which unfair dismissal and psychiatric illness might coincide. First, where there is an unfair dismissal, can the ex-employee be compensated for illness caused by the unfair dismissal? Secondly, can it be fair to dismiss because of psychiatric illness? As far as the first question is concerned, it should be noted that constructive dismissal is part of the definition of dismissal for the purposes of a claim, so that an

---

[82] The protection is now contained in Part X of the Employment Rights Act 1996. The qualifying period is currently one year, although for certain dismissals, eg discrimination, pregnancy, and health and safety, there is no qualifying period.

employee who treats an employee in such a way as to be in breach of contract, ie entitling the employee to leave, and that employee does, in fact, leave, can have an action brought against it for unfair dismissal.[83] It raises the point made in *Johnson*, ie that the definition of compensation is wide enough to cover 'compensation for distress, humiliation, damage to reputation in the community or to family life'.[84]

The case of *The Governors of Hanson School v Edwards*[85] was about an employee who had a considerable amount of sick leave for which he was eventually dismissed. He claimed unfair dismissal and was successful on the basis that the employer did not follow a proper procedure. However, he had also claimed that his employer's treatment of him had caused him to become ill (he was clinically depressed) and that his unfair dismissal compensation should reflect this. However, the employment tribunal had awarded him compensation merely to reflect the pay he would have earned if he had been remained in employment whilst the proper procedures were followed. The Employment Appeal Tribunal upheld his appeal and remitted the case to a fresh tribunal to consider whether he could show that his illness had been so caused, and, if so, to award compensation accordingly. The case is interesting because it would have been open to the ex-employee here to sue the employer for damages for personal injury through the ordinary civil courts, and, if successful, he would be awarded damages for the ill-health and any consequential economic losses such as loss of earnings, pension rights and so on. The Employment Appeal Tribunal, however, held that the fact that he had this option did not preclude an employment tribunal from awarding compensation which might well overlap with such a civil claim.

Section 100 of the Employment Rights Act 1996 specifically protects employees who are dismissed because of health and safety reasons. It is automatically unfair to dismiss if the reason (or, if more than one, the principal reason) for the dismissal is, *inter alia*,[86] that:

(d)   in circumstances of danger which the employee reasonably believed to be serious and imminent and which he would not reasonably have been expected to avert, he left (or proposed to leave) or (while the danger persisted) refused to return to his place of work or any dangerous part of his place of work . . .

---

[83] Employment Rights Act 1996, s 95(1)(c).

[84] [2001] 2 WLR 1076, per Lord Hoffmann at 1096.   [85] [2001] IRLR 733.

[86] Section 100 also protects an employee from dismissal when he has been designated by the employer to carry out health and safety functions, carries them out; being a safety representative or member of a safety committee, performed or proposed to perform such functions or acted as an elected representative; or where there is not a safety representative or committee, brought to his employer's attention, by reasonable means, harmful or potentially harmful circumstances; in circumstances of danger took or proposed to take appropriate steps to protect himself or others from the danger. Note the case of *Von Goetz v St George's Healthcare NHS Trust* [2001] All ER(D) 478 (Oct) where it was held that s 100 was not limited to 'employers', so, e.g., it would cover workers who did not satisfy the definition of 'employee', such as agency workers.

In *Harvest Press Ltd v McCaffrey*,[87] the applicant had complained that he had been dismissed in circumstances covered by section 100(1)(d). He had been threatened by a colleague and had been so alarmed by the threats that he had left his shift and telephoned his manager about the behaviour from home. He subsequently repeated the allegation about the behaviour of his colleague to a more senior manager, and said that he would not return to work unless the other man was put on a different shift or dismissed. There was an investigation and the employer accepted the other man's account in its entirety, and informed the applicant that he regarded him as having resigned. The employment tribunal found that there had not been a resignation, and the Employment Appeal Tribunal upheld the decision. Furthermore, it was confirmed that, in the light of the European Framework Directive on the Introduction of Measures to Encourage Improvements in the Safety and Health of Workers at Work,[88] the words of section 100(1)(d) are wide enough to cover this situation and that he had, indeed, been dismissed for this reason, since the employer had not investigated his version of events.

It is accepted that an employer can fairly dismiss an employee for reasons of ill health, as long as a fair procedure is followed and as long as the employee is given proper and fair opportunities to make representations,[89] and to be aware of the employer's intentions. This would give the employee the opportunity to suggest redeployment or, say, retirement on grounds of ill-health, but this does not absolve the employer from independently considering ways in which to keep the employee, perhaps in another, less demanding capacity.

DISCRIMINATION AND HARASSMENT

Employers may underestimate the potential claims for discrimination, particularly in the context of personal injury, but the importance of considering them when considering risk-management strategies cannot be overstated: 'in reality negligence risk is known, largely controllable, and readily insurable ... discrimination cases, which are generally speaking an unknown quantity, [are] not protected against and uninsured ... in sex discrimination at least the burden of proof may be placed on the [employer] and claims in all discrimination cases are open-ended as far as the measure of compensation is concerned.'[90] The reference here to the employer bearing the burden of proof is to the Sex Discrimination (Indirect Discrimination

---

[87] [1999] IRLR 778.
[88] Council Directive 89/391/EEC, OJ L183, 29.06.1989, p 1.
[89] See, eg, *East Lindsey District Council v Daubney* [1977] ICR 566.
[90] See S Young, 'Risk Management: Think Discrimination' (2001) NLJ 1891.

and Burden of Proof) Regulations 2001.[91] As far as direct discrimination is concerned, case law has in any event established that, as there is usually very little direct evidence of discrimination a tribunal is entitled to infer discrimination from the primary facts and this will apply to all forms of discrimination.[92]

Although certain forms of discrimination may well be contrary to common law implied contractual terms such as the obligation to treat employees with trust and respect, or, in circumstances where the tortious tests are satisfied, discrimination might be a breach of the duty of care owed to employees, it is not always necessary to try and fit such acts into these pigeonholes, as the law relating to discrimination might come to the rescue. Here, within a firm statutory framework based upon the principle of equality, the vagaries of the common law are held at bay. However, it must be remembered, that in order to be of use, the acts or procedures complained of, must fit into one of the prohibited forms of discrimination. In the United Kingdom, these are sex, race and disability discrimination.[93] Sex discrimination is also unlawful under European law pursuant to article 141 of the Treaty of Amsterdam, and the Equal Treatment and Equal Pay Directives.[94] However, there are two new European Directives which will specifically outlaw discrimination on the grounds of race, age, religion, sexual orientation.[95]

Discrimination can take one of two forms; direct or indirect. In the first case, under section 1(1)(a) of the Sex Discrimination Act 1975 and Race Relations Act 1976 the employee is treated less favourably on the grounds of his or her sex,[96] or on racial grounds (defined by section 3(1) of the Race Relations Act as 'any of the following grounds, namely colour, race, nationality or ethnic or national origins'). In the case of indirect discrimination (section 1(1)(b) of the Sex Discrimination Act), the employer applies a

[91] SI 2001/2660. In force since 12 October 2001, but note that similar burdens will probably be placed on employers in race and disability cases, not least because of precedent; see *King v Great Britain China Centre* [1991] IRLR 513, CA.

[92] See *King v Great Britain-China Centre* [1991] IRLR 513.

[93] The Sex Discrimination Act 1975, the Race Relations Act 1976 and the Disability Discrimination Act 1995.

[94] Council Directive on the Implementation of the Principle of Equal Treatment for Men and Women as regards Access to Employment, Vocational Training and Promotion, and Working Conditions, 76/207/EEC, OJ 1976 L 39; Council Directive on the Approximation of the Laws of the Member States Relating to the Application of the Principle of Equal Pay for Men and Women, 75/117/EEC, OJ 1975 L45.

[95] The European Race Directive, 2000/43/EC, and the Equality Framework Directive, 2000/78/EC, come into force in 2003 (2006 for age but note the Age Discrimination Bill 2002).

[96] That is the wording of our domestic legislation but the European Court of Justice has ruled that the correct approach is to consider discrimination on the ground of 'sex' and not 'his or her sex' (*P v S and Cornwall County Council* [1996] IRLR 347, where transsexual discrimination was said to be unlawful as it was on the ground of 'sex'). However, see *Grant v South-West Trains* [1998] IRLR 206, where the European Court of Justice drew back from such a liberal interpretation, by refusing to make discrimination against gay people unlawful on the same sort of reasoning.

particular provision, criterion or practice to the employee, or prospective employee, which applies to everyone else but which is such that it is to the detriment of a considerably larger proportion of women than men, and the employer cannot objectively justify imposing that condition or requirement. (As far as race discrimination is concerned the wording is slightly different in that it refers to a 'requirement or condition'; the proportion of the racial group who can comply is considerably smaller and the detriment is because the person cannot comply with it. The Sex Discrimination Act had virtually identical wording but was changed to comply with the European Directive (97/80/EC) which reversed the burden of proof in sex discrimination cases. Disability discrimination, which is dealt with separately below, is only concerned with direct discrimination.)

Claims for psychiatric injury caused by discrimination will almost certainly be cases of direct discrimination. Although intention is irrelevant to both forms of discrimination, in cases of indirect discrimination the discrimination is against a group of people (as opposed to an individual), and therefore 'psychological fallout' in the form of injury is usually not an issue. Someone who is less favourably treated on one of the prohibited grounds may, however, suffer feelings of persecution and so on, which may develop into psychiatric illness. Frequently, in the case of serious psychological consequences, the complaint is not about a case of, say, a woman being refused a promotion on the ground of her sex, but about one or more acts of harassment. This has to be fitted into the framework of direct (usually) discrimination. The test is the 'but for' test set out in the House of Lords case of *James v Eastleigh Borough Council*,[97] so that he or she has been treated less favourably and that 'but for' his or her sex/racial group, he or she would not have been treated less favourably. If harassment is on the ground of sex or race then normally this test can be satisfied.

Disability discrimination

Although this is only obliquely about being compensated for psychiatric injury, for the sake of completeness it should be said that disability due to mental health is covered by the Disability Discrimination Act 1995, and that, damages can be awarded for unlawful discrimination under that Act, and that the damages, as in sex and race discrimination cases, can be for both actual psychiatric injury and for injured feelings.

Under the 1995 Act a 'disability' is 'a physical or mental impairment which has a substantial and long-term adverse effect on his ability to carry out normal day-to-day activities' (section 1(2)).[98] Although direct discrimi-

---

[97] [1990] 2 AC 751.

[98] Two exceptions the Act, ie that it does not apply to employers with less than 20 employees, and it does not apply to, *inter alia*, members of the armed forces, police, prison officers, and firefighters will be removed under the Disability Discrimination (Amendment) Bill 2002.

nation on the ground of disability is outlawed, it is possible for an employer to justify it. The reasons given by the employer must be both material to the circumstances of each case and 'substantial' (section 5(3)).

The case of *Goodwin v Patent Office*[99] concerned an employee who suffered from paranoid schizophrenia. He was dismissed by the Patent Office following complaints from colleagues about his behaviour. He complained to an employment tribunal that he had been discriminated against by reason of his disability. The tribunal had to consider whether he was disabled within the meaning of section 1 of the Disability Discrimination Act 1995, which states that the disability must have a substantial and long-term adverse effect on his ability to carry out normal day-to-day activities, and found that his impairment was not substantial because he could perform domestic tasks without help and was capable of getting to work and carrying out his job adequately. Allowing the appeal, the Employment Appeal Tribunal held that mental impairment included impairment caused by or constituting a well-recognized mental illness. The adverse effect condition would be fulfilled if the tribunal was satisfied that one of the capacities in paragraph 4(1) of Schedule 1 to the Act had been affected, and the fact that a person could carry out activities did not mean that his ability to carry them out had not been impaired. Whether an adverse effect was substantial had to be assessed by considering whether the effect of the impairment on a person's ability to carry out normal day-to-day activities was more than minor or trivial. In the instant case, the applicant was clearly disabled within the meaning of the Act.

In *Rugamer v Sony Music Entertainment UK Ltd*,[100] the Employment Appeal Tribunal had to consider the meaning of the expression 'functional overlay' in the context of disability discrimination. The expression can mean that there are psychological aspects of a person's 'medical' condition which cannot be attributed to the alleged condition. It is sometimes used by doctors, however, as a euphemism for malingering. Here, the employee suffered from shoulder pain, for which there was no physical explanation, and the question to be decided was whether functional overlay can constitute a physical or mental impairment within the meaning of section 1(1) of the Disability Discrimination Act. The Employment Appeal Tribunal held that it cannot. In the context of the Act, which differentiated between the presence of an impairment and its cause or effects, a disablement which was not 'a manifestation of a person's physical condition' but was 'a manifestation of his psychological make up' could not be a physical impairment, even if its effects were such as to limit his physical abilities. It should be noted here that there was no consideration given as to whether it was a mental impairment, which is no doubt due to the fact that functional overlay is not a recognizable psychiatric condition. However, various factitious disorders are,[101] and it would be difficult for a tribunal to refuse jurisdiction to hear such a disability discrimination claim if the applicant was diagnosed to be suffering from such a disorder.

If the Dignity at Work Bill 2001 is enacted, it will prohibit harassment, bullying and any conduct which causes an employee 'to be alarmed or distressed'. It includes behaviour on more than one occasion which is offensive or abusive; unjustified criticism on more than one occasion, punishment imposed without reasonable justification, or changes in the duties or responsibilities of the employee to the employee's detriment without reasonable justification. As in discrimination cases, the tribunal can make a declaration, recommendation or order compensation, which can include damages for injury to feelings. There is a statutory defence if the employer has in force a 'Dignity at Work Policy' and has taken reasonable steps to enforce it; the acts complained of are repudiated by the person in charge of the policy within three days of complaint, and the employer takes all steps reasonably necessary to remedy any loss suffered by the complainant. The Bill also modifies the Employment Rights Act 1996 so that breach of this 'implied dignity' contractual term, can amount to a constructive dismissal.

Finally, it should be noted that the Protection from Harassment Act 1997 applies to employees (see Chapter 1).

Compensation for discrimination

In discrimination cases, compensation can be awarded for 'injured feelings'. In common law claims damages are not normally recoverable for this sort of 'mere distress'. In a work-induced 'stress' case, therefore, the employee must still show that he is suffering from a recognizable psychiatric disorder, and, of course, causation must be proved. Other factors in the employee's life will be examined to see whether one or more of these have caused the disorder, but it should be noted that compensation can be awarded for injury to feelings, and crucially, aggravated damages can be awarded. Together these can amount to fairly substantial sums (see Chapter 7).

In *Sheriff v Klyne Tugs (Lowestoft) Ltd*,[102] the employee, of Somali origin, was employed as a ship's engineer and, because of his racial origin, was subjected to harassment, intimidation and bullying by the master during the course of his employment. Consequently, he experienced stress and anxiety making him unfit for work, but, when he submitted a medical certificate, he was told that his P45 would be sent to him. He brought an action for race discrimination and a settlement agreement was reached in the sum of

---

[101] See DSM–IV for diagnostic criteria.   [102] [1999] IRLR 481, CA.

£4,000. The agreement was on standard terms and stated that he accepted the settlement in full and final settlement of all claims against his former employer and the employment tribunal dismissed the application on withdrawal by him. He subsequently issued county court proceedings, alleging negligence by his former employer and claiming compensation for the psychiatric injury. The action was struck out as an abuse of process on the basis that the claim had been within the jurisdiction of the employment tribunal, and that the claim had been settled. The Court of Appeal dismissed the plaintiff's appeal on the basis that the employment tribunal had had jurisdiction to hear the claim since it arose out of his employment and under section 56 of the Race Relations Act 1976, an employment tribunal could award compensation on the same basis as the county court, where it was just and equitable to do so. Although section 57(4) specified injury to feelings as a new head, this did not restrict the scope of compensation but allowed recovery not otherwise possible at common law. Compensation for psychiatric injury in the form of PTSD was recoverable through a claim presented to an employment tribunal, if it could be established that the damage had been caused as a result of the statutory tort of racial discrimination. Since the claim fell within the settlement agreement, and could have been raised in the previous proceedings, he had lost the right to raise the issue before the county court. The only circumstances in which a claimant might present such a claim to a county court was where the condition was discovered after the earlier proceedings had been concluded. In *Taylor v Rover Group Ltd*,[103] the case of *Sherrif* was distinguished on the basis that the release contained a clause which stated that 'This settlement does not affect any right the Applicant may have in relation to any industrial injuries claim.'

---

[103] [2000] CLY 575, Birmingham county court.

7

Assessing Damages

Damages for psychiatric injury are, of course, subject to the general law of damages, the main principle of which is that damages should be compensatory (but note what is said below about punitive damages). The usual rule that damages should compensate only for actual loss applies to damages for psychiatric injury. It is proposed to look at some of the main considerations on the award of damages in a psychiatric injury case, with the caveat that, as far as general principles are concerned, reference should also be made to a more general work.[1]

Until the late 1980s there was not a great deal of authority on assessment and quantum of damages in this area but in 1989 the *Herald of Free Enterprise* arbitrations, which are considered in full in this chapter, reviewed the issues involved in assessing damages in a psychiatric injury case.

At the time of writing the first edition of this book, when damages were awarded for physical injury and psychiatric injury, judges almost always gave a 'global' figure for general damages so that it was not possible to ascertain levels of damages for the psychiatric aspect of the injury. Fortunately, this is no longer the case and, in all the cases following, where there is also physical injury, a separate figure for psychiatric injury is also given.

THE ONCE-AND-FOR-ALL RULE

Where damages result from the same cause of action, they are assessed once and for all, so that any loss which will or may occur in the future must be assessed. If there is only a probability that there will be future deterioration or loss then that will be valued according to the percentage risk of the deterioration or loss which may occur.

PROVISIONAL DAMAGES

In most cases of psychiatric injury the once-and-for-all rule will apply. For example in the *Herald of Free Enterprise* arbitrations, it was decided by the arbitrators that the risk of future problems and the vulnerability of a claimant to future injury should be taken into account when assessing damages.

However, there are some cases where it is not appropriate to assess the damages for this future risk, which may be of some serious and debilitating development, and for which the essentially modest sum of damages which would be assessed at trial would be entirely inadequate. Section 32A the Supreme Court Act 1981 gives the court a power to assess damages in two stages if:

---

[1] See, eg, *McGregor on Damages*, 16th edn (London: Sweet & Maxwell, 1997). See also B Langstaff et al, *Personal Injury Schedules* (London: Butterworths, 2001) for guidance on calculating and drafting particular heads of damage.

there is proved or admitted to be a chance that at some definite or indefinite time in the future the injured person will, as a result of the act or omission which gave rise to the cause of action, develop some serious disease or suffer some serious deterioration in his physical or mental condition.

For the county court the power to award provisional damages is in section 51 of the County Courts Act 1984. In order for the court to make an award of provisional damages a claim for provisional damages must have been pleaded. It is also important to note that the adjective 'serious' qualifies the disease or deterioration and *not* the risk; in fact the word 'chance' suggests that the claimant does not have to show that he is likely to suffer such deterioration on a balance of probabilities.

It may be appropriate to consider provisional damages in a psychiatric injury case if the claimant has been involved in a particularly horrifying incident and appears to have suffered no psychiatric ill-effects but there is psychiatric evidence to suggest that a serious breakdown could occur later in life. For a high-earning and ambitious claimant, the consequences of this could be devastating, and provisional damages should be considered. What has to be established is a 'clear and severable risk rather than a continuing deterioration'.[2] There is evidence that mental breakdowns can occur many years after a traumatic event,[3] which might make it appropriate to award provisional damages.

The procedure is that when damages are assessed in the first place, the risk is ignored, but the judgment will state the precise nature of the disease or deterioration for which damages are reserved and should usually fix a time limit for a further claim.

EFFECT OF ILLNESS OR ACCIDENT SUPERVENING BEFORE ASSESSMENT OF DAMAGES (*NOVUS ACTUS* OR *NOVA CAUSA*)

The law in this area is complex. One of the leading cases is *Baker v Willoughby*,[4] which concerned a later, unconnected accident. The plaintiff had sustained a fractured leg as a result of the defendant's negligence. This had left him with some permanent disability, pain and risk of osteoarthritis. Before the trial his leg was shot by armed robbers and had to be amputated. The House of Lords held that since his earning capacity and enjoyment of life had been reduced by the first accident, he was entitled to damages for this *as a continuing condition* notwithstanding the fact that the supervening

---

[2] See *Cowan v Kitson Insulations Ltd* [1992] PIQR Q19.
[3] See C B Scrignar, *Post-traumatic Stress Disorder*, 2nd ed (New Orleans, LA: Bruno Press, 1988) pp 96–9.
[4] [1970] AC 467.

attack had made his condition a lot worse. However, as the pain could not continue, nor was there now any future risk of osteoarthritis, damages under those heads were not recoverable.

In *Jobling v Associated Dairies Ltd*[5] a different approach was taken by the House of Lords, without actually disapproving *Baker v Willoughby*. *Jobling v Associated Dairies Ltd* concerned a supervening *illness* and damages were reduced on the basis that the illness would have supervened regardless of the original accident. The difference between illness and accident is not entirely clear; it may be that illness is thought to be something already written into a person's physical development *before* the original accident took place, whereas a subsequent tortious event is pure chance. On this basis, however, it would be necessary to distinguish between different *types* of illness, and treat, say, a permanent disability brought on by a chance infection as the same as one brought about by a tortious act. On the other hand if the distinction is made to avoid a victim of two torts missing out on compensation from both tortfeasors then this would not make sense either.

In *Neil v Rankin*[6] the Court of Appeal considered the application of these cases to a hypothetical future tort. In that case the claimant was a police officer who had suffered from post-traumatic stress disorder ('PTSD') as a result of a shooting incident. He was subsequently involved in a minor road traffic accident which exacerbated his psychiatric condition and led to him leaving the police force. At first instance the judge reduced the award for loss of earnings on the basis that had he remained in the police force some other tortious event would probably have had the same effect. The Court of Appeal held that this approach was correct, on the 'vicissitudes' principle, ie the purpose of an award of damages is, insofar as it is possible, to put the claimant in the same position as he would have been in had the tortious event not happened, no better and no worse. (In the event the Court of Appeal found that the judge had used the wrong multiplier and upheld the appeal on that basis.)

The case of *Pigney v Pointer's Transport Services Ltd*[7] is illustrative of this point in relation to psychiatric injury. The facts were that Mr Pigney sustained head injuries in July 1955 due to the negligence of the defendants. He commenced proceedings, but in January 1957 before the hearing of the action, he committed suicide. His widow continued the action, and also brought one of her own under the Fatal Accidents Acts. The question for the courts was whether the suicide, which it was accepted had been committed in a fit of depression brought about by a condition of acute anxiety neurosis induced by the accident and the injury incurred therein, was a *novus actus interveniens* which broke the chain of causation between Mr Pigney's injury and his death. It had been established that Mr Pigney was not insane as

---

[5] [1982] AC 794.   [6] [2000] 2 WLR 1173.   [7] [1957] 1 WLR 1121.

judged by the standard laid down in the M'Naughten rules, and it was held that if he had been then that would have made the chain of causation complete. Pilcher J found that the suicide did not break the chain of causation, and that, furthermore, the widow's action was not barred by public policy considerations (suicide was then an offence) because any damages would accrue to her and not to her late husband's estate.

DAMAGES WHERE THERE IS A PRE-EXISTING CONDITION

A pre-existing condition may cause an apportionment of damages, a discount for the contingency of the condition developing in any event, or an increase in damages.

An apportionment will be appropriate in cases where it can be shown on the evidence that the plaintiff was already *suffering* from the effects of a psychiatric disorder and the defendant will only be liable for the additional disorder. In practice, of course, it may be difficult, if not impossible, for the medical evidence to make it clear how the damages should be apportioned.

If the plaintiff was not actually suffering from any psychiatric disorder at the time of the accident, but had a predisposition towards such illness, then the court *may* discount the damages to take account of the condition developing in any event. This has to be contrasted with the situation where the plaintiff has the psychological equivalent of an eggshell skull: the eggshell personality. In such a case the plaintiff may appear to be disproportionately ill, but full damages will be payable however serious the condition may be (see *Page v Smith*[8] and *Brice v Brown*[9] and the general discussion below).

Again, in practice, the difference between these two situations can be difficult to see. An analogy can be drawn with some orthopaedic cases. Ageing causes degenerative changes in the spine, and most people remain unaware of these for most of their lives. However, an injury can sometimes result in osteoarthritis, for example, which may never have otherwise happened. The defendant in such a case may point to X-rays which show the pre-existing changes and state that the illness would have manifested itself sooner or later. The claimant will say that the illness would never have occurred but for the injury. In a psychiatric injury case, the point at issue will not be x-rays but the claimant's medical history.

In *Jeffries v Home Office*[10] Ian Kennedy J, distinguished between compensation for psychiatric injury in excess of what would normally be anticipated and compensation for the claimant's personality itself. The claimant was a

---

[8] [1995] 2 All ER 736.   [9] [1984] 1 All ER 997.   [10] [1999] CLY 1414.

prison officer who had suffered a back injury when part of a ceiling fell on him. The medical evidence was that he was fit to return to work in March 1994. He did return but was unable to work due to anxiety and depression. It was held that his failure to continue to work or attempt any other form of work was due to his personality rather than a medical condition and his claim for loss of earnings from March 1994 onwards was rejected. This is a decision which does not sit easily with the eggshell skull rule (see below) but it may stem from a lack of good medical evidence.

CERTAINTY OF LOSS

The difficulties outlined above are similar to those faced when the loss sustained is simply uncertain. It is well established that mere difficulty in assessment and lack of precision and certainty are not reasons for denying an award of damages.[11] Courts often make awards for the loss of a chance, for example, the loss of a job opportunity or career, but see the case of *Hotson v East Berkshire Health Authority*.[12]

Damages can be awarded for risk of relapse. Psychiatric injury can leave a plaintiff very vulnerable to a relapse which may be triggered by a relatively ordinary event. The degree of vulnerability will depend entirely upon the medical evidence. Consider this in relation to an award of provisional damages described above (page 175) and the *Herald of Free Enterprise* findings (see page 212).

REMOTENESS OF DAMAGES

The question as to whether the damage is 'too remote' is not concerned with factual causation in terms of the physical chain of events, but with whether the damage sustained was foreseeable.[13] However, as Jones suggests, to say that the test is one of foreseeability is unhelpful, because one has to ask 'what exactly has to be foreseen?'[14] Generally if the damage has left the claimant vulnerable to risks then if he suffers further damage as a result of the realization of those risks, then unless that was wholly due to the negligence or intentional act of himself or a third party, the plaintiff will recover for the additional damage.

The case of *Robinson v Post Office*,[15] illustrates this point. The plaintiff suffered a cut shin due to the negligence of the defendant. He was given an

---

[11] See *Chaplin v Hicks* [1911] 2 KB 786, CA.   [12] [1987] AC 750.

[13] *Overseas Tankship (UK) Ltd v Morts Dock & Engineering Co, The Wagon Mound* [1961] AC 388.

[14] M Jones, *Textbook on Torts* (London: Blackstone Press, 2000), p 240.

[15] [1974] 2 All ER 737, CA.

anti-tetanus injection to which he was allergic, as a result of which he developed encephalitis and brain damage. It was held by the Court of Appeal that, although it was not foreseeable that he would suffer such a reaction to the injection, the chain of causation was not broken, as it was the original injury which was being treated, and in addition, the defendant must take the plaintiff as he finds him, with his allergy. There was some argument that the doctor was negligent because he had not carried out the test properly to ascertain whether the plaintiff was allergic, but the court decided that there was no negligence, and in any event the weakness would not have been revealed within the stipulated period of time.

However, in *McKew v Holland & Hannen & Cubitts (Scotland) Ltd*[16] (a Scottish case) the pursuer suffered an injury which left him with a weak knee liable to give way. As a result, when he attempted to go down a steep flight of stone steps without the help of a stick, he fell and broke both legs. It was held that he could not recover damages for the injury he received when he fell, as he had behaved unreasonably and this had broken the chain of causation. (*Contrast Wieland v Cyril Lord Carpets Ltd*[17] where damages were recovered in a similar situation where the plaintiff's actions were found to be reasonable in the circumstances.)

As far as remoteness of damage is concerned, three principles have to be considered. Firstly, the principle that the type of harm suffered must be foreseeable. For example, in *Tremain v Pike*[18] the plaintiff contracted Weil's disease following his exposure to rats' urine. His claim for damages failed because the court found that although injury through rat bites or contaminated food was foreseeable, this rare disease was not. Nothing could be a better illustration of Jones's point that the foreseeability test means little unless one knows what it is one is supposed to foresee. It would clearly have been open to the court simply to regard the presence of rats as being foreseeably predictive of disease generally without specifying a particular type.

Second, there is the principle that if some damage is foreseeable it does not matter that the extent of the damage is not. This is well illustrated by *Vacwell Engineering v BDH Chemicals*[19] where an explosion was foreseeable but, in the event, an unforeseeably large explosion occurred.

The third principle is the 'eggshell skull' principle which is another way of saying that the defendant must take his victim as he finds him, as in *Robinson v Post Office* (considered above). The principle was set out in the psychiatric injury case of *Dulieu v White & Sons*[20] where it was said:

If a man is negligently run over or otherwise negligently injured in his body, it is no answer to the sufferer's claim for damages that he would have suffered less injury, or no injury at all, if he had not had an unusually thin skull or an unusually weak heart.[21]

[16] [1969] 3 All ER 1621.   [17] [1969] 3 All ER 1006.   [18] [1969] 3 All ER 103.
[19] [1971] 1 QB 88.   [20] [1901] 2 KB 669.   [21] ibid, per Kennedy J at 679.

An illustration of this principle is the case of *Smith v Leech Brain*[22] where the plaintiff's lip was burnt with molten metal. A pre-cancerous condition was triggered and the plaintiff suffered a cancerous growth which eventually killed him. The defendant was held liable because the burn was foreseeable. However, this sits uneasily with the principle that the 'type of injury' must be foreseeable.

Burke v Royal Infirmary of Edinburgh NHS Trust[23] was an action brought for damages following a fall at work. The Scottish Outer House found that there was insufficient evidence to establish fault. However, the action was also defended on the basis that the pursuer's reaction to the fall (continuing pain, sleeplessness and an inability to work) was abnormal. The opinion of the court was that, whilst a defender would not be liable for losses arising from a voluntary and rational decision following a physical injury, the reaction was neither conscious nor rational but was the result of the pursuer's psychological disposition. This case should be contrasted with *Jeffries v Home Office*[24] discussed below.

It might be thought that the eggshell rule is the same as the 'extent of the injury' principle. The very name implies that there is a possibility of some, at least, slight damage to the skull, but that due to the particular vulnerability of this claimant's cranium, more serious damage occurs. However, there is a tendency to suggest that the two principles are not coterminous and that the eggshell rule is a device which allows recovery of compensation for damage which would otherwise belong to an unforeseeable category or type.[25] It is arguable that there is no real distinction, but the psychiatric injury cases complicate the issue. Since *Page v Smith*[26] where it was stated that, as far as primary victims are concerned, there need not be separate foreseeability of psychiatric injury as long as there is foreseeability of physical injury (both being regarded as types of *personal* injury), the eggshell rule is a separate rule which allows recovery for unforeseeable psychiatric injury. This is illustrated by an example of physical injury given in *Bourhill v Young* by Lord Wright:

One who suffers from the terrible tendency to bleed on slight contact, which is denoted by the term 'a bleeder', cannot complain if he mixes with the crowd and suffers severely, perhaps fatally, from being merely brushed against. There is no wrong done there.[27]

The plaintiff in *Bourhill* was required to have sufficient fortitude to withstand the noise of accidents and the sight of injury to others. Psychiatric injury was not foreseeable. It might be argued that she was a mere bystander and that

---

[22] [1962] 2 QB 405.   [23] 1999 SLT 539.   [24] [1999] CLY 1414.
[25] See, eg, W V H Rogers, *Winfield and Jolowicz on Tort*, 14th edn (London: Sweet & Maxwell, 1994), p 165.
[26] [1995] 2 All ER 736.   [27] [1943] AC 92, at 109.

the 'normal fortitude' rule does not apply to secondary victims who are in a close relationship with the primary victim.

It seems to be the law, therefore, that in secondary victim cases there is no eggshell skull rule and that the type of damage must be foreseeable, albeit that the extent of the damage is greater than could be foreseen. It is, of course, also arguable that both *Bourhill v Young* and *Page v Smith* were about establishing a duty, rather than a consideration of remoteness of damage, but the very application of the remoteness test to the eggshell skull shows that the distinction between duty and remoteness can be blurred to the extent that either concept could justify the same decision.

Remoteness of damage in the specific context of psychiatric injury, is best considered by a close analysis of a number of reported decisions.

The *Meah v McCreamer* cases considered below are interesting from an historical perspective but it must be noted that the first case is probably no longer good law following *Clunis v Camden and Islington Health Authority*.[28] There, the plaintiff was convicted of manslaughter following his unprovoked attack on a passenger at a tube station. He was an ex-psychiatric patient formerly detained under the Mental Health Act 1983, and still subject to the Act's after-care provisions under section 117. The plaintiff claimed damages on the basis that if he had received appropriate care he would not have gone on to kill. The Court of Appeal rejected the claim on the basis, *inter alia*, that the act of killing was the plaintiff's own illegal act and the maxim *ex turpi causci non aritur* applied (he would only have escaped this by successfully pleading insanity, ie he did not appreciate that what he was doing was wrong, as opposed to having diminished responsibility). The Court of Appeal specifically referred to *Meah v McCreamer* and doubted its correctness. The Court of Appeal's approach was followed in *Worrall v British Railways Board*[29] and *Cooper v Reed*.[30]

Meah v McCreamer [31]

The plaintiff was a passenger in a car driven negligently by the defendant. As a result of the injury suffered, which included severe brain damage, he developed a psychiatric injury in the form of a serious personality change. He became aggressive, violent and dangerous and attacked a number of women. As a consequence of these attacks he was sentenced to life imprisonment and classified as a category A prisoner. He claimed damages (*inter alia*) for the psychiatric injury and his incarceration for life as a category A prisoner. He was awarded general damages of £45,750. Although the evidence indicated that before the accident, Mr Meah had been convicted of a number of offences and had a poor employment record,

---

[28] [1998] 3 All ER 180.   [29] [1999] CLY 1413, CA.
[30] [2001] EWCA Civ 224, CA.   [31] [1985] 1 All ER 367.

there was no evidence of his being violent towards women; indeed he had had several successful relationships. The medical evidence was that his personality was altered by the head injury in the direction of a coarsening and an exaggeration of pre-existing traits, and a loss of emotional control. He had an 'eggshell personality'. Woolf J concluded that but for the accident he would not have committed the acts of violence, although some discount was made for the finding that he would probably have spent time in prison. The full damages were £60,000, discounted by 25 per cent because of the plaintiff's contributory negligence in travelling as a passenger with a driver whom he knew to be drunk.

Meah v McCreamer (No 2) [32]

Two of Mr Meah's victims, Mrs W and Miss D, one of whom had been raped by him in terrifying circumstances, and the other of whom had been seriously assaulted sexually, were awarded damages of £10,250 and £6,750 respectively against him.[33] Meah brought an action against the driver and the driver's insurers to recover the amounts awarded to the two victims. The action failed. Adopting what Woolf J referred to as a 'robust' approach, the damages awarded to Mrs W and Miss D were too remote to be recoverable. They were not in respect of the plaintiff's own injuries or *direct* financial loss, and if the plaintiff were to recover it would expose the defendants and other defendants in similar cases to an indefinite liability for an indefinite duration. It was also held that it would be contrary to public policy for the plaintiff to be indemnified for the consequences of his crimes.

Malcolm v Broadhurst[34]

This is an interesting case on the question of remoteness of damage generally, but it does involve consideration of the 'eggshell personality' rule.

The case concerned a husband and wife who were injured in a road accident. The husband suffered head injuries which caused his intellectual deterioration and a serious diminution of learning power, and changed his personality and behaviour so that he became irritable in the home, bad tempered and, on occasions, violent towards his wife. The prognosis was poor. The wife recovered from her physical injuries after some three to four months, but she did suffer from a pre-existing nervous condition which was exacerbated by the accident. This had improved after a year, but for some seven months she was incapacitated from work solely because of the effect on her vulnerable personality of the husband's changed behaviour. In addition to her full-time job, before the accident, the wife had worked part-time for her husband, but was no longer able to do this, as, due to the

---

[32] [1986] 1 All ER 943.   [33] See *W v Meah* [1986] 1 All ER 935.   [34] [1970] 3 All ER 508.

effect of the accident, he no longer worked himself. She returned to work after seven months, but the medical view was that her husband's behaviour would be likely to cause her to develop nervous symptoms from time to time. However, the wife was unable to obtain part-time work in addition to her full-time job.

The difficult question of remoteness of damage that the court had to decide was whether she was entitled to loss of wages in respect of both her full-time and part-time job, and her nervous disability from which she suffered due to the effect on her of her husband's changed behaviour.

It was held that the exacerbation of her nervous condition was a foreseeable consequence of injuring her on the principle of the 'eggshell personality', and that it was reasonably foreseeable that if the husband was severely injured when the wife was temperamentally unstable, her instability might be adversely affected by the injury done to the husband. She was, therefore, entitled to damages to compensate her for loss of wages from full-time work for that period of seven months, and to a sum (assessed at £150) for her nervous disability over those months and the slight risk of future nervous trouble.

However, Geoffrey Lane J also held that she was not entitled to compensation for the part-time wages lost. This loss was not foreseeable. He said:

> If the wife herself had not been injured there is no doubt that she would not have been entitled to recover under this head. The defendant could not reasonably have foreseen that by injuring the husband he would be depriving the wife of her only means of part-time employment. Does the fact that she herself has a cause of action against the defendant arising out of the same accident give her the right to recover?[35]

Since both the cause of action and the recoverability of damages depend on foreseeability, the answer logically should be the same in each case. Logic, however, is not always an infallible guide in problems of remoteness of damage. The 'eggshell skull' principle itself is hard to reconcile logically with the foreseeability test. Geoffrey Lane J went on to say:

> It seems to me that the only way in which the defendant could be made liable under this head would be by saying that he must take his victims as he finds them not only in relation to their physical infirmities but also in relation to their infirmities of employment. That would be an extension, and in my judgment an unwarrantable extension, of the present law.

This may be contrasted with *Pigney v Pointer's Transport Services Ltd*[36] (see above page 177).

Cowan v National Coal Board[37]

This was an action brought by the widow of a workman who suffered an injury to his left eye, become mentally ill as a result of the injury and

---

[35] ibid, at 512.   [36] [1957] 1 WLR 112.
[37] 1958 SLT (Notes) 19, Scotland, Court of Session Outer House.

committed suicide some three months after the accident. Damages were claimed in respect of the suicide, but recovery was denied. Lord Cameron said:

> ... if it were held to be established that the deceased had received a comparatively moderate injury through the negligence of the defenders and had thereafter become depressed and worried because of fear for his future working capacity or physical health and then had committed suicide under the influence of such depression and worry no doubt it might be inferred that the suicide was consequent upon that injury.... In the present case not only is there no proof of injury to the skull or brain but there is no physical connection between the initial injury (assuming it to have been caused by the defenders' negligence) and the assumed suicide.[38]

The correctness of this decision can be doubted, but what may have been being considered was a straightforward anxiety about the future in material terms, rather than the more subtle and less rational feelings of anxiety and depression which can result from a traumatic incident.

McLaren v Bradstreet[39]

The three plaintiffs were passengers in the defendant's car, which met with an accident. The defendant died as a result, but the plaintiffs suffered minimal physical injuries. They were all young siblings and lived with their parents. Their mother was neurotic and was obsessed with the accident, constantly talking about it. The plaintiffs suffered from dizziness, shyness, occasional blackouts and other symptoms. Two of the plaintiffs said they were unable to work for two years following the accident, and the third for seven years. The defendant's medical evidence was that the mother's personality was such that the plaintiffs' symptoms would have cleared up within a few months if she had not influenced them to exaggerate and perpetuate them. She was held to have instigated a form of family hysteria. This evidence was accepted by the court, and the Court of Appeal held that while it was true that a tortfeasor had to take his victim as he found him, he did not have to take his family. The hysteria here was not foreseeable and the chain of causation was broken.

GENERAL DAMAGES

General damages consist of damages for pain, suffering and loss of amenities of life. It is interesting that in negligence there are no recoverable damages for 'ordinary' mental distress or shock if there have been no physical

---

[38] ibid, at 21.   [39] (1969) 119 NLJ 484.

injuries.[40] If there have been physical injuries, then, although it is not described as such, in a sense there are always damages for mental distress, as this is part of pain and suffering. According to McGregor,[41] 'pain' is the immediately felt effect on the nerves and brain, while 'suffering' is distress not directly connected with any bodily condition, and would include fright at the time of the injury, and 'fright reaction' (*Thompson v Royal Mail Lines Ltd*[42]), fear of future incapacity — in relation to health, sanity or the ability to make a living — and humiliation, sadness and embarrassment caused by disfigurement. If there is a physical injury, therefore, any non-medical distress which is suffered in excess of that which is to be expected, for example, a bad case of fright which did not go so far as to develop into a recognizable psychiatric illness, would be claimed under this heading. Damages for pain and suffering are, of course, entirely dependent upon the type of injury sustained. It should always be considered, however, whether the bad case of fright could be said to be an acute stress reaction.

The other aspect of general damages is 'loss of amenities of life'. These include injuries to the senses,[43] sexual dysfunction,[44] loss of marriage prospects, loss of enjoyment of family life,[45] loss of enjoyment of work[46] and loss of a holiday.[47]

In an award for psychiatric injury, loss of amenity can have great significance. Disorders such as depression and post-traumatic stress disorder ('PTSD') can affect all aspects of the sufferer's life. For example, clinical depression can mean that the plaintiff suffers from insomnia in varying degrees, loss of libido, sometimes to the extent of impotence, loss of interest in work and leisure activities, and impaired concentration. There may be an effect on enjoyment of work or any hobby which requires a degree of concentration. In addition, of course, the plaintiff may suffer from depressive feelings such as hopelessness, exhaustion, low self-esteem, etc which can permeate everything he does. Similarly, affective and neurotic disorders can be just as debilitating. An anxiety neurosis, for example, means that there is unreasonable fear without any particular focus. These attacks are often accompanied by a variety of symptoms: palpitations, excessive sweating, breathlessness, faintness, nausea etc. A phobic anxiety can also seriously curtail the claimant's activities, particularly if it concerns something of a commonplace nature, such as travelling in a vehicle, or being left alone. Again, the symptoms in the later stages of PTSD — phobic

[40] See *Nicholls v Rushton* The Times, 19 June 1992, but note 'acute stress reaction' (see page 56).

[41] *McGregor on Damages*, 16th edn (London: Sweet & Maxwell, 1997), p 1103.

[42] [1957] 1 Lloyd's Rep 99.   [43] See *Cook v J L Kier & Co Ltd* [1970] 1 WLR 774.

[44] ibid.   [45] See *Hoffman v Sofaer* [1982] 1 WLR 1350.

[46] See *Morris v Johnson Matthey & Co Ltd* (1967) 112 SJ 32, CA, where a substantial sum was awarded for the loss of the joy which a craftsman found in his craft.

[47] See *Marson v Hall* [1983] CLY 1046.

anxiety, inordinate attention to physical discomfort and normal physiological processes so that the claimant may, the example, become obsessive about bodily sensations — will all interfere with enjoyment of the normal activities of life. Loss of amenities of life will, in these sorts of cases, be substantial. As Birkett J stated in *Griffiths v R & H Green & Silley Weir Ltd*:[48]

... I can conceive of very few things so painful as to be continually unwell; to lose the savour and zest for life.... I think I must award a fairly substantial sum.

SPECIAL DAMAGES FOR PECUNIARY LOSS

Obviously, all the usual special damages apply in exactly the same way as in the case of physical injury. When considering, however, loss of earning capacity or handicap in the labour market or loss of a career, it should be remembered that psychiatric injury can have serious consequences for a claimant's employability.[49] Claimant lawyers will be aware that, whilst there is always a duty to mitigate loss, allegations by the defence that the claimant is not making enough efforts to resume working should receive a robust response, subject, of course, to the evidence, both medical and non-medical, supporting the claimant whose injuries are such that work is as yet impossible. It should also be remembered that damages can be awarded for loss of housekeeping capacity, whether or not the claimant intends to employ anyone.[50]

If the claimant's marriage breaks down as a result of his or her injuries, and, undoubtedly, psychiatric injuries can put a great strain upon a marriage, then the claimant can recover damages to cover certain aspects of the consequent financial loss. In *Jones v Jones*,[51] the injured husband recovered damages for part of the amount of the lump sum he had been ordered to pay to the wife in divorce proceedings. The whole of the lump sum was not recovered as it was held that the wife would have shared in the general damages that the husband was awarded. The damages did not cover the maintenance order on the grounds that the husband might have a reduced tax liability because of this, and also the wife might remarry.

Medical expenses must be 'reasonable', but there is no obligation on the claimant to make use of NHS or other 'free' treatment even if this is available.[52] The cost of convalescence, again, subject to it being reasonable, is also recoverable.

---

[48] (1948) 81 Ll L Rep 378.
[49] See eg *R v Liverpool City Council* [1989] CLY 1255 considered below at page 196.
[50] See *Daly v General Steam Navigation Co Ltd* [1981] 1 WLR 120.
[51] [1985] QB 704, CA.   [52] Law Reform (Personal Injuries) Act 1948, s 2(4).

OTHER DAMAGES

Aggravated and exemplary damages

Aggravated damages were defined in *Rookes v Barnard*,[53] as compensation for injuring the plaintiff's feelings. In other words they depended upon the motives or manner of committing the wrong of the defendant. They would, therefore, be appropriate usually only in cases of assault, or some other form of deliberate infliction of injury. The suitability of an award of aggravated damages was considered in *Kralj v McGrath*.[54] It was stated that it would be inappropriate to introduce the concept of aggravated damages into claims for breach of contract and negligence. In that case it was found that a doctor had treated his patient in a horrific and wholly unacceptable way, but it was held that if aggravated damages were allowed into this sort of case, it would be difficult to keep them out of many negligence cases. Woolf J said:

> If the principle is right, a higher award of damages would be appropriate in a case of reckless driving which caused injury than would be appropriate in cases where careless driving caused identical injuries. Such a result seems to me to be wholly inconsistent with the general approach to damages in this area, which is to compensate the plaintiff for the loss that she has actually suffered.[55]

In the case of *B (A Child) v D*[56] H H J Carter described a very serious case of sexual abuse as 'crying out' for an award of aggravated damages. The child, a girl aged five years at the date of the injury and eight years at the trial, suffered a very serious and violent sexual assault, including vaginal rape and anal penetration, by a family 'friend' in December 1997. She was woken in the middle of the night and suffered appalling injury, in the form of vaginal damage akin to an episiotomy cut, bruising and biting of the body, bruising of the neck and petechial haemorrhaging consistent with attempts at strangulation, and injury to the inside of her mouth consistent with some object having been roughly forced into it.

Unsurprisingly she also suffered from psychiatric problems, namely PTSD, and required prolonged counselling and therapy from a child psychologist. Although, after three years, her recovery was good, the prognosis was that she would never fully recover from the emotional effects of the attack, which would probably adversely affect her future psychosexual development. Furthermore, gynaecological opinion was that the physical injuries would give rise to a long-term future risk of pelvic discomfort and pain on sexual intercourse in adulthood. Nocturnal enuresis became a

---

[53] [1964] AC 1129, HL.   [54] [1986] 1 All ER 54.   [55] ibid, at 61.
[56] [2000] 3 QR, Manchester county court (*Re Duke*, 15 May 1997, *Re M*, 21 April 1997, *Heil v Rankin* [2001] QB 272 and JSB Guidelines, Category 3(B)(b) considered).

continuing problem whereas prior to the attack bedwetting had been only occasional. She also exhibited inappropriately 'flirtatious' behaviour with strangers which medical opinion considered to be attributable to the effects of the attack and which created a risk of vulnerability to inappropriately early sexual experimentation.

The judge, describing the case as the worst of its kind, held that there should be an award of substantial aggravated damages in addition to compensatory damages. General damages of £40,000 were awarded, plus aggravated damages of £20,000.

It should be noted that aggravated damages can be awarded in appropriate cases of employment discrimination. In *Armitage v Johnson*[57] the applicant, who was a prison officer, was subjected to an 18-month campaign of racial abuse. The tribunal, whose decision was upheld by the Employment Appeal Tribunal, accepted that the stress must have been severe, that it had understandably, affected his home life, and that most people would have left the job rather than continue to face up to such harassment. The EAT upheld an award of £21,000 for injury to feelings and £7,500 aggravated damages. Damages in a discrimination case are awarded on normal tort principles but, crucially, to avoid any suggestion that 'mere distress' might not be enough to attract an award of damages, the relevant legislation specifically allows for compensation for injured feelings.[58]

Although the general approach to aggravated damages is that they compensate for injury to feelings, it is important to note the case of *Tchoula v ICTS (UK) Ltd*[59] where it was said that an award for aggravated damages was *not* the same as an award for injury to feelings in a discrimination case. It was said in that case that the award was to compensate for high-handed, malicious, insulting or oppressive behaviour and that an award for injury to feelings could be made in addition to the award for aggravated damages. Furthermore, damages for personal injury itself, ie psychiatric injury caused by the discriminatory treatment of the employee, could be awarded by an employment tribunal as compensation for the statutory tort.[60]

It is suggested that there is scope for the award of aggravated damages for non-consensual sterilizations which, in appropriate cases could reflect the severity of any resulting psychiatric injury. There are a number of cases where women have been sterilized without seeking their consent, usually when undergoing a Caesarean operation and when the surgeon, aware that the woman had a number of children, decided that it would be in her 'best

---

[57] [1997] IRLR 162.
[58] See the Sex Discrimination Act 1985, ss 65(1), 66(1); Race Relations Act 1976, ss 56, 57; and the Disability Discrimination Act 1995, s 8.
[59] [2000] IRLR 643.
[60] *Sheriff v Klyne Tugs (Lowestoft) Ltd* [1999] IRLR 481.

interests' to sterilize her.[61] Such operations, apart from evidencing an extraordinary arrogance on the part of the surgeons concerned, are batteries, and it is suggested that claimants should be awarded aggravated damages in appropriate cases.*

Exemplary damages were not distinguished from aggravated damages until the case of *Rookes v Barnard*, and they have little or no part to play in personal injury cases. They are punitive in nature and are usually considered as punishment for oppressive or arbitrary action by government servants or persons making a profit out of their wrong, which may exceed the compensation payable to the claimant. However, should that action have resulted in psychiatric injury, then it would not be inappropriate to award them, subject to the restrictions placed upon awarding them by *Rookes v Barnard, Cassell & Co Ltd v Broome*,[62] and *AB v South West Water Services Ltd*,[63] which confirmed the unsatisfactory criterion that exemplary damages can be awarded only if the type of tort is one in respect of which an award was made prior to 1964, which does not include negligence.[64]

MITIGATION OF LOSS

The claimant is under a duty to mitigate his loss. What if a psychiatrically injured claimant refuses the necessary medical treatment which may reduce loss? An *unreasonable* refusal (and the burden of proof will be on the claimant to show that it was reasonable to refuse) will mean a reduction in damages to a level which it is deemed would have been appropriate if the treatment had gone ahead and the anticipated degree of recovery had been made.[65] The test of reasonableness is objective: would a reasonable man have refused? It also does not matter whether it is the claimant's own medical adviser or the defendant's adviser who recommends the treatment, although the claimant would certainly want to seek his own doctor's advice before proceeding. However, it must be remembered that with injuries of a psychiatric nature, the refusal of treatment can be part of the condition or can be reasonable simply because the claimant does not wish to relive the trauma. An important finding of the *Herald of Free Enterprise* arbitrations (see page 212) was that it may be reasonable for the survivors to refuse medical treatment.

---

[61] See, eg, *Hamilton v Birmingham Regional Hospital Board* (1969) BMJ 456, *Devi v West Midlands Regional Health Authority*, 9 December 1981, CA. See further Nelson-Jones and Burton, *Medical Negligence Case Law* (London: Fourmat Publishing, 1990).

* Aggravated damages cannot be awarded for discrimination claims in Scottish law (*D. Watt (Shetland) Ltd v Christian Reid* [2001], Scottish EAT.

[62] [1972] AC 1027.   [63] [1993] 2 WLR 506.

[64] See Alan Reed, 'The End of the Line for Exemplary Damages?' (1993) 143 NLJ 929 and the Law Commission's report, *Aggravated, Exemplary and Restitutionary Damages* (Law Com No 247) (London: HMSO, 1997).

[65] See *Morgan v T Wallis Ltd* [1974] 1 Lloyd's Rep 165.

'Compensation neurosis'

The precise meaning of this term (sometimes called 'litigation or accident neurosis') is elusive. Sometimes medical reports state that a claimant's condition is likely to improve, perhaps to the point of complete recovery, once the case is settled. This is often a euphemistic way of saying the claimant is malingering. However, it can be a reference to the inevitable stress of the litigation process, and consequences such as financial hardship, which can inhibit the claimant's recovery, or even exacerbate the claimant's condition. This is particularly likely to be the case in a claim following psychiatric injury. Dr James Thompson at the Middlesex Hospital has researched into post-disaster victims and the effect of the subsequent legal and administrative procedures and found that these procedures exacerbated their injuries.[66] This is no fault of the victim and should not be used as an argument to reduce damages. A report containing such an opinion should not be agreed by the claimant's lawyers unless there is also agreement about precisely what is meant by it. Two cases which deal with this issue are have already been considered: *Lucy v Mariehamns Rederi* (see page 192) and *Malyon v Lawrance, Messer & Co* (see page 131).

Exacerbation of physical injuries

A claimant's physical injuries may be exacerbated by the psychiatric injury that he has suffered. Thus, it is important to identify the psychiatric injury as soon as symptoms become apparent. Damages can be awarded to cover both exacerbation and prolongation of physical injuries.[67]

LEVEL OF DAMAGES

Some key cases

It is well established that judges are free to inform themselves of appropriate levels of damages from any reasonable source.[68] In other words there is no doctrine of precedent in matters of quantum. Naturally, as in any other area of personal injury law, the authorities on quantum set the guidelines for practitioners and the courts. Many would be surprised at the extent of the authorities on cases involving psychiatric injury. Here are reviewed the landmark cases on quantum that have marked the progression towards the point where the fifth edition of the Judicial Studies Board's *Guidelines for*

---

[66] Radio 4 transmission 'Shockwaves', 28 April 1991.
[67] See *Kralj McGrath* [1986] 1 All ER 54.
[68] See, eg, *Waldon v War Office* [1956] 1 WLR 51.

Assessment of General Damages in Personal Injury Cases,[69] now record the following:

(a)	severe psychiatric damage:	£27,500 to £57,500
(b)	moderately severe damage:	£9,500 to £27,500
(c)	moderate damage:	£3,000 to £9,500
(d)	minor damage:	£750 to £3,000

It should be noted that the cases on compensation for criminal injuries considered below are based on the old 1964 scheme before the 'tariff system' was introduced. The assessment of damages was, therefore, based upon ordinary tort principles.

Hinz v Berry[70]

This was the first really significant case on quantum. The plaintiff was picking flowers at the side of the road with one of her children when she saw a car run into the stationary van where her husband and the other seven children (some were the foster children of the couple) were preparing a picnic. Her husband was killed and the children were injured. It was said that she had a robust character, and that but for witnessing the accident she would have stood up well to the bereavement. However, at the trial some five years after the event she was still suffering from morbid depression. The trial judge awarded her £4,000 damages in respect of the depression. The defendant appealed. The Court of Appeal upheld this award, saying that although it was high, it was not wholly erroneous. The duration of the illness was said to make it a very exceptional case. Pearson LJ said:

It should not be for the whole of the mental anguish which she has endured during the last five or six years. It should be only for that additional element which has been contributed by the shock of witnessing the accident, and which would not have occurred if she had not suffered that shock.[71]

In 2001 this award of £4,000 would have been worth £37,700.

Lucy v Mariehamns Rederi[72]

Here, the issue to be decided concerned an anxiety neurosis suffered by the plaintiff and how far this was due to the plaintiff's own intentional actions. The plaintiff was struck by a large quantity of oil in the course of his employment, and, although not physically injured, developed an anxiety neurosis as a result. Despite having suffered no apparent physical injury, the plaintiff complained of it having hurt his eyes. He was sent to an eye specialist who concluded that there was nothing wrong with his eyes. He also

---

[69] London: Blackstone Press, 2000.   [70] [1970] 2 QB 40, CA.
[71] ibid, at 45.   [72] [1971] 2 Lloyd's Rep 314.

found it difficult to sleep; difficult to lie comfortably in bed at night; he felt lethargic, with no interest in household jobs or social activities. There seemed little dispute between the parties that the symptoms, *at some point*, had been genuine, and were still continuing at the trial of the matter, over three years after the accident. The defendant contended that to begin with it had been a genuine anxiety neurosis, but that the plaintiff had recovered from it some six months after the accident. Due to an intentional assumption or exaggeration of symptoms at that time he caused his illness to continue, and this exaggeration had subsequently become part of his make-up and he was incapable of voluntarily reversing it.

The plaintiff had been examined by his psychiatrist some six months after the accident, and had appeared to have recovered, being optimistic about going back to work. Much was made of this at the trial, together with the fact that the plaintiff when first giving evidence had been tearful and trembling, but that this condition improved as the evidence continued, and particularly under cross-examination. Geoffrey Lane J, however, accepted the plaintiff's expert witness's conclusion that his condition deteriorated because when he got back to work he found he could no longer drive a crane, but was relegated to a less responsible job. Geoffrey Lane J also concluded that the plaintiff's condition was due entirely to the result of the accident. This was in part based upon some hesitation on the part of the defendant's medical expert, and in part upon the evidence of both the plaintiff and his wife. The genuineness of the wife's evidence was particularly important: 'I cannot believe that a man like Mr Lucy would, under any circumstances, deliberately inflict that sort of torture on his family'.[73]

Geoffrey Lane J also concluded from the report of the defendant's expert witness that the matter which really caused the anxiety neurosis to continue so long was the very litigation itself, and that within six months he would be fully restored to health.

The damages awarded for pain and suffering were £1,100, some three and a half years after the accident, with a prognosis of complete recovery within six months. The 2001 equivalent of this was £9,400.

Brice v Brown[74]

This is an important case both on remoteness and on quantum. The plaintiff was a middle-aged woman who had suffered from a hysterical personality disorder since childhood. The effect of that disorder upon her life, however, was relatively minor, inasmuch as symptoms were relatively moderate and infrequent, and generally the plaintiff and her family of husband and three children led a happy life. In 1980 she and her daughter were passengers in a taxi which was involved in a collision with an oncoming bus. The plaintiff

---

[73] ibid, at 317.   [74] [1984] 1 All ER 997.

suffered minor injuries only, but her daughter had a very badly cut head, although she recovered quickly from this. Shortly afterwards, the plaintiff became moody, unable to sleep and neglected her household jobs. This gradually became worse; she attempted suicide on a number of occasions and her behaviour became increasingly bizarre, to such an extent that she was admitted to hospital under the Mental Health Act on three occasions.

The plaintiff sought damages for her condition and for the cost of future care. There was no dispute that her illness was genuine, although there was some dispute between the experts as to its precise nature, the defendant contending that it was endogenous depression, unconnected with the accident. On the medical evidence, Stuart-Smith J did not accept this and found that the accident had aggravated and made patent the underlying personality disorder.

It was submitted by the defendant that even if this was the condition, as she had an underlying personality disorder, she did not have a normal standard of susceptibility, and a hypothetical reasonable man could not foresee that the psychiatric results would eventuate. However, it was held that the circumstances of the accident were such that 'nervous shock' might result to a mother of a normally robust constitution, and the fact that the consequences were so much worse than a normal person would suffer was immaterial.

General damages were awarded of £22,500. In 2001 the equivalent would have been £43,940, and is substantial. In view of that here is extracted a substantial part of the description of the plaintiff's illness as given by Stuart-Smith J:

The accident . . . occurred on 2 February 1980. . . .

On 8 February 1980 she consulted a partner of the general practitioner's practice and was prescribed an analgesic, presumably for the chest pain of which she was complaining. . . .

On 1 April 1980 she again consulted a partner in the general practitioner's practice who recorded a reactive depression to a road traffic accident. . . .

The family went for a holiday in Italy shortly after this time but it was not a success. On 28 April she again consulted her general practitioner and different drugs were prescribed. She went again on 2 May. It is quite clear that by this time her condition had reached a somewhat worrying state. She describes seeing or dreaming about evil spirits. She thought she was dying, and she believed she had got cancer. She was prescribed Mogadon for sleeping and anti-depressants. By this time her husband described her condition as very bad. She appears to have thought that both her husband and Julie [a daughter] were trying to poison her. On 29 May she attempted suicide by drinking a bottle of wine after she had taken a large quantity of tablets. There is no reason to suppose that that was anything other than a genuine attempt to take her life. She was admitted to hospital.

. . . the hospital notes indicate violent changes of mood and bizarre behaviour on the part of the plaintiff. The hospital seems to have diagnosed a depressive illness, seemingly brought about by the accident. Towards the end of her stay there she was allowed home at weekends. On 22 June another serious attempt at suicide was made. She was returned to hospital. There appears to have been a further attempt on 30 June. Early in July she was found in a compromising position with a male patient. It seems that she had sexual relations with him. This got back to the plaintiff's husband, who was extremely angry both with her and with the hospital. She appears to have made another, probably this time half-hearted, attempt at suicide, and on 10 July to the evident relief of the hospital she discharged herself. I think they were thankful to get rid of a troublesome patient.

Over the next few months she continued to behave in a most bizarre way. She wandered off for sometimes weeks at a time and sometimes days. She probably behaved like a prostitute in London and elsewhere. She slept rough in the woods and did not take any proper food. The hospital were reluctant to take her back. She was rejected at home for her unsocial behaviour and because her husband, understand-ably I think, thought that she was some sort of moral danger to the girls. On 14 September she was again admitted to the Queen Elizabeth II hospital pursuant to s. 136 of the Mental Health Act 1959, having been found in a destitute state. She remained there until 29 October. The picture again presented by the notes is one of changing moods but on the whole, isolated, sullen, uncooperative, secretive and not taking drugs. The plaintiff's husband described her as being unrepentant, aggressive and like a nasty spoilt child. . . .

On her discharge from the Queen Elizabeth II hospital on the second occasion the plaintiff lived at home. Her husband described her as awful. He said: 'The intensity of crying and screaming got worse; I could not bear it'. On 10 November he came home to find the house in darkness. The plaintiff was in the hall. She had pulled out the main cable where the electricity comes into the junction box in an attempt to kill herself. He found her shaking and she would not let him near her. She was admitted to Hillend hospital following that, under s. 29 of the Mental Health Act 1959. Again her history was taken from the patient and she appears to have related her symptoms to the accident. Her behaviour in hospital as recorded in the hospital notes continued to be bizarre. She was convinced that she was suffering from venereal disease. She certainly had some infection in the genital region but it does not appear to have been venereal disease. The hospital appears to have diagnosed recurrent depression in a neurotic personality following the road traffic accident. She was allowed home over Christmas 1980 . . . she was discharged from Hillend hospital early in January 1981, and since that time she has lived at home. . . .

Since January 1981 her condition has to some extent stabilised though her behaviour remains highly abnormal. Her present state is described by her husband. She spends most of her time in one room. She covers the window with a blanket, and even in the extremely hot weather which we have been experiencing recently she does not open the window and she stays in there, the room being like an oven. In the winter time she is in there nearly all the time. In the summer she will go out for walks in the fields. She goes uninvited into the neighbours' gardens and is often most inappropriately dressed, wearing either a bra and knickers or in hot weather one or two hot jerseys. She is unable to cook or wash her own clothes. She can now take a bath and does bath herself, but until comparatively recently she had to be bathed, and her husband described it in a graphic phrase, 'like bathing a cat'. She has peculiar habits in relation to her toilet. She apparently was reluctant to use the WC and would urinate on the floor . . . she now for the most part uses the bucket. . . . She lives largely on biscuits. . . . She pleads with people in a pathetic way to cut off her head and kill her. She wrings her hands and appears to be miserable a great deal of the time. She seems to want to play with children and continues to do bizarre and inappropriate things like untying the laces of her son-in-law's shoes; but there is no doubt that there has been some improvement. She is no longer vicious or aggressive. She is slightly less reluctant to mix with the family, and she seems to be making some response at last to overtures of affection. But there is no doubt that at the moment she is severely deranged. She needs supervision. She cannot be left alone for long. . . . She has to be cooked for, tidied after, shopped for and have her clothes washed.[75]

This graphic description should leave no doubt that Mrs Brice's damages of £22,500 were not in any way excessive. It is also a fascinating, if harrowing, account of the way in which a relatively minor road accident could reduce a normal life to one so far removed from anything that could be described as satisfactory.

Other cases

The following are summaries of a number of other cases on quantum. Where appropriate the damages have been multiplied to give the 2001 figure.

R v Liverpool City Council[76]
A middle-aged man suffered psychiatric injury following an accident at work when he was struck in the face by chain. He suffered from a lot of debilitating symptoms, including depression, tiredness, poor social function, loss of appetite and sleep function. He was effectively unemployable and there was no treatment to help him. He received £15,000 for the psychiatric injury, Hodgson J commented that awards for this type of injury seemed 'surprisingly low'. (2001 figure: £22,640.)

The 'Marchioness' cases
A number of cases were heard in 1991–2 resulting from the sinking of the pleasure boat, the *Marchioness*, by the dredger, the *Bowbelle*, in the Thames on 20 August 1989 in which over fifty people died. In 1991 the case of Deborah Jane Ross was heard by Master Topley, who received £5,000 damages for PTSD (2001 figure: £6,420). She lost a friend in the tragedy, and was thrown out into the river close to the still turning propeller of the dredger. Some two years later she still suffered from a moderate depressive illness, and had experienced the classic PTSD symptoms. She became dependent upon alcohol. In addition to general damages she was awarded

---

[75] ibid, at 1000–3.   [76] [1989] CLY 1255, QBD.

£1,000 for the 'trauma of the day', but which was not awarded in subsequent cases resulting from this disaster.

Higher damages were awarded to another young woman, Miss Russell, who was awarded £15,000 for her psychiatric injury (PTSD) (2001 figure: £19,270). She had also lost a friend. The severity of her case was said to be close to *Case G* of the *Herald of Free Enterprise* arbitrations (see page 212 below).

Hale v London Underground Ltd[77]

This case concerned one of the firemen involved in the King's Cross fire of October 1987. He suffered little or no physical injury but received general damages for PTSD, described as of 'moderate severity' but from which he would probably never fully recover. General damages: £27,500. (2001 figure: £33,975.)

Waller and Waller v Canterbury and Thanet Health Authority[78]

The plaintiffs alleged negligence on the part of the hospital treating their 20-year-old son. It was said that insufficient precautions had been taken to prevent him from committing suicide. The plaintiffs discovered their son's body hanging by a rope in a disused building on the hospital site. Liability was admitted. Both parents suffered from depressive disorders which caused sleep disturbance, intrusive images, uncontrolled weeping, lethargy and lack of concentration. They were each awarded general damages of £8,500. (2001 figure: £10,500.)

Anderson v Davis[79]

The plaintiff was physically injured in a road accident and also suffered from PTSD and depression. It was found that he had a genetic disposition to manic depressive illness and therefore damages for future loss of earnings were discounted by 15 per cent. His general damages included a sum for physical injury and approximately £20,000 was awarded for the psychiatric injury. (2001 figure: £24,700.)

Tredget & Tredget v Bexley Health Authority[80]

The facts of this case have already been mentioned (see page 108). As a result of the distress caused by the traumatic birth and subsequent death of their son, the plaintiff parents suffered psychiatric illness and a pathological grief reaction, the father being the worst affected. He was awarded £32,500 and the mother was awarded £17,500. (2001 figures: £39,120 and £21,060.)

---

[77] [1993] PIQR Q30.   [78] Quantum, Issue 5/93, 16 September 1993.
    [79] [1993] PIQR Q87.   [80] [1994] 5 Med LR 178.

Vernon v Bosley (No 1) [81]

This case made newspaper headlines because the total amount of damages awarded was over £1 million, and the losses all flowed from a psychiatric injury caused by the plaintiff witnessing the death of his three children when the car in which they were travelling crashed into a river. In a judgment which ran to 262 pages, Mr Justice Sedley said that this was 'every parent's nightmare become a reality'.[82] For the psychiatric injury the plaintiff was awarded £37,500. (2001 figure: £41,470). However, note that there was subsequently a dispute about the medical evidence (see *Vernon v Bosley (No 2)*).[83]

Pucci v Reigate and Banstead Borough Council [84]

The plaintiff, aged twenty-six at the date of the accident and thirty-one at the date of trial, had suffered a fracture dislocation of her left knee, fractures of the weight-bearing surface of the tibia and a rupture of a number of knee ligaments after she had ridden her bicycle into a pothole. She had been an in-patient for three weeks when a staple was inserted and subsequently was in plaster for over two months. She was left with a painful and unstable knee that necessitated the wearing of a brace. As a result of the injuries, she suffered a severe reactive depression resulting in a spell as a psychiatric in-patient for one month. She needed counselling for two years after which it was thought that she should be able to return to work. Her general damages for the psychiatric injury were £7,500 (2001 figure: £9,380). (She received £20,000 for the physical injury.)

De Smet v Gold [85]

The claimant, aged twenty-six at the date of the accident and twenty-eight at trial, had suffered a severe burn of her scalp following bleaching treatment at a hairdressing salon. For one month the wound was open and extremely painful. She was left with a tender bald patch approximately 7 cm in diameter. Five months after the injury she was admitted to hospital for insertion of a tissue expander beneath a section of her scalp adjacent to the bald area. The purpose was to produce new tissue which would be inserted over the damaged area. It was a painful procedure and she was in hospital for five days. Over the next two months she underwent five outpatient 'expansions' sessions which resulted in pain for two days after each session. Further treatment was necessary and she was left with a scarred scalp. She was severely depressed after the injury and in consequence her longstanding relationship broke down. Her sleep was disturbed, she lost weight and had

---

[81] [1997] 1 All ER 577.   [82] at first instance.   [83] [1997] PIQR P326.
[84] [1992] CLY 1711, QBD (H H J Gower, QC).
[85] (1999) 99(1) QR 5, Brighton county court (H H J Lloyd).

no interest in her usual recreational activities. Although not fully recovered at the time of trial the prognosis was that she would make a full recovery. Her general damages for the psychiatric aspects were £2,500 (2001 figure: £2,630). (She also received £10,000 for the physical injury.)

Pearson v British Midland Airways[86]
The plaintiff suffered psychiatric injury following his assistance at the time of the British Midland Airways crash on the M1 at Kegworth in Leicestershire. He was travelling on the motorway at the time and went into the aircraft, where he was the first to arrive and where he stayed for three hours to give first aid and comfort to the survivors, being the only civilian to do so. As a result of the event he developed severe PTSD. The symptoms included intrusive recollections and reliving of events, loss of interest in both his domestic and working life, disturbed sleep, irritability, aggression, loss of concentration, feelings of guilt and physical symptoms such as sweating and dizziness. In particular, he experienced emotional numbing and for a long time refused to acknowledge that he had a problem. Both his domestic and work life deteriorated, and two years after the incident he lost his job due to poor performance. He lost another job when he was unable to continue working after witnessing a motorway accident whilst travelling on business. Nine years after the accident he had received treatment for PTSD and had changed career. His symptoms were significantly reduced and, whilst the prognosis was that he would experience mild symptoms for some years, they would eventually resolve. General damages: £17,000 (2001 figure: £19,320).

Andrews v Secretary of State for Health (Damages Assessments)[87] (also known as *CJD Litigation (No 9)*, *Re Creutzfeldt-Jakob Disease Litigation (No 9)*)
The plaintiff had received treatment with human growth hormone from shortly after his birth in 1966 until 1972. In 1985 he heard that there was known to be a link between this treatment and Creutzfeldt-Jakob disease ('CJD'). Earlier proceedings had established liability. He subsequently became distressed and concerned about CJD and this was a factor in him leaving his job in 1993. In 1994 he began to develop phobias and had difficulty sleeping and symptoms of depression. He was diagnosed as suffering from psychological disturbance and referred for psychiatric treatment. His claim was resisted by the defendant on the basis that he was not suffering from a psychiatric illness. The court found that he was suffering from a psychiatric disorder that went beyond mere anxiety or concern. Although his condition would probably improve with treatment, he was never likely to make a full recovery. General damages: £20,000 (2001 figure: £20,360).

---

[86] [1998] CLY 1530, QBD (Garland J).   [87] (2000) 54 BMLR 111, QBD (Morland J).

James v London Electricity plc[88]

The plaintiff, together with her husband and two children had to be evacuated from their tenth floor flat due to a serious fire. Whilst being evacuated by firemen the family were trapped in a lift for several minutes when it became stuck on descent. J had a vulnerable personality which predisposed her to anxiety and phobias, and a lengthy record of a low-grade anxiety disorder marked by frequent visits to her GP. At the time of the accident, she had not had sexual intercourse with her husband for twenty-one months because of fears about pregnancy and AIDS. However, she had withstood life events such as witnessing her grandmother's death and was a meticulous housewife and mother.

Following the fire, J and her family were forced to relocate. The fire caused a direct and immediate onset of PTSD, depression and severe obsessive compulsive disorder. The PTSD was intense for about a year. During that time, J's husband left her. She was completely unable to care for her children and eventually moved with them into her mother's home. She experienced frequent flashbacks, nightmares, fears of a foreshortened future, disturbed sleep, lethargy and tearfulness, could not be left alone and was often unable to attend her counselling appointments. Following psychiatric referral and treatment with paroxetine, the plaintiff's PTSD and depressive symptoms had improved markedly a year after the incident. However, eighteen months after the accident, she was still experiencing flashbacks at a rate of about two a week, continually wrung her hands, was neglectful of her appearance and low in mood. She became phobic about dirt and contamination, as a result of which she wore gloves for some months; had irrational fears of AIDS, blood and the colour red; and was overprotective about her children's safety and cleanliness. Those symptoms improved significantly within three and a half years of the accident, and further improvement was expected with a course of cognitive behavioural therapy and the assistance of a psychiatric nurse. The accepted prognosis was that her remaining symptoms would largely resolve within a further two to three years. However, she would always be more vulnerable to future life events. General damages: £24,000 (2001 figure: £25,600).

Greenwood v Newalls Insulation Co Ltd[89]

The plaintiff, who was aged sixty at trial, had been exposed to asbestos for two years from the age of twenty-four when working at NIC's premises. G developed asbestos-related pleural plaques which were diagnosed in early 1994 when G was about fifty-six. The agreed medical evidence was that the pleural plaques were asymptomatic, but G complained of chest pain and

---

[88] [1998] CLY 1528, Central London county court (H H J Zucker QC).
[89] [1999] CLY 1538, Sunderland county court (H H J Walton).

shortness of breath which he attributed to asbestos exposure. There was a 2 per cent risk of G developing pleural disease sufficient to cause a disability; a 1 per cent risk of asbestosis; a 3 per cent risk of mesothelioma, and a 1–2 per cent risk of lung cancer. G had also developed a psychiatric illness as a result of the diagnosis of pleural plaques and perceived that all his physical problems were due to asbestos. The illness was characterized by depression, poor sleep, lack of enjoyment of life and a fear that he was going to die. General damages: £16,000 (2001 figure: £16,830).

Lynn Howarth v Philip Green [90]
The claimant engaged the defendant to perform stage hypnosis for one hour to raise money for charity. Consent of the local authority which was required by the Hypnotism Act 1952 was not obtained. The defendant asked for volunteers, one of whom was the claimant. They were asked to imagine that they were children. The claimant claimed that the defendant negligently caused her to regress to the age of eight and to recall deeply buried memories of sexual abuse. She claimed that, in consequence, she suffered a depressive illness for a period of eighteen months to two years. General damages were agreed at £6,500.

Mizon v Comcon International Ltd [91]
The plaintiff, aged fifty-five at the date of injury and sixty-two at trial, was an engineer working on a merchant vessel when the engine exploded whilst at sea, trapping him in the flaming engine room. He suffered full-thickness burns to the face, hands and forearms. Skin grafts were carried out from donor sites on the thighs and calves. Three further operations were carried out on his hands to relieve contractures over the following years. At the date of trial, his hands remained severely scarred and clawed, such that he had difficulty in carrying out most everyday tasks. The facial scarring was not obvious, but he was very self-conscious of his hands and arms and would not wear shorts because of the visible donor sites. Within six months, he was diagnosed as suffering from PTSD with mixed anxiety and depression. The latter developed into a fixed phobic anxiety of fire and being trapped indoors. He was taking sleeping tablets and occasionally anxiolytic drugs and analgesics. He became dependent on alcohol and short-tempered with no interests and few friends. He got no benefit from counselling, the prognosis was poor and he was unfit for work. The judge found that this was within the severe category of the JSB Guidelines for PTSD with his life severely affected by anger and phobia of fire. The award for general damages comprised £28,000 for psychological injury (2001 figure: £28,500) (£15,000 for loss of hand function and £12,000 for scarring).

---

[90] LTLPI, 1 June 2001.
[91] [2000] CLY 1641, Kingston upon Hull county court (H H J Bowers).

Corner v Osment[92]

The claimant, aged forty-eight at the date of the accident and fifty-one at trial, was involved in a road traffic accident and sustained bruising to his left lower leg, subungual haematoma leading to the temporary loss of his big toe nail, other bruises and contusions and shock. A polyarthritic condition had led to his retirement from school teaching before the accident. A few days after the accident, he developed neck pain which was diagnosed as cervical spinal whiplash (C5/6 and C6/7) with an exacerbation of a previously subsided crico-thyroid injury. The neck pain significantly affected his daily activities, including watching television. He also suffered from PTSD and anxious depression. He suffered from nightmares and flashbacks of the accident, continued to suffer headaches for a while, and there were some uncharacteristic episodes of uncontrollable aggression. He was prescribed a large number of drugs, including sleeping pills, relaxants and pain killers, and he saw numerous specialists. A psychiatrist said of him that his 'neat, methodical, punctual, approach to life has made it more difficult for him to adjust to the effect of the accident' and that he had an 'eggshell personality with extensive psychosomatic problems prior to the index episode'. Despite some improvement there was a possibility of them continuing indefinitely. The judge took account of a possibility of further expenditure on investigation and treatment which C was still undergoing at trial, and applied Guidelines 3(A)(c) and 3(B)(c) of the JSB Guidelines for the psychiatric injuries, awarding him £4,000 (£7,250 for the physical injuries).

Elderbrant v Cape Darlington Ltd[93]

The plaintiff, aged forty-nine at the date of trial, had worked for the defendant as a lagger between the ages of sixteen and twenty-six. He was exposed to asbestos in the course of his work which involved feeding asbestos into a limpet-spraying machine, mixing up asbestos and applying it to pipes and boilers, cutting sections, making mattresses and occasionally delagging. He was diagnosed as having a pleural plaque, a 10 per cent risk of developing mesothelioma, a 5 per cent risk of developing lung cancer, a 5 per cent risk of developing asbestosis and a 1 per cent risk of developing pleural thickening. As a result of the knowledge that he had an asbestos-related disease he developed a significant psychiatric reaction due in part to the fact that his father, uncle and grandfather had worked as laggers and had all died from asbestos-related conditions. The symptoms included becoming bad tempered and irritable, sleep disturbance, impaired concentration and losing interest in hobbies and in his social life. He was undertaking cognitive therapy with a clinical psychologist and it was anticipated that he would

---

[92] [2000] CLY 1565, Brentford county court (H H J Edwards).
[93] [2000] CLY 1652, Newcastle upon Tyne county court.

need an immediate course of some twenty sessions and thereafter approximately one session every two months until the age of fifty-five. Damages were opted for on a final basis, and were awarded for his psychiatric condition and for the risks of contracting further asbestos-related diseases. General damages: £20,000. An award of £2,800 was made for future psychiatric counselling costs.

Terry v Sands Farm Country House Hotel[94]

This case is interesting for the fact that no psychiatric evidence was given. The plaintiff, aged thirty-two at the date of the accident in August 1997 and thirty-three at trial, was on holiday at a hotel when a waitress spilt scalding water over her lap and left forearm. She suffered superficial burns to both legs and her arm, which subsequently formed large blisters, which wept and burst. She was confined to bed for one week, and suffered limited mobility for a further two weeks. She was pregnant at the time of the accident and suffered anxiety about the health of her unborn child, heightened by vaginal bleeding one week after the accident. Her pregnancy also meant that she was only able to take limited analgaesia for the treatment of what were extremely painful injuries. She was acutely aware of the presence of the residual scars and, although no psychiatric evidence was adduced, it was apparent that she had also suffered psychological trauma as a result of the accident which was still present at trial, manifesting itself as anxiety, intrusive thought and hypervigilence, improvement of which was again anticipated in due course. General damages were awarded of £5,500 for the physical injury and £2,000 for the psychological sequelae.

Pearson v Central Sheffield University Hospitals NHS Trust[95]

The claimant, aged thirty-eight at the date of a sterilization procedure and forty-two at the hearing, had at the date of the procedure, a grown-up daughter from her first marriage and two surviving children from her second marriage. There was a fourth child from her second marriage, who had died a cot death in March 1989. The claimant was psychologically vulnerable generally, but particularly after the cot death, up to which time she had worked part time. After the cot death, she suffered problems with alcoholism and, when she discovered she was pregnant again in early 1995, she made a difficult decision, being a practising Roman Catholic, to undergo a termination procedure and at the same time sterilization. In November 1995, she discovered she was pregnant yet again and from that time she suffered an adjustment disorder throughout pregnancy, worrying about her new baby. Following the birth, she was diagnosed with severe post-natal depression,

---

[94] [2000] CLY 1643, Telford county court (District Judge Weston).
[95] [2001] 1 QR 8, Sheffield county court (Recorder Keely).

confusing her new daughter with her deceased daughter. It was agreed that by December 1997 she was back to her pre- pregnancy state, aside from residual anxiety which the judge put down to fear of becoming pregnant again, despite resterilization in March 1999, as well as litigation stress. General damages: £8,500 for psychological injury (£4,500 for physical consequences of pregnancy).

Gibbens v Wood[96]

This is a case where an unspecified 'psychological' condition was compensated in a sum in excess of that awarded for the physical injury. The plaintiff, aged nineteen at the date of the road traffic accident and twenty-three at trial, sustained soft-tissue injuries to his lower back, soft-tissue injuries to his neck which resolved after ten days, bruising to his shoulder, knees and right thigh, which settled over four weeks, and a scar to his right thigh. He was off work for seven days and was unable to pursue his hobby of weight training for six weeks. He suffered psychological symptoms for eighteen months as a result of the accident, including headaches, intrusive thoughts, flashbacks, mood and sleep disturbance and travel anxiety. The judge found that, while the psychological symptoms stopped short of PTSD, he was entitled to be compensated in respect of them. General damages were awarded of £3,000 for the psychological injury (£2,250 for the orthopaedic injuries).

Streeting v Hogg Robinson plc[97]

The plaintiff, aged forty-eight at the date of the road traffic accident and fifty-five at trial, sustained a fracture of the sternum and a neck injury in a head-on collision. The symptoms of the neck injury were continuing at trial and were considered permanent. He had been off work for three months and then returned to full-time employment in the Prison Service. In addition, the plaintiff, who had a history of depression, suffered from PTSD from the time of the accident and was troubled by invasive thoughts of the head-on collision and near-death experience. By the date of trial it had been agreed that he suffered from PTSD arising out of the accident. Whilst he had been able to work for almost three years after the accident and had carried out his job effectively, the effect of the PTSD and subsequent adjustment reaction and depression led him to retire on the grounds of ill health caused by depression. The judge found that the plaintiff was a truthful witness who had not exaggerated the effect of the accident upon his symptoms. He had worked all his life without periods of unemployment up to the date of the accident, notwithstanding that he had a history of depression, which was under control. The judge found the claimant had enjoyed his work for the

---

[96] [2000] CLY 1671, Plymouth county court (District Judge Corrigan).
[97] [2001] 7 CL 183, Norwich county court (H H J Barham).

Prison Service and, but for the accident, would have continued in that employment. In assessing general damages, the judge stated that he was discounting the level of damages for the psychiatric injury to take account of the plaintiff's pre-existing depression and was adjusting the future loss of earnings claim from a multiplier of 3.98 to 3, again to take account of the risk of him being unable to continue work to the age of sixty because of his pre-existing depressive illness. General damages for psychiatric injury were £20,000. (£10,000 was awarded for the physical injuries and an award of £45,810 was made for future loss of earnings.)

Haseley v Morrell [98]

The plaintiff, aged twenty-one at the date of the accident and twenty-five at trial, was involved in a multiple car road traffic accident. She had to be cut from the wreckage of her car. She suffered whiplash-type injuries to her neck and back, PTSD, depressive disorder to a moderate or severe degree, soft-tissue injury to the right knee with some scarring, damage to the patella of the left knee with some scarring, mild temporo mandibular joint dysfunction of the jaw and general cuts and bruises. Orthopaedic evidence indicated permanent pain and restriction of the cervical and lumbar spine, although at trial the pain had resolved greatly from the level it was in the weeks and months immediately after the accident. Psychiatric evidence suggested that the PTSD would resolve with treatment over a period of two years as would the depressive disorder. That disorder was aggravated by the fact that she had had to give up working with horses, which career had been a lifetime ambition. The right-knee symptoms resolved within a matter of months but the scarring remained visible at the date of trial. The left knee was diagnosed with chondromalacia patellae causing stiffness and pain along with intermittent locking. Symptoms were unlikely to improve in the future. The jaw injury had resolved by the date of trial save for the odd clicking sound. At the date of the accident she had just obtained the job she wanted and after the accident did her utmost to make a success of it. She failed because of the injuries suffered. She said in evidence that the accident had ruined her life. General damages included £4,000 for the psychiatric damage.

Wilson v Hall [99]

The plaintiff, aged twenty at the date of the road traffic accident and twenty-three at trial, sustained an injury to her left foot, a bang to her nose and seat-belt bruising. She had two weeks off work. After her return, she found it painful to walk on her left foot and an x-ray revealed a healing

---

[98] [2001] 9 CL 158, Telford county court (District Judge Weston).
[99] [2001] 12 CL 153, Norwich county court (H H J Coleman).

fracture of the second metatarsal. No particular treatment was prescribed. At trial, three and a half years after the accident, W still experienced intermittent aching and discomfort in the foot. There was also a slight resultant deformity in the second toe. Both were likely to be permanent. W also suffered a psychological reaction to the accident. This manifested itself in tearfulness, sleep disturbance and irritability for a period and in nervousness in cars, particularly as a passenger. These symptoms had completely cleared within eighteen months to two years of the accident. The psychiatric evidence was that these symptoms at no stage amounted to PTSD, but did constitute a marked psychological reaction to the accident with situational anxiety in relation to car travel. For the psychological injury she was awarded general damages of £1,750.

Children cases

Spittle v Bunney [100]

The plaintiff, then aged just over three, had been standing on the pavement with her mother when a van driven by the defendant mounted the pavement and killed the mother. The plaintiff was slightly injured. Subsequently the child had lived with her maternal aunt who had treated her like her own child. After the accident the child was detained in hospital overnight and was discharged the following day.

There was some minor injury to her hand, but the major injury from the accident was emotional. Her aunt gave evidence about the child's immediate reaction to the death of her mother. She would not eat or drink. She would wake screaming and crying, and had difficulty in going back to sleep. She lost control of her bladder and bowels. For the first year and a half after the accident her behaviour was disturbed. Her condition was dealt with in two agreed psychological reports. There was no doubt that she was intelligent, but she would not in the early days mix with other children at school and was therefore socially isolated. By the time of the second report, when she was ten years old, the report was as follows:

Kate's behavioural and sleep problems have been settled for the last two years although she is still unable to deal with small problems on her own. She is a steady, sensible, loving and helpful child whom the Spittles enjoy very much. However, for her age, she does still need an extra bit of security and confidence boosting from time to time. Kate can still feel insecure when subjected to any kind of change or stressful situation but the Spittles are able to handle these occasions by providing her with extra support. [101]

---

[100] [1988] 1 WLR 847, CA (Croom-Johnson, Dillon and Woolf LJJ).   [101] ibid, at 851.

The trial judge awarded £5,000 (2001 figure: £8,170) general damages for the psychological effects and £3,000 for the physical injury. The defendant appealed both awards. The Court of Appeal upheld the appeal in respect of the physical injury, but in respect of the psychological effects the award of £5,000 was left undisturbed. The court held that the emotional or psychological damage was not of a kind which fitted readily into a bracket of damages, and that no comparable case had been referred to.

S (A Minor) v Hearnshaw [102]

The plaintiff was a male aged four at the date of a road traffic accident and nine at trial. He suffered minor physical injuries, including cuts and bruises to the right side of his body, particularly the face, elbow, lower leg and ankle. He suffered PTSD with severe symptoms for two years during which time he was doubly incontinent, lost his appetite and suffered temporary growth retardation. He had difficulty sleeping, suffered nightmares and tiredness on days after he had not been able to sleep properly. He developed anti-social behaviour, becoming spiteful, possessive and prone to tantrums. He became withdrawn, had difficulty interacting, had a reduced attention span and was prone to dreaming. His educational achievement suffered and he was registered as a child with special needs. After two years his condition improved but he had ongoing symptoms of sleeping difficulties, problems with peer relationships, some lack of concentration and mild traffic phobia. He was expected to go on suffering difficult peer relationships through adolescence and he would be vulnerable to stress, otherwise his symptoms were expected fully to resolve within seven to eight years of the accident. Although painful and distressing at the time, the physical injuries soon resolved without any lasting damage. The judge found that in light of Spittle v Bunney (considered above), the JSB Guidelines did not adequately cover cases of traumatized children. General damages: £9,500 for the psychiatric injury (2001 figure: £9,990) (£1,000 for the physical injuries). This case might be a particular interpretation of Spittle v Bunney inasmuch as the Court of Appeal seemed to be suggesting that there was no comparable case at that time.

C (A Patient: Dependency) v Ewin [103]

The plaintiff, aged ten at the date of the road traffic accident in which his father was killed and his mother seriously injured, and fifteen at trial, suffered only minor physical injuries and was not detained in hospital. His mother's injuries resulted in epilepsy and a changed personality. She came to rely heavily on the plaintiff for emotional and practical support, despite the fact that his maternal grandparents were heavily involved in looking after

[102] (1999) 99(5) QR, Mayor's and City of London Court (H H J Byrt).
[103] [2000] CLY 1520, QBD (infant settlement approved by District Judge Holloway).

his mother. This meant moving to a different town and school, and the child became depressed and distressed over the death of his father and, as he saw it, effectively the death of his mother as he had known her, due to the severity of her change of personality. He became upset when trying to talk about his father. He suffered from repetitive thoughts and nightmares about the accident and was nervous at first when travelling by car. There were indications of a PTSD. Over a period of about two years his mental state improved. He did well at school and coped with caring for his mother and his other interests, including football and his pets. He largely overcame his emotional state over the accident and was found to cope well with the responsibility he had assumed in helping to care for his mother. General damages: £11,000 (agreed and approved).

C v Flintshire CC (formerly Clwyd CC) [104]

The local authority appealed against an award of damages of £70,000 which included £35,000 for pain, suffering and loss of amenity resulting from sexual, physical and emotional abuse inflicted upon the plaintiff when she was a child in care. The court dismissed the appeal and held that the JSB Guidelines for the assessment of damages for psychiatric harm resulting from abuse were not directly applicable in cases of abuse of children in care. The most significant element of the damage was the extent to which the abuse compounded a pre-existing condition. The JSB Guidelines took no account of the duration of the abuse and suffering. Accordingly, the trial judge had been entitled to consider the Guidelines for awards for severe and moderately severe cases of psychiatric harm and to conclude that they were, in fact, guidelines only.

J (A Child) v Reid [105]

The child, aged three at the date of the road traffic accident and five at the child settlement hearing had no physical symptoms but suffered from minor psychological trauma in the form of anxiety. He was tearful for a few weeks and experienced increased bed-wetting for approximately six months. The district judge stated that despite the fact that this was an injury with no physical symptoms, but purely minor psychological trauma, an award was appropriate. General damages: £500 (agreed and approved).

Employment cases

Lancaster v Birmingham City Council [106]

The plaintiff worked for the city council from 1971 and until 1993 she was employed in various jobs which involved little contact with the general

---

[104] [2001] EWCA Civ 302, CA (Ward, Buxton, Henry, LJJ).
[105] [2001] 11 CL 155, Brighton county court (District Judge Jackson).
[106] (1999) 99(6) QR 4, Birmingham county court (Assistant Recorder Kirkham).

public. In 1993, however, she was transferred to work as a housing officer in a Neighbourhood Housing Office, where she was required to deal with difficult people. She was promised training which never materialized and she commenced a number of periods of absences from April 1994 until February 1997 when her employment ended in early retirement on the ground of ill health. She had developed a severe anxiety state with depression, and had received both cognitive therapy and medication under the care of hospital psychiatrists. The medical prognosis was that she would eventually be able to undertake work of an undemanding nature. General damages: £12,000 (2001 figure: £12,550).

Cowley v Mersey Regional Ambulance Service NHS Trust [107]

The plaintiff, a deputy director of operations, aged thirty-six at the date of injury and forty-four at trial, suffered severe agitated depression in September 1993 as a result of an excessive workload and stress due to insensitive handling by his chief executive. Following psychiatric treatment, including anti-depressants, he returned to work in January 1994 as a training and quality manager rather than to his original post. The new role was designed to be less stressful but in September 1994 he developed a second major reactive depression as a result of further stress and harassment. He was described as being very ill and required a course of seven ECT treatments. Although there were episodes of improvement, his progress was variable and in late 1995 he had been unable to complete a benefit claim form. At trial, he continued to suffer from a lack of concentration, raised irritability and impaired confidence. He had not resumed employment, was still taking anti-depressants, and his prognosis was described as uncertain. The judge concluded that the employer was primarily liable but that the plaintiff would, at some stage, have succumbed to the serious depression which befell him and held that that would have been six years after the onset of the second illness. Therefore, he awarded general damages and loss of earnings both of which were limited to a six-year period. General damages: £15,000.

HM Prison Service v Salmon [108]

HM Prison Service appealed against the level of compensation awarded to a former prison officer, following a finding that the Service had been guilty of sex discrimination in a number of respects. The tribunal had awarded £15,000 for psychiatric injury, discounted by 25 per cent on the basis that the illness was caused in part by the applicant's pre-existing vulnerability. In addition, £20,000 was awarded for injury to feelings, which included £5,000 by way of aggravated damages, and more than £45,000 in respect of

---

[107] [2001] 9 CL 161, Liverpool county court (H H J Douglas Brown).
[108] [2001] IRLR 425, Employment Appeal Tribunal.

lost earnings. The main grounds of appeal were that the £15,000 general damages was excessive and that the behaviour of HM Prison Service and its employees had not amounted to aggravating conduct and, in any event, separate awards for psychiatric damage and injury to feelings had resulted in double recovery.

The appeal was dismissed firstly on the basis that the illness fell within the category of 'moderately severe psychiatric damage' as defined by the JSB Guidelines. The fact that a victim had a pre-existing vulnerability to injury did not necessarily mean that the level of compensation should be automatically discounted nor was it an irrelevant factor. The tribunal had made no error of law in making a broad-based assessment of the relevant discount and there had been ample evidence before it to justify a reduction of 25 per cent. The Employment Appeal Tribunal also rejected the second ground on the basis that the Prison Service's impression that it viewed some of the behaviour of its officers as trivial justified the making of an award for aggravated damages. An award of £20,000 was not excessive when the discriminatory acts were viewed within the context of other incidents. Although the tribunal had not expressly considered the possibility of double recovery, it could not be said that the award was excessive when viewed as a whole (*Tchoula v ICTS (UK) Ltd*[109] applied).

Fasipe v London Fire & Civil Defence Authority [110]

The applicant, a male, Afro-Caribbean VDU operator and computer programmer, sought compensation from his employer after a finding that he was suffering from chronic adjustment disorder, complicated by a major depressive illness following a finding of race discrimination. His relationships with friends and family had been seriously disrupted and, despite medical help, his condition had failed to improve. He would be vulnerable to any situation which would trigger recollection of the discrimination. He would not be able to work on a part-time basis for two years, and it would be three years before he could return to full-time work. This was dependent upon him receiving treatment and retraining. The tribunal applied the JSB Guidelines for psychiatric damage and classified the applicant's injury as severe psychiatric damage. He was awarded £25,000 for injury to feelings (including aggravated damages) and £40,000 for personal injury. Other awards were for loss of pension rights, cost of medical treatment, loss of pension rights and loss of past and future earnings, cost of re-training and a *Smith v Manchester* award of £30,000.

[109] [2000] ICR 1191.
[110] [2001] CL 132, Employment Tribunal (G H K Meeran, Regional Chairman).

Vento v Chief Constable of West Yorkshire Police (No 2) [111]

The employment tribunal had found that a female police officer had been the victim of bullying, unwarranted criticism and sexual harassment. The award consisted of £165,829 for loss of future earnings, £65,000 for injury to feelings, including £15,000 for aggravated damages, £9,000 for personal injury and £18,015 for interest. The Employment Appeal Tribunal found the loss of earnings to be too high but, significantly, also regarded the overall award of £74,000 for injury to feelings, personal injury and aggravated damages as too high. The most relevant authority was *Armitage & Others v Johnson*,[112] (see above) following which the appropriate awards were £25,000 for injury to feelings and £5,000 for aggravated damages.

D Watt (Shetland) Ltd v Christian Reid [113]

The applicant was found to have been subjected to bullying and mistreatment. It was said that he had been treated in a male stereotypical fashion: On the one hand he had been expected to deal in competent fashion with a female colleague who had threatened him with a knife, but, on the other hand, to take seriously her complaint that when she had so threatened him, he had been verbally abusive. He had been found to be a particularly loyal employee who had suffered distress, humiliation, psychiatric injury and the breakdown of his relationship with his fiancée. The tribunal had awarded him £7,500 for injury to feelings and £2,500 for aggravated damages, on the grounds that no apology had been forthcoming and that there had not even been a response to his complaint to the tribunal. The Scottish Employment Appeal Tribunal had found that the tribunal had been entitled to take a very high view of the reliability and credibility of the applicant and that £7,500 was not sufficiently disproportionate, but aggravated damages could not be awarded under Scottish law, and the award of £2,500 was quashed.

Long v Mercury Communications [114]

The claimant had been employed as a senior manager by Mercury Communications. Over a long period of time he had been subjected to a vendetta by his superior at work and had suffered from an adjustment disorder with mixed anxiety and depressive reaction. Liability was admitted and the issue before the court was quantum. The judge found that the claimant, aged 48 at the time of the hearing, would never be able to return to senior management, although he accepted medical evidence that, over a two or three year period, he would be able to return to work in a less senior capacity. It was said that the claimant's ability to cope with life and work had

---

[111] [2002] IRLR 177, Employment Appeal Tribunal.　　[112] [1997] IRLR 163.
[113] 2001, Scottish Employment Appeal Tribunal.
[114] [2002] PIQR Q1, QBD (H H J Anthony Thompson QC sitting as a High Court judge).

been severely impaired; the relationship with his family had been damaged. His former employer had subjected him to a fair measure of humiliation. It was agreed by both counsel that the claimant's case fell within the moderately severe category of psychiatric damage as set out by the Judicial Studies Board. General damages were set at £20,000. He was also awarded damages for future loss of earnings and pension and a sum to cover the cost of cognitive behaviourial therapy.

THE *HERALD OF FREE ENTERPRISE*
ARBITRATION AWARDS

These arbitrations examined psychiatric injury in some detail and assessed damages in ten test cases. On 6 March 1987, the *Herald of Free Enterprise*, passenger and freight ferry, which had just left Zeebrugge harbour, capsized, resulting in chaos and panic. Out of the 600 or so people aboard, some 193, both passengers and crew, lost their lives. Some people witnessed the deaths and injury of loved ones, in terrible physical conditions. Many survivors spent hours in the water, not knowing whether they would be rescued. It was a traumatic event of enormous magnitude.

Many passengers entered into a compensation agreement which included an arbitration clause for the resolution of disputes arising under the agreement.

In many cases the parties were unable to agree levels of damages for 'nervous shock'. It was agreed that a selection of cases should be dealt with by arbitration before a panel of three Queen's Counsel. Ten cases were chosen as a representative sample. Almost all of the claims for physical injuries and special damages in the ten cases were resolved by agreement. The principal interest of the arbitrators in making their awards therefore related to the claims for psychiatric damage. Under the agreement each claimant received a fixed payment of £5,000 for having been involved in and having witnessed the events of the day of the disaster. This payment was disregarded by the arbitrators in assessing their awards for psychiatric damage suffered in the days after the capsize. Where survivors had also suffered the loss of relatives who died in the capsize there were fixed payments under the agreement of £5,000 to each survivor for each relative lost. Sums payable under this paragraph of the agreement were disregarded by the arbitrators when assessing damages for pathological grief. With regard to fatal accident claims there were fixed payments to the personal representatives of each deceased passenger in respect of bereavement and a further £5,000 to the estate of each deceased passenger in respect of pre-death injury, pain and suffering in addition to the usual claims for the dependants.

The arbitrators were Sir Michael Ogden QC, Michael Wright QC (now Mr Justice Michael Wright), and William Crowther QC. The award was made in February 1989.

The following passages are extracted from the reasons given by the arbitrators.

Nervous shock

The respondents have conceded that all the claimants suffered nervous shock. This rather odd legal phrase does not connote shock in the sense in which it is often used in ordinary conversation. In *McLoughlin v O'Brian* [1983] 1 AC 410 at p 431 Lord Bridge said this of nervous shock:

The basic difficulty of the subject arises from the fact that the crucial answers to the questions which it raises lie in the difficult field of psychiatric medicine. The common law gives no damages for the emotional distress which any normal person experiences when someone he loves is killed or injured. Anxiety and depression are normal human emotions. Yet an anxiety neurosis or a reactive depression may be recognisable psychiatric illnesses, with or without psychosomatic symptoms. So, the first hurdle which a plaintiff claiming damages of the kind in question must surmount is to establish that he is suffering, not merely grief, distress or any other normal emotion, but a positive psychiatric illness.

Post-Traumatic Stress Disorder ('PTSD')

While the respondents conceded that all the claimants suffered from nervous shock, it was necessary for us to consider the nature of the illness from which each claimant suffered, mainly because identification of the nature of the illness enables conclusions to be drawn about prognosis in most cases.

The arbitrators then described the features of PTSD, and continued:

Many of the Zeebrugge victims undoubtedly suffered from PTSD; of course, some victims suffered from some other psychiatric illness, eg, depression, at the same time.

We are asked by the claimants to make a finding that DSM III R contains a suitable guide to diagnosis of PTSD. The reason for this request is that claims from other victims are outstanding and it is desired to use findings made in this award when dealing with the outstanding cases. While we are anxious to be as helpful as possible to the parties, we do not feel able to be as dogmatic about this point as the claimants would wish us to be because points may arise in outstanding cases which have not arisen in this arbitration. Furthermore, PTSD is a very recent concept and, just as DSM III was revised in 1987, further research and experience may necessitate revision in the future. When considering the cases involved in this arbitration there did not appear to be much dispute that, in very general terms DSM III R contains a useful guide to diagnosis provided that it is not construed as a statute, but more a document which gives a guide to diagnosis. In particular, it seemed to us that passages concerning time of commencement or duration of symptoms were unduly arbitrary. We do not feel able to say more than this.

Some of the claimants lost one or more relatives in the disaster and suffered from what is termed 'pathological grief' or 'pathological mourning'. This, too, is a recognised psychiatric illness and in non-medical terms can be said to be grief the extent and duration of which is in excess of normal grief reaction.

This has posed extremely difficult problems of an obvious nature. As Lord Bridge said in the passage already quoted, a person is not to be compensated for normal grief. However, a person is to be compensated for pathological grief. 'Normal' grief varies widely between one individual and another.

Gauging the extent to which a claimant's suffering is from grief which that claimant would have suffered is a task which is enormously difficult and cannot be undertaken with any degree of precision. In each case, we have had to estimate the extent to which the claimant's grief is in excess of the normal grief which the claimant would have suffered had the death occurred in ordinary circumstances and compensate the claimant accordingly. Obviously, this can be done only in a very rough and ready fashion; the more so, since in all these cases there is another form of illness present.

The duration of the illness

The arbitrators considered the question of prognosis as follows:

Unhappily, some of the claimants continue to suffer to a significant degree. However, in all cases improvement is probable. This is not to say that the victim will ever forget the experience or that painful intrusive thoughts will cease. Plainly, that is impossible. However, in such cases the improvement will reach a point at which it can be said that, in spite of remaining intrusive thoughts etc., the victim is no longer suffering from psychiatric illness. Since compensation for nervous shock is compensation for psychiatric illness, it is the period until illness ceases which is compensatable. This has to be assessed, as is everything else, on a balance of probabilities and, for obvious reasons, the estimate approaches being the useful but nasty word a 'guesstimate'.

However, in reaching our conclusions, we have borne in mind that most, if not all, prognoses are guarded in cases in which a claimant is still *ill*. Counsel for the claimants has urged us to bear in mind that, quite apart from the guarded nature of the prognosis, very understandably, some claimants are reluctant to undergo treatment, which involves recollecting the distressing circumstances of the disaster, and may balk at undergoing such treatment. We have no hesitation in accepting this argument.

Vulnerability

The arbitrators also considered the risk of future problems:

An injury to a limb leaves it vulnerable. It is the same with psychiatric problems. All the claimants will be at risk of further illness in the face of stress which would not have affected them or would have affected them less but for their Zeebrugge experience.

This is a factor which must be taken into account when assessing compensation. Following a serious head injury, there is often a risk of epilepsy and an award of damages takes account of that risk. Our awards do likewise in respect of vulnerability to future psychiatric troubles. In our view, it is an important factor which must be borne in mind in each case, although more so in some cases than in others.

Assessment of damages

In considering their awards of damages the arbitrators said:

In 1970, in *Hinz v Berry* [1970] 2 QB 40, Lord Denning MR said there were only two cases in which the quantum of damages for nervous shock had been considered and Lord Pearson said that he thought it was the first case in which the Court of Appeal had considered the problem.

Although counsel have gone to great trouble in assembling a comprehensive list of reported cases of damages for nervous shock, the number of such cases is comparatively small. More important, counsel agreed that no clear guidelines can be discerned in the reported cases.

In these circumstances, our assessment must be based not upon consideration of the cases to which our attention was directed but also upon consideration of how each claimant's illness compares with cases in which damages were awarded for physical injuries.

In undertaking this task, we must record our appreciation for the very considerable help given to us by the doctors who gave evidence. It was fortunate both for us and the parties that, plainly, they are of the very highest calibre and competence.

Summary of the main findings of the arbitrators

    (a)   PTSD is a recognized psychiatric illness.

    (b)   Many Zeebrugge victims suffered PTSD.

    (c)   The DSM–III R is a useful guide to diagnosis.

    (d)   Pathological grief is a recognized psychiatric illness in excess of normal grief.

    (e)   Some survivors suffer from other psychiatric illnesses such as depression and it is possible to suffer from more than one psychiatric illness.

    (f)   It may be reasonable for survivors to refuse to undergo treatment for psychiatric damage.

    (g)   Account should be taken in individual cases of any vulnerability to future psychiatric illness.

Case A

A 22-year-old single woman with some pre-existing fear of water. Civil servant. All her party survived. After 24 hours, reaction set in and she wept uncontrollably for two or three days. For several months she had a fear of water so intense that she could not take a bath without someone present to encourage her. She suffered PTSD for about nine months, with nightmares, loss of appetite, loss of libido, feelings of guilt and intrusive thoughts about the capsize. She constantly relived the accident in her mind. In July 1987, psychotherapy was recommended but not taken up. While her fear of water led her to cancel a trip to Sweden in 1987, in 1988 she was able to fly to Corfu and enjoy her holiday although she did not swim. She had received no treatment. The arbitrators found that for practical purposes she had entirely recovered by September 1988. Her physical injuries included bruising to her chest, back, right leg, arm, hands and left index finger. At the site of the bruising on her leg she had developed an irritable skin condition although with treatment the prognosis was good.

Total compensation £9,135.75 made up as follows:

Fixed payment	£5,000.00	(2001: £7,550)
Psychiatric injuries	£1,750.00	(2001: £2,640)
Physical injuries	£1,250.00	
Special damages	£1,135.75	

There was no award for loss of future earnings or earning capacity.

Case B

A 41-year-old married woman. All her party survived. By nine months after the accident she described symptoms of PTSD which were said by the medical experts to be 'moderately severe' and she was said to be 'moderately depressed and anxious'. She was described as 'cheerful and coping' by November 1988 and had been able to resume work as a cashier. Her principal persisting symptom was an unwillingness to be parted from her husband even for short periods to such extent that she had obtained work at the same place as him. However, treatment was advised and the arbitrators found that with treatment she should be back to normal within about twelve months. She had sustained lacerations of her left hand with damage to the tendons in the ring and little fingers and to the digital nerves, ruptured ligaments of the left thumb and multiple contusions including a probable contusion of the right kidney. The left wrist and thumb were in plaster for three weeks and in August 1987 she underwent tendon graft under general anaesthetic when her hand was put in plaster for twelve weeks. She was left with some slight scarring disability and restriction of movement in the hand.

Total compensation £20,160.82 made up as follows:

Fixed payment	£5,000.00	
Psychiatric injuries	£3,000.00	(2001: £4,530)
Cost of treatment for psychiatric injuries	£ 750.00	
Physical injuries	£8,250.00	
Special damages	£3,160.82	

There was no award for loss of future earnings or earning capacity.

Case C

A 22-year-old single man. He and his travelling companion both survived. He was employed as a recreation assistant at swimming baths and was hoping to progress to a career in recreational management. He suffered from 'quite severe' PTSD in the months immediately after the incident and his consumption of alcohol increased substantially. By November 1988 the symptoms were said to be of 'moderate severity' and consumption of alcohol had reverted to pre-accident level. The arbitrators approached the case on the basis that it was one of moderate psychiatric damage lasting for about three and a half years. He had to give up his job which he greatly enjoyed and was now a chauffeur for a car-hire firm which gave him very little job satisfaction. The arbitrators took into account that at present he was not suffering any loss of earnings or loss of leisure because he was working about the same hours as before and earning slightly more but he had lost his chance of promotion within his chosen career which would have brought higher earnings for shorter hours. The arbitrators thought it likely, however, that once his psychiatric symptoms had abated he would find more congenial and remunerative employment. He had no physical injuries.

Total compensation £21,728.30 made up as follows:

Fixed payment	£5,000.00	
Psychiatric injuries	£4,000.00	(2001: £6,040)
Loss of chance of	£2,000.00	
increased leisure and		
potential loss of earnings		
Actual loss of earnings	£7,309.84	
Special damages	£3,418.46	

There was no award for loss of future earnings or earning capacity.

Case D

A long-distance lorry driver travelling alone, married and aged 42. He suffered severe PTSD involving anxiety, sleeplessness and nightmares, sweating attacks and phobias of water and the sea. The sight of plate-glass windows or the sound of children crying caused him to think of the capsize. He had become severely depressed, irritable and aggressive. In the early stages he was drinking to excess but this problem had now resolved. His level of smoking had also greatly increased and remained high. He found his work as a long-distance driver distressing because it meant he was on his own for a great deal of the time and on such occasions his mind dwelt on the capsize. He had therefore changed to work within the depot. It is highly unlikely that he will ever return to his old job. Because of his condition his marriage had come under serious strain. The doctors agreed that he would benefit from a period of regular psychiatric help for his anxiety states coupled with specific treatment for depression. Although he was naturally resistant to such treatment the arbitrators found that with the support of his wife he would undergo treatment and that over the next twelve to eighteen months he was likely to make a substantial improvement. Everyone accepted that over the last two years his illness had operated at a very severe level and had greatly exacerbated his vulnerability to stress for the foreseeable future. He had also suffered bruising and whilst acting as a rescuer in the capsize he had strained both his shoulders as a result of hauling on ropes. These had caused significant discomfort for some three months and he was still having some features of painful arc syndrome in his right shoulder. He had also strained both wrists and suffered some discomfort in his back.

Total compensation £21,580.00 made up as follows:

Fixed payment	£5,000.00	
Psychiatric injuries	£8,500.00	(2001: £12,835)
Physical injuries	£2,500.00	
Special damages	£ 580.00	
**A loss of future earnings/ earning capacity	£5,000.00	
	£21,580.00	— plus interest to be calculated

**This was awarded because the arbitrators accepted that he now had to work longer and harder hours in less congenial employment to maintain his former level of earnings and that if he should give up or lose his present job his range of possible jobs would be restricted because he could not return to long-distance driving, but that suitable alternative work could be found by his employers who were a large organization.

Case E

A 38-year-old divorced woman with a teenage daughter (who was also a survivor) living at home. She had been travelling with her mother to whom she was very close and who was killed in dramatic circumstances. The mother's body was not recovered until it was washed ashore some three weeks after the capsize. There was a difference of opinion between the doctors whether she was suffering from an abnormal grief reaction or from hysterical disassociation as a defensive mechanism. It was accepted that either she was suffering from or would suffer from pathological grief and that hysterical dissociation, if present, was designed to protect her feelings of unusually severe grief. She took a great deal of time off work, had had counselling sessions and some in-patient treatment. In addition to her grief reactions she was still suffering from 'classic and severe PTSD' which had been unremitting since the accident, and depression which had greatly improved so as no longer to be pathological. She was hoping to move home soon in which event the prognosis was that within a further year from the move she would be back at work. She would need regular counselling and treatment for depression as an outpatient for one year. She was always likely to be vulnerable to stress but she had very considerable job security as a civil servant so that the likelihood of her losing her job was remote in the extreme. In addition she had suffered generalized cuts and bruising.

Total compensation £30,774.07 made up as follows:

Fixed payment	£ 5,000.00	
Psychiatric injuries	£ 7,500.00	(2001: £11,325)
Cost of future treatment for psychiatric injuries	£ 1,000.00	
Physical injuries	£ 400.00	
Loss of earnings to date	£ 4,398.89	
Future loss of earnings	£ 4,463.43	
Fixed payment for loss of relative	£ 5,000.00	
Special damages	£ 3,011.75	
	£30,774.07	— plus interest to be calculated

Case F

A married man aged 41 years. His wife and two friends were killed in the capsize. He had developed chronic PTSD. In particular he was hypersensitive to unexpected noises and suffered panic attacks when faced with reminders of the capsize such as a 10-minute boat trip. His sleep was frequently disturbed and he had become irritable and impatient. He had suffered a profound pathological grief reaction. The arbitrators found that 'every aspect of his everyday life has been affected by the fact that she (his wife) is no longer with him'. There was a discount in respect of the grief which he would have suffered if his wife had died in more ordinary circumstances. He was having difficulties with concentration and was thus afraid about the loss of his job in a managerial position. Out-patient treatment was recommended for twelve to eighteen months after which he should have achieved a substantial degree of recovery. He would remain vulnerable to stressful incidents for the foreseeable future. By way of physical injuries he suffered a chest infection which required hospital treatment, multiple bruises and grazes, localized numbness in both heels and discomfort in the right shin. He had also suffered 40 per cent loss of hearing in the left ear and tinnitus due to vascular damage as a result of stress. This had been diagnosed as Menieres Disease giving rise to a 10 per cent risk of bilateral hearing loss. A 'tullio' phenomenon had also been diagnosed which is a startle reaction to veer off (in this case to the right-hand side) on hearing a loud noise. He had also suffered some vertigo.

Total compensation (which does not include the fatal accident claim in respect of his wife's death) £41,042.94 made up as follows:

Fixed payment	£ 5,000.00	
Psychiatric injuries	£ 7,500.00	(2001: £11,325)
Cost of treatment for psychiatric injuries	£ 1,000.00	
Physical injuries	£20,000.00	
Further fixed payment for loss of relative	£ 5,000.00	
Special damages	£ 2,542.94	
	£41,042.94 — plus interest to be calculated	

The arbitrators made no award for loss of earning capacity on the basis that he had managed to continue working in a sophisticated and highly competitive environment during the period since the capsize and therefore was not under any real disadvantage in respect of his earning capacity.

Case G

A divorced lady aged 34 who had been living with a man for some three years before the capsize in which he was killed. His body was not recovered until the vessel was righted on 7 April 1987. She was said to have been one of the most severely affected of the survivors with whom the doctors had been concerned and to have had a 'terrible two years'. She was subject to mood swings, being tearful, miserable and very depressed with suicidal thoughts, and she had been drinking to excess. She had become withdrawn and isolated from her friends, was very reckless about her own safety and was found to be suffering from 'a severe depressive illness'. She had occasional out-patient sessions with a psychiatrist which had not produced much improvement. She needs intensive supportive psychotherapy on a weekly basis for at least twelve months in which case there was a reasonable prospect of getting her 'on her feet' within eighteen months from the arbitration. She would quite possibly find herself in stressful situations in the future and being sensitised to further disaster might well have serious problems in the future however successful the short-term treatment may be. The arbitrators found her to be one of the claimants most vulnerable to further problems both in the near and more distant future. She had been in responsible and taxing work as an international auditor which she had to give up. She was now hoping to start a small business. If all went well she would in about four and a half years be back to earning as much as she would have earned but for the accident. Her actual loss over that period would be £36,000 but there was a real risk that because of her psychiatric condition the business would fail which would cause both psychiatric and financial problems.

The arbitrators held that they had to make an appropriate allowance for the very substantial risk of unforeseen difficulties. She had also suffered bruising around her midriff and on the legs.

Total compensation (which did not include the fatal accident claim in respect of her co-habitee) £98,333.00 made up as follows:

Fixed payment	£ 5,000.00	
Psychiatric injuries	£15,000.00	(2001: £22,650)
Physical injuries	£ 400.00	
Loss of earnings to date	£21,557.00	
Loss of future earnings/ earning capacity	£50,000.00	
Fixed payment for loss of relative	£ 5,000.00	
Special damages	£ 1,376.00	
	£98,333.00	— plus interest to be calculated

Case H

A 14-year-old boy travelling with his family. His mother and elder brother were killed. His father and sister survived. In September 1987 he was diagnosed as suffering from chronic PTSD and prolonged depressive adjustment reaction. By June 1988 he was severely depressed and at times suicidal. His schooling was disrupted by non-attendance. He was still depressed and suffering from PTSD at the time of the arbitration and the arbitrators found him to be 'severely disturbed'. The prognosis was 'quite good' in that with proper in-patient treatment for six to eight weeks with continuing outpatient care he would be 'on his feet' in eighteen months to two years. The arbitrators hoped for a 'very substantial recovery' but found a significant risk that treatment would not be successful and he would still be vulnerable to relapse. Before the capsize the claimant was probably of 'A' level ability and might with very hard work have obtained university entrance. With treatment he was expected to return to full-time education but there was a significant risk that he would not and would therefore have no academic qualifications. Even if he went back to his studies and recovered most of his pre-accident potential he would be a late starter with a good deal of catching up to do. He would be permanently vulnerable to stress and would have to avoid jobs of a particularly stressful nature. Even if he avoided such jobs he would be vulnerable to relapse and consequent periods of unemployment. He suffered the following physical injuries:

(a) avulsion of the transverse processes from his first, second, third and fourth lumbar vertebrae on the right side. There was acute pain initially which subsided after about one month and thereafter continued at a reduced level for a further two months or so. He continued to have pain on stressing his back but the prognosis was good. However it was unlikely that transverse processes would fuse again at their fracture site which could create problems if he had to do a lot of lifting. His earning capacity is thus further impaired. He had been advised against participating in sports such as athletics, rugby or football. There would be permanent disability as he would tend to get aching in his lumbar spine particularly after heavy use;

(b) severe bruising in the area of the kidneys. He had an intra-venous urogram to which he had an allergic reaction such that he almost died;

(c) a urinary tract infection;

(d) he developed eczema of both hands and thighs, and it was likely that stress following the disaster had been a factor in producing the disorder. Although there has been improvement, prognosis is uncertain;

(e) generalized cuts and bruises.

Total compensation £102,453.00 made up as follows:

Fixed payment	£ 5,000.00	
Psychiatric injuries	£ 20,000.00	(2001: £30,200)
Cost of treatment for		
psychiatric injuries	£ 8,000.00	
Physical injuries	£ 7,500.00	
Future loss of earnings/		
earning capacity	£ 50,000.00	
Fixed payments for loss of		
relatives	£ 10,000.00	
Special damages	£ 1,953.00	
	£102,453.00	— plus interest to be calculated

Case I

A married man aged 26 whose wife and four-month-old daughter were travelling with him. He and the baby survived but his wife was killed. He was an enlisted soldier but was discharged in July 1988 as no longer medically fit for service. He had formed an intense relationship with his wife and the army. Having lost both he was now 'on his own and totally lost'. He drank and smoked heavily. By December 1988 he was still profoundly depressed with a high level of anxiety and instrusive obsessional thoughts. With treatment, recovery would take at least another two years and this was optimistic. He was, however, extremely resistent to treatment which was symptomatic of his condition. Without successful treatment and without regaining some motivation in life the outlook was gloomy. With successful treatment he would have had 'four to five years of severe disability'. He had suffered a contusion of the chest and two fractured ribs with some contusion of the underlying lung and one episode of haemophysis (coughing blood). He continued to experience aching in his chest when carrying out heavy work or during inclement weather.

Total compensation (excluding fatal accident claim in respect of his wife) £148,571.12 made up as follows:

Fixed payment	£ 5,000.00	
Psychiatric injuries	£ 15,000.00	(2001: £22,650)
Physical injuries	£ 2,250.00	
Loss of earnings to date	£ 8,000.00	
Loss of future earnings/ earning capacity/ Army pension rights	£109,500.00	
Fixed payment for loss of relative	£ 5,000.00	
Special damages	£ 3,821.12	
	£148,571.12 — plus interest to be calculated	

Case J

A 54-year-old married man working as a tractor driver at a main line railway terminal. His mother, wife, daughter and 10-month-old grandchild (all of whom had lived in the same household with him) were killed. The emotional and psychological impact of the disaster had been 'catastrophic'. He suffered from a depressive illness, pathological grief and severe PTSD. He had suicidal thoughts and had become a heavy drinker and smoker. He was receiving in-patient treatment at the time of the arbitration. The arbitrators found him to be demoralized, bitterly unhappy and depressed and at present totally unable to reconstruct his life. He would never be able to work again. The prognosis was extremely gloomy. Over a period of up to five years with treatment he may become 'more comfortable' in his daily life and may be able to take up some hobby or interest to occupy his mind. His present grief, depression and anxiety would always be with him to some extent. He was the worst of all the survivors the doctors had seen. He was suffering from a pathological grief reaction but the arbitrators 'bore in mind' that anyone who suffered the loss of four relatives would be likely to suffer considerable grief and that they had to assess the extent to which his reaction exceeded that which would be expected after the death of four relatives in other circumstances. He also suffered a hand injury, a whiplash injury of the cervical spine, an injury to the right elbow and an injury to the right middle finger. He has some continuing discomfort in his neck. His right elbow was stiff and would not straighten properly and he had intermittent triggering of the right finger. He had difficulty lifting weights such as suitcases, and stretching up and doing DIY jobs.

Total compensation (excluding fatal accident claims for deceased relatives) £151,114.27 made up as follows:

Fixed payment	£ 5,000.00	
Psychiatric injuries	£ 30,000.00	(2001: £45,300)
Physical injuries	£ 5,500.00	
Loss of earnings to date	£ 19,026.00	
Future loss of earnings	£ 65,880.00	
Cost of DIY	£ 2,000.00	
Fixed payment for lost relative	£ 20,000.00	
Special damages	£ 3,708.27	
	£151,114.27—plus interest to be calculated[115]	

[115] The *Herald of Free Enterprise* arbitrations first appeared in the *Personal and Medical Injuries Law Letter*, published by Legal Studies & Services, June 1989.

8

Practical Steps

Many detailed accounts are available of the intricacies of practice and procedure,[1] and the following is not intended to be a comprehensive account. Rather, it aims to deal with those issues which may possess special features in a psychiatric injury case.

[1] See, eg, I S Goldstein and M R de Haas (eds), *Butterworths Personal Injury Service* (London: Butterworths, 1999) and John M Pritchard and N Soloman, *Personal Injury Litigation*, 9th edn (London: Longman, 1999).

LIMITATION

Time limits for bringing legal proceedings are governed by the Limitation Act 1980. The limitation period for personal injury claims is set out in section 11. The period is three years from the accrual of the cause of action, or three years from the date of knowledge, whichever is later. According to section 14 of the 1980 Act, the date of knowledge is the time when a plaintiff first has knowledge of the following facts:

(a)   that the injury in question was significant; and

(b)   that the injury was attributable in whole or in part to the act or omission which is alleged to constitute negligence, nuisance or breach of duty; and

(c)   the identity of the defendant; and

(d)   if it is alleged that the act or omission was that of a person other than the defendant, the identity of that person and the additional facts supporting the bringing of an action against the defendant.

By section 14(2), an injury is 'significant' if the person whose date of knowledge is in question would reasonably have considered it sufficiently serious to justify instituting proceedings for damages against a defendant who did not dispute liability and was able to satisfy judgment.

It was stated in *McCafferty v Metropolitan Police District Receiver*[2], that the test of significance is partly subjective (did this claimant consider it significant?), and partly objective (was it reasonable for the claimant not to regard it as significant?). It is clear on the test that 'significant' does *not* mean serious, and that quite minor injuries would pass the test.

Section 14(3) of the 1980 Act provides that a person's knowledge includes knowledge which he might reasonably have been expected to acquire:

(a)   from facts observable or ascertainable by him; or

(b)   from facts ascertainable by him with the help of medical or other appropriate expert advice which it is reasonable for him to seek;

but a person shall not be fixed under this subsection with knowledge of a fact ascertainable only with the help of expert advice so long as he has taken all reasonable steps to obtain (and, where appropriate, to act on) that advice.

Though not having actual knowledge, a claimant may be deemed to have constructive knowledge. The word 'knowledge' should be given its natural meaning.[3] It has been held that the test of constructive knowledge is subjective; in other words at what date would *this claimant* have taken advice about his condition, rather than at what date would the reasonable person

---

[2]   [1977] 1 WLR 1073, CA.

[3]   *Davis v Ministry of Health*, The Times, 7 August 1985, CA.

have taken advice.[4] Whether the particular claimant can pass this test will depend upon the circumstances. The knowledge concerned will only be knowledge of facts, and not law. The effect of this is that if the claimant does seek advice from a non-legal expert, for example, a doctor, and is advised that he or she is not suffering from any illness, then the claimant cannot be said to have knowledge of the illness but advice from a lawyer that there is no claim in law would not have the same effect. Time can begin to run before the claimant has knowledge that is detailed enough to enable the legal advisers to draw a statement of claim. In a medical negligence case in the course of a surgical operation, a person alleging negligence is fixed with knowledge that starts the clock running when he knew or could have known, with the help of medical advice reasonably obtainable, that the injury had been caused by damage resulting from something done or not done by the surgeon concerned.[5]

There are many factors which may prevent a claimant realizing that he is suffering from an illness, and in many cases this is entirely understandable. People are often positively discouraged from assuming they have a psychiatric injury. The doctors treating organic injuries may be full of optimism for an early and a complete recovery, and a patient who does not wish to dispute this will almost certainly be held to be reasonable.

The provision of the 1980 Act giving the court discretion to disapply the time bar is equally important. Section 33(1) states as follows (emphasis added):

If it appears to the court that it would be *equitable* to allow an action to proceed having regard to the degree to which —

(a)   the provisions of section 11 (personal injuries) or 12 (fatal accidents) of this Act *prejudice the plaintiff* or *any person whom he represents*; and

(b)   any decision of the court under this subsection would *prejudice the defendant* or any *person whom he represents*;

the court may direct that those provisions shall not apply to the action, or shall not apply to any specified cause of action to which the action relates.

It is a question, therefore, of balancing the prejudice to each of the parties. It is important for the claimant to show that he has a good arguable case, and for the defendant to show that the delay has made the defence more difficult. The court has unfettered discretion,[6] and it is *not* limited to exceptional cases.[7]

This section would be relevant in, for example, cases where the plaintiff did know of his illness, but through, say, fear of treatment, was unwilling to obtain the appropriate psychiatric examination, or, *because of his condition*, was unable to take the necessary steps to get proceedings off the ground.

[4] See *Newton v Cammell Laird & Co (Shipbuilders and Engineers) Ltd* [1969] 1 WLR 415.
[5] *Broadley v Guy Clapham & Co* [1994] 4 All ER 439, CA.
[6] *Conry v Simpson* [1983] 3 All ER 369, CA.   [7] *Firman v Ellis* [1978] QB 886.

It is important not to confuse section 11, which is about when the plaintiff knew of a cause of action, and section 33, which is about the court's discretion to disapply the time bar *even when there is the relevant knowledge*, as they are entirely independent of one another and apply different criteria.

There are many different circumstances in which an apparent time bar may be lifted, and it is always worth looking at the Act's provisions to see if there is a possibility of doing so. The interpretation of limitation in multi-party actions was considered by the Court of Appeal in the case of *Nash v Eli Lilly & Co.*[8] It was held that there was no difference between the court's discretion in an ordinary individual action and a multi-party action, the cases had to be considered individually. It was also held that the weakness of a case was a relevant consideration as it might be prejudicial and inequitable to allow a dilatory claimant to claim in settlement a sum which would reflect the risk in costs to the defendants rather than the fair value of the claim, and it was said that 'knowledge' for the purposes of section 14 of the 1980 Act imported a state of mind of sufficient certainty that the claimant would be reasonably justified in embarking on the preliminaries to making a claim for compensation, and once that knowledge was gained it could not be lost. In *Dobbie v Medway Health Authority*,[9] the Court of Appeal disallowed the plaintiff's application for discretion under section 33. In 1973 she had been admitted to hospital to have a lump removed from her breast for diagnostic purposes only. When she came round from surgery, she was horrified to discover that the whole of her breast had been removed. She suffered psychiatric injury as a result of this. After surgery, the hospital tested the removed tissue and found that the lump was benign. It was not until fifteen years later, in 1988, that the plaintiff discovered that her breast should not have been removed before the tissue had been tested. The court held that the plaintiff had knowledge within the meaning of section 14(1), Sir Thomas Bingham MR said:

The personal injury on which the plaintiff seeks to found her claim is the removal of her breast and the psychological and physical harm which followed. She knew of this injury within hours, days or months of the operation and she, at all times, reasonably considered it to be significant. She knew from the beginning that the personal injury was capable of being attributed to, or more bluntly was the clear and direct result of, an act or omission of the health authority. What she did not appreciate until later was that the health authority's act or omission was (arguably) negligent or blameworthy. But her want of that knowledge did not stop time beginning to run.[10]

The court denied her application for discretion under section 33, Sir Thomas Bingham MR concluding his judgment:

---

[8] [1993] 1 WLR 782.   [9] [1994] 4 All ER 450.   [10] ibid, at 458.

I approach this aspect on the basis that the plaintiff is a grievously injured woman who has suffered much and whose claim, if allowed to proceed, might prove to be very strong. But the delay in this case, after the date of actual knowledge is very lengthy indeed. The plaintiff could have taken advice and issued proceedings before she did. Sympathetic though anyone reading these papers must be to the plaintiff, it would in my judgment (as in that of the judge) be unfair to require the health authority to face this claim arising out of events which took place so long ago.[11]

However, Dobbie was distinguished in *Spargo v North Essex District Health Authority*.[12] Here, the damages claimed were for personal injury arising from a misdiagnosis which resulted in the plaintiff being compulsorily detained in hospital. The question arose as to whether she had the requisite knowledge within the meaning of section 11(4). The defence claimed that her firm belief that her condition was attributable to misdiagnosis was sufficient to establish actual knowledge. Collins J disagreed and held that the claim was not time-barred because she had no actual knowledge until an expert confirmed the link between the misdiagnosis and the mental condition which constituted the personal injury.

The question of the prejudicial effect on the parties if discretion were exercised under section 33(1), was considered in *Hartley v Birmingham City District Council*.[13] The reason for delay in issuing proceedings was the fault of the claimant's solicitors who issued proceedings one day out of time. The Court of Appeal held that the only proper question for the judge to ask himself in exercising his unfettered discretion under section 33(1) was whether it would be equitable to allow the action to proceed. Where the defendant had been presented with a cast iron but windfall limitation defence, this was a factor to be taken into account along with the fact that allowing the action to proceed would not affect the defendant's ability to defend the action. It is significant that this was a case strong on its facts.

The case of *Stubbings v Webb*[14] concerned a plaintiff who applied to the court pursuant to section 11(4)(b), contending that the limitation period had not begun to run until she had the requisite knowledge under the Act that the injury she had received was 'significant'. The injury was psychological damage caused by childhood sexual abuse by her adoptive father and brother. The Court of Appeal held that although she knew, probably within three years of her majority, and certainly knew more than three years before issuing the writ, that she had suffered a significant impairment of her mental condition, such that it would have been reasonable to issue proceedings, she did not know (nor could she reasonably be expected to know) that the

---

[11] ibid, at 459.   [12] [1996] 7 Med LR 219.   [13] [1992] 2 All ER 213.
[14] [1993] AC 498.

impairment was attributable to the defendant's acts of sexual abuse. She had sued within three years of acquiring that knowledge.

However, the House of Lords upheld the defendant's appeal, holding that the discretion afforded by section 11 to extend or refuse to apply the limitation period in personal injury actions did not apply to actions for intentional trespass to the person. It followed, therefore, that in this case, the causes of action were subject to a six-year limitation period suspended until she attained her majority (by virtue of section 28 of the 1980 Act). The period had expired many years before she issued her writ, and there were no provisions for extending this period. Her actions were, therefore, statute-barred.

The case was taken to the European Court of Human Rights on the basis that this decision violated her right to access to a court under article 6(1) of the European Convention on Human Rights and also violated her right to a private life under article 8. As far as article 8 was concerned the court unanimously held that criminal sanction against child abusers discharged the state's obligation to protect the right to respect for private life, and, by seven votes to two, that although article 6 did include the right to bring civil actions, the state could limit that right for a legitimate reason as long as the limitation was proportionate, which it was here. There was also argument under article 14 (no discrimination in the application of the Convention rights, here articles 6 and 8), that had the injuries been negligently caused there would have been a discretion to admit the claim. The court, by eight votes to one, rejected this argument as the applicants could not be said to be in an analogous position to those bringing actions in negligence as different considerations applied to each type of claim, and that even if they were comparable, different treatment of the two claims might be justifiable. This is an unsatisfactory decision. For example, an allegation of battery in, say, a medical negligence action where the appropriate consent was not obtained to a surgical procedure, would be subject to the fixed six-year limitation period, with no discretion to extend.

In cases of, for example, exposure to contamination which *may* result in injury on the part of the 'worried well' (see page 134 onwards), there is no mechanism to stop the limitation clock. In a multi-party action courts may impose a cut off date by which claims should be made. Claimants in such a case may have to rely on a liberal interpretation of section 33 discretion to bring their claims at a later date. In the USA the increasing use of class actions is being developed to obtain from the court, a certified class of 'future victims' who are as yet unidentified, but for whom a compensation fund is established by the defendants.[15]

---

[15] See, eg, *Re Agent Orange Product Liability Litigation* 597 F Supp 740 (EDNY 1984).

DELAY AFTER ISSUE OF PROCEEDINGS

Once proceedings have been issued, and throughout the pre-trial process, it is open to the defendant to make an application for the action to be struck out for failure to comply with procedural matters or dismissed for want of prosecution. The application to strike out can be made when there has been inexcusable delay in complying with the time limits imposed by the County Court Rules or the Rules of the Supreme Court in respect of the various steps that have to be taken, such as complying with the automatic directions imposed by CPR part 29. There is some dispute as to whether delay will be sufficient to warrant striking out only if the limitation period has already expired. It is generally thought that striking out before the expiry of the limitation period would be fruitless as the plaintiff would merely commence a further action, but in *Janov v Morris*,[16] it was stated that if a plaintiff fails to comply with a peremptory order without explanation and the action is struck out, then it is within the court's discretion to strike out a second action on the same cause brought within the limitation period.

In *Hannigan v Hannigan*[17] the Court of Appeal held that technical errors should not be penalized when it was clear that the defendant knew the precise nature of the claim and that the overriding objective would be best furthered by the defendant pointing out the procedural defects so that they could be remedied.

Striking out can take place in the case of unmeritorious claims and for inexcusable delay. In *Biguzzi v Rank Leisure plc*[18] the Court of Appeal held that an action should not be struck out when a lesser sanction would be appropriate. Delay is that which is materially longer than that which the courts and lawyers are accustomed to, and delay is inexcusable when it is caused by the plaintiff and/or his advisers. Delay which is due to the non-culpable behaviour of the claimant ascribable to a medical condition is not inexcusable and should be explained by reference to the opinion of medical advisers.[19]

In medical negligence cases, the court will be concerned that the hospital and/or the doctors should not have a case hanging over them for many years; this may be regarded as prejudicial in certain circumstances.[20]

It is possible for a split trial to be ordered if there is likely to be delay because prognosis is a problem, or if the claimant is undergoing a long

---

[16] [1981] 2 WLR 1389.   [17] [2000] 2 FCR 650.   [18] [1999] 1 WLR 1926.
[19] See *Birkett v James* [1978] AC 297, HL.
[20] See *Biss v Lambeth, Southwark and Lewisham Area Health Authority (Teaching)* [1978] 1 WLR 382 (delay of over 11 years, action struck out). Cf *Westaway v South Glamorgan Health Authority*, CA, 9 June 1986, where the action was not dismissed after 10 years because the delay, though inordinate and inexcusable, was not prejudicial.

course of therapy the result of which it is desirable to know before considering quantum. All that needs to be shown is that it would be just and convenient if liability were tried first, and then, if the claimant is successful, for quantum to be considered at a later date. This could be advantageous for the defendant in circumstances where it is felt that liability may prove difficult for the claimant to establish, but where quantum may involve costly expert evidence. The application is made by summons in the normal way. In certain cases it may be more appropriate to ask for provisional damages (see page 175).

In *James v Woodall Duckham Construction Co*[21] the Court of Appeal held that where a plaintiff in an action for damages in respect of personal injuries receives a medical report to the effect that his pain and suffering was caused by neurosis and will disappear when the action is disposed of, he is under an obligation to proceed with the action expeditiously, and will not be able to recover damages in respect of a period of unreasonable delay.

DISCLOSURE OF DOCUMENTS

Claims for psychiatric injury employ the usual mechanisms for disclosure of documents, The Personal Injury Pre-action Protocol encourages voluntary disclosure of those documents which would be likely to be subject of an order for disclosure, either pre-action or by disclosure during the course of the proceedings. It is worth looking at disclosure of medical records in some detail here as they can have great significance. There are two main areas to consider. First, there is access by the claimant to his own medical records and secondly, there is access by the defendant to the claimant's records.

The claimant will certainly require his own records if pursuing damages for psychiatric injury in a medical negligence claim, as, unless the negligence was blatant, it is almost impossible to assess the prospects of success without sight of the relevant medical and nursing notes, x-rays, reports and correspondence. The claimant may also require these documents to rebut allegations from the defendants or to substantiate or clarify susceptibility to psychiatric injury.

If disclosure has not been made and is required before commencement of proceedings, as in a medical negligence claim, there are two possible routes: an application to the court pursuant to section 33 of the Supreme Court Act 1981 (or section 52(2) of the County Courts Act 1984), or reliance upon the Data Protection Act 1998, which is subject to limitations, eg if disclosure might cause serious physical or mental harm.

The conditions which need to be satisfied under sections 33 or 53 are: the respondent to the application is likely to be a party to subsequent

---

[21] [1969] 1 WLR 903.

proceedings; the applicant is likely to be such a party; the document or classes of document would be disclosable in accordance with standard disclosure if proceedings had commenced, and pre-action disclosure is desirable in order to either (a) dispose fairly of the anticipated proceedings; (b) assist the dispute to be resolved without proceedings; or (c) save costs.[22]

It is up to the potential claimant to satisfy the court that an order for pre-action disclosure is likely to assist in disposing of the matter fairly or be a saving on costs, but it is not necessary to show that the claimant already has a good cause of action.[23]

In medical negligence cases, it is common for the health authorities to give voluntary disclosure, upon receipt of details of the allegations of negligence to be made in accordance with the pre-action protocol on clinical negligence which contains detailed guidance on the supply of medical records, as follows:

OBTAINING THE HEALTH RECORDS

3.7   Any request for records by the **patient** or their adviser should—

- provide sufficient information to alert the healthcare provider where an adverse outcome has been serious or had serious consequences;
- be as specific as possible about the records which are required.

3.8   Requests for copies of the patient's clinical records should be made using the Law Society and Department of Health approved **standard forms** (enclosed at Annex B), adapted as necessary.

3.9   The copy records should be provided **within 40 days** of the request and for a cost not exceeding the charges permissible under the Access to Health Records Act 1990 (currently a maximum of £10 plus photocopying and postage).

3.10   In the rare circumstances that the healthcare provider is in difficulty in complying with the request within 40 days, the **problem should be explained** quickly and details given of what is being done to resolve it.

3.11   It will not be practicable for healthcare providers to investigate in detail each case when records are requested. But healthcare providers should **adopt a policy on which cases will be investigated** (see paragraph 3.5 on clinical governance and adverse outcomes reporting).

---

[22] Civil Procedure Rules 1998, r 31.

[23] See *Dunning v United Liverpool Hospitals Board of Governors* [1973] 1 WLR 586, CA, and *Shaw v Vauxhall Motors Ltd* [1974] 1 WLR 1035, CA, in which latter case it was also held that before the summons is issued a letter before action should be sent to the party against whom the order is sought, setting out the documents which are required and the reasons why they are relevant.

3.12   If the healthcare provider fails to provide the health records within 40 days, the patient or their adviser can then apply to the court for an **order for pre-action disclosure**. The new Civil Procedure Rules should make pre-action applications to the court easier. The court will also have the power to impose costs sanctions for unreasonable delay in providing records.

3.13   If either the patient or the healthcare provider considers **additional health records are required from a third party**, in the first instance these should be requested by or through the patient. Third party healthcare providers are expected to co-operate. The Civil Procedure Rules will enable patients and healthcare providers to apply to the court for pre-action disclosure by third parties.

Sometimes it is not possible to give anything other than the most basic allegations, but this should not defeat an application for pre-action disclosure if voluntary disclosure is not forthcoming. 'Fishing expeditions'[24] are not encouraged, but it must be remembered that the purpose of the application is to assess a case before litigation, and the claimant and his adviser will not be expected to enter into complex medical argument at that stage. It must also be understood that few medical experts will offer any opinion until they have seen the medical notes concerned. It is important to note that the legislation provides for disclosure to the legal advisors and any suggestion that disclosure should be made to the claimant's medical expert only should be strongly resisted. There are matters in all medical notes which should be checked with the claimant personally and this should be done before the notes are sent to the medical expert, together with any of the claimant's comments which are appropriate. These are such things as chronology of events, accuracy of those parts of the notes allegedly recorded from the claimant's own subjective accounts, advice alleged to have been given to the claimant, and so on.

The fact that the limitation period has expired is not a good reason on its own for refusing an order, unless it is clear that the case is doomed to failure.[25]

It is open to the defendant to raise privilege in respect of certain types of documents which may be sought, for example, confidential reports and the like, but this should be carefully scrutinized.[26] Disclosure can be refused if it is thought that it is not in the public interest, and to assist in the decision, the court can inspect the documents if necessary.

This provision is not available if the claimant wishes to obtain discovery from someone who is not a likely party to the action. In that case the

[24] See *Roper v Slack and Parr* [1981] CLY 2165.
[25] See *Harris v Newcastle-upon-Tyne Health Authority* [1989] 1 WLR 96, CA.
[26] See *Lee v South West Thames Regional Health Authority* [1985] 1 WLR 845.

application must be made after commencement of the action, pursuant to section 34 of the Supreme Court Act 1981, or, in the county court, pursuant to section 53 of the County Courts Act 1984, (see below).

On disclosure generally it should be noted that the obligation is continuing. In *Vernon v Bosley (No 2)*[27] the plaintiff had been awarded damages for psychiatric injury caused by witnessing the death of his two children. Before the final order was drawn up, the defendant became aware of a judgment relating to family proceedings which indicated that there had been a substantial improvement in the plaintiff's condition. The Court of Appeal held that this new evidence would be admitted as it was likely to have a significant impact on the amount of damages awarded. It also held that, where there had been a change in material circumstances essential to the case, there was no difference between actively misleading the court and passively allowing it to believe that the earlier state of affairs still existed.

Disclosure against non-parties

Disclosure orders can be made against non-parties to an action. It may, for example, be necessary to obtain details of the work history of a claimant, particularly useful if there is any allegation of malingering, but the employer(s) may be unwilling to supply the information.

The application should be made pursuant to section 34(2) of the Supreme Court Act 1981 and rule 34(2), and should specify the documents in respect of which the order is sought. It should be supported by evidence which should show how the documents are relevant to an issue arising or likely to arise, and that the person against whom the order is sought is likely to have possession or custody of, or power over, the documents.

The county court procedure is very similar, and is governed by section 53 of the County Courts Act 1984.

INTERIM PAYMENTS

In serious cases where it will take some time to assess damages, where treatment under the NHS is unavailable or unsuitable, or in cases where there is financial hardship, it may be appropriate to make an application to the court for an interim payment. Psychiatric injuries can have potentially disastrous effects upon earning capacity, and financial difficulties can delay recovery, so an application for an interim payment should be seriously considered. Similarly, it may be that, for example, psychotherapy is unavailable through the NHS and a payment to cover the cost of that could

---

[27] [1997] 1 All ER 614.

be made. The possible advantage of this to the defendant should always be kept in mind: recovery or improvement at the earliest possible stage will reduce the damages eventually payable. Although financial hardship is a factor that may be taken into account, it is not a prerequisite of entitlement to an interim payment. It is rare but not unheard of for a defendant to propose interim funding to assist the claimant's recovery and this is to be encouraged in the interests of all concerned.

An application can be made for an interim payment at any time after proceedings have been served on the defendant and the time limit for the defendant to acknowledge service has expired. The circumstances in which the court can order an interim payment are contained within CPR Part 25 and in particular r 25(7) and for personal injury claims are as follows:

(a)   the defendant is insured in respect of the claim, or the Motor Insurers' Bureau are dealing with the claim, *or* is a public authority; *and*

(b)   the defendant has admitted liability, or has had judgment obtained against him for damages to be assessed, *or* the court is satisfied that if the action proceeded to trial, the plaintiff would obtain judgment for substantial damages.

The admission of liability may be in the pleadings or it may be in correspondence, or even an oral admission.[28] It may be implied from pleadings, or it may come from elsewhere, for example, a conviction for careless driving.

The application must be supported by evidence which must deal with the sum of money sought by way of an interim payment; the item or matters in respect of which the interim payment is sought; the sum of money for which final judgment is likely to be given; any other relevant matters; details of special damages and past and future loss in a claim under the Fatal Accidents Act 1976; details of the person(s) on whose behalf the claim is made and the nature of the claim; and the reasons for believing that the following conditions listed in rule 25.7 of the Civil Procedure Rules are satisfied:

1.   liability is admitted either in whole or part; or
2.   judgment has already been obtained; or
3.   the court is satisfied that if the matter went to trial, the claimant would obtain a judgment for a substantial amount of money . . .

If there is financial hardship, that should be stated, but hardship is not a necessary prerequisite for an award to be made.[29] In the case of *Stringman v McArdle*,[30] it was held that it was not appropriate for the judge to question what will be done with the money.

---

[28] See *Re Beeny* [1894] 1 Ch 499.
[29] See *Schott Kem Ltd v Bentley* [1991] 1 QB 61.   [30] The Times, 19 November 1993.

In the county court, an interim payment can be awarded pursuant to CCR, ord 13, r 12(1).

DISCLOSURE OF MEDICAL HISTORY

In a psychiatric injury case it will be normal for both sides to require access to the claimant's medical history. The evaluation of the claimant's pre-accident disposition is important for an understanding of the effect of the trauma or other circumstances experienced and its severity. The medical records may give rise to issues of causation, the reasons why the events may have had a (more or less) dramatic impact on the claimant and the prognosis for recovery.

Medical records may reveal a predisposition to mental illness; this *may* mean a reduction in damages. However, they may also reveal that the manifestation of mental illness took place a long time ago, and had not recurred until the incident which has now triggered and/or exacerbated the previous condition.

In addition to examination of the GP's records, it may also be desirable for a statement to be taken from the general practitioner who has known the claimant for some and who may well be able to indicate with some force and accuracy the effect of the incident upon the claimant. For example, in *Brice v Brown*,[31] Stuart-Smith J was most impressed by the evidence of the plaintiff's GP:

I was much impressed by Dr Green. He had the great advantage of knowing the patient for a period well before this accident and has seen much of her since. He is clearly a thoughtful and intelligent man; he is not a trained psychiatrist, but like many general practitioners has much experience of psychiatric problems.[32]

The provisions of the personal injury pre-action protocol in the fast track provide for the instruction of a single joint expert (but note the decision in *Daniels v Walker*[33]). If for reasons which are not 'fanciful', a party is dissatisfied with the report of a joint expert, it might be appropriate to allow that party to instruct and adduce the report of a second expert.

In a psychiatric injury case, there may be a need for more than two medical experts, if, as will usually be the case, there is a need for an expert report on the physical injuries too. This could be because evidence of the psychiatric injury may need to be given by both psychiatrist and psychologist. In a head injury case, there would also be the evidence of a neurosurgeon if there is physical brain damage. Similarly, if there is a

---

[31] [1984] 1 All ER 997.   [32] ibid, at 1005.   [33] The Times, 17 May 2000, CA.

problem with employment or rehabilitation, consultants in both disciplines are available.

Where each side instructs their own expert, the claimant's report should be disclosed only on the undertaking of the defendant to forward his report in exchange. In other words exchange should normally be simultaneous, and not sequential. If reports are to be agreed then they must be agreed on all material points.

MEDICAL EVIDENCE

Instructing an expert psychiatrist or psychologist

It is important to say a word or two here about the different experts that may be involved in a psychiatric injury claim. Psychiatrists are medically qualified, and can prescribe drug treatments in appropriate cases. They can also use techniques of psychotherapy, analysis and behavioural therapy, although if these become necessary, a clinical psychologist may become involved. Clinical psychologists are not usually medically qualified, but are trained in the treatment of various psychiatric and psychological disorders.

As psychiatrists are medically qualified it may, therefore, be appropriate to instruct a psychiatrist in the first instance. In addition, the claimant may be suffering from other physical disorders which the psychiatrist should be able to identify. If the psychiatrist believes that psychological treatment is necessary then this may either be carried out by a psychiatrist or a clinical psychologist. The extent of the medical evidence to be given at trial will then depend upon the diagnosis, treatment and prognosis.

Unlike a claim involving a physical injury, where the initial referral to the medical expert is for a report on a known injury and with emphasis on prognosis, the psychiatric injury case may involve an instruction letter that emphasizes the need for careful diagnosis, possibly by reference to the criteria contained in DSM–IV and ICD–10.

Where the claimant's degree of psychiatric injury is less clear, or where there are signs more indicative of behavioural problems rather than mental disorder, it may be sensible to instruct a psychologist as a first step. As an aid to diagnosis, psychologists often use self-assessment questionnaires which they require patients to complete (see Chapter 3). Such questionnaires are discoverable as part of the claimant's medical evidence if referred to in a subsequent medical report.

In *Gumpo v Church of Scientology Religious Education College Inc*[34] the claimant sought damages for psychiatric harm as a result of alleged

---

[34] [2000] CP Rep 38, QBD.

intimidation at work. He sought to rely on psychiatric evidence to substantiate his allegations. It was held that the trial judge would be able to decide whether there had been intimidation without hearing psychiatric evidence, and that the cost of adducing this would be wholly disproportionate to the potential benefit gained. Two comments can be made on this: first, it is a claim alleging intimidation, not negligence, where a recognizable psychiatric illness would need to be shown, and secondly, the decision does not mean that psychiatric evidence cannot be given in order for quantum to be assessed.

The medical examination

By the claimant's doctor
It is worth mentioning again the need for sensitivity when instructing your expert(s). It is also important to give full and detailed instructions to your doctor, so he knows precisely what has happened to this plaintiff, including a copy of the claimant's statement. It may also help to arrange for a spouse or other close relative to attend to assist the expert about pre- and post-accident behaviour.

By the defendant
A claimant who sues for damages for personal injury must permit a medical examination to be carried out on behalf of the defendant (subject to what has already been said about joint experts), and the court will stay the action if the claimant unreasonably refuses to submit to an examination.[35] It is not reasonable to refuse examination because the doctor who is to carry it out is believed to be a 'defence doctor', although in *Hall v Avon Area Health Authority (Teaching)*,[36] it was held reasonable to refuse if the doctor concerned had a reputation for being hostile to plaintiffs. It was also held that it was reasonable to refuse if the plaintiff was in a highly nervous state, or was confused by the effects of a brain injury. In *Hall* the following was also established: the plaintiff could not insist upon the presence at the examinations of either her own doctor, or her own medical expert, nor could she make it conditional upon a disclosure of the ensuing report. On the other hand, it was held that it may be reasonable to insist upon a doctor of the same sex carrying out the examination, or it may be reasonable for a third party to be present. Note also *Larby v Thurgood*[37] where it was held that a plaintiff could refuse to be interviewed by the defendant's employment expert as job prospects etc. were issues of fact that could be determined by evidence at trial. The concerns of claimants who are suffering from some

---

[35] *Edmeades v Thames Board Mills Ltd* [1969] 2 QB 67, CA.
[36] [1980] 1 WLR 481, CA.   [37] [1993] ICR 66.

psychiatric disorder can be given due consideration in deciding what is reasonable. On the other hand, the defence can, if it is reasonable to do so, insist upon a psychiatric examination.[38]

If the examination by the defendant's expert goes beyond pure examination and involves tests etc then there is greater reason for refusal because of risk to health. It may be reasonable to refuse even if there is only a very slight risk.[39] In *Osman v British Midland Airways Limited*[40] an application to stay proceedings until the plaintiff agreed to be examined by the defendant's psychiatrist was refused as the plaintiff's *bona fides* were not in issue and the real reason for requesting the examination was a refusal of payment into court.

The medical report

As in any other personal injury case, the medical report should deal fully with the circumstances in which the injuries were caused and it should be clear that every aspect of the injuries has been covered in the report. Care should be taken to make sure that the medical evidence is consistent and coextensive with both the claimant's own evidence and witnesses. The claimant's lawyers should make sure that any symptoms which are cited by lay witnesses (for example, depression, inability to concentrate, irritability) are dealt with in the report. If there is more than one medical report then inconsistencies, if any, should be noted and reconciled. The costs of private medical treatment such as psychotherapy, and, if appropriate, rehabilitation, should be clearly stated and care should be taken to avoid underestimating them.

Other evidence

The claimant's case is always going to be that *this* particular event or *this* set of circumstances produced *this* particular effect upon his or her mind. The importance of personal testimony cannot be overestimated.

In cases where proximity is the issue, full and detailed proofs of evidence are vital. If the issue is proximity to the event itself, then, as well as personal evidence, the claimant should assemble as much external evidence as possible. This could be in the form of plans and photographs, to show exactly where the claimant was at the relevant times, and evidence of the timings involved. Whilst the temporal factor is not the only one in

---

[38] See *Lane v Willis* [1972] 1 WLR 326.
[39] See *Aspinall v Sterling Mansell Ltd* [1981] 3 All ER 866, CA.
[40] [1994] 10(4) PMILL (May).

event-proximity cases, in practice it is of considerable importance; the later the claimant arrives on the scene, the more likely that emergency crews and hospital staff will have reduced the likelihood of a traumatic scene.

External evidence of the horror of the situation can also be of great importance. In *Brice* v *Brown*,[41] the plaintiff (admittedly with some predisposition to mental illness) suffered dreadful psychiatric illness following a relatively minor road accident. She herself was hardly injured at all, but her daughter suffered a visually frightening, but in practice not a serious, head injury. At the trial the father of the child gave evidence as to the child's appearance, as stated by Stuart-Smith J:

> She now has a 10 cm scar running from the eye up into the hairline, and it is perhaps difficult from that to realise quite how alarming that injury must have seemed at the time. The husband, who saw her in hospital, thought that she had lost the whole of her scalp because the skin contracted upwards over the head.[42]

Similarly, in cases where the witnessing of injury to others is in issue and the relationship of the witness to the injured person is not that of parent or spouse, evidence must be produced of the closeness of that relationship, both by personal testimony, and by statements from those who know the parties and their relationship. External evidence, such as wills or gifts, should also be obtained if available.

It is interesting to consider the question of evidence and its relation to the decision in *Alcock* v *Chief Constable of the South Yorkshire Police*.[43] It was accepted by the defence that if the plaintiffs established those required degrees of proximity then they would succeed. The courts were asked, therefore, to consider the proximity questions without hearing from the plaintiffs themselves. The sole witness was a psychiatrist highly experienced in treating Falklands War veterans, but no personal testimony was given to the court of any notion of who those spectators felt when they saw the television pictures. It may well be that it would have made no difference, but personal testimony must be of considerable importance when judges are considering whether an experience is sufficiently shocking. Further, no evidence was given about the degree of closeness of the relationships concerned. The decision indicates that there could have been evidence which would have compelled their lordships to acknowledge that a relationship between two brothers may be as close as that which may exist between a parent and child. There is no doubt therefore that much scope has been left to the imaginative and diligent litigator to establish claims of wider proximity.

It is tempting to overestimate the impact of the litigation ensuing upon the tragedy that took place at the Hillsborough stadium. That case was primarily about 'event proximity' under very exceptional circumstances. The very

---

[41] [1984] 1 All ER 997.   [42] ibid, at 1000.   [43] [1992] 1 AC 310.

great majority of claims will not ever touch upon that issue and therefore it is vital not to exaggerate the effect of that case.

Even when proximity is a worrying and doubtful issue there is no doubting the importance of the individual case and its presentation. The practitioner will have the obstacle course of foreseeability and proximity to negotiate, but, given that policy, however described,[44] is to prevent the opening of those well-known floodgates, then the more individually compelling a case can be, the more likely will be the claimant to succeed.

PLEADINGS

Claimant lawyers should note that the following matters should be included in the particulars of injuries on the statement of particulars of claim: the claimant's date of birth; the nature of the injury, details of the medical treatment already received, the continuing effect of the injury and any disability for work suffered as a result. There is a temptation on the part of defendants to ask for further and better particulars of the claimant's exposure to the traumatic event, but the courts are not sympathetic to excessive or inappropriate requests.[45]

TRIAL

The possibility of a split trial has already been considered at page 231. The more problematic situation of decisions on preliminary points was considered in *Attia v British Gas plc*,[46] CA. In that case the parties asked the court to decide, as a preliminary point, whether witnessing destruction of property (as opposed to witnessing or experiencing threat of, physical injury) could give rise to a claim for damages for nervous shock. At first instance the judge found for the defendants and, on appeal, the Court of Appeal found for the plaintiff, but also commented on the suitability of the matter for decision as a preliminary point. Bingham LJ stated:

. . . one must be very cautious in determining questions of fact on assumed facts, and the risk of doing so unfairly to one side or the other is increased where, as here, the parties were by no means strangers to each other before the careless act occurred. In deciding what the defendants should reasonably have foreseen I would wish to have

---

[44] ibid, per Lord Oliver at 410.
[45] See *British Airways Pension Trustees Ltd v Sir Robert McAlpine & Sons Ltd*, 15 December 1994, CA.
[46] [1988] QB 304, CA.

a much fuller picture than pleadings can give of the plaintiff's personality and circumstances as manifested to and known by the defendants.[47]

Strain on the claimant

In the period coming up to trial and during the trial itself, it is important to be aware of the strain that the claimant will be under. Giving evidence, and anticipation thereof, may be extremely distressing for the claimant. The whole of the distressing events which have caused the claimant's injury will have to be recounted in detail. The effect this is likely to have on the claimant at trial and during the weeks beforehand, should be taken into consideration by the practitioners involved. The claimant should be reassured that his or her advisers appreciate the situation and can provide patience and sympathy. It may be necessary for the claimant to leave the court during parts of the trial.

Children

Special care is needed where a child is suffering from psychiatric injury, and may, for example, have suffered from violence or sexual abuse. Special care will have to be taken to ensure that the child's evidence can be given under circumstances sympathetic to the child. Fortunately, there are now procedures in the civil courts parallel to those in the criminal courts whereby video-linked evidence can be given by children (CPR, r 32.3). It would be up to the child's lawyer to obtain the appropriate direction at the time of setting down.

COSTS

A claimant suffering from psychiatric injuries may be a time-consuming client, and claimant lawyers may be concerned about whether the additional time spent with the client, taking instructions, explaining procedures and preparing the client for trial, can ever be recovered. It should be possible to recover the costs reasonably incurred in dealing with such a client. Simon John of Cunningham John & Co has supplied a copy of the review of taxation in *Evason v Essex Health Authority*.[48] This concerned a woman who had been wrongly diagnosed as suffering from cancer with devastating financial and psychiatric consequences. It was accepted by the court that her special and unusual needs for personal attendance should be taken into account, and the appropriate allowances were given for the additional time spent with her.

---

[47] ibid, at 32.   [48] [1994] 10(1) PMILL (February).

ARBITRATION

Whilst arbitration has long been a popular procedure for solving certain forms of dispute, it is not a forum usually used for the resolution of personal injury cases. However, a number of the plaintiffs in the *Herald of Free Enterprise* litigation agreed to have their cases dealt with by arbitration (see page 212), and it is worth noting the most salient features of the arbitration procedure.

The first point of note is that the parties must *agree* to refer a dispute to arbitration, and they must also agree to be legally bound by that decision. Arbitration should be distinguished from conciliation and mediation as these processes do not result in legally binding and enforceable decisions. Anyone can be an arbitrator (subject to the general rules of natural justice, and subject, of course, to the agreement of the parties). In the *Herald of Free Enterprise* arbitration, the arbitrators were three Queen's Counsel, highly experienced in personal injury matters. Arbitrations are at present governed by the Arbitration Acts of 1950 and 1996, with a number of provisions in the Supreme Court Act 1981 and the Courts and Legal Services Act 1990 which are relevant to arbitrations.

The courts have limited powers under Part II of the 1996 Act, eg to set aside an award for want of jurisdiction or to remove an arbitrator for misconduct. Similarly, there is a very limited right of appeal against an arbitrator's award, on the ground that it raises a question of law of general public importance. Because of the nature of arbitration, there are unlikely to be enforcement problems, but if there are, then the award can be enforced in exactly the same way as if it was a court judgment.

Generally, the advantages of arbitration are said to be speed, flexibility and cheapness. Because there are no formal rules as to the conduct of an arbitration, the procedures used can be adapted by the parties to suit the particular needs of the case. The relaxed nature of the proceedings may make arbitration more attractive to parties with psychiatric problems, who may find the prospect of formal court proceedings frightening. This was a significant feature of the *Herald of Free Enterprise* arbitrations. There is now specific reference in the clinical negligence pre-action protocol to referral to Alternative Dispute Resolution.

9

Future Developments

SHOCK CASES

It is clear that the limiting factors in 'nervous shock' cases are anomalous and based upon an uneven and unprincipled development of the law. As Lord Hoffmann stated in *White v Chief Constable of South Yorkshire Police*: 'It seems to me that in this area of the law, the search for principle was called off in *Alcock v Chief Constable of South Yorkshire Police* [1992] 1 AC 310'.[1] He also stated that there was a time in English law when the law 'came within a hair's breadth' of treating psychiatric injury like physical injury and applying the foreseeability test without more.[2] Presumably he is referring to the case of *McLoughlin v O'Brian*[3] where the judgments, with the exception of Lord Wilberforce's, suggested a more flexible approach to the category of psychiatric injury.

---

[1] [1999] 2 AC 455, at 511. See the criticism of this lack of principle in, eg, M A Jones, 'Liability for Psychiatric Illness: More Principle, Less Subtlety?' [1995] 4 Web JCLI, and J Stapleton, 'In Restraint of Tort' in P Birks (ed), *The Frontiers of Liability* (Oxford University Press, 1994), vol 2, in which she takes the draconian approach whereby if compensation is to be subject to such arbitrary rules then it would be fairer to abolish compensation for psychiatric injury entirely.

[2] [1999] 2 AC 455, at 502.   [3] [1983] 1 AC 410.

It is arguable that further support for this approach comes from the distinction between 'primary' and 'secondary' victims. As has been seen, the result of *Page v Smith*[4] is that the primary victim can recover compensation however trivial the event in which he was involved. The secondary victim, however, who just happens to be slightly too far away to bring himself into the physical 'arena', can recover no compensation despite the fact that he might be informed of the catastrophic injuries of, say, his wife and children. Resistance to change is commonly perceived to be based upon the floodgates argument.

The floodgates argument

As far as the floodgates argument is concerned, again, there is some interesting judicial comment on this in *McLoughlin v O'Brian*. For example, Lord Edmund Davies said:

My Lords, the experiences of a long life in the law have made me very familiar with this 'floodgates' argument. I do not, of course, suggest that it can invariably be dismissed as lacking cogency; on the contrary, it has to be weighed carefully, but I have often seen it disproved by later events. It was urged when abolition of the doctrine of common employment was being canvassed, and it raised its head again when the abolition of contributory negligence as a total bar to a claim in negligence was being urged.[5]

As indicated above, part of the floodgates argument appears to be concerned with the possibility of fraudulent claims. However, it seems that, on the contrary, the main plank of the argument, is the fear of a large number of *genuine* claims. Again in *McLoughlin v O'Brian* it was said by Lord Wilberforce that:

The scarcity of cases which have occurred in the past, and the modest sums recovered, give some indication that fears of a flood of litigation may be exaggerated experience in other fields suggests that such fears usually are.[6]

In *Hevican v Ruane*, Mantell J also disposed of the floodgates argument in a robust fashion:

That was, I think, demolished by the majority in *McLoughlin v O'Brian* and I shall only say that the evidence in this case would suggest that any such extension would be likely to fuel a very small number of additional claims. Nor do I consider that it would leave the door open to fraud. To sustain a claim based on nervous shock, no matter what the circumstances in which the shock was received, a plaintiff would be bound to submit himself or herself over a protracted period to the close scrutiny of psychiatrists well able to detect humbug.[7]

---

[4] [1995] 2 WLR 644.   [5] [1983] 1 AC 410, at 425.
[6] ibid, at 421.   [7] [1991] 3 All ER 65, at 71.

However, it is arguable that, since Mantell J's statement, with three House of Lords cases dealing with the issue (*Alcock*, *Page v Smith*, *White*), a report by the Law Commission, and the first English case to find liability for occupational stress (*Walker*), the public at large are more aware of the possibility of pursuing psychiatric injury claims. Nicholas Mullany, an indefatigable supporter of the abolition of any distinction between physical and psychiatric injury claims, has (and some might say that he does not necessarily advance his cause by doing so) said as much himself:

Cases, successful and unsuccessful, that have surfaced in the last decade, and, particularly, within the 1990s, reflect a growing appreciation that the scope for psychiatric damage suits is much wider than traditionally perceived ... pleas are beginning to appear for compensation for mental illness stemming from scenarios where once legal redress would not have been thought possible ...[8]

Lord Steyn, in *White*, had also supported variations on the floodgates theme, such as the fact that to remove the control mechanisms might impose a disproportionate burden on defendants and insurers when there had only been 'momentary lapses'.[9] It is arguable that the fact that this can happen in the case of physical injury demolishes this view. However, the Law Commission was sufficiently impressed by the floodgates argument to consider it as a good justification for continuing to treat psychiatric and physical injury as being different in terms of the criteria required to establish liability.

The Law Commission report

The Law Commission published its report on psychiatric illness on 9 March 1998.[10] The recommendations relate mainly to the reform of claims by so-called secondary victims, ie those who are injured because of the death, injury or imperilment of another person. However, at the outset, the Commission had to address the basic question of whether psychiatric injury should be regarded differently from physical injury in terms of liability in negligence. It concluded that the distinction should remain in secondary victim cases. In other words, the test of reasonable foreseeability without more should not be sufficient. The Commission had to attempt a justification for this approach. It considered, and rejected, the arguments relating to the possibility of fraudulent claims, conflicts of medical opinion, and the argument that psychiatric injury as such, and/or secondary victims in particular, are less worthy of receiving compensation than those who have suffered physical injury. However, the Commission was persuaded by the

---

[8] N Mullany, 'Fear for the Future: Liability for Infliction of Psychiatric Disorder' in N Mullany (ed), *Torts in the Nineties* (LBC Information Services, New South Wales, 1997).
[9] [1999] 2 AC 455, at 494.
[10] *Liability for Psychiatric Illness* (Law Com No 249) (London: The Stationery Office, 1998).

floodgates argument. Despite a conspicuous lack of evidence to support the argument, the Commission concluded 'that the adoption of a simple foreseeability test would or could result in a significant increase in the number of claims which, at least at this point in time, would be unaccept-able'.[11]

In any event, the Commission suggested that if there were to be a significant increase in the number of claims, then the courts would respond by restricting liability by a manipulation of the concept of foreseeability. The author has commented elsewhere:

Although in its Report the Commission sees this *as a consequence* of an increase in the number of claims and depends upon an actual flood for its efficacy, it is possible to envisage courts *anticipating* such an increase. Such blatant judicial meddling is not a palatable prospect, but is it out of the question? If this were a possibility, then it would be another argument, albeit an unattractive one, in favour of keeping the physical/psychiatric distinction.[12]

That is not necessarily to say that the distinction should not be abolished, but to suggest that there are ways in which the judiciary can use the negligence concepts to achieve whatever result they want.

The Commission's central recommendation is that the requirement that secondary victims be close in space and time to the shocking event should be abandoned. This recommendation was a result of three things: the opinion of the overwhelming majority of the respondees to the Consultation Paper; the patently arbitrary distinctions between successful and unsuccessful claimants; and the medical opinions received about the nature of causation and psychiatric injury.[13] The Commission proposed that the requirement be removed by the introduction of a statutory duty of care where there is no condition as to closeness in space and time, as long as the illness is reasonably foreseeable. The Commission rejected an adoption of the statutory provisions in the Australian jurisdictions of New South Wales, Australian Capital Territories and the Northern Territories[14] which state that once one of the statutory relationships has been established, there is no additional requirement of reasonable foreseeability, regarding this as an essential element of the tort of negligence.

The defences proposed by the Commission are the usual tort defences such as voluntary acceptance of the risk and the defence of illegality, but also that there might be situations where policy dictates that there should be no duty. An example of this is where the primary victim voluntarily accepts the

---

[11] ibid, para 6.8.

[12] K Wheat, 'Liability for Psychiatric Illness: The Law Commission Report' [1998] 3 JPIL 211.

[13] *Liability for Psychiatric Illness* (n 10 above), para 6.10.

[14] Law Reform (Miscellaneous Provisions) Act 1944 (NSW), Law Reform (Miscellaneous Provisions Act 1955 (ACT) and Law Reform (Miscellaneous Provisions) Act 1956 (NT).

risk (as in the case of a sporting activity), but a secondary victim seeks damages. In such a case, argues the Commission, it would be wrong to impose a duty of care towards the secondary victim as it constitutes an unwarranted infringement of the liberty of the primary victim.

The Commission also favoured the abandonment of the requirement that a claimant must be subjected to some form of 'shock'. The Commission rejected arguments that this would open the floodgates (the closeness in terms of love and affection being, to change the metaphor, a brake on this), the fact that claims might arise some time after the event and also give rise to causation problems (no different said the Commission from cases where physical illnesses take some time to manifest themselves). However, the most telling reason for abandoning this requirement was given as the medical responses to the Consultation Paper, which stressed the fact that there was no clinical merit in it.[15]

As far as the close tie of love and affection is concerned, the Commission favoured keeping this requirement, ie not allowing the claims of a mere bystander, and also recommended that there be a number of relationships where there is an irrebuttable presumption that the relationship is close enough to result in psychiatric injury. In response to the possible scenario that there might, for example, be a parent/child relationship which had never been close and where the parties had not seen each other for many years, the Commission stated that in such a case the argument would be that the injury was simply unforeseeable.

Interestingly, the Commission considered the question as to *when* the relationship should arise in order to found a claim. The report stated that, as the physical and temporal closeness to the event would be abandoned upon its recommendation, there would be no need to insist upon the close relationship also being present *at the time* the event occurred. The result of this is a recommendation that there only need be a close relationship at the time of the event *or at the onset of the claimant's psychiatric illness*. The Commission gives an example of a child who is brain damaged and, following the death of its parents, is cared for by a grandparent who suffers no illness as a result of the accident, but subsequently develops depression as a result of caring for the brain-damaged child.

The rule against claims by a secondary victim where a primary victim has inflicted damage upon himself, which was, until recently, an Australian rule was tested in the English courts and found to be valid in the case of *Greatorex v Greatorex*[16] (see Chapter 4). The Commission acknowledged that there could be cases where the rule is justified on the basis of the right to

---

[15] eg, the Royal College of Psychiatrists Mental Health Law Group's submitted that the term 'shock-induced' is 'vague, has no psychiatric meaning and is emotively misleading'; see *Liability for Psychiatric Illness* (n 10 above), para 5.29

[16] [2000] 1 WLR 1970.

self-determination (although, as has been argued above, not in a *Greatorex* situation), and dealt with this by recommending that the new statutory duty of care should not be imposed where the court is satisfied that its imposition would not be just and reasonable because the defendant chose to cause his, or her death, injury or imperilment.[17]

Finally, in view of its main recommendations, the report addressed the point as to the place of the common law in the context of its proposed new statutory framework. The Commission formed the view that the common law is still developing and should not be excluded by legislation. The situation of rescuers, bystanders, involuntary participants, those who suffer as a result of negligent communication of bad news, employees and those who suffer as a result of property damage will still be governed by the common law, as will the 'primary' victim. The report, of course, was published before the decision of the House of Lords in *White v Chief Constable of South Yorkshire Police*,[18] and therefore at the time of the Commission's recommendations, there was the assumption that the category of rescuer was still open to a wider interpretation than that made by the House of Lords.

The report is now four years' old, and, like most Law Commission reports, has not been adopted by government. Shortly after its publication, this writer suggested that it might stand more chance of success, given the 'understandable public outcry at, for example, the disparity between the favourable treatment of the police officers in *Frost* [*White* in the House of Lords] and the rejection of the claims of relatives in *Alcock*'.[19] The House of Lords decision in *White* might well be regarded by some as having responded to that concern, and with it, the chances of any liberalizing legislation.

A different approach?

If there is no likelihood at the moment that there will be legislative change to the law in this area, is it arguable that the common law might make a change? Despite the fatalism of Lord Hoffmann in *White v Chief Constable of South Yorkshire*[20] where he frankly stated that there was no point in pursuing this issue from the point of view of principle, it is arguable that the common law could be more flexible in this area without any general extension of principle, and, indeed, there have been attempts to do this. For example, although a case which was limited in its effect by the facts, the judgment of Morland J in the CJD litigation nevertheless admits of claims by those whom he regarded as secondary victims when the control mechanisms did not apply. Similarly, although they occurred before the House of Lords decision in

---

[17] *Liability for Psychiatric Illness* (n 10 above), para 6.53.   [18] [1999] 2 AC 455.
[19] *Wheat* (n 12 above), at 216.   [20] [1999] 2 AC 455, at 511.

Alcock, the judgments in *Hevican v Ruane*[21] and *Ravenscroft v Rederiak-tiebolaget Transatlantic*[22] took a less restrictive approach.

Although *McLoughlin v O'Brian* established the current statement of law on the 'immediate aftermath/unaided senses' point, the case (in the House of Lords) also contains judicial support for the extension of the scope of the test. For example Lord Bridge said:

> consider the plaintiff who learned after the event of the relevant accident. Take the case of a mother who knows that her husband and children are staying in a certain hotel. She reads in her morning newspaper that it has been the scene of a disastrous fire. She sees in the paper a photograph of unidentifiable victims trapped on the top floor waving for help from the windows. She learns shortly afterwards that all her family have perished. She suffers an acute psychiatric illness. That her illness in these circumstances was a reasonably foreseeable consequence of the events resulting from the fire is undeniable. Yet is the law to deny her damages as against a defendant whose negligence was responsible for the fire simply on the ground that an important link in the chain of causation ... was supplied by her imagination ... rather than by direct perception of the event? ... I have no doubt that this is an area of the law of negligence where we should resist the temptation to try yet once more to freeze the law in a rigid posture which would deny justice to some, who, in the application of the classic principles of negligence derived from *Donoghue v Stevenson* [1932] AC 562, ought to succeed.[23]

In *Hevican v Ruane*, the plaintiff's 14-year-old son had been killed when his school bus was involved in a road accident. The accident happened at 4 pm. The plaintiff, the boy's father, was told about the accident very shortly afterwards and, just before 6 pm, was told by the police that his son was dead. At 7 pm he identified his son's body in the mortuary. The plaintiff suffered a reactive depression and had to give up work. When the case came to trial, there was no dispute about the plaintiff's medical condition; the trial issue was about liability on the second limb of the proximity test, ie 'event proximity'.

Mantell J, the trial judge, acknowledged the authority of *McLoughlin v O'Brian* on 'event proximity'. He interpreted this as a recognition of the principle that there must be a causal connection between the event and the damage caused, but, using the authority of the House of Lords' cases of *Home Office v Dorset Yacht Co Ltd*[24] and *Smith v Littlewoods Organisation Ltd*,[25] he said that as long as each link in the causal chain could be established by foreseeability, then spatio/temporal separation would not defeat a claim. He went on to say:

> So if proximity in either sense is to be used to bar this plaintiff's claim, it can only be because of an arbitrary rule special to cases of nervous shock.[26]

---

[21] [1991] 4 All ER 907. [22] [1991] 3 All ER 65. [23] [1983] AC 410, at 442–3.
[24] [1970] AC 1004. [25] [1987] AC 241. [26] [1991] 3 All ER 65, at 69.

The judge refused to accept such an arbitrary rule. It would have been open to him to find that the identification of the body was part of the immediate aftermath of the accident, but refused to do so, finding for the plaintiff purely and simply on the basis of foreseeability and the justified development of the common law, quoting from the part of Lord Bridge's speech in *McLoughlin v O'Brian* extracted above on the need to resist the temptation to freeze the law in a rigid posture.

In *Hevican* the judge found in favour of the plaintiff, but, following the *Alcock* decision in the House of Lords, the case was successfully appealed.

In *Ravenscroft*, a woman suffered a prolonged grief reaction (classified as a depressive illness in the tenth revision of the World Health Organization's *International Statistical Classification of Diseases and Related Health Problems*[27] ('ICD–10'), following the death of her adult son in an industrial accident. She learned of his death about two hours afterwards, and, although she was at the hospital, did not see his body because her husband prevented her from doing so (the accident had been violent, and her husband feared that the body would be seriously damaged). As in *Hevican*, the trial issue concerned 'event proximity', and Ward J, again reviewing the cases, referred to the American case of *Dillon v Legg*,[28] which identified the three elements of foreseeability of injury as:

(a) the physical proximity of the plaintiff to the scene of the accident; (b) whether the shock arose from the direct impact of the event, or from learning about it from others; (c) the proximity of relationship of the plaintiff and the victim.

This form of evaluation was approved in *McLoughlin v O'Brian* as giving discretion to expand liability when the justice of the case demands it. In his judgment, Ward J saw this 'evaluation' as a way of giving the courts a discretion to weigh each of the three aspects against each other. In consequence, he saw this as giving him the discretion in this case to find in favour of the plaintiff. Unfortunately, as in *Hevican*, the House of Lords decision in *Alcock* came very shortly afterwards, and *Ravenscroft* was also reversed on appeal.

This is an impressively imaginative approach to the proximity tests. It would mean that *each* of the three factors would not necessarily have to be satisfied, ie one which weighed very heavily could mean that the requirement of another did not have to be met. The fact that in *Alcock*, it was stated that the requirement for relationship proximity would not always be imposed, ie the possibility of a claim by a mere bystander was admitted of,[29] goes a long way in support of this. Flexibility would be retained, in appropriate cases regard might be had to the floodgates argument, and it would leave discretion in the hands of the judges to provide justice in appropriate cases.

---

[27] See further www.who.int/whosis/icd10.   [28] (1968) 68 Cal 2d 728.
[29] *Alcock v Chief Constable of South Yorkshire Police* [1992] 1 AC 310, at 397 (Lord Keith), 416 (Lord Oliver) and 493 (Lord Ackner).

To return to the California case of *Dillon v Legg*,[30] and to consider the 'just and reasonableness' requirement formulated in *Caparo Industries plc v Dickman*[31] (along with the elements of foreseeability and proximity), if one weighs the respective *types* of proximity, then this seems to be very much in line with current judicial thinking in other areas of tort. For example in *Marc Rich & Co AG and others v Bishop Rock Marine Co Ltd and others*,[32] the question of the distinction between pure economic loss and physical damage was considered. It was held that, whether it was physical damage or pure economic loss, in both cases as the remedy is financial compensation there is no logic in seeking to draw any distinction between financial loss caused directly and financial loss resulting from physical injury or damage. What had to be considered was reasonable foreseeability, the nature of the relationship, and fairness, justice and reasonableness.

Similarly, the House of Lords has recently confirmed the Court of Appeal decision in *White v Jones*[33] that a solicitor owes a duty of care, not only to his client, but also to his client's intended beneficiary. Both Lords Browne-Wilkinson and Nolan adopted the 'incremental approach' to negligence, and emphasis was placed upon foreseeability of damage.[34] Lord Nolan said:

> I simply point to the facts as being relevant to the pragmatic, case by case approach which the law now adopts towards negligence claims.[35]

In *M (a minor) and another v Newham London Borough Council and others*[36] Sir Thomas Bingham MR cogently argued from the point of view of the 'just and reasonableness' requirement, and the circumstances of the case were, in his judgment, such as to import a duty of care. In other words, here again is emphasis on the case-by-case approach.[37]

Looking at each case and, according to the particular facts, giving different weight and emphasis to event proximity and to relationship proximity seems to be entirely in line with current judicial thinking in other areas of negligence. So, for example, a mere bystander can recover damages if the event proximity facts and the nature of the event itself are particularly compelling; and a loving spouse or parent can recover when the event proximity factors are more remote.

The other aspect of the shock cases which could be developed within the present confines of the common law is the distinction between the mere bystander and someone who is not in a relationship of love and affection with the primary victim, but is in some other form of relationship where the secondary victim might reasonably suffer shock. Such situations have already been considered in Chapter 4, where the employment relationship, for example, might suffice.

---

[30] (1968) 68 Cal 2d 728.   [31] [1990] 2 AC 605.   [32] [1994] 3 All ER 686, CA.
[33] [1995] 1 All ER 691.   [34] ibid, at 714.   [35] ibid, at 736.
[36] [1994] 2 WLR 554.   [37] ibid, at 573.

Whilst there is no reason to suppose that he would support the approach taken above in relation to secondary victims, there is a similar degree of flexibility as to who might be a primary victim, in the judgment of Lord Goff in *White*, where he concluded that the category of primary victims must encompass more than those who are at risk of physical injury (or perceive themselves so to be) because, otherwise, *Page v Smith*[38] would have had the nonsensical result of expanding recovery to allow those who are at risk of physical injury to recover for unforeseeable psychiatric injury, while at the same time restricting recovery by denying the claims of those who suffered foreseeable psychiatric injury.[39]

NON-SHOCK CASES

As has been seen above in Chapters 5 and 6, there is much more scope for development here, because the floodgates argument plays a much smaller part, usually due to the fact that there is some sort of pre-existing relationship between the parties. Prior to *Sutherland v Hatton*[40] it would have been arguable that the area most ripe for expansion is that of employers' liability for occupational stress. However, that case has sent clear signals that such claims will be rigorously scrutinized and that, in the absence of inappropriate actions on the part of the employer, such claims will fail. In other words, employers cannot be expected to know that employees cannot cope without some plain indication to that effect. Furthermore, generally, there is no obligation on an employer to adopt preventative measures, although if an employer does so, then normally he will escape liability. Future cases therefore are more likely to extend to those special situations where employees in high-risk situations can argue that there is a positive obligation to take steps to ameliorate the effect of particularly oppressive employment conditions.

THE PHYSICAL/PSYCHIATRIC DISTINCTION: MEDICAL DEVELOPMENTS

There is no doubt that the wariness of the courts when considering claims for psychiatric injury relates to the general suspicion that such claims, whether in negligence or elsewhere, are open to exaggeration, and even fakery. There are tests well-known to psychiatry for investigating claims and eliminating any that may be bogus (see, for example, DSM–IV and the 'script-driven imagery' referred to in Chapter 2). There is no evidence to

---

[38] [1995] 2 WLR 644.   [39] [1999] 2 AC 455, at 479.   [40] [2002] 2 All ER 1.

suggest that it is easier to fake psychiatric illness than to fake physical pain, and it seems to be an affront to the professions of psychiatry and clinical psychology to use this argument at all.

It is also hoped that the increasingly sophisticated methods of diagnosis and analysis in the medical field will do much to allay any remaining fears about exaggerated or fraudulent claims. For example, the technique of script-driven imagery involves objective criteria such as measurements of the subject's heart rate, sweat gland activity and muscle tension as he recalls the traumatic experience. There are also the developments within the assessment of post-traumatic stress disorder ('PTSD') and other psychiatric injuries, through such mechanisms as the administration of the Structured Clinical Interview for PTSD ('SCID') and the Clinician Administered PTSD Scale ('CAPS'). Most intriguing, are the developments in the field of neurochemistry, where research has indicated that it may be possible *physically* to identify trauma-induced conditions within the brain. The last point relating to physical damage within the nervous system caused by traumatic experiences raises the specific requirement imposed upon a secondary victim in a 'nervous shock' claim that the event has to be shocking to one of 'normal fortitude'. If it becomes possible in the future to identify physical damage within the claimant's neurochemistry then it would be illogical to retain this requirement because the claimant would have to be regarded as a primary victim. In any event, an examination of *Bourhill v Young*[41] suggests that this test was intended to apply only to the 'mere bystander':

The driver of a car or vehicle, even though careless, is entitled to assume that the ordinary frequenter of the streets has sufficient fortitude to endure ... the noise of a collision and the sight of injury to others, and is not to be considered towards one who does not possess the customary phlegm.[42]

---

[41] [1943] AC 92.   [42] ibid, per Lord Porter at 117.

Appendix 1

Diagnostic Criteria for Post-Traumatic Stress Disorder and Acute Stress Disorder from DSM–IV–TR

DIAGNOSTIC CRITERIA FOR 309.81 POST-TRAUMATIC STRESS DISORDER

A. The person has been exposed to a traumatic event in which both of the following were present:

(1) the person experienced, witnessed, or was confronted with an event or events that involved actual or threatened death or serious injury, or a threat to the physical integrity of self or others.

(2) the person's response involved intense fear, helplessness, or horror. **Note:** In children, this may be expressed instead by disorganised or agitated behaviour

B. The traumatic event is persistently re-experienced in one (or more) of the following ways:

(1) recurrent and intrusive distressing recollections of the event, including images, thoughts, or perceptions. **Note:** In young children, repetitive play may occur in which themes or aspects of the trauma are expressed.

(2) recurrent distressing dreams of the event. **Note:** In children, there may be frightening dreams without recognisable content.

(3) acting or feeling as if the traumatic event were recurring (includes a sense of reliving the experience, illusions, hallucinations, and dissociative flashback episodes, including those that occur on awakening or when intoxicated). **Note:** In young children, trauma-specific re-enactment may occur.

(4) intense psychological distress at exposure to internal or external cues that symbolise or resemble an aspect of the traumatic event

(5) physiological reactivity on exposure to internal or external cues that symbolise or resemble an aspect of the traumatic event.

C.   Persistent avoidance of stimuli associated with the trauma and numbing of general responsiveness (not present before the trauma), as indicated by three (or more) of the following:
   (1)   efforts to avoid thoughts, feelings, or conversations associated with the trauma
   (2)   efforts to avoid activities, places, or people that arouse recollections of the trauma
   (3)   inability to recall an important aspect of the trauma
   (4)   markedly diminished interest or participation in significant activities
   (5)   feeling of detachment or estrangement from others
   (6)   restricted range of affect (eg, unable to have loving feelings)
   (7)   sense of a foreshortened future (eg, does not expect to have a career, marriage, children, or a normal life span)

D.   Persistent symptoms of increased arousal (not present before the trauma), as indicated by two (or more) of the following:
   (1)   difficulty falling or staying asleep
   (2)   irritability or outbursts of anger
   (3)   difficulty concentrating
   (4)   hypervigilance
   (5)   exaggerated startle response

E.   Duration of the disturbance (symptoms in Criteria B, C, and D) is more than 1 month.

F.   The disturbance causes clinically significant distress or impairment in social, occupational, or other important areas of functioning.

Specify if:
   Acute: if duration of symptoms is less than 3 months
   Chronic: if duration of symptoms is 3 months or more

Specify if:
   With Delayed Onset: if onset of symptoms is at least 6 months after the stressor

Specifiers

The following specifiers may be used to specify onset and duration of the symptoms of Post-Traumatic Stress Disorder:

   Acute: This specifier should be used when the duration of symptoms is less than 3 months.

Chronic: This specifier should be used when the symptoms last 3 months or longer.

With Delayed Onset: This specifier indicates that at least 6 months have passed between the traumatic event and the onset of the symptoms.

Associated features and disorders

Associated descriptive features and mental disorders. Individuals with Post-Traumatic Stress Disorder may describe painful guilt feelings about surviving when others did not survive or about the things they had to do to survive. Phobic avoidance of situations or activities that resemble or symbolise the original trauma may interfere with interpersonal relationships and lead to marital conflict, divorce, or loss of job. The following associated constellation of symptoms may occur and are more commonly seen in association with an interpersonal stressor (eg, childhood sexual or physical abuse, domestic battering, being taken hostage, incarceration as a prisoner of war or in a concentration camp, torture): impaired affect modulation; self-destructive and impulsive behaviour; dissociative symptoms; somatic complaints; feelings of ineffectiveness, shame, despair, or hopelessness; feeling permanently damaged; a loss of previously sustained beliefs; hostility; social withdrawal; feeling constantly threatened; impaired relationships with others; or a change from the individual's previous personality characteristics.

There may be increased risk of Panic Disorder, Agoraphobia, Obsessive-Compulsive Disorder, Social Phobia, Specific Phobia, Major Depressive Disorder, Somatisation Disorder, and Substance-Related Disorders. It is not known to what extent these disorders precede or follow the onset of Post-Traumatic Stress Disorder.

Associated laboratory findings. Increased arousal may be measured through studies of autonomic functioning (eg, heart rate, electromyography, sweat gland activity).

Associated physical examination findings and general medical conditions. General medical conditions may occur as a consequence of the trauma (eg, head injury, burns).

Specific culture and age features

Individuals who have recently emigrated from areas of considerable social unrest and civil conflict may have elevated rates of Post-Traumatic Stress Disorder. Such individuals may be especially reluctant to divulge experiences of torture and trauma due to their vulnerable political immigrant status. Specific assessments of traumatic experiences and concomitant symptoms are needed for such individuals.

In younger children, distressing dreams of the event may, within several weeks, change into generalised nightmares of monsters, of rescuing others, or of threats to self or others. Young children usually do not have the sense that they are reliving the past; rather, the reliving of the trauma may occur through repetitive play (eg, a child who was involved in a serious automobile accident repeatedly re-enacts car crashes with toy cars). Because it may be difficult for children to report diminished interest in significant activities and construction of affect, these symptoms should be carefully evaluated with reports from parents, teachers, and other observers. In children, the sense of a foreshortened future may be evidenced by the belief that life will be too short to include becoming an adult. There may also be 'omen formation' — that is, belief in an ability to foresee future untoward events. Children may also exhibit various physical symptoms, such as stomachaches and headaches.

Prevalence

Community-based studies reveal a lifetime prevalence for Post-Traumatic Stress Disorder ranging from 1% to 14%, with the variability related to methods of ascertainment and the population sampled. Studies of at-risk individuals (eg, combat veterans, victims of volcanic eruptions or criminal violence) have yielded prevalence rates ranging from 3% to 58%.

Course

Post-Traumatic Stress Disorder can occur at any age, including childhood. Symptoms usually begin within the first 3 months after the trauma, although there may be a delay of months, or even years, before symptoms appear. Frequently, the disturbance initially meets criteria for Acute Stress Disorder (see p. 429) in the immediate aftermath of the trauma. The symptoms of the disorder and the relative predominance of re-experiencing avoidance, and hyperarousal symptoms may vary over time. Duration of the symptoms varies, with complete recovery occurring within 3 months in approximately half of cases with many others having persisting symptoms for longer than 12 months after the trauma.

The severity, duration, and proximity of an individual's exposure to the traumatic event are the most important factors affecting the likelihood of developing this disorder. There is some evidence that social supports, family history, childhood experiences, personality variables, and pre-existing mental disorders may influence the development of Post-Traumatic Stress Disorder. This disorder can develop in individuals without any predisposing conditions, particularly if the stressor is especially extreme.

Familial Pattern

There is evidence of a heritable component to the transmission of PTSD. Furthermore, a history of depression in first-degree relatives has been related to an increased vulnerability to developing PTSD.

Differential diagnosis

In Post-Traumatic Stress Disorder, the stressor must be of an extreme (ie, life-threatening) nature. In contrast, in **Adjustment Disorder**, the stressor can be of any severity. The disgnosis of Adjustment Disorder is appropriate both for situations in which the response to an extreme stressor does not meet the criteria for Post-Traumatic Stress Disorder (or another specific mental disorder) and for situations in which the symptom pattern of Post-Traumatic Stress Disorder occurs in response to a stressor that is not extreme (eg, spouse leaving, being fired).

Not all psychopathology that occurs in individuals exposed to an extreme stressor should necessarily be attributed to Post-Traumatic Stress Disorder. **Symptoms of avoidance, numbing, and increased arousal that are present before exposure to the stressor** do not meet criteria for the diagnosis of Post-Traumatic Stress Disorder and require consideration of other diagnoses (eg, a Mood Disorder or another Anxiety Disorder). Moreover, if the symptom response pattern to the extreme stressor meets criteria for **another mental disorder** (eg, Brief Psychotic Disorder, Conversion Disorder, Major Depressive Disorder), these diagnoses should be given instead of, or in addition to, Post-Traumatic Stress Disorder.

Acute Stress Disorder is distinguished from Post-Traumatic Stress Disorder because the symptom pattern in Acute Stress Disorder must occur within 4 weeks of the traumatic event and resolve within the 4-week period. If the symptoms persist for more than 1 month and meet criteria for Post-Traumatic Stress Disorder, the diagnosis is changed from Acute Stress Disorder to Post-Traumatic Stress Disorder.

In **Obsessive-Compulsive Disorder**, there are recurrent intrusive thoughts, but these are experienced as inappropriate and are not related to an experienced traumatic event. Flashbacks in Post-Traumatic Stress Disorder must be distinguished from illusions, hallucinations, and other perceptual disturbances that may occur in **Schizophrenia, other Psychotic Disorders, Mood Disorder With Psychotic Features, a delirium, Substance-Induced Disorders,** and **Psychotic Disorders Due to a General Medical Condition.**

Malingering should be ruled out in those situations in which financial remuneration, benefit eligibility, and forensic determinations play a role.

DIAGNOSTIC CRITERIA FOR 308.3 ACUTE STRESS DISORDER

A.   The person has been exposed to a traumatic event in which both of the following were present:

(1)   the person experienced, witnessed, or was confronted with an event or events that involved actual or threatened death or serious injury, or a threat to the physical integrity of self or others

(2)   the person's response involved intense fear, helplessness, or horror

B.   Either while experiencing or after experiencing the distressing event, the individual has three (or more) of the following dissociative symptoms:

(1)   a subjective sense of numbing, detachment, or absence of emotional responsiveness

(2)   a reduction in awareness of his or her surroundings (eg, 'being in a daze')

(3)   derealisation

(4)   depersonalisation

(5)   dissociative amnesia (ie, inability to recall an important aspect of the trauma)

C.   The traumatic event is persistently re-experienced in at least one of the following ways: recurrent images, thoughts, dreams, illusions, flashback episodes, or a sense of reliving the experience; or distress on exposure to reminders of the traumatic event.

D.   Marked avoidance of stimuli that arouse recollections of the trauma (eg, thoughts, feelings, conversations, activities, places, people).

E.   Marked symptoms of anxiety or increased arousal (eg, difficulty sleeping, irritability, poor concentration, hypervigilance, exaggerated startle response, motor restlessness).

F.   The disturbance causes clinically significant distress or impairment in social, occupational, or other important areas of functioning or impairs the individual's ability to pursue some necessary task, such as obtaining necessary assistance or mobilising personal resources by telling family members about the traumatic experience.

G.   The disturbance lasts for a minimum of 2 days and a maximum of 4 weeks and occurs within 4 weeks of the traumatic event.

H.   The disturbance is not due to the direct physiological effects of a substance (eg, a drug of abuse, a medication) or a general medical condition, is not better accounted for by Brief Psychotic Disorder, and is not merely an exacerbation of a pre-existing Axis I or Axis II disorder.

Appendix 2

Treatment Providers

Set out below are a list of some providers of treatment for trauma. Some may also provide medico-legal reports. The list is by no means exhaustive, is not an approved list of accredited experts and has been selected on the basis of geographical coverage, and on the fact that all providers take direct referrals, and both NHS and private patients. It should also be noted that most of these providers provide psychological services.

The author therefore disclaims any responsibility.

Dr Terence Aubrey Greenfield, 1st Floor, 157 Ashley Road, Hale, Altrincham, Cheshire WA14 2UW. Tel: 0161 928 3898, 0161 929 0361.

Mr Z Bhunnoo, A.M.H.C, 1 Elwick Road, Ashford, Kent TN23 1PD. Tel: 01634 861440, 01233 204163.

Mr Terry Cromey, 'Brakken', 43 Sheridan Drive, Helens Bay, Bangor, County Down BT19 1LB. Tel: 028 9185 3473. Fax: 028 9185 3743. Email: TCromey@compuserve.com

Dr Kenny Midence, Dept of Clinical Psychology, Uned Hergest Ysbyty, Gwynedd, Bangor, Gwynedd LL57 2PW. Tel: 01248 384251. Email: kmidence@gwynfa. u-net.com

Ms Linda Mathews, Dept Psychological Health Care, 11/12 Keresforth Close, Barnsley, South Yorkshire S70 6RS; 57 Fitzwilliam Street, Wath upon Dearne, Rotherham, South Yorkshire S63 7HG. Tel: 01226 777914, 01709 876995. Email: LindaAMatthews@aol.com

Mr Bruce Bassam, Acorn Lodge, Bethlem Royal Hospital, Monks Orchard Road, Beckenham, Kent BR3 3BX. Tel: 020 8776 4516, 020 7737 3527. Email: bruce.bassam@exmachina,demon.co.uk

Mr T N Bowman, Crumlin Road, Health Centre, 130 Crumlin Road, Belfast, Northern Ireland BT14 6AP; 12 Garland Avenue, Belfast BT8 6YH. Tel: 028 9074 1188, 028 9070 5640. Email: normanbow@yahoo.com

Mr Derek P Farrell, Dept of Psychological Therapies, St Catherine's Hospital, Church Road, Birkenhead, Merseyside CH42 0LQ. 11–13 Downham Road, South Heswall, Wirral, Merseyside CH60 5RG. Tel: 0151 604 7276, 0151 342 9601. Email: Derek.Farrell@mta2.wwirralcc-tr.nwest.nhs.uk

Mr Paul Stephen Keenan, Dept of Psychological Therapies, St Catherines Hospital, Church Road, Birkenhead, Merseyside CH42 0LQ. Tel: 0151 604 7276, 0151 342 9601. Email: paul.keenan@mta2.wwirralcc-tr.nwest.nhs.uk

Dr Geraldine Fletcher, Coleshill CMHT, 112A Coleshill Road, Water Orton, Birmingham B46 1RD; East Midlands, Nuffield Hospital, Rykneld Road, Littleover, Derby DE23 7SN. Tel: 0121 747 2080, 01332 517891.

Mr Steven James Cox, Newington Resource Centre, Newington Road, Marston Green, Birmingham B37 7RW, 7 Nayland Croft Hall Green, Birmingham B28 0QH. Tel: 0121 779 6468 x220, 0121 733 7292.

Ms Caroline Driver, 37 Princes Terrace, Brighton, East Sussex BN2 5JS; Behavioural Psychotherapy Dept, Hove Polyclinic, Hove BN3 7HY. Tel: 01273 690770, 01273 242018.

Mrs Christa Schreiber-Kounine, STEPS Unit, Southmead Hospital, Southmead Road, Westbury-on-Trym, Bristol BS10 5NB. Tel: 0117 959 6113, 07974 793247.

Ms Rosalind Fortune, Cabot CMHT, 12 Grove Road, Redland, Bristol BS6 6UJ; 1 Halsbury Road, Westbury Park, Bristol BS6 7SS. Tel: 0117 973 5142, 0117 940 5389.

Mrs Jennifer J Conroy, 22 Green End Fen, Ditton, Cambridge CB5 8SX; Dept of Cognitive & Behav Psychthrp Psychological Treatment Service Box, 190/Portacabins, Addenbrooke's Hospital, Hills Road, Cambridge CB2 2QQ. Tel: 01223 292124, 01223 217939.

Mr Neil James Kitchiner, 38 Oakridge, Thornhill, Cardiff CF14 9BT. Tel: 029 2075 0602. Mobile: 077 80 687311. Email: neiljkitchiner@yahoo.co.uk

Dr Angela Barrass, The Derby Suite, Cheadle Royal Healthcare, 100 Wilmslow Road, Cheadle, Cheshire SK8 3DG. Tel: 0161 276 5365, 0161 495 4902.

Mrs Joanna Trosh, Behavioural Psychotherapy Dept, Chelmsford & Essex Centre, New London Road, Chelmsford CM2 0QH. Tel: 01245 318609. Email: bjtrosh@tinyworld.co.uk

Mr Rufus Harrington, The Runnymede Hospital, Guildford Road, Chertsey, Surrey KT16 0RQ; The BUPA Hospital, Clare Park, Farnham, Surrey GU10 5XX. Mobile: 07961 378329. Tel: 01932 877814. Email: aemeth@compuserve.com

Mr Pierce J O'Carroll, Chester College of H E, Parkgate Road, Chester CH1 4BJ; Psychology Department, West Cheshire Hospital, Liverpool Road, Chester CH2 1UL. Tel: 0151 727 3049, 01244 364046. Email: clinpsych@btiternet.com

Mrs Christine Orton, Upton-by-Chester, Chester, Cheshire; NCH The Flintshire Family Project, Mancot Clinic, Mancot, Deeside, Flintshire CH5 2AH. Tel: 01244 383860, 01244 539537. Email: waffs@mail.nchafc.org.uk

Mr Paul Rice, Blackwater House, 81 Riverside Way, Klevedon, Colchester, Essex CO5 9LX; CMHT, 8 Line Grove House, Highwood Hospital, Geary Drive, Brentwood, Essex CM15 9DY. Tel: 01376 571515, 01277 223581.

Dr B T Pilkington, Department of Clinical Psychology, Psychiatric Unit, Craigavon Area Hospital, Portadown, Craigavon, County Armagh BT63 5QQ. Tel: 028 3833 4444. Fax: 028 3833 1179.

Mr Brendan Armstrong, Cityside CMHT, 22 Crawford Square, Derry, Northern Ireland BT48 7HT; 24 Cherry Drive, Eglington, Derry, Northern Ireland BT47 3US. Tel: 028 7137 2230, 028 7181 1342.

Mr Antony Brown, Dept Behavioural Psychotherapy, Doncaster Royal Infirmary, Armthorpe Road, Doncaster, South Yorkshire DN2 5LT. Tel: 01302 734795, 01904 621648. Email: antonybrowncbt@hotmail.com

Mr Bernard J B Kat, Dept of Clinical Psychology County Hospital, Durham DH1 4ST. Tel & Fax: 0191 281 0411, 0191 333 3499. Email: b.kat@psynapse.co.uk

Dr Jane Kunkler, Department of Health Psychology, Astley Ainslie Hospital, 133 Grange Loan, Edinburgh EH9 2HL. Tel: 0131 537 9128, 0131 667 3454.

Mr Ulrich J Fischer, The Arndale CMHT, 80–90 Kinfauns Drive, Glasgow G15 7TS; Ross Hall Hospital, 221 Crookston Road, Glasgow G52 3NQ. Tel: 0141 211 6184, 01360 620845. Email: ulrich.fischer@ndirect.co.uk

Dr Michael Killoran Ross, c/o Bons Secours Hospital, 36 Mansionhouse Road, Langside, Glasgow G41 3DN. Tel: 01292 285607, 0141 632 9231.

Dr Michael Killoran Ross, 68 Keswick Road, East Kilbride, Glasgow G75 8QX; Nuffield House, 1000 Great Western Road, Glasgow G12 0NR. Tel: 01355 265936, 0141 576 2900. Email: Michael.Ross@gghb.scot.nhs.uk

Mrs Lesley A Rogers, 48 Parrock Avenue, Gravesend, Kent DA12 1QQ; Day Hospital, Orchard House, Joyce Green Hospital, Temple Hill, Dartford, Kent DA1 5HU. Tel: 01474 364720, 01322 622494.

Ms Karen Pittman, Admiralty House, Northgate Hospital, Northgate Street, Great Yarmouth, Norfolk NR30 1BU. Tel: 01493 337677, 01692 581755. Email: kp@cognitivebehaviourtherapy.org

Mr Philip Pattinson, Psychology Services, Northowram Hospital, Northowram, Halifax, West Yorkshire HX3 7SW. Tel: 01422 201101 Ext 334, 01422 205415. Email: 101516.2474@compuserve.com

Ms Christine Marklow, Dept of Clinical Psychology Northowram Hospital, Halifax HX3 7SW; Highfield Hospital, Manchester Road, Rochdale, Lancs OL11 4LZ. Tel: 01422 201101, 01706 655121.

Ms Julie Dickson, Parkway Centre: Adult Mental Health, Park Way, Havant, Hampshire PO9 1HH; The Centre in Portsmouth, 20 Landport Terrace, Portsmouth, Hampshire PO1 2RG. Tel: 023 9247 1661, 023 9283 0558. Email: julie.dicksonson@talk21.com

Mr Thomas Lambton Phillips, 90 Redwood Drive, Bradley Manor, Huddersfield, West Yorkshire HD2 1PW; Dept Behavioural Psychotherapy, 6A Greenhead Road, Huddersfield, West Yorkshire HD1 4EN. Tel: 01484 455150, 01484 347725. Email: lambton@redwoodpsychotherapy.fsnet.co.uk

Mr Damian Gardner, Dept of Clinical Psychology, St Marys Hospital, 77 London Road, Kettering, Northamptonshire NN15 7PW. Tel: 01536 493033.

Dr Rosaleen Isles, Glebe House, Kirkmahoe, Dumfries DG1 1SY. Tel: 01387 710202.

Mr James Taylor, Behavioural Psychotherapy Service FVPC NHS, Trust No 2, The Bungalows, Stirling Road, Larbert FK5 4SD; 38 Allandale Cottages, Allandale, Bonnybridge, Stirlingshire FK4 2HF. Tel: 01324 574321, 01324 841492. Email: jastaylor@msn.com

Mrs Christine Anderson, Community Mental Health Centre, 62 Etnam Street, Leominster, Herefordshire HR6 8AN. Tel: 01568 780621, 07866 441313. Email: chrisacbt@aol.com

Ms A-L Humphreys, Dept of Allied Health Professions School of Health Sciences Johnston Building, Brownlow Hill, Liverpool L69 3GB; Lifespan Therapy Consultants, The Cottage, Little Lane, Parkgate, Wirral, Cheshire CH64 6SD. Tel: 0151 794 4916. Mobile: 077 20 289050. Email: lhumph@liv.ac.uk

Ms Gill Ross, Child & Family Services, NE Team Mulberry House, Alder Hey Children's Hospital, Eaton Road, West Derby, Liverpool L12 2AP; 27 Llys Nercwys, Mold, Flintshire CH7 1HR. Tel: 151 228 4811, 01352 755602. Email: gill.ross@virgin.net

Mr Danny C K Lam, Faculty Health & Socl Care Sciences, Kingston Univ & St Georges Hosp, 2nd Floor, Grosvenor Wing, Blackshaw Road, London SW17 0QT. Tel: 07974 979737. Email: danny–lam11@hotmail.com

Ms Alice G Shires, City & Hackney NHS Trust Psychological Therapies Dept, 50–52 Clifden Road, London E5 0LJ; PPCS, 14 Deconshire Place, London W1N 1PB. Tel: 020 8510 8661, 020 7935 0640. Email: ppcs@globalnet.co.uk

Mr Trevor E L Smith, Dept Behavioural/Cognitive Therapy Avenue House, CMHRC, 43–47 Avenue Road, Acton, London W3 8NJ. Tel: 020 8653 0924, 020 8993 7892.

Ms Jenifer A Bright, 54 Ellerton Road, Wandsworth Common, London SW18 3NN; Maudsley Psychiatry Centre, Maudsley Hospital, Denmark Hill, London SE5 8AZ. Tel: 020 8877 9853, 020 7919 2194. Email: jeniferbright@hotmail.com

Mr John Manley, West London Mental Health NHS Trust, 2 Wolverton Gardens, London W6 7DY. Tel: 07801 065420.

Ms Sara Mitchell-O'Malley, Room 29, Outpatient Dept of Neuropsychiatry, The Maudsley Hospital, Denmark Hill, London SE5 8AZ. Tel: 020 7919 2330, 07961 146862.

Mr James Willis, Cognitive Behavioural Psychotherapy, George Villa, Priority House Annex, Hermitage Lane, Maidstone, Kent ME16 9PD; 19 Milton Street, Maidstone, Kent ME16 8JT. Tel: 01622 723813, 01622 204752. Email: jimlandis@tesco.net

Dr Angela Barrass, Dept of Clinical Psychology, Rawnsley Building, Manchester Royal Infirmary, Oxford Road, Manchester M13 9WL; The Derby Suite, Cheadle Royal Healthcare, 100 Wilmslow Road, Cheadle, Cheshire SK8 3DG. Tel: 0161 276 5365, 0161 495 4902.

Dr Paul King, Department of Clinical Psychology, North Manchester General Hospital, Delaunays Road, Crumpsall, Manchester M8 5RB. Tel: 0161 720 2810. Fax: 0161 720 2671.

Mrs Lesley Maunder, Dept Psychological Therapy & Research, St George's Hospital, Morpeth, Northumberland NE61 2NU. Tel: 01670 512121 Ext 3534.

Prof Ivy-Marie Blackburn, Newcastle Cognitive Therapy Centre, Plummer Court, Carliol Place, Newcastle upon Tyne NE1 6UR; 1 Towers Avenue, Jesmond, Newcastle upon Tyne NE2 3QE. Tel: 0191 219 6284, 0191 281 1117. Email: ivyblackburn@tiscali.co.uk

Dr Fiona C Kennedy, Sevenacres, St Marys Hospital, Parkhurst Ropad, Newport, Isle of Wight PO30 6TG. Tel: 01983 534052. Fax: 01983 534020. Email: fiona.kennedy@iow.nhs.uk

Mr Malcolm Wheatley, St Andrews Hospital, Billing Road, Northampton NN1 5DG. Tel: 01604 629696. Email: mwheatley@standrew.co.uk

Mr Stephen Regel, Traumatic Stress Service, Notts Healthcare NHS Trust, Duncan Macmillan House, Porchester Road, Nottingham NG3 6AA. Tel: 0115 952 9436. Fax: 0115 952 9477. Email: liz.jeffrey@nhc-tr.trent.nhs.uk

Dr Kate Gillespie, Cognitive Therapy Centre, Erne House, Tyrone & Fermanagh Hospital, Omagh, Northern Ireland BT79 0NS. Tel: 028 8224 5211 x 2528. Fax: 028 8225 0257. Email: estewart@slt.n-i.nhs.uk

Dr Joan W Kirk, Psychology Department Warneford Hopspital, Headington, Oxford OX3 7JX. Tel: 01865 226432. Fax: 01865 226411.

Mrs Dinah Jenkins, Occupational Health & Safety Unit, Derriford Hospital, Plymouth, Devon PL6 8DH. Tel: 01752 763586, 01503 262067. Email: dinah.jenkins@phnt.swest.nhs.uk

Dr Steven H Jones, Laurence E Burns Unit, Dept of Clinical Psychology, Birch Hill Hospital, Rochdale OL12 9QB. Tel: 01706 755774.

Mr Alec Brady, 25 Hunshelf Park, Stocksbridge, Sheffield, South Yorkshire S36 2BT; Dept of Clinical Psychology, Stepping Hill Hospital, Stockport, Cheshire SK2 7JE. Tel: 0114 288 3276, 07768 593117. Email: alec.brady@virgin.net

Mr Camal Gouneea, 59 Marlborough Road, Broomhill, Sheffield, South Yorkshire S10 1DA; Claremont Hospital, 401 Sandygate Road, Sheffield S10 5UB. Tel: 0114 266 8243, 0114 263 2109. Email: c.gouneea@sheffield.ac.uk

Dr Carol Brady, Lincolnshire Healthcare Trust, Orchard House, South Rauceby, Sleaford, Lincolnshire NG34 8PP. Tel: 01529 416055. Email: DrCarol-Brady@aol.com

Ms Zhila Rouhifar, Ealing Hammersmith & Fulham MH NHS, Local Secure Directorate, St Bernards' Wing, C Block, Uxbridge Road, Southall, Middlesex UB1 3EU. Tel: 020 8354 8640.

Ms Susan M Ross, Clinical Psychology Department, Department of Psychiatry, Royal South Hants Hospital, Brintons Terrace, Southampton SO14 0YG. Tel: 023 8082 5531.

Mr Ian P Dyer, Queens House, St Saviours Hospital, La Route de la Hougue Bie, St Saviour, Jersey JE2 7UW; No 1 Coastlands, Greve D'Azette, St Clement, Jersey JE2 6PD. Tel: 01534 623223, 01534 878018.

Mr Adrian Newell, South Staffs NHS Trust, St Georges Hsopital, Corporation Street, Stafford ST16 3AG. Tel: 01785 221429.

Miss Jane Ridgway, Department of Psychology, Stepping Hill Hospital, Poplar Grove, Stockport, Cheshire SK2 7JE. Tel: 0161 419 5766. Mobile: 07776 220426.

Ms Nicola Louise Ridgeway, 2 Dalham Road, Ousden, Newmarket, Suffolk CB8 8UA. Tel: 01638 500182. Email: NicolaRidgeway@aol.com

Dr Peter Amies, Kingshill House, Kingshill Road, Swindon SN1 4LG. Tel: 01865 556322, 01793 491917. Email: 100411.624@compuserve.com

Dr Paul T Alexander, Pain Clinic, Taunton & Somerset Hospital, Musgrove Park, Taunton, Somerset TA1 5DA. Tel: 01823 343770.

Mr Michael Gillingham, 21 Wigeon Grove, Leegomery, Telford, Shropshire TF1 6GZ; Psychology Department, Stepping Hill Hospital, Poplar Grove, Stockport, Cheshire SK2 7JE. Tel: 01952 244425, 0161 419 5766.

Mr Peter John Kolb, White Lodge, BCPU Springfield Hospital, Glenburnie Road, Tooting, London SW17 7DJ. Tel: 020 8672 9911 x 42961.

Mr Glen Macklin, 7 Lonicera Close, Walsall WS5 4SQ; Sycamore House Medical Centre, 111 Birmingham Road, Walsall, West Midlands WS1 2NL. Tel: 01922 616253, 01922 624320. Email: gm@impsyc.freeserve.co.uk

Mrs Molly McKay, Dept of Psychological Therapies, Warrington Community Health Care, Garven Place Clinic, Sankey Street, Warrington, Cheshire WA1 1RH. Tel: 01925 653295, 01925 655052 Ext 3838. Email: mollywallet@mmckay0.freeserve.co.uk

Mr Nicholas J Black, Psychology Services, Royal Hants County Hospital, Romsey Road, Winchester, Hants SO22 6DG; Brook House, 15 Burley Cose, Chandlers Ford, Eastleigh, Hants SO53 4NS. Tel: 01962 824351, 023 8025 5568. Email: Nick.Black@weht.swest.nhs.uk

Miss Tina Louise Chipman, Psychological Therapies Department, Wrexham Maelor Hospital, Croesnewydd Road, Wrexham, Clwyd LL13 7TD. Tel: 01978 725349. Email: tina.chipman@new-tr.wales.nhs.uk

Appendix 3

Selected Reading
(in addition to works cited in the text)

LAW

Books

W A Barton, *Recovering for Psychological Injuries*, 2nd edn (American Trial Lawyers Association, 1990).

I Goldrein and M de Haas, *Butterworths Personal Injury Service*.

J Hendy *et al, Personal Injury Practice*, 3rd edn (London: Butterworths, 2000).

N J Mullany (ed), *Torts in the Nineties* (Sydney: LBC Information Services, 1997)

—— and P R Handford, *Tort Liability for Psychiatric Damage* (London: Sweet & Maxwell, 1993).

Articles

M Davie, 'Negligently Inflicted Psychiatric Illness: The Hillsborough Case in the House of Lords' (1992) 43 NILQ 237.

S Dziobon and A Tettenborn, 'When the Truth Hurts: The Incompetent Transmission of Distressing News' (1997) 13 PN 70.

R English, 'Nervous Shock: Before the Aftermath' [1993] CLJ 204.

T K Feng, 'Nervous Shock: Bystander Witnessing a Catastrophe' (1995) 111 LQR 48.

—— 'Nervous Shock to Primary Victims' [1995] SJLS 649.

P R Handford, 'Compensation for Psychiatric Injury: The Limits of Liability' (1995) 2 Psychiatry, Psychology and Law 37.

S Hedley, 'Hillsborough: Morbid Musings of a Reasonable Chief Constable' [1992] CLJ 16.

C A Hopkins, 'A New Twist to Nervous Shock' [1995] CLJ 491

M A Jones, 'Liability for Psychiatric Illness: More Principle, Less Subtlety?' [1995] 4 Web JCLI.

—— 'Negligently Inflicted Psychiatric Harm: Is the Word Mightier than the Deed?' (1997) 13 PN 111.

B Lynch, 'A Victory for Pragmatism? Nervous Shock Reconsidered' (1992) 108 LQR 367.

M McCulloch, 'Post Traumatic Stress Disorder: Turning the Tide without Opening the Floodgates (1995) 35 Med Sci Law 287.

B McKenna, 'Stress Injuries at Work' (1994) 144 NLJ 1652.

F McManus, 'Nervous Shock: Back to Square One?' [1996] Jur Rev 159.

N J Mullany, 'Compensation for Fear and Worry-Induced Psychiatric Illness: The Australian Position' (1997) 4 Psychiatry, Psychology and Law 147.

—— 'Psychiatric Damage in the House of Lords — Fourth Time Unlucky: *Page v Smith*' (1995) 3 Journal of Law and Medicine 112

—— and P R Handford, 'Hillsborough Replayed' (1997) 113 LQR 410.

K J Nasir, 'Nervous Shock and *Alcock*: The Judicial Buck Stops Here' (1992) 55 MLR 705.

J O'Sullivan, 'Liability for Fear of the Onset of Future Medical Conditions' (1999) 15 PN 96.

G Peart, 'Case Management and Client Care for Solicitors and their Clients Litigating PTSD Claims Arising from Fatalities or Disaster Situations' [1999] 2 JPIL 113.

A Ritchie, 'Damages for Psychiatric Injuries' (1994) 144 NLJ 1690.

F S Shuaib, 'Claims for "Nervous Shock" by Secondary Victims in Medical Negligence Cases' (1999) 15 PN 18.

A Sprince, '*Page v Smith*: Being "Primary" Colours House of Lords' Judgment' (1995) 11 PN 124.

H Teff, 'The Hillsborough Football Disaster and Claims for Nervous Shock' (1992) 32(3) Med Sci Law 252.

—— 'Liability for Psychiatric Illness after Hillsborough' [1992] OJLS 440.

F A Trindade, 'The Principles Governing the Recovery of Damages for Negligently Caused Nervous Shock' [1986] CLJ 476

—— 'Nervous Shock and Negligent Conduct' (1996) 112 LQR 22.

A Unger, 'Undue Caution in the Lords' (1991) 141 NLJ 1729.

K Wheat, 'Nervous Shock: Proposals for Reform' [1994] JPIL 207.

—— '*Frost*: More Confusion and Unfairness in Psychiatric Injury Claims' (1998) 2 MJLS 32.

—— 'Liability for Psychiatric Illness: The Law Commission Report' [1998] 3 JPIL 211.

MEDICINE

Books

R Bluglass and P Bowden (eds), *Principles and Practice of Forensic Psychiatry* (Churchill-Livingstone, 1990).

J Davidson and E Foa (eds), *Post-Traumatic Stress Disorder: DSM–IV and Beyond* (American Psychiatric Publishers, 1993).

J Gunn and P J Taylor (eds), *Forensic Psychiatry: Clinical, Legal and Ethical Issues* (Butterworth-Heinemann, 1993).

C B Scrignar, *Post-Traumatic Stress Disorder*, 2nd edn (New Orleans, LA: Bruno Press, 1988).

M E Wolfe and A D Mosnaim (eds), *Post-Traumatic Stress Disorder: Etiology, Phenomenology and Treatment* (Washington, DC: American Psychiatric Press, 1990).

W Yule (ed), *Post-Traumatic Stress Disorders: Concepts and Therapy* (Chichester: John Wiley & Sons, 1998).

Articles

D A Alexander, 'Psychological Intervention for Victims and Helpers after Disasters' (1990) 40 *British Journal of General Practice* 345.

—— 'Stress Among Police Body Handlers: A Long-term Follow-up' (1993) 163 *Br J Psychiatry* 806.

—— 'Trauma Research: A New Era' (1996) 41 *J Psychosom Res* 1.

N Breslau and G Davis, 'Post-Traumatic Stress Disorder: The Stressor Criterion' (1987) 175 *Journal of Nervous and Mental Disease* 255, 262.

D Brom et al, 'Victims of Traffic Accidents: Incidence and Prevention of Post-Traumatic Stress Disorder' (1993) 49 *Journal of Clinical Psychology* 131.

P Burnett et al, 'Concepts of Normal Bereavement' (1994) 7 *Br J Psychiatry* 123.

A Dyregrov, 'The Process of Psychological Debriefings' (1997) 10 *Journal of Traumatic Stress* 589.

B L Green, 'Psychological Research in Traumatic Stress: An Update' (1994) 7 *Journal of Traumatic Stress* 341.

S Joseph et al, 'Crisis Support and Psychiatric Symptomatology in Adult Survivors of the Jupiter Cruise Ship Disaster' (1992) 31 *British Journal of Clinical Psychology* 63.

A C McFarlane, 'The Aetiology of Post-traumatic Morbidity: Predisposing, Precipitating and Perpetuating Factors' (1989) 154 *Br J Psychiatry* 221.

—— and P Papay, 'Multiple Diagnosis in Post-Traumatic Stress Disorder in the Victims of a Natural Disaster' (1992) 176 *Journal of Nervous and Mental Disease* 498, 502.

P Mason and G Wilkinson, 'The Prevalence of Psychiatric Morbidity: OPCS Survey of Psychiatric Morbidity in Great Britain' (1996) 168 *Br J Psychiatry* 1.

R Mayou, 'Accident Neurosis Revisited' (1996) 168 *Br J Psychiatry* 399.

—— et al, 'Psychiatric Consequences of Road Traffic Accidents' (1993) 307 BMJ 647.

D Pardoen *et al*, 'Life Events and Primary Affective Disorders: A One-Year Prospective Study' (1996) 169 *Br J Psychiatry* 160.

C Pugh and M Trimble, 'Psychiatric Injury after Hillsborough' (1993) 163 *Br J Psychiatry* 425.

S Regel, 'Critical Incident Stress Debriefing: Current Status, Controversies and Future Directions' (unpublished conference paper available from the Traumatic Stress Service, Nottinghamshire Healthcare NHS Trust, Duncan Macmillan House, Porchester Road, Nottingham, NG3 6AA).

M Weller, 'Post-Traumatic Stress Disorder' (1993) 143 NLJ 878.

S Wessely *et al*, 'A Systematic Review of Brief Psychological Interventions ("debriefing") for the Treatment of Immediate Trauma-related Symptoms and the Prevention of Post-Traumatic Stress Disorder' (1998) *The Cochrane Library*, Issue 4.

W Yule *et al*, 'The "Jupiter" Sinking: Effects on Children's Fears, Depression and Anxiety' (1990) 31 *J Child Psychol Psychiat* 1051.

—— 'Post-Traumatic Stress Disorders in Children' (1992) 4(4) *Current Opinion in Paediatrics*, August 1992.

POPULAR ACCOUNTS OF TRAUMA

Books

David Muss, *The Trauma Trap* (London and New York: Doubleday, 1991). (A self-help book.)

Geraldine Sheridan and Thomas Kenning, *Survivors: Lockerbie* (London: Pan Books, 1993). (An account of the experiences of those who have survived trauma.)

Index

nervous shock
Alcock v Chief Constable of the South Yorkshire Police 35–38
Bourhill v Young 34
circumstances of claim 3
claim requirements 2–3
claimants 6
customary phlegm 34
Dulieu v White & Sons 32–33
essential ingredients for claim 2–3
floodgates argument 246–47
foreseeability 38–39
future developments 245–54
  different approach to 250–54
  flexibility 245–46
  floodgates argument 246–47
  Law Commission report 247–50
  primary and secondary victims 246
Hambrook v Stokes Brothers 33–34
Herald of Free Enterprise 213
Hillsborough stadium disaster 35–38
historical development 32–42
  Alcock v Chief Constable of the South Yorkshire Police 35–38
  Bourhill v Young 34
  Dulieu v White & Sons 32–33
  foreseeability 38–39
  generally 32
  Hambrook v Stokes Brothers 33–34
  Hillsborough stadium disaster 35–38
  McLoughlin v O'Brian 35
  Page v Smith 38–39
  police officers 40–42
  policy 35
  proximity 35
  White v Chief Constable of South Yorkshire Police 40–42
Law Commission report 247–50
McLoughlin v O'Brian 35
meaning 2
mere bystander 37–38
'nervous' 33
Page v Smith 38–39
police officers 40–42
primary and secondary victims 40–42
  see also primary victims; secondary victims
rescuers 37, 37–38
secondary victims 38
shocking criterion 88–89
television broadcasting 35–36
use of term 2
White v Chief Constable of South Yorkshire Police 40–42
neuroses 46, 49, 192–93
accident neurosis 64, 191
newsletters 68

nightmares
post-traumatic stress disorder 79
non-shock cases
generally 4
normal fortitude, person of
medical negligence 95
secondary victim 100–01
nuisance
generally 6
harassment 21
mental distress 28–29
ordinary mental distress 28–29
nurses
occupational stress 151

obsessional neuroses 49
obsessive compulsive disorder 61
obstetrics
medical negligence 95–96
occupational stress 145–55
armed forces 155
causation 149
clear signal to employer of 151, 152
cognitive behavioural therapy 154
contributory negligence 159
control by employer 151
counselling 153, 155–56
course of employment 157–58
damaging interventions, for 155–57
debriefing 154, 156
defences
  contributory negligence 159
  volenti non fit injuria 158–59
definition 145
discrimination cases 153
dismissal on ill health grounds 152
egg-shell employees 152
flexible arrangements 152
foreseeability 147, 148
guidance on meaning 145–46
harmful stress 145
indications of impending breakdown 151
injuries during training 149
intervention, employer 154
intimidation 148–49
living conditions 147
management style 148
meaning 145
nurses 151
physical harm 151
police 150
prevention 149
prison officers 149
punitive work regimes 148
refusal of treatment 155
risk assessment 153
schemes to help with 153